Strategic Financial Management
for Commercial Banks

Ronald L. Olson
Chairman of the Board
Olson Research Associates, Inc.
Columbia, Maryland

Harold M. Sollenberger
Professor of Accounting
Michigan State University
East Lansing, Michigan

William E. O'Connell, Jr.
Chessie Professor of Finance
College of William and Mary
Williamsburg, Virginia

Ivy Press, Inc.

10290 Old Columbia Road
Columbia, MD 21046
(410) 290-6999
Fax (410) 290-6726

Ivy Press, Columbia, MD 21046

PRINTED IN THE UNITED STATES OF AMERICA
First Printing   1993
ISBN 0-916077-02-0

TABLE OF CONTENTS

PREFACE

Preface

STRATEGIC FINANCIAL MANAGEMENT has evolved with bank managers and the banking industry. Demand from bank customers for new products and services, a more competitive environment, an increasingly complex legal structure, shareholder desire for larger returns, innovation in the financial markets, continued economic growth, pressure for higher employee rewards, and expanding regulatory rules are the forces of change within the banking industry which intensify each day. As a result of these forces, executing new varieties of financial contracts, understanding complex measurement techniques, thinking strategically, and being a continuous learner are routine for anyone who expects to survive professionally in today's banking environment.

This text illustrates financial strategies and tools which are available to help bankers attain above average performance results. It also presents the latest developments in financial measurement techniques. It is an opportunity to learn about complex financial decisions, the power of discipline in planning and control processes, and the latest regulatory requirements related to risk management.

This text uses both a case study and a simulation exercise. In the three chapters of Part I, the case is used to illustrate how financial management concepts relate to real world circumstances. In the two chapters of Part II, the simulation exercise provides opportunities for the reader to get involved in an active learning process. As an effective learning experience, simulation is second only to on-the-job training, but uses less time, with little risk and low cost.

Chapter One, *Strategic Financial Planning*, presents a summary of financial planning and financial management concepts, an explanation of four alternative financial strategies, an outline of key strategic financial goals, and an introductory discussion of financial risk.

Chapter Two, *Community Regional National Bank: A Case Study*, presents the current status of the hypothetical bank (CRNB) to be used throughout the text for illustrative purposes, performance results of the immediate past, and the expected future interest rate environment.

Chapter Three, *Risk Measurement and Management*, identifies financial risks, illustrates methods to measure these risks, and discusses concepts of managing these risks.

Chapter Four, *Management Simulation: Operating Decisions,* explains the operating decisions which each bank team makes for the forecast year 2003. It presents the products and services offered to the CRNB customers and the capital market transactions available to the bank's officers. The products, services, and market opportunities are described; anticipated results are discussed; and decision alternatives are identified.

Chapter Five, *Management Simulation: Policies and Procedures*, It discusses the ground rules and policies under which all bank teams will operate in the simulation. The exercise can either be a non-competitive planning simulation or a competitive management simulation.

The appendices in Part III provide monthly financial reports of CRNB for the years 2000, 2001, 2002, and 2003, a display of yield curve points, definitions of key ratios, interest variance analysis formulas, present value/duration analysis, and technical instructions for the use of the computer simulation program.

The case has been designed for ease and speed of learning, but it is not for beginners. It should present a challenge to both the student of banking and the experienced bank executive. It requires a knowledge of banking terminology and active participation. The results achieved in the simulation exercises will measure immediate success. However, the ultimate benefits of the case come from the continual application of what has been learned.

This edition of the simulation exercise began in 1989 and has been actively tested. Participants in the tests included students at The School for Bank Administration, staff members of Ernst & Young in continuing professional education courses, the executive management team (including the board of directors) at First National Bank in Albuquerque, the staff members of the asset management division of Federated Investors.

Many staff members and clients of Olson Research Associates, Inc. have played a role in bringing this text to completion. Kurt Schneckenburger was responsible for systems design, data base development, and programming. Al Gardner's experience and research provided a real-world perspective. Scott Ulbrich of First Security Corporation and Jeanne Krips of Key Banks gave input for our investment portfolio and capital market topics. Lorraine Warner's endurance has seen us through an untold number of manuscript changes. Karin Evans' editing added finishing touches. Credit goes to Christine Stewart for keeping us on a schedule and bringing the book to completion.

To the above people and to all the others who have helped, we say, "Thanks." In the final analysis, the authors assume full responsibility for content and presentation.

The Concepts of Financial Management

Chapter ONE

Strategic Financial Planning

In a rapidly changing environment, the job of bank managers is to acquire and allocate resources within a structured system of planning and control. Quality human and financial resources are scarce and expensive, and they must be carefully allocated and coordinated. The business transactions of banking contain many risks. The discipline of a risk management system helps keep risk under control. The goal of this text is to help bankers and others learn more about resource allocation and risk management in the banking world of the 1990s; i.e. , *Strategic Financial Management*.

Strategic Financial Management is a broad term which includes planning, implementing decisions, and very importantly, a monitoring and control system. Implementation action converts plans into reality, and a control system helps conform reality to plans.

Planning is the beginning of the managerial process. *Strategic Financial Planning* is the process of selecting a financial strategy (balance sheet structure and operating characteristics), setting financial goals (capital leverage, dividends, earnings, and growth rates), and defining acceptable levels of financial risk (credit, liquidity, and interest-rate risk).

Strategic Planning

Strategic Financial Planning is a subset of the broader notion of Strategic Planning. This subset has two dimensions. First, strategic financial planning is directly concerned with one of the four basic business elements — capital. Financial managers must determine how much of it is needed, what its form should be, when it must be available, and from where it will come.

Second, the strategic financial planning process is the most critical web that binds together the various strategic business elements, especially in a financial institution. The four basic business elements are the markets served, products and services offered, human and physical resources needed, and capital required. Strategy selections in any one of the basic areas will impact the others. Managers will be forever faced with the dilemma of which decision to make first. For example, financial strategy (balance sheet structure) may determine which markets to serve. Alternatively, the geography of a bank's market may dictate its financial strategy.

Strategic planning is a process which helps determine where you are, where you want to go, how you will get there, and what the implications are of reaching the goals. In order to set goals and targets for where you want to go, you must first know what goals and targets are appropriate. While in an Indy car, a driver doesn't try to win the Kentucky Derby.

One critical aspect of each of these items is the financial capital of the bank. A bank with $10 million in capital cannot be a nationwide bank — immediately, at least. Alternatively, a bank with $500 million in capital cannot afford to be an independent community bank serving a local market. The balance sheet structure and operating characteristics of a community bank are very different from the characteristics of a superregional or money center bank.

Some strategies are riskier than others: and the more risk, the higher should be the expected rate of return. Concentration strategies are riskier than diversification strategies. A rapid growth strategy is riskier than a slow growth strategy. A push to capture a greater market share is riskier than maintaining current competitive relationships. Goals for return on equity must reflect appropriate levels of risk; bankers cannot expect a high rate of return without assuming a high degree of financial risk. Alternatively, if a strategy is selected so as to avoid financial risk, the goals for earnings should be set at lower levels.

If risky strategies are pursued, the bank manager must be prepared to manage the risk. A system of risk identification, tools to protect against excessive levels, and a process of reporting and evaluation are important steps which follow in the financial planning process; i.e., *Strategic Financial Management* includes planning, implementation, and control.

Financial Management Concepts

Current financial management concepts reflect the problems, opportunities, and innovations in the financial services industries over the past six decades. Within the banking industry, five distinct approaches to financial management evolved during the sixty years between the 1930s and the 1990s. Today's strategic financial management is a result of this evolution.

Survival and Conservatism

Immediately prior to and in the early years of the Depression, many banks failed. The banking holiday, the creation of the FDIC, and other events were directed toward salvaging the financial system. A decade of political energy and a massive World War proved successful for the industry, but the managerial philosophy within must banks was that of passive conservatism.

During and immediately following World War II, the memories of the Great Depression were strong; and bank operations were limited by regulatory and monetary policy restrictions. Banks continued to follow a conservative, slow-growth approach. Bankers tended to view themselves as deposit takers and to regard the banks' deposit structures as a function of customer action. Rates paid on individual accounts were less than regulatory ceilings, and often banks did not accept corporate time accounts. It was characteristic of banks to have very liquid assets. Portfolios contained a high percentage of government bonds. At the end of 1945, for example, U.S. Treasury securities comprised 73 percent of bank credit outstanding.[1]

Asset Management

Asset management as a financial management concept came into being after the war years. Bankers sought to improve earnings and realized they could accomplish this goal by shifting assets when profitable opportunities were identified. A gradual waning of Depression-era fears meant banks were more willing to assume added risks. Bankers, by and large, regarded funds supply as a factor outside their control and sought to make more funds available for lending through more effective asset management. Funds were shifted from noninterest-bearing reserves into higher yielding loans. At the same time, the use of U.S. Treasury securities declined, as investments in securities issued by state, local, and federal agencies increased.

Over time, writers have described two methods of asset management — asset allocation and conversion of funds.[2] Asset allocation involves analyzing asset mix and allocating funds according to a liquidity priority. Assets traditionally have been categorized as primary reserves, secondary reserves, tertiary funds, and fixed assets. Providing for primary reserves and fixed assets is the first priority. Primary reserves include vault cash, required liquidity reserves, and funds on deposit with correspondent banks. Fixed assets include buildings and equipment.

---

[1] Jack Beeloe, "A Perspective on Liability Management and Bank Risk, " *Federal Reserve Bank of San Francisco Economic Review* (Winter 1977): p. 5.

[2] American Bankers Association, "Utilization of Bank Funds" (Washington, DC 1964).

Secondary reserve levels depend upon the availability of loans and deposits. The aim is to match maturities with the expected need for funds. Tertiary funds are used to meet the credit needs of the community and generate earnings for the bank. This third level (tertiary) is generally subject to the most credit and interest-rate risk.

Conversion of funds (a second version of the concept of asset allocation) categorizes assets and liabilities according to volatility and attempts to match assets with liabilities having similar (liquidity) characteristics. Funds from small savings accounts, for example, may be matched with mortgage and installment loans. Conversion of funds has served some bankers very well by encouraging management not to overextend bank resources. However, strict adherence to this approach has forced some banks to liquidate desirable assets to cover deposit shrinkages when other less desirable assets could have been used.

Asset allocation focuses on the maintenance of liquidity and earnings, given a passive concept of funding. Such concepts were appropriate to the banking environment of the 1950s and are still used by some community bankers today. In more aggressive and some larger banks, asset allocation is too simplistic and ignores management of the funding process.

Liability Management

The 1960s saw a change in economic conditions that set the stage for a shift to liability management. Bank deposits grew modestly from 1945 until the early sixties. As corporate treasurers adopted more sophisticated cash management techniques and sought greater rates of return, corporations were beginning to shift funds from bank deposits into money market instruments. At the same time, banks experienced strong loan demand, and money center banks began running out of unpledged securities that could be liquidated to meet the demand. Some banks had an adequate amount of securities but would have had to liquidate them at a loss and were reluctant to do so.

A major turning point in bank management philosophy occurred in early 1961 when large New York City banks introduced negotiable-rate certificates of deposit. Other banks rapidly followed suit, and securities dealers began making a secondary market. The new instruments signaled a shift towards purchased funds as a means of increasing loan growth. Banks realized that they could do more than just sit back and wait for deposits. By buying funds, they found they could meet borrowers' needs as demand developed, rather than as funds became available.

In addition to the negotiable certificates of deposit, banks actively began purchasing federal funds, using repurchase agreements, and buying Eurocurrency (borrowing from foreign branches). Purchased funds were used for both growth and liquidity. Banks no longer had to rely solely on deposits from local markets to finance loan demand but could grow beyond those limits through the purchased funds mechanism. Banks also found they could replace liquidity on the asset side of the balance sheet with liquidity on the liability side, by reducing reserves and short-term Treasury issues and by using purchased funds, as needed, for liquidity. While the liability management approach created the possibility of higher returns, it also made the banks more vulnerable to changes in the economic environment and, therefore, increased their level of risk.

Asset/Liability Management

The economic fluctuations caused by the deregulation of financial markets in the late 1970s and the early 1980s had serious repercussions for financial institutions. Many had financed growth of long-term, fixed-rate loans and investments with short-term, interest-sensitive funds. Alternatively, many had invested in short-term federal funds and variable-rate loans while being funded by long-term core deposits.

In both of the above cases, interest-rate fluctuations led to volatile earnings. In turn, volatile earnings pushed bankers to assume more credit risk to improve the bottom line. After a while, the increased credit risk created losses which prompted failures, mergers, and corporate restructuring.

Enlightened bankers avoided the above pitfalls by using greater caution. "Asset/liability management" became the rallying cry for the times. Improved credit and lending policies eliminated much credit risk. Ceilings were established for purchased funds. Portfolio limits were set to avoid concentrations in any one type of loan or investment. Maturity schedules were carefully managed toward the goals of maximizing net interest income and minimizing risk.

The process of asset/liability management proved to be successful in helping bankers to stabilize earnings. The success was a direct result of the avoidance of risk. In the early stages, the good results were "worth the price." However, as the asset/liability management process matured, it became apparent that bankers were destined to limited growth in earnings unless new ventures were undertaken.

Resource Allocation and Risk Management

Resource allocation and risk management has evolved as a collective term describing activities; some of which were defined as part of the asset/liability management process just a few years ago. Now, however, *resource allocation* refers to the process of acquiring and using human and financial resources within the business entity; however, this process is not restricted to "balance sheet products." *Risk management* replaces the notion that Asset/Liability Management Committee (ALCO) policies are designed to avoid risk. It acknowledges that the assumption and management of reasonable risk positions are inherent in normal banking activities.

Bankers continue to make loans, accept deposits, manage investment portfolios, and borrow money. However, efficient uses of human and financial capital can also occur in non-balance sheet products and services. Direct customer services such as financial planning, estate planning, trust administration, stand-by loan commitments, letters of credit, third party mutual funds, and insurance are illustrations of non-balance sheet services offered by banks. Also, many resources can be profitability directed to capital market activities such as direct transactions with off-balance sheet financial instruments, merger and acquisition advice, investment banking activities, and a variety of merchant banking services.

During the 1980s tightly constraining ALCO policies created a philosophy of risk avoidance. Regulators forced higher levels of capital when static measures of liquidity, interest rate, or credit risk appeared to be outside normal levels. Options, futures, and interest rate swap contracts were considered "Las Vegas" type activities to be avoided under all circumstances by many banks. The environment has now changed.

Also in the 1980s, some banking risks went unrecognized. Daily transfers and settlements involve large sums of financial resources which are done under informal rules and traditions and with few contingencies for failures to perform. "Understandings" about interbank settlements, loan commitments, loan participations, and other transactions involve substantial and growing risks. Prudent bankers and regulators are now forcing the recognition of these risks.

In today's world, strategy selection and a well-defined risk management system are keys to profitability, growth, improved customer service, and professional survival. A deliberate, planned strategy, implemented within the context of a professional risk management system, is now competitive banking norm.

Financial Strategies

Strategy is defined in dictionaries as a careful method for working toward a goal; the art of devising or employing stratagems in a competitive political, military, or economic environment. *Stratagem* is defined as a cleverly contrived scheme for gaining an end.

Banking operates in a competitive economic environment. Banking strategy is driven by geographic location, customer opportunities, regulation, knowledge, experience of bank personnel, risk tolerances of bank executives, goals of investors, and the availability of capital. Each of these strategic factors may present a bank management team with alternatives from which to choose or with a focus which cannot be changed.

J. P. Morgan ($100 billion in assets) of New York City has been referred to as a "money center bank." Palmer National Bank ($100 million) of Washington, DC has been referred to as a "merchant bank." NationsBank ($110 billion) of Charlotte, NC has been referred to as a "superregional bank." California United Bank ($350 million) of Encino, CA has been referred to as a "business bank." Central National Bank ($225 million) of Enid, OK has been referred to as a "community bank." First Security ($7 billion) of Salt Lake City, UT has been referred to as a "regional bank." BancOne ($70 billion) of Columbus, OH has been referred to as a "superregional banking company" while many of its subsidiary banks have been referred to as "community banks."

The above terms do not have exact definitions but do have general acceptance as a way to identify the basic strategy of a bank and its managerial team. Many banks which have had clear strategic identification have been successful and many case histories of bank failures have been written for those banks which "failed to know who they were."[3]

---

[3] For example, Phillip L. Zweig, *Belly Up: The Collapse of the Penn Square Bank*, Ballantine Books, New York, NY 1985.

From time-to-time, various publications, including the *ABA Banking Journal, American Banker, Bank Management, Bankers Monthly,* and *United States Banker,* have identified banks by type of strategy. While each publication has its own criteria for classification, the definitions are similar. For purposes of this text, four types of banks representing alternative banking strategies have been identified: community banks, regional banks, superregional banks, and money center banks. The four strategic types are defined below, and several actual banks are cited as examples. Where financial data identifies the various banks, publicly reported performance results for the year ending December 31, 1991 and financial conditions on that date were used.

Figure 1-1 shows illustrative percentage composition balance sheets for the four types of banks. Although bankers disagree on an ideal mix composition, these prototypes give insight into the alternative strategies. Figure 1-2 shows percentage composition for the 1991 actual average balance sheets of peer groups representing the four alternative types of banks. Figures 1-3 and 1-4 show the key ratios for the illustrative and the 1991 actual peer strategic type banks. The reader should refer to these figures while reading about the alternative types of banks discussed below.

Community Banks

A community bank (up to $1 billion in total assets) serves a reasonably well-defined set of customers by providing traditional loan and deposit services. The customer group can be defined either geographically, or by market focus. For example, a rural community bank may serve a town, county or geographically remote location. A city community bank may serve a neighborhood or several well-defined city blocks. Alternatively, a community bank may focus on senior citizens, an ethnic or minority group, or unique industry segments such as cotton farming or insurance brokerage. The size of the service area will expand with the growth of the bank. Sometimes, community banks with a speciality customer focus are referred to as niche banks.

The asset composition of a community bank generally exhibits a conservative approach to balance sheet management. As interest rates fluctuate, the investment portfolio shifts from Treasuries to federal funds and back. With over 20% of assets invested in relatively short-term and marketable U.S. Treasury securities, other liquidity contingencies are not needed.

Loans are kept to a low percentage of earning assets (30 to 60%). Commercial loans (usually less than 15% of total assets) are made to small local businesses, or loan participations are acquired from larger correspondents. Much of the lending is real estate based residential mortgage loans, some commercial real estate loans, loans to small businesses for plant and equipment, and farm loans. Although many community banks sell conforming mortgage loans, the retained real estate loans offer high yields and comprise 30% or more of total assets.

Figure 1-1

STRATEGIC POSITION: ILLUSTRATIONS

	COMMUNITY BANK	REGIONAL BANK	SUPER-REGIONAL BANK	MONEY CENTER BANK
ASSETS:				
CASH & DUE FROM BANKS	4.0%	6.0%	8.0%	4.0%
US TREASURY & AGENCY SEC	24.0	12.0	10.0	7.0
STATE & MUNI SECURITIES	5.0	2.0	2.0	2.0
OTHER SECURITIES	1.0	2.0	6.0	8.0
TOTAL SECURITIES	30.0	16.0	18.0	17.0
SHORT-TERM INVESTMENTS	12.0	2.0	9.0	34.0
COMMERCIAL LOANS (DOM)	10.0	26.0	25.0	18.0
FOREIGN LOANS	0.0	0.0	3.0	11.0
AGRICULTURAL LOANS	2.0	1.0	1.0	0.0
REAL ESTATE LOANS	30.0	29.0	18.0	5.0
CONSUMER LOANS	10.0	16.0	13.0	2.0
TOTAL LOANS & LEASES	52.0	72.0	60.0	36.0
LOAN & LEASE RESERVES	-1.0	-2.0	-2.0	-1.0
NET LOANS & LEASES	51.0	70.0	58.0	35.0
PREMISES & FIXED ASSETS	1.0	2.0	2.0	1.0
OREO & FORECLOSED ASSETS	0.0	1.0	1.0	1.0
OTHER ASSETS	2.0	3.0	4.0	8.0
TOTAL OTHER ASSETS	3.0	6.0	7.0	10.0
TOTAL ASSETS	100.0	100.0	100.0	100.0
LIABILITIES & CAPITAL:				
NON-INTEREST DEPOSITS	10.0	15.0	18.0	4.0
NOW & SAVINGS DEPOSITS	20.0	14.0	9.0	2.0
MONEY MARKET DEPOSITS	10.0	15.0	14.0	2.0
SMALL CDs & OTHER TIME	42.0	25.0	18.0	2.0
LARGE CDs	8.0	10.0	12.0	20.0
FOREIGN INT BRG DEPOSITS	0.0	1.0	4.0	25.0
TOTAL DEPOSITS	90.0	80.0	75.0	55.0
SHORT-TERM BORROWINGS	1.0	10.0	10.0	20.0
LONG-TERM DEBT	0.0	1.0	4.0	10.0
OTHER LIABILITIES	1.0	1.5	4.0	9.0
EQUITY	8.0	7.5	7.0	6.0
TOTAL LIAB & EQUITY	100.0	100.0	100.0	100.0

Figure 1-2

STRATEGIC POSITION: 1991 PEER AVERAGES

	COMMUNITY BANK	REGIONAL BANK	SUPER-REGIONAL BANK	MONEY CENTER BANK
ASSETS:				
CASH & DUE FROM BANKS	3.6%	6.0%	5.6%	4.5%
US TREASURY & AGENCY SEC	23.7	15.2	12.7	4.7
STATE & MUNI SECURITIES	5.1	1.4	1.5	1.6
OTHER SECURITIES	1.5	1.4	2.4	4.9
TOTAL SECURITIES	30.2	17.9	16.6	11.2
SHORT-TERM INVESTMENTS	5.0	6.7	6.5	27.6
COMMERCIAL LOANS (DOM)	11.3	21.9	23.9	21.9
FOREIGN LOANS	0.0	0.0	3.5	10.7
AGRICULTURAL LOANS	2.0	0.1	0.4	0.0
REAL ESTATE LOANS	33.2	29.4	26.6	9.4
CONSUMER LOANS	12.3	15.2	11.8	5.9
TOTAL LOANS & LEASES	58.6	66.6	66.2	48.0
LOAN & LEASE RESERVES	-0.8	-1.6	-1.7	-2.5
NET LOANS & LEASES	57.8	65.0	64.5	45.5
PREMISES & FIXED ASSETS	1.5	1.2	1.5	1.6
OREO & FORECLOSED ASSETS	0.2	0.5	0.6	0.5
OTHER ASSETS	1.6	2.7	4.6	9.1
TOTAL OTHER ASSETS	3.3	4.4	6.7	11.2
TOTAL ASSETS	100.0	100.0	100.0	100.0
LIABILITIES & CAPITAL:				
NON-INTEREST DEPOSITS	9.5	14.4	13.5	9.3
NOW & SAVINGS DEPOSITS	19.4	14.4	6.5	1.1
MONEY MARKET DEPOSITS	9.6	15.2	21.4	7.3
SMALL CDs & OTHER TIME	42.9	25.3	0.4	3.9
LARGE CDs	8.8	9.5	9.3	8.7
FOREIGN INT BRG DEPOSIT	0.0	2.0	4.4	25.7
TOTAL DEPOSITS	90.1	80.8	75.5	56.1
SHORT-TERM BORROWINGS	0.8	11.4	8.3	17.3
LONG-TERM DEBT	0.0	0.1	5.4	10.6
OTHER LIABILITIES	0.9	1.5	2.4	8.0
EQUITY	8.2	6.1	8.4	7.9
TOTAL LIAB & EQUITY	100.0	100.0	100.0	100.0

Figure 1-3

STRATEGIC PERFORMANCE: ILLUSTRATIONS

	COMMUNITY BANK	REGIONAL BANK	SUPER-REGIONAL BANK	MONEY CENTER BANK
EARNINGS:				
RETURN ON EQUITY %	12.50	15.00	17.00	20.00
RETURN ON ASSETS %	1.00	1.13	1.19	1.20
INTEREST SPREAD %	4.00	3.50	3.75	1.50
INT MARGIN ON E.A. %	5.00	4.50	4.00	2.75
NET OVERHEAD TO E.A. %	2.50	2.25	2.00	0.75
LOAN POSITION:				
LOSS PROVISION/LOANS %	0.50	1.00	1.50	2.00
NET CHARGE-OFFS/LOANS %	0.45	0.90	1.30	1.80
LOSS RESERVE/LOANS %	1.50	2.00	2.50	3.00
NONPERFORMING/LNS(EOP) %	1.50	3.00	5.00	6.00
CAPITAL LEVERAGE:				
CORE CAPITAL (TIER 1) %	14.00	10.00	8.00	8.00
TOTAL CAPITAL (RBC) %	15.00	11.00	10.00	9.00
ASSET LEVERAGE %	8.00	7.00	6.00	5.50
EQUITY TO ASSETS %	8.00	7.50	7.00	6.00
DIVIDEND PAYOUT %	33.33	33.33	33.33	33.33
LIQUIDITY:				
LOANS/TOTAL DEPOSITS %	65.00	90.00	80.00	65.00
PURCHASED FUNDS/E.A. %	00.00	25.00	20.00	60.00
PER EMPLOYEE:				
SALARIES & BENEFITS ($)	25,000	35,000	34,000	65,000
TOTAL ASSETS ($ MILLIONS)	1.75	2.25	2.00	4.00

Figure 1-4

STRATEGIC PERFORMANCE: 1991 PEER AVERAGES

	COMMUNITY BANK	REGIONAL BANK	SUPER-REGIONAL BANK	MONEY CENTER BANK
EARNINGS:				
RETURN ON EQUITY %	13.17	11.40	5.63	8.18
RETURN ON ASSETS %	1.08	0.70	0.47	0.65
INTEREST SPREAD %	3.68	3.49	3.63	1.53
INT MARGIN ON E.A. %	4.50	4.35	4.69	2.58
NET OVERHEAD TO E.A. %	2.43	2.31	2.52	0.73
LOAN POSITION:				
LOSS PROVISION/LOANS %	0.46	1.43	1.90	1.46
NET CHARGE-OFFS/LOANS %	0.39	1.32	1.77	2.27
LOSS RESERVE/LOANS %	1.35	2.34	2.51	5.19
NONPERFORMING/LNS(EOP) %	1.21	3.47	5.04	6.61
CAPITAL LEVERAGE:				
CORE CAPITAL (TIER 1) %	14.28	9.17	6.70	6.09
TOTAL CAPITAL (RBC) %	15.66	10.68	9.14	8.87
ASSET LEVERAGE RATIO	8.39	6.24	5.87	4.41
EQUITY TO ASSETS %	8.20	6.14	8.36	7.91
DIVIDEND PAYOUT %	44.53	49.43	61.64	40.44
LIQUIDITY:				
LOANS/TOTAL DEPOSITS %	65.07	82.47	87.64	85.49
PURCHASED FUNDS/E.A. %	10.18	22.95	24.66	59.71
PER EMPLOYEE:				
SALARIES & BENEFITS ($)	26,151	34,211	36,215	64,114
TOTAL ASSETS ($ MILLIONS)	1.86	2.23	1.86	4.15

Consumer lending in community banks tends to be highly personalized and consists of installment loans for automobiles, home appliances, recreation, and home improvements. Some community banks offer credit card loans directly, but many serve as agent banks for large servicers. Recent tax laws have made home equity lending popular in many areas of the country. This response to home equity loans illustrates how bankers must continually adapt to external events. History is full of other illustrations of new banking products in response to external change (checking accounts, NOW accounts, certificates of deposit, adjustable-rate mortgage loans, and others). The future will bring more.

Community banks are funded primarily with core deposits. Consumer deposits are the largest portion of funding, and the small business segment represents checking accounts and CDs with good stability. Deposits provide funding for over 90% of assets and capital provides funding for 7 to 10%. Short-term and long-term borrowing tend to be unusual.

Community banks provide a large amount of "free" services to promote customer loyalty. Thus, non-interest income as a percentage of total income tends to be low and interest margin tends to be higher (Interest margin of over 5.0% is the norm with some community banks reporting interest margins of 5.5 to 6.0%). Overhead expenses are generally controlled by low salaries and benefits and a frugal approach to operating expenses.

To provide the "extra service," community banks tend to have more employees per dollar of assets. Some report as low as $1.0 million of assets per employee, but the norm is about $1.75 million. Due to the lack of experience, knowledge, and/or perceived need, few community banks use off-balance sheet contracts for strategic or risk management purposes.

Each year the Federal Financial Institutions Examination Council (FFIEC) aggregates all commercial banks into twenty-five peer groups for comparison analysis. Peer Group No. 8 of the FFIEC Uniform Bank Performance Reports (UBPR) was selected for our purposes, as representative of community banks. This group contained 687 banks in 1991, each had total assets between $100 and $300 million, was located in non-metropolitan areas, had three or more banking offices. Information about this peer group is labeled "Community Bank" in Figures 1-2 and 1-4.

Regional Banks

A regional bank is similar to a community bank in that it serves a defined customer base but is different in size and breadth of geographic coverage. They typically range in size from $1 billion to $20 billion in total assets. A regional bank will serve a major economic region (or perhaps two or three separately definable economic regions) geographically spread over an entire state or even several states, which are similar in economic characteristics.

A regional bank may be a multi-bank holding company that usually merges banks into a single entity where legal conditions permit. They have a large number of branches which are either purchased or opened de novo to enter new markets or expand existing service areas.

Regional banks are loan driven. Growth of service areas comes from new lending opportunities. Total loans are normally over 65% of total assets and in many cases exceed 75%. Loan to deposit ratios of 100% and more are frequent. Commercial loans comprise 20 to 30% of total assets and real estate lending is substantial. The commercial loans are direct loans to small- and medium-sized regional companies. Some large commercial loans are made, managed, and participated out to smaller correspondent banks. Conforming real estate mortgages on personal residences and credit card loans are frequently sold or securitized for liquidity purposes.

Regional banks aggressively work to acquire commercial deposit business but rely heavily on retail or consumer core deposits. Consumer core deposits will represent 50 to 60% of total assets; business deposits represent 20 to 30%; and a small amount (1 or 2%) will come from foreign sources.

Net borrowed funds will provide funding when the loan to deposit ratios hit 100% and beyond. The primary constraint on the use of borrowed funds is capital leverage. Regional banks have a need to show strong earnings performance and capital ratios to protect a good credit rating.

Regional banks continually fight the battle between free services and service charges as a source of income. With more commercial business, they tend to do more fee-based service than community banks, but the heavy reliance on consumer funding tempers the ability to push fee income too far. They tend to benefit from economies of scale as growth expands the trade area and increases penetration of existing markets. Net overhead as a percentage of earning assets of 2.25% is common.

Net interest margin is hurt by prime-based commercial lending versus consumer lending and by higher priced consumer CDs which seem to be necessary to attract core consumer funding. Regional banks suffer from credit quality problems when growth and geographic spread occur before improved credit control systems are in place.

Productivity measures generally improve with mergers. Assets per employee average above $2 million. Salaries and benefits also jump from community bank levels. This reflects more specialized experts and more levels of managerial supervision.

Regional banks experiment with off-balance sheet contracts to manage growing risks associated with aggressive growth in lending. Many however, have not made extensive use of such contracts in the past. Peer group No. 2 of the FFIEC Uniform Bank Performance Reports was selected to represent actual results for regional banks. This group was comprised of 131 banks with total assets between $3 and $10 billion. For December 31, 1991, total assets of this group averaged $5.6 billion, and total off-balance sheet amounts were $2.5 billion. Off-balance sheet contracts equaled 44.8% of total assets. Information about this peer group is labeled "Regional Bank" in Figures 1-2 and 1-4.

Superregional Banks

A superregional bank is a multi-bank holding company. Commercial bank holding companies own both bank and non-bank subsidiaries. A multi-bank holding company operates more than one bank subsidiary. Subsidiary banks of a superregional holding company serve customers in a traditional manner similar to regional and community banks. Because of size ($38 billion in total assets in 1991), superregional banks also engage in some large transactions in the money and capital markets.

The primary source of growth for a superregional is via acquisition of independent banks or other bank holding companies. Superregional banks tend to have a large number of branches.

A superregional bank serves many states and economic regions. The perspective is on a national scale but is currently constrained by legal barriers. An alternative name is sometimes "nation-wide" banks, but legislation to permit nation-wide banking is still in the future (as of the spring of 1993). The management philosophy for a superregional must recognize the divergent cultures representing the different geographic regions.

The asset mix of a superregional bank is generally driven by capital constraints and funding needs. They tend to hold commercial and foreign loans (25% of total assets), although foreign lending is not as significant as in money center banks. Subsidiary banks in many different geographic locations provide a good base of retail lending for real estate and consumer loans (30% of total assets). These loans are also excellent for loan securitizations. The investment portfolios meet minimum regulatory requirements and are usually managed for profits. At least 50% of the investment portfolio will be held for sale or trading. Asset-backed securities are a major portion of investment securities.

Like regional and community banks, superregional banks strive for core-deposit funding. Also, commercial deposits are aggressively sought with many cash management services for corporate treasurers. Total deposits fund 75% of assets, with 15% coming from corporate accounts. Core consumer deposits account for about 40% and purchased CDs provide 10 to 20%. The capital accounts appear strong at first glance; but when intangible assets are netted against equity, the capital ratios are similar to regional banks.

Superregional banks offer a large number of deposit-based services, trust services, loan servicing, and other fee-based products. As a result, fee income is high. Widely spread operations put constant pressure on expenses; and, as a result, the net overhead as a percentage of earning assets is a continual problem (averaging over 2.5% when economies of scale suggest that it should be 2% or less). The interest margin (4.5% of earning assets) tends to hold up fairly well due to retail lending and the active profit management in the investment portfolios.

The superregional banks have good access to the money and capital markets. In most instances, the headquarters office of superregional banks is located in a money center city. If not, the bank will maintain a significant trading office in one or more major money center cities. As a result, off-balance sheet contracts play an important role in managing a superregional bank (although not as significant as the money center banks). The authors have identified thirty-five banks as superregional. The total assets of the thirty-five largest superregional banks on December 31, 1991, was $1.2 trillion. The total of all off-balance sheet amounts reported on the FR Y-9 C[4] quarterly report on that date was $3 trillion. Off-balance sheet amounts total two and one half times the amount of total assets. Information about this peer group is labeled "Superregional Bank" in Figures 1-2 and 1-4.

Money Center Banks

A money center bank acquires and invests large blocks of funds at relatively low spreads. Generally, contract maturities are short; the turnover ratios are high; and the risks are known and accepted. Sometimes, the term wholesale bank, merchant bank, or business bank is used instead of money center bank.

---

[4] The FR Y-9C is the regulatory report filed with the Federal Reserve Board by the bank holding company.

Money center banks are generally large (total assets of $20 billion or more). Some "wholesale" or niche community banks, however, have characteristics of money center banks but are small ($200 million). Generally, the money center or wholesale bank has relatively few domestic branches.

The geography of a money center bank is usually national and international with large amounts of activity in foreign exchange markets and branches in foreign countries. The home office of the money center bank is generally New York or Chicago. Other cities such as San Francisco, Los Angeles, Boston, Philadelphia, Atlanta, and Dallas also have banks with wholesale financial activities.

For December 31, 1991, eight banks above $20 billion in total assets were identified as money center banks. In New York, those banks were Bankers Trust Co., Chase Manhattan, Chemical Bank, Citicorp, J. P. Morgan, Inc., and Republic Bank. In Chicago, Continental Bank and First Chicago were identified as money center banks. Citicorp had many characteristics of a superregional bank but qualified as a money center bank on six of ten measurements used for screening criteria by the authors.

The money center banks have a higher than average amount of commercial and foreign loans (more than 30% of total loans). Many of the commercial loans tend to be participations in large commercial funding projects. They generally have a large amount of foreign loans and investments (more than 20% of total earning assets). They have only about 15% of earning assets invested in consumer and real estate loans. They tend to hold a large percentage of short-term investments such as federal funds, securities purchased with resale agreements, bankers acceptances, broker call loans, etc. (more than 25% of total earning assets). Many of their investment securities are held as trading account securities.

Money center banks have a lesser dependence on core deposits as a source of funding (core deposits account for less than 20% of assets.). A primary source of funding is purchased CDs and borrowed funds (over 45% of total assets). Foreign funds (more than 15%) and from correspondent relationships due to bank balances (more than 10% of total assets) are significant sources of funds. Consumer core deposits comprise less than 10% of total funding.

Money center banks offer many services similar to investment banking firms. As a result, they generate a higher than average percentage of revenue from fees and non-interest income. They operate with lower margins (generally less than 3% net interest margin). They have a lower overhead burden (less than 1.5% of earning assets). They also have higher productivity measures such as more dollars of assets per employee (over $4 million per employee).

Money center banks deal in, trade, and acquire contracts which remain off-balance sheet financial instruments more than other types of commercial banks. On December 31, 1991, total assets of the eight money center banks mentioned above were $645 billion. On that same date, the sum of off-balance sheet contracts (notional values reported on the FR Y-9 C quarterly report) was $4.3 trillion. The off-balance sheet contract values were seven times the amount of total assets. Information about this peer group is labeled "Money Center Bank" in Figures 1-2 and 1-4.

Financial instruments included in the above total of off-balance sheet contracts are standby letters of credit, risk participations in acceptances, securities lent, assets sold with recourse, direct credit substitutes, interest-rate contracts (such as futures, option, swap, and forward contracts), foreign exchange contracts, performance letters of credit, loan commitments, revolving underwriting facilities, note issuance facilities, and other transaction-related contingencies. Although the notional values of these contracts are not considered a relevant measurement for many purposes, this information is currently reported and provides a relative measure of banks in various classifications. In addition, the long list and the large amounts give a perspective to the need for a professional risk management system.

Financial Goals

In the previously cited dictionary definition, the word *stratagem* was defined as a cleverly contrived scheme for gaining an end. Financial goals and targets are the ends toward which bankers direct their strategies.

Investors have alternatives other than placing their capital in the banking industry. The rate of return on capital by banks must therefore provide a rate of return equivalent to alternative investments with comparable risk characteristics. Although much discussion and research could be directed toward the question of how much is enough, for purposes of this text, 12.5% is shown as the rate of return on capital for community banks in Figure 1-3. Accepting this 12.5% target, the question is: What other goals are consistent with this target?

Financial Formulas

Financial goals for rate of return on equity, growth rate of assets, leverage ratio of capital, and dividend payout are generally quantified for each planning period. Short-term goals may be the same as or different from long-term goals. Financial targets for balance sheet mix and performance ratios are generally related to strategic positions and peer performance.

A rule of thumb in the banking industry is that the dividend payout should be approximately one-third of earnings. If one-third of the 12.5% rate of return on equity is paid out in dividends, 8.3% is retained earnings which increases the amount of capital by a growth rate of 8.3%. Therefore, the annual growth rate of assets must be 8.3% if you assume that the capital leverage ratio (equity as a percentage of total assets) was at a desired level at the beginning of the year.

Another rule of thumb in banking is that a minimum acceptable rate of return on assets is 1%. If this rule is accepted, and given 12.5% as the target return on equity, the equity multiplier must be 12.5, and equity, as a percentage of assets, must be 8.

But, the above equity and return on asset ratios do not fit all four alternative types of banks. Figure 1-4 shows that the actual performance for 1991 did not measure up to these standards. Given the four alternative strategies outlined earlier, what financial goals should be set for capital leverage, for asset growth, and for return on assets?

While the ratios shown in Figure 1-3 are set arbitrarily, they were developed by the authors from experience in monitoring bank types and their ratios. The numbers should be thoughtfully tested. For example,

- Are they internally consistent?
- How do they compare to actual 1991 peer performance ratios?
- How do they compare with today's banking numbers?
- How might these ratios change in the future?

External Forces

Financial goals must bring into consideration the desires of investors and the rules of the bank regulators. In the final analysis, the 12.5% rate of return on equity stated above will be judged by shareholders. In addition, the dividend payout ratio, asset growth rates, and the risk profiles will reflect shareholders' desires. Bank regulatory requirements, on the other hand, will be the primary determinant for capital leverage.

For many community banks and some smaller regional banks, shareholders are local investors. The number of shareholders may not be large, and the individual shareholders will have goals which are similar. In some instances, the group's investment goals will emphasize current income and, therefore, the group will want high current dividends. Alternatively, the group's investment goals may emphasize growth of investment value and, therefore, the group will want a low dividend payout so as to boost book and market values of the shares. An investor group may be conservative and want a low-risk profile. Alternately, an investor group may have goals which include a high growth of earnings and be prepared to accept the risks associated with that goal.

For money center banks, superregionals, and some of the larger regional banks, the share ownership is spread over a large number of investors, including asset management funds. In such circumstances, the market price of the shares reflects the combined influences of investment goals, earnings, dividends, risk profile analysis, and general market expectations. In such an environment, the bank is dependent upon market value of its stock for such things as access to additional capital for growth, executive compensation, credit ratings, and "currency" for acquisitions. Understanding how to influence the market price of the bank's stock is extremely important.

Most financial analysts are very aware of the market power generated by high market capitalization (market price per share multiplied by the number of shares outstanding). The market capitalization of selected banks on December 31, 1991 is shown in Figure 1-5, along with their total assets and market/book ratio.

Figure 1-5

Market Capitalization of Selected Banks*
December 31, 1991

	Total Assets ($ Billions)	Common Equity ($ Millions)		
		Market Value	Book Value	MV/BV
Citicorp	$216.9	$4,155	$7,349	57%
BankAmerica Corp	115.5	7,851	6,737	117
First Interstate Bancorp	48.9	1,883	2,045	92
BancOne Corp	46.3	7,600	3,545	214
Bancorp Hawaii, Inc.	11.4	1,205	724	166
Riggs National Corp	5.5	72	205	35

* Source: 1991 Annual Reports and *The Wall Street Journal*, January 2, 1992.

The influence of bank regulators in the goal setting process is seen primarily in the capital leverage ratio. Bank regulators are charged with the safety and soundness of the banking system. To carry out this responsibility, regulators focus on the level of various risks in individual banks relative to the amount of capital available to absorb losses. If a bank incurs losses, the depositors are at risk, which in turn means the Bank Insurance Fund is at risk. To help quantify the capital requirements, the FDIC Improvement Act of 1991 (FDICIA) specified five levels of equity capital (capital zones) which have specific meaning to individual banks. Those capital zones and the prevailing equity to asset percentage definitions are:

Well capitalized	above 5%
Adequately capitalized	4% to 5%
Undercapitalized	3% to 4%
Significantly undercapitalized	2% to 3%
Critically undercapitalized	under 2%

Where a bank is categorized on the above scheme determines what powers it is permitted. The bottom category is particularly difficult as FDICIA requires that the regulators take quick action to liquidate critically undercapitalized banks on the notion that quick corrective action will mean the least cost to the Bank Insurance Fund. The other categories are less severe but do put constraints on branching, the issuance of brokered CDs, executive compensation, and other matters.

Strategic financial goals of a bank must consider the long-term corporate strategy, the desires of shareholders, and the requirements of bank regulators. In addition, the goals should consider the degree of tolerance for risk on the part of bank management.

Financial Risks

Financial risk is the possibility of loss from a financial transaction entered into with other parties. Financial institutions make loans, issue deposit liabilities, purchase investment securities, borrow funds, and hold or provide for the transfer of large quantities of cash and cash like items. All of these traditional banking activities are financial transactions with other parties, and all of these involve financial risk(s). In addition, many other financial transactions (which may not be considered traditional banking activities) create risks and rewards for bank managers.

Chapter Three of this text discusses the subjects of risk measurement and management. In addition, much new literature has been produced in recent years which describe financial risk, define measurement techniques, and identify tools for control and management of risk. One such document is *Risk Management*, a pamphlet published by the office of the Comptroller of the Currency (OCC).[5] The following quotes are from that pamphlet.

Regulatory Emphasis

Banking is the business of managing risk. Those banks which manage risk well are successful. Those that do not manage it well frequently do not survive. ...

...Nearly every action taken by a banker involves risk, whether it is participation in a highly leveraged financing transaction, the opening of a new branch office, or the purchase of a U. S. Treasury bond. Risk may also result from a banker's inaction in certain circumstances. One of management's roles in the banking business, like in any other business, is to manage that risk. One of the OCC's roles is to ensure that risks within the banking system are being properly identified and managed by bank management and adequately supported by capital.

There are many types of risks inherent in banking. The following represent the major banking risk categories...

Credit Risk is financial exposure resulting from an institution's dependence upon another party to make or keep it whole. It usually occurs in assets shown on the balance sheet, however, it also shows up off-balance sheet in some forms of contingent obligation. It is acquired through actual or implied contractual agreements where bank funds are extended, committed, or exposed.

---

[5] Comptroller of the Currency, *Risk Management*, Washington DC, 1992. This pamphlet was prepared under the general guidance of Thomas M. Fitzgerald, District Administrator, Central District. The project was headed by Director Bank Supervision Robert W. Hefner, Assistance was provided by John T. Berry, Paul R. Fongheiser, Marcia H. Oley, Craig E. Reay, Christopher G. Sablich and David W. Schiltz. This pamphlet is not dated, but was distributed to bankers on September 1, 1992.

Liquidity Risk is traditionally defined as the ability of a bank to meet its obligations as they come due. A practical definition would be the ability (at a reasonable cost) to accommodate decreases in funding sources, increases in assets and payment of expenses.

Market risk is the potential effect external forces have on the value of a bank's assets, liabilities, and off-balance sheet positions. It arises from movements in the financial markets.

Operational risk is the exposure to loss resulting from the failure of a manual or automated operating system to process, produce or analyze items in an accurate, timely and thorough manner.

Interest rate risk is the threat to net interest income arising from repricing differences in a bank's assets and liabilities; the threat to net income arising from fluctuations in market values of financial instruments; and the threat to market value of the bank's equity arising from long-term fixed rate contract positions. The above threats may be on or off the balance sheet.

Transfer risk is the possibility that a customer cannot obtain the appropriate currency to meet an obligation. The customer may have the domestic currency to repay an external currency obligation but is unable to pay because of the inability to obtain, or to transfer, the hard currency needed to pay the external obligation. This risk is highest in countries which have established controls to ration foreign currencies so the country will have foreign exchange to pay for vital imports.

Historically, the OCC was a measurer of risk. For many years OCC examinations focused on the measurement of risk at a bank...(with)...static measurements.

Under the OCC's current supervisory approach, the examiner's role in risk assessment is changing dramatically.

It is the OCC's responsibility to assess the adequacy of a bank's risk management system. In this role the examiner will evaluate how management has identified risks, measured those risks, and implemented systems to control and monitor risks. Emphasis on the evaluation of risk management systems enables the OCC to make a proactive assessment of a bank's condition and performance. Banks with weak risk management systems are ill-prepared for changes in their environment. Such changes could result in losses and possibly failure. By contrast, banks with strong effective risk management systems should enjoy success.

New Financial Instruments

The OCC's emerging emphasis on off-balance sheet items and risk management systems underscores the dynamics of banking today. During the past twenty years (the past decade in particular), the capital markets have virtually exploded with new services and financial instruments.

Loan securitizations and sales have converted bank loans into liquid assets. Mortgage-backed securities provide investment alternatives ranging from credit risk protected government agency securities to exotic derivatives, and the volume of transactions in mortgage-backed securities has grown dramatically from 1980 to 1990. Interest rate swap contracts were first introduced in 1982. Since that time the size of the average contract has fallen, and the number of contracts has grown rapidly. The following quote provides a perspective on the growth of the new financial instruments.[6]

> The result has often been called a revolution in finance. Innovative instruments and transactions — such as interest rate "swaps" and "caps," foreign currency options, interest-only "strips" and other asset "securitizations," and many more — have become commonplace. For successful innovations like mortgage-backed securities and swaps, the rates of growth have been explosive (See Figures 1-6 and 1-7.). Furthermore, the innovations are changing the role of more traditional financial instruments like loans, bonds, and common and preferred stock. While the effects on financial services companies are more noticeable, commercial and industrial entities whose businesses are primarily nonfinancial also have been profoundly affected. The forces that gave rise to the many changes in financial markets and activities persist, and they will inevitably continue to spur further innovation.

Figure 1-6

Mortgage-Related Securities Outstanding

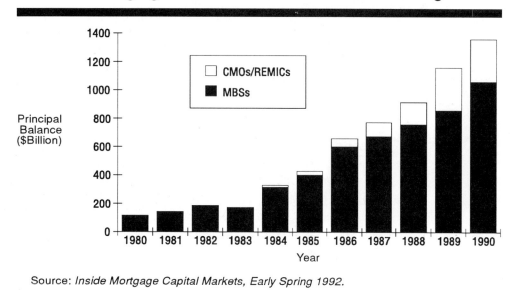

Source: *Inside Mortgage Capital Markets, Early Spring 1992.*

---

[6] *Recognition and Measurement of Financial Instruments: a discussion memorandum,* Financial Accounting Standards Board (FASB), Norwalk, CT, November 18, 1991, p. v.

22

Figure 1-7

Interest Rate Swaps Outstanding

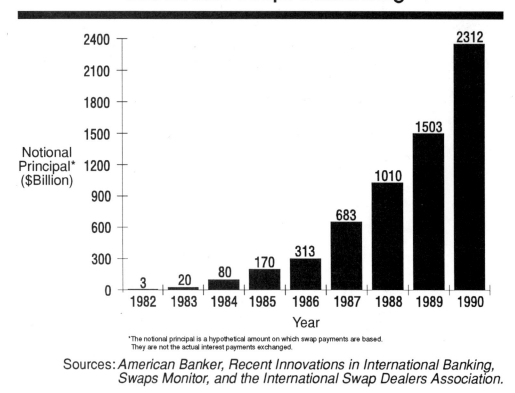

*The notional principal is a hypothetical amount on which swap payments are based.
They are not the actual interest payments exchanged.

Sources: *American Banker, Recent Innovations in International Banking,
Swaps Monitor, and the International Swap Dealers Association.*

**Risk
Measurement**

Static measures, using historical data, do not identify risk in a timely or adequate fashion. Snapshots at a moment in time miss the dynamics. The analysis of growth or change rates and the analysis of financial flows over time are required to understand the essence of risk assumption and control. Assumptions about future probable actions on the part of financial contract parties, as well as, forecasts of the level and term structure of interest rates are required to measure some risks.

Some financial contracts fluctuate in value when customer and market conditions change. For some contracts, the legal performance requirements will change when external events take place in the future. Prepaying, renegotiating, and defaulting are potential alternatives on the part of the maker or original obligation. Calling, renegotiating, or selling are potential alternatives on the part of the holder or owner. The realistic analysis of financial value and future potential takes all of these terms, events, and alternatives into consideration.

For bank managers, identification, acknowledgement, and measurement of risk are part of the job. Logical analytical techniques and appropriate control procedures (consistently followed) are the essence of a risk measurement system. Because many financial transactions are large, fast paced, and dependent upon external conditions, current day tools such as computers, mathematical models, and timely reporting systems are essential. Bank executives cannot rely solely on "black-box" systems, however. Good communication patterns, timely responses, and a team culture based upon professional judgment are also essential.

Conclusions and Summary

Not all banks are alike; and, therefore, each bank must be managed uniquely. The identification and selection of a basic strategy are dependent upon location, capital, market place opportunities, investor goals, and risk tolerance of management.

Financial strategy sets the framework for managerial goals, financial targets, and day-to-day decisions. Strategy identification and selection, therefore, must be the first step, in the managerial process. In those instances where strategy is dictated by tradition, momentum, other circumstance, or lack of alternatives, strategy identification should precede personnel and managerial selections.

Financial goals are set within the context of financial formulas which express the interrelationship of earnings, dividends, capital leverage, and growth. Shareholder desires and regulatory requirements are the external forces which ultimately determine specific financial targets.

Risk management is a process which recognizes the existence of risk as the basis for earning rewards. Credit, liquidity, and interest-rate risk are major factors in the daily operations of a bank. The assumption, measurement, and management of these risks provide the profit opportunities for bank managers.

Chapter TWO

Community Regional National Bank:

A Case Study

This chapter describes the case bank, Community Regional National Bank (CRNB). The chapter provides detailed financial reports for the two most recent years, and forecast financial reports for the next operating year. In addition, a discussion of interest rates is provided, and an interest-rate forecast is presented.

Location   The bank is located in an outlying suburb of a large city with a broad-based economy. Major employers include high technology industry, assembly plants, a variety of service oriented firms, governmental offices, and other financial institutions. In addition to its main office, CRNB has twenty-one branch offices, which offer a full range of banking services. Competition within the market area is offered by three other similar sized commercial banks, and by a number of other types of financial institutions.

Direct competition exists among the four banks in seeking sources and uses of funds. Decisions made by each bank management team will have an impact on the other banks' performance, and, in some market segments, competition is also influenced by the other financial institutions in the market area.

Financial Data   Comprehensive historical financial data is provided for the bank for the last two calendar years (2001 and 2002). The data is presented in financial reports, usually found in a bank annual report, along with other internal reports used by management for analysis and decision making. In addition, a preliminary forecast for the calendar year 2003 is also provided. All financial reports reflect generally accepted accounting principles including accruals, cash flows, maturity structures, and incremental interest rates, as well as appropriate averaging and annualization techniques.

Figure 2-1

ENDING STATEMENT OF CONDITION
Dollars in Thousands

	12/02 ACTUAL	12/01 ACTUAL	DIFFERENCE	PERCENT
ASSETS:				
CASH, FLOAT & RESERVES	27021	25188	1834	7.3
U.S. TREASURIES	86490	78773	7717	9.8
ASSET BACKED SECURITIES	5143	4750	393	8.3
ALL OTHER SECURITIES	6324	8658	-2334	-27.0
TOTAL SECURITIES	97957	92181	5776	6.3
SHORT-TERM INVESTMENTS	23529	16363	7166	43.8
COMMERCIAL LOANS	105879	95964	9915	10.3
REAL ESTATE LOANS	82896	71557	11339	15.8
CONSUMER LOANS	104011	91894	12118	13.2
TOTAL LOANS	292786	259414	33372	12.9
RESERVE FOR LOAN LOSSES	-5036	-4462	-574	12.9
NET LOANS	287750	254952	32798	12.9
TOTAL OTHER ASSETS	18071	17112	959	5.6
TOTAL ASSETS	454329	405796	48533	12.0
LIABILITIES & CAPITAL:				
DEMAND DEPOSITS	43591	41073	2518	6.1
IBC & SAVINGS	107122	94662	12460	13.2
MMDAs	97677	84474	13203	15.6
CONSUMER & OTHER CDs	32187	28777	3410	11.8
LARGE & PUBLIC CDs	131921	118051	13870	11.7
TOTAL DEPOSITS	412497	367036	45461	12.4
BORROWINGS	4913	4782	131	2.7
OTHER LIABILITIES	11438	10537	901	8.6
EQUITY	25481	23441	2040	8.7
TOTAL LIAB & EQUITY	454329	405796	48533	12.0

CRNB's Statements of Condition are presented in Figures 2-1 through 2-4. Figures 2-1 and 2-2 show the Bank's end of period (EOP) assets, liabilities and capital as of December 31 on an actual basis for the historical years 2001 and 2002, and on a forecast basis for the year 2003. The forecast Ending Statement of Condition was developed from the asset and liability management decisions shown in Figure 4-36 in Chapter Four. The actual results that each bank management team achieves, for the simulated year 2003, will obviously differ from the forecast since they will depend on the management team's decisions, on competitive interaction, and on changes in interest rates.

ENDING STATEMENT OF CONDITION
Dollars in Thousands

Figure 2-2

	12/03 FORECAST	12/02 ACTUAL	DIFFERENCE	PERCENT
ASSETS:				
CASH, FLOAT & RESERVES	17615	27021	-9406	-34.8
U.S. TREASURIES	102059	86490	15569	18.0
ASSET BACKED SECURITIES	15129	5143	9986	194.2
ALL OTHER SECURITIES	6474	6324	150	2.4
TOTAL SECURITIES	123662	97957	25705	26.2
SHORT-TERM INVESTMENTS	30911	23529	7382	31.4
COMMERCIAL LOANS	113099	105879	7220	6.8
REAL ESTATE LOANS	84229	82896	1334	1.6
CONSUMER LOANS	111345	104011	7333	7.1
TOTAL LOANS	308674	292786	15887	5.4
RESERVE FOR LOAN LOSSES	-5055	-5036	-19	0.4
NET LOANS	303619	287750	15868	5.5
TOTAL OTHER ASSETS	20494	18071	2423	13.4
TOTAL ASSETS	496301	454329	41972	9.2
LIABILITIES & CAPITAL:				
DEMAND DEPOSITS	46168	43591	2578	5.9
IBC & SAVINGS	113369	107122	6248	5.8
MMDAs	105500	97677	7823	8.0
CONSUMER & OTHER CDs	41704	32187	9518	29.6
LARGE & PUBLIC CDs	144134	131921	12213	9.3
TOTAL DEPOSITS	450876	412497	38379	9.3
BORROWINGS	5167	4913	254	5.2
OTHER LIABILITIES	11934	11438	496	4.3
EQUITY	28324	25481	2843	11.2
TOTAL LIAB & EQUITY	496301	454329	41972	9.2

Detailed Comparative Statements of Condition showing all asset, liability and capital accounts are included in Appendix A. These detailed statements contain all of the accounts that are involved in operating decisions. Periodic Statements of Condition for each month of the years 2000, 2001, 2002, and a forecast for 2003 are shown in Appendices B and C. These periodic statements are useful for observing the actual position attained at each month end, and for noting seasonal and secular trends. The chart of accounts for all financial statements will be used consistently throughout this case.

Figure 2-3

AVERAGE STATEMENT OF CONDITION
Percentage Composition

	1/02 - 12/02 ACTUAL	1/01 - 12/01 ACTUAL	DIFFERENCE
ASSETS:			
CASH, FLOAT & RESERVES	6.0	6.3	-0.3
U.S. TREASURIES	19.3	19.3	-0.0
ASSET BACKED SECURITIES	1.1	1.1	-0.0
ALL OTHER SECURITIES	1.7	3.0	-1.2
TOTAL SECURITIES	22.2	23.5	-1.3
SHORT-TERM INVESTMENTS	4.1	3.0	1.0
COMMERCIAL LOANS	23.5	23.9	-0.3
REAL ESTATE LOANS	18.1	17.4	0.6
CONSUMER LOANS	23.0	22.4	0.5
TOTAL LOANS	64.7	63.8	0.8
RESERVE FOR LOAN LOSSES	-1.1	-1.0	-0.0
NET LOANS	63.6	62.8	0.8
TOTAL OTHER ASSETS	3.9	4.1	-0.2
TOTAL ASSETS	100.0	100.0	0.0
LIABILITIES & CAPITAL:			
DEMAND DEPOSITS	9.9	10.4	-0.5
IBC & SAVINGS	23.5	23.3	0.2
MMDAs	21.2	20.5	0.6
CONSUMER & OTHER CDs	7.1	7.2	-0.1
LARGE & PUBLIC CDs	29.2	29.1	0.0
TOTAL DEPOSITS	91.0	90.7	0.3
BORROWINGS	0.7	0.8	-0.0
OTHER LIABILITIES	2.5	2.6	-0.0
EQUITY	5.7	5.8	-0.1
TOTAL LIAB & EQUITY	100.0	100.0	0.0

Percentage composition Average Statements of Condition, sometimes called common size balance sheets, are shown in Figure 2-3 and 2-4. These statements are prepared using average balances for each period. In these statements each account is divided by total assets so that the percentage composition of the Statement of Condition can be observed. This type of report is very useful for observing changes and trends in assets and liabilities balances and mixes. These statements are also helpful in making comparisons with peer banks.

AVERAGE STATEMENT OF CONDITION
Percentage Composition

Figure 2-4

	1/03 - 12/03 FORECAST	1/02 - 12/02 ACTUAL	DIFFERENCE
ASSETS:			
CASH, FLOAT & RESERVES	3.6	6.0	-2.3
U.S. TREASURIES	20.7	19.3	1.4
ASSET BACKED SECURITIES	2.9	1.1	1.7
ALL OTHER SECURITIES	1.3	1.7	-0.3
TOTAL SECURITIES	25.0	22.2	2.8
SHORT-TERM INVESTMENTS	4.9	4.1	0.8
COMMERCIAL LOANS	23.0	23.5	-0.5
REAL ESTATE LOANS	17.5	18.1	-0.6
CONSUMER LOANS	22.8	23.0	-0.1
TOTAL LOANS	63.4	64.7	-1.3
RESERVE FOR LOAN LOSSES	-1.0	-1.1	0.0
NET LOANS	62.3	63.6	-1.2
TOTAL OTHER ASSETS	3.9	3.9	-0.0
TOTAL ASSETS	100.0	100.0	0.0
LIABILITIES & CAPITAL:			
DEMAND DEPOSITS	9.7	9.9	-0.1
IBC & SAVINGS	23.1	23.5	-0.3
MMDAs	21.3	21.2	0.0
CONSUMER & OTHER CDs	7.6	7.1	0.5
LARGE & PUBLIC CDs	29.4	29.2	0.2
TOTAL DEPOSITS	91.3	91.0	0.3
BORROWINGS	0.7	0.7	0.0
OTHER LIABILITIES	2.2	2.5	-0.2
EQUITY	5.7	5.7	-0.0
TOTAL LIAB & EQUITY	100.0	100.0	0.0

Detailed comparative percentage composition Statements of Condition showing all asset, liability and capital accounts are provided in Appendix A. Detailed percentage composition Statements of Condition on a monthly basis are included in Appendices B and C for the years 2000 through 2002 on an actual basis, along with a forecast for 2003. Periodic statements are useful for observing changes in the mix of assets and liabilities over time, and to reveal seasonal patterns in sources and uses of financial resources.

Figure 2-5

STATEMENT OF INCOME
Dollars in Thousands

	1/02 - 12/02 ACTUAL	1/01 - 12/01 ACTUAL	DIFFERENCE	PERCENT
INTEREST INCOME:				
U.S. TREASURIES	6460	5978	482	8.1
ASSET BACKED SECURITIES	606	578	28	4.9
ALL OTHER SECURITIES	664	1244	-580	-46.6
TOTAL SECURITIES	7730	7800	-70	-0.9
SHORT-TERM INVESTMENTS	1432	1072	360	33.6
COMMERCIAL LOANS	10269	9938	331	3.3
REAL ESTATE LOANS	7980	6953	1027	14.8
CONSUMER LOANS	14147	11700	2447	20.9
TOTAL LOANS	32396	28591	3805	13.3
TOTAL INTEREST INCOME	41558	37463	4095	10.9
INTEREST EXPENSE:				
IBC & SAVINGS	5219	4613	606	13.1
MMDAs	6815	5606	1210	21.6
CONSUMER & SMALL CDs	2465	2144	321	14.9
LARGE & PUBLIC CDs	10247	10191	56	0.6
TOTAL DEPOSITS	24746	22554	2193	9.7
BORROWINGS	248	28	-32	-11.6
TOTAL INTEREST EXPENSE	24994	22834	2160	9.5
NET INTEREST INCOME	16563	14629	1935	13.2
PROVISION FOR LOAN LOSS	1831	1612	219	13.6
NET INT INCOME AFTER PROV	14732	13016	1716	13.2
OTHER INCOME	3095	2864	231	8.1
OTHER EXPENSE	12681	11055	1626	14.7
NET INCOME BEFORE TAXES	5147	4826	321	6.6
INCOME TAXES	1807	1617	190	11.8
NET INCOME	3340	3209	130	4.1

CRNB's Statements of Income for 2001 and 2002 are shown in Figure 2-5, along with the changes in each account on a dollar and percent basis. Figure 2-6 provides a forecast of the same information for the year 2003 along with a comparison with 2002. Detailed comparative Statements of Income are contained in Appendix A. Detailed periodic Statements of Income, on a monthly basis, are included in Appendices B and C for each year.

STATEMENT OF INCOME
Dollars in Thousands

Figure 2-6

	1/03 - 12/03 FORECAST	1/02 - 12/02 ACTUAL	DIFFERENCE	PERCENT
INTEREST INCOME:				
U.S. TREASURIES	7475	6460	1014	15.7
ASSET BACKED SECURITIES	1465	606	859	141.7
ALL OTHER SECURITIES	620	664	-44	-6.6
TOTAL SECURITIES	9560	7730	1830	23.7
SHORT-TERM INVESTMENTS	1778	1432	347	24.2
COMMERCIAL LOANS	10909	10269	640	6.2
REAL ESTATE LOANS	8149	7980	168	2.1
CONSUMER LOANS	15992	14147	1846	13.0
TOTAL LOANS	35050	32396	2654	8.2
TOTAL INTEREST INCOME	46389	41558	4831	11.6
INTEREST EXPENSE:				
IBC & SAVINGS	5711	5219	492	9.4
MMDAs	7160	6815	345	5.1
CONSUMER & SMALL CDs	2772	2465	308	12.5
LARGE & PUBLIC CDs	11136	10247	889	8.7
TOTAL DEPOSITS	26780	24746	2033	8.2
BORROWINGS	250	248	2	0.9
TOTAL INTEREST EXPENSE	27030	24994	2036	8.1
NET INTEREST INCOME	19359	16563	2795	16.9
PROVISION FOR LOAN LOSS	1489	1831	-342	-18.7
NET INT INCOME AFTER PROV	17870	14732	3138	21.3
OTHER INCOME	3384	3095	288	9.3
OTHER EXPENSE	14728	12681	2047	16.1
NET INCOME BEFORE TAXES	6525	5147	1379	26.8
INCOME TAXES	2362	1807	555	30.7
NET INCOME	4163	3340	823	24.6

Total interest income is forecast to rise from $41,558,000 in 2002 to $46,389,000 in 2003 for an increase of 11.6 percent. During the same time period interest expense is forecast to increase from $24,994,000 to $27,030,000 or 8.1 percent. These changes result in an increase in net interest income of $2,795,000, which is a key factor in the forecast increase of 24.6 percent increase in net income. The actual net income earned for 2003 will be a function of each bank management team's decisions.

Figure 2-7

KEY RATIOS REPORT

	1/02 - 12/02 ACTUAL	1/01 - 12/01 ACTUAL	DIFFERENCE
PERFORMANCE:			
RETURN ON EQUITY %	13.61	14.31	-0.69
RETURN ON ASSETS %	0.78	0.84	-0.06
EARNINGS PER SHARE(ANN$)	1.11	1.07	0.04
COMMON DIV PER SHARE ($)	0.43	0.41	0.03
BOOK VALUE PER SHR(EOP$)	8.49	7.81	0.68
EARNING/TOTAL ASSETS %	91.10	90.54	0.56
INT BEAR/TOTAL DEPOSITS %	89.13	88.51	0.62
INTEREST MARGIN & OVERHEAD:			
AVG NATIONAL PRIME RATE	10.01	10.87	-0.86
YIELD ON EARNING ASSETS	10.74	10.96	-0.23
COST OF FUNDS RATE	7.14	7.37	-0.23
SPREAD %	3.60	3.60	0.00
INT MARGIN ON E.A. %	4.32	4.36	-0.04
NET OVERHEAD TO E.A. %	2.46	2.37	0.09
LOAN POSITION:			
LOANS/TOTAL DEPOSITS %	71.12	70.43	0.69
LOANS TO EARNING ASSETS	71.06	70.57	0.49
LOSS PROVISION/LOANS %	0.66	0.66	0.00
NET CHARGE-OFFS/LOANS %	0.45	0.44	0.01
LOSS RESERVE/LOANS %	1.69	1.69	0.00
NONPERFORMING/LNS(EOP) %	1.40	1.43	-0.03
CAPITAL LEVERAGE:			
TIER 1 RISK-BASED CAPITAL %	8.51	8.69	-0.18
TOTAL RISK-BASED CAPITAL %	9.76	9.95	-0.18
ASSET LEVERAGE %	5.30	5.41	-0.11
EQUITY TO ASSETS %	5.74	5.87	-0.14
DIVIDEND PAYOUT %	38.92	38.01	0.91
LIQUIDITY:			
CASH/TOTAL DEPOSITS %	6.64	7.00	-0.36
PURCHASED FUNDS/E.A. %	32.32	32.48	-0.16
NET FED FUNDS/EQUITY %	-68.13	-47.66	-20.47
PER EMPLOYEE:			
SALARIES & BENEFITS ($)	28325	26275	2050
TOTAL ASSETS ($ MILLIONS)	1.83	1.75	0.07

Key Ratios Reports are shown in Figures 2-7 and 2-8 on an actual basis for 2001 and 2002, and on a forecast basis for 2003. Detailed comparative Key Ratios Reports are provided in Appendix A. Key Ratios Reports on a monthly basis are contained in Appendices B and C.

KEY RATIOS REPORT

Figure 2-8

	1/03 - 12/03 FORECAST	1/02 - 12/02 ACTUAL	DIFFERENCE
PERFORMANCE:			
RETURN ON EQUITY %	15.33	13.61	1.72
RETURN ON ASSETS %	0.87	0.78	0.09
EARNINGS PER SHARE(ANN$)	1.39	1.11	0.27
COMMON DIV PER SHARE ($)	0.44	0.43	0.01
BOOK VALUE PER SHR(EOP$)	9.44	8.49	0.95
EARNING/TOTAL ASSETS %	93.45	91.10	2.36
INT BEAR/TOTAL DEPOSITS %	89.33	89.13	0.20
INTEREST MARGIN & OVERHEAD:			
AVG NATIONAL PRIME RATE	10.00	10.01	-0.01
YIELD ON EARNING ASSETS	10.47	10.74	-0.27
COST OF FUNDS RATE	6.89	7.14	-0.24
SPREAD %	3.57	3.60	-0.03
INT MARGIN ON E.A. %	4.39	4.32	0.07
NET OVERHEAD TO E.A. %	2.55	2.46	0.09
LOAN POSITION:			
LOANS/TOTAL DEPOSITS %	69.43	71.12	-1.69
LOANS TO EARNING ASSETS	67.84	71.06	-3.22
LOSS PROVISION/LOANS %	0.49	0.66	-0.17
NET CHARGE-OFFS/LOANS %	0.49	0.45	0.03
LOSS RESERVE/LOANS %	1.62	1.69	-0.07
NONPERFORMING/LNS(EOP) %	1.41	1.40	-0.01
CAPITAL LEVERAGE:			
TIER 1 RISK-BASED CAPITAL %	8.66	8.51	0.15
TOTAL RISK-BASED CAPITAL %	9.91	9.76	0.15
ASSET LEVERAGE %	5.36	5.30	0.06
EQUITY TO ASSETS %	5.70	5.74	-0.03
DIVIDEND PAYOUT %	31.71	38.92	-7.22
LIQUIDITY:			
CASH/TOTAL DEPOSITS %	4.01	6.64	-2.63
PURCHASED FUNDS/E.A. %	31.73	32.32	-0.59
NET FED FUNDS/EQUITY %	-65.38	-68.13	2.75
PER EMPLOYEE:			
SALARIES & BENEFITS ($)	30527	28325	2202
TOTAL ASSETS ($ MILLIONS)	1.87	1.83	0.04

The Key Ratios Report includes many of the traditional ratios used to measure bank performance utilizing the CAMEL framework. Ratios are utilized to assess Capital position, Asset quality, Earnings, and Liquidity. The overall performance of the bank is the ultimate measure of Management. Unless noted as EOP, these ratios use an average balance for the calculation.

Figure 2-9

INTEREST RATE REPORT

	1/02 - 12/02 ACTUAL	1/01 - 12/01 ACTUAL	DIFFERENCE
EARNING ASSET YIELDS:			
U.S. TREASURIES	7.82	8.08	-0.26
ASSET BACKED SECURITIES	12.08	12.73	-0.65
ALL OTHER SECURITIES	12.75	14.78	-2.03
TOTAL SECURITIES	8.44	9.18	-0.74
SHORT-TERM INVESTMENTS	8.08	9.16	-1.09
COMMERCIAL LOANS	10.18	10.87	-0.69
REAL ESTATE LOANS	10.28	10.41	-0.14
CONSUMER LOANS	14.38	13.62	0.76
TOTAL LOANS	11.70	11.71	-0.01
TOTAL EARNING ASSETS	10.74	10.96	-0.23
COST OF FUNDS RATES:			
IBC & SAVINGS	5.18	5.18	0.00
MMDAs	7.49	7.13	0.37
CONSUMER & OTHER CDs	8.12	7.74	0.38
LARGE & PUBLIC CDs	8.20	9.15	-0.95
TOTAL DEPOSITS	7.13	7.35	-0.22
BORROWINGS	8.03	9.15	-1.12
TOTAL INT-BEAR LIAB	7.14	7.37	-0.23
NET INTEREST SPREAD	3.60	3.60	0.00
NET INTEREST INCOME	4.32	4.36	-0.04
MARKET RATES:			
PRIME RATE (LG BKS)	10.00	10.87	-0.87
FED FUNDS RATE (NATIONAL)	8.10	9.22	-1.12
TREASURY BILL RATE 3 MO	7.51	8.11	-0.60
US GOVT YIELD (3 YRS)	8.25	8.55	-0.30

Because interest income is the major source of earnings for most banks and interest expense is the major expense, the Interest Rate Report is important for bank analysis and management. The actual Interest Rate Report for CRNB for the years 2001 and 2002 is presented in Figure 2-9. The forecast year of 2003 is compared to 2002 in Figure 2-10. The earning asset yields are calculated by dividing total interest income earned on each asset by the average balance for the particular asset. In a similar manner, the cost of funds rate for each liability is calculated by dividing total interest expense for each liability by the average balance for the appropriate liability. The report also shows the difference in each asset yield or cost of fund rate between the two periods.

INTEREST RATE REPORT

Figure 2-10

	1/03 - 12/03 FORECAST	1/02 - 12/02 ACTUAL	DIFFERENCE
EARNING ASSET YIELDS:			
U.S. TREASURIES	7.57	7.82	-0.26
ASSET BACKED SECURITIES	10.46	12.08	-1.62
ALL OTHER SECURITIES	12.24	12.75	-0.51
TOTAL SECURITIES	8.16	8.44	-0.27
SHORT-TERM INVESTMENTS	7.49	8.08	-0.59
COMMERCIAL LOANS	9.95	10.18	-0.23
REAL ESTATE LOANS	9.76	10.28	-0.51
CONSUMER LOANS	14.70	14.38	0.32
TOTAL LOANS	11.61	11.70	-0.09
TOTAL EARNING ASSETS	10.47	10.74	-0.27
COST OF FUNDS RATES:			
IBC & SAVINGS	5.18	5.18	0.00
MMDAs	7.05	7.49	-0.45
CONSUMER & OTHER CDs	7.63	8.12	-0.49
LARGE & PUBLIC CDs	7.94	8.20	-0.26
TOTAL DEPOSITS	6.89	7.13	-0.24
BORROWINGS	7.02	8.03	-1.01
TOTAL INT-BEAR LIAB	6.89	7.14	-0.24
NET INTEREST SPREAD	3.57	3.60	-0.03
NET INTEREST INCOME	4.39	4.32	0.07
MARKET RATES:			
PRIME RATE (LG BKS)	10.00	10.00	0.00
FED FUNDS RATE (NATIONAL)	7.31	8.10	-0.79
TREASURY BILL RATE 3 MO	6.81	7.51	-0.70
US GOVT YIELD (3 YRS)	7.47	8.25	-0.78

At the bottom of each Interest Rate Report, several market interest rates are shown. These rates are influenced by a variety of economic and monetary factors. Market rates cannot be controlled or influenced by the bank, but they may serve as the basis for the bank management team's asset and liability pricing decisions. For example, the rate on commercial loans charged by the bank is a differential to the prime rate shown in market rates. Summary comparative Interest Rate Reports are contained in Appendix A, and monthly periodic Interest Rate Reports are included in Appendices B and C.

Figure 2-11

LINE OF BUSINESS REPORT
Summary
Dollars in Thousands

	1/02 - 12/02 ACTUAL	1/01 - 12/01 ACTUAL	DIFFERENCE
SOURCES ($):			
RETAIL	204546	179261	25285
BUSINESS	76984	69778	7205
WHOLESALE	108171	96920	11250
TOTAL	389701	345960	43741
USES ($):			
RETAIL	176060	152708	23352
BUSINESS	100866	91435	9431
INVESTMENTS	112775	101816	10958
TOTAL	389701	345960	43741
SOURCES NET OF USES ($):			
RETAIL	28486	26553	1933
BUSINESS	-23882	-21657	-2226
WHOLESALE/INVESTMENTS	-4604	-4896	292
SOURCES (%):			
RETAIL	52.49	51.82	0.67
BUSINESS	19.75	20.17	-0.41
WHOLESALE	27.76	28.01	-0.26
TOTAL	100.00	100.00	0.00
USES (%):			
RETAIL	45.18	44.14	1.04
BUSINESS	25.88	26.43	-0.55
INVESTMENTS	28.94	29.43	-0.49
TOTAL	100.00	100.00	0.00

As a technique for understanding which markets are being served by the bank, a report has been designed which allocates all accounts reported on the Statement of Condition to a particular market category. On the asset side of the statement of condition which represents uses of funds, the markets have been categorized as retail, business, and investments. Total uses are equal to average earning assets. On the liability side, which represents sources of funds, the retail and business categories have been retained and a balancing category called investments has been added.

Figure 2-12

LINE OF BUSINESS REPORT
Summary
Dollars in Thousands

	1/03 - 12/03 FORECAST	1/02 - 12/02 ACTUAL	DIFFERENCE
SOURCES ($):			
RETAIL	235172	204546	30626
BUSINESS	85982	76984	8999
WHOLESALE	123869	108171	15698
TOTAL	445024	389701	55323
USES ($):			
RETAIL	192288	176060	16228
BUSINESS	109636	100866	8770
INVESTMENTS	143099	112775	30325
TOTAL	445024	389701	55323
SOURCES NET OF USES ($):			
RETAIL	42884	28486	14398
BUSINESS	-23654	-23882	229
WHOLESALE/INVESTMENTS	-19230	-4604	-146263
SOURCES (%):			
RETAIL	52.84	52.49	0.36
BUSINESS	19.32	19.75	-0.43
WHOLESALE	27.83	27.76	0.08
TOTAL	100.00	100.00	0.00
USES (%):			
RETAIL	43.21	45.18	-1.97
BUSINESS	24.64	25.88	-1.25
INVESTMENTS	32.16	28.94	3.22
TOTAL	100.00	100.00	0.00

The summary Line of Business Reports are shown in Figures 2-11 and 2-12. Both total dollars and percentages are shown for each of the categories, and a net position is determined for each category. As shown in the report, the retail markets have been net providers of funds, and business and investments have been net users of funds during 2001 and 2002. The forecast for 2003 indicates that the retail markets will increase as net providers of funds, the business markets will maintain their relative position, and investments will increase as a net user of financial resources. Detailed comparative Line of Business Reports are included in Appendix A.

Figure 2-13

INTEREST VARIANCE ANALYSIS
SEC Method

2002 ACTUAL vs. 2001 ACTUAL

INTEREST INCOME CHANGE DUE TO:	TOTAL VOLUME	RATE	TOTAL CHANGE
SHORT-TERM TREASURIES	387	-205	181
LONG-TERM TREASURIES	290	10	300
ASSET BACKED SECURITIES	59	-30	28
ALL OTHER SECURITIES	-368	-212	-580
TOTAL SECURITIES	619	-689	-70
SHORT-TERM INVESTMENTS	499	-139	360
COMMERCIAL LOANS-FIXED	417	-229	189
COMMERCIAL LOANS-FLOAT	569	-427	142
MORTGAGE LOANS-FIXED	439	-28	411
MORTGAGE LOANS-ADJ	417	-64	353
HOME EQUITY LOANS	269	-6	263
CONSUMER LOANS	1118	719	1836
CREDIT CARD LOANS	573	0	573
AUTO LOANS	35	3	38
TOTAL LOANS	3835	-30	3805
TOTAL EARNING ASSETS	4892	-797	4095

INTEREST EXPENSE CHANGE DUE TO:	TOTAL VOLUME	RATE	TOTAL CHANGE
IBC & SAVINGS	607	-1	606
MMDAs	910	300	1210
SMALL CDs	186	124	311
LARGE CDs	903	-788	116
PUBLIC CDs	269	-328	-59
OTHER CDs	24	-14	10
TOTAL CERTIFICATES	1371	-995	377
SHORT-TERM BOR FNDS	2	-35	-32
LONG-TERM DEBT	0	0	0
TOTAL INT-BEAR LIAB	2892	-732	2160
NET INTEREST INCOME	1662	273	1935

Interest Variance Analysis is a useful technique for explaining the difference in net interest income from one year to the next. An analysis of interest variance is required by the Securities and Exchange Commission (SEC) and the Commission's two variance method is illustrated for CRNB in Figures 2-13 and 2-14. See Appendix F for an explanation of the calculations for the Interest Variance Analysis.

INTEREST VARIANCE ANALYSIS
SEC Method

Figure 2-14

2003 FORECAST vs. 2002 ACTUAL

INTEREST INCOME CHANGE DUE TO:	TOTAL VOLUME	RATE	TOTAL CHANGE
SHORT-TERM TREASURIES	1050	-247	803
LONG-TERM TREASURIES	118	93	211
ASSET BACKED SECURITIES	950	-91	859
ALL OTHER SECURITIES	-7	-37	-44
TOTAL SECURITIES	2096	-266	1830
SHORT-TERM INVESTMENTS	458	-111	347
COMMERCIAL LOANS-FIXED	402	49	451
COMMERCIAL LOANS-FLOAT	479	-290	189
MORTGAGE LOANS-FIXED	-91	-10	-101
MORTGAGE LOANS-ADJ	482	-327	155
HOME EQUITY LOANS	148	-34	114
CONSUMER LOANS	694	18	713
CREDIT CARD LOANS	788	249	1037
AUTO LOANS	106	-10	96
TOTAL LOANS	2904	-250	2654
TOTAL EARNING ASSETS	5918	-1087	4831

INTEREST EXPENSE CHANGE DUE TO:	TOTAL VOLUME	RATE	TOTAL CHANGE
IBC & SAVINGS	495	-3	492
MMDAs	768	-423	345
SMALL CDs	441	-157	285
LARGE CDs	691	-337	354
PUBLIC CDs	536	-1	535
OTHER CDs	23	0	23
TOTAL CERTIFICATES	1685	-489	1196
SHORT-TERM BOR FNDS	35	-33	2
LONG-TERM DEBT	0	0	0
TOTAL INT-BEAR LIAB	2912	-877	2036
NET INTEREST INCOME	5270	-2475	2795

The SEC two variance method shows which part of the change in interest income or interest expense in each account is attributable to changes in volume of balances and which part results from changes in interest rates. Interest rates for 2003 are forecast to be lower than 2002 resulting in a negative rate variance, while higher forecast balances produce a positive volume variance.

Figure 2-15

STATEMENT OF CASH FLOWS (SFAS 95)
Dollars in Thousands

	2002 ACTUAL	2001 ACTUAL	DIFFERENCE	PERCENT
CASH FLOWS FROM OPERATING ACTIVITIES:				
INTEREST ON INVESTMENTS	9162	8872	290	3.3
INTEREST & FEES ON LOANS	32396	28591	3805	13.3
NON-INTEREST INCOME	3095	2864	231	8.1
CASH IN FROM OPERATIONS	44653	40327	4326	10.7
INTEREST ON DEPOSITS	-24746	-22554	-2193	9.7
INTEREST ON BORROWINGS	-248	-281	32	-11.6
NON-INTEREST EXPENSE	-12681	-11055	-1626	14.7
TAXES PAID	-1807	-1617	-190	11.8
NET CHANGE IN OTHER LIAB	901	802	99	12.4
CASH OUT FROM OPERATIONS	-38581	-34703	-3877	11.2
NET CASH FROM OPERATIONS	6072	5623	449	8.0
CASH FLOWS FROM INVESTING ACTIVITIES:				
MAT/SALE OF SECURITIES	173892	193414	-19522	-10.1
REPAYMENT OF LOANS	431128	375722	55405	14.7
SALE OF ASSETS	5137	5167	-25	-0.5
CASH IN FROM INVESTING	610156	574298	35858	6.2
PURCHASE OF SECURITIES	-179668	-198290	-18622	-9.4
NEW LOANS	-465757	-406599	-59158	14.5
ACQUISITION OF ASSETS	-6095	-6056	-39	0.6
CASH OUT FROM INVESTING	-651520	-610945	-40575	6.6
NET CASH FROM INVESTING	-41365	-36647	-4718	12.9
CASH FLOWS FROM FINANCING ACTIVITIES:				
NEW CERTIFICATES	541848	483353	58494	12.1
NEW BORROWING	62235	61691	544	0.9
INCREASE IN DDA/SVNGS	28181	24759	3422	13.8
COMMON STOCK & SURPLUS	0	0	0	0.0
CASH IN FROM FINANCING	632263	569803	62460	11.0

A Statement of Cash Flows prepared in the manner prescribed by the FASB in SFAS 95 is shown in Figures 2-15 and 2-16 for the years 2001 and 2002. This report explains the overall change in cash and cash equivalents from one period to the next by indicating the net change in cash resulting from operating activities, investing activities, and financing activities. The report

STATEMENT OF CASH FLOWS (SFAS 95)

Dollars in Thousands

Figure 2-16

	2002 ACTUAL	2001 ACTUAL	DIFFERENCE	PERCENT
IMPACT OF CASH FLOWS:				
CASH, RESERVES & DUE FROM	-47209	-41336	-5873	14.2
ITEMS IN PROCESS	1330	1589	-259	-16.3
NET CHANGE IN CASH	-45879	-39747	-6132	15.4
TERM FED FUNDS SOLD	0	0	0	0.0
OVERNIGHT FED FUNDS SOLD	7166	6143	1023	16.7
TRADING ACCOUNT	0	0	0	0.0
NET CHANGE IN FUNDS SOLD	7166	6143	1023	16.7
CASH EQUIVALENT CHANGE	-38713	-33604	-5109	15.2
BEGINNING BALANCES:				
CASH, RESERVES & DUE FROM	10884	13557	-2673	-19.7
ITEMS IN PROCESS	14303	12714	1589	12.5
TERM FED FUNDS SOLD	0	0	0	0.0
OVERNIGHT FED FUNDS SOLD	16363	10220	6143	60.1
TRADING ACCOUNT	0	0	0	0.0
BEGINNING CASH & EQUIV	41551	36492	5059	13.9
ENDING BALANCES:				
CASH, RESERVES & DUE FROM	11388	10884	504	4.6
ITEMS IN PROCESS	15633	14303	1330	9.3
TERM FED FUNDS SOLD	0	0	0	0.0
OVERNIGHT FED FUNDS SOLD	23529	16363	7166	43.8
TRADING ACCOUNT	0	0	0	0.0
ENDING CASH & EQUIV	50550	41551	9000	21.7
RECONCILIATION OF NET INCOME TO NET				
CASH PROVIDED BY OPERATING ACTIVITIES:				
NET INCOME	3340	3209	130	4.1
ADJUSTMENTS TO RECONCILE				
PROVISION FOR LOAN LOSS	1831	1612	219	13.6
GAIN(LOSS) ON SECURITIES	0	0	0	0.0
TOTAL ADJUSTMENTS	1831	1612	219	13.6
NET CASH FROM OPERATIONS	5171	4822	349	7.2

is a bridge from one balance sheet to another and includes relevant income statement items as well as changes in balance sheet accounts.

Cash and equivalents at the beginning of 2002 totaled $41,551,000. Net cash provided by all activities during 2002 was $9,000,000 which resulted in an ending balance in cash and equivalents of $50,550,000.

Fair Market Value of Assets and Liabilities Report

The Fair Market Value of Assets and Liabilities Report is shown in Figure 2-17. This report is an outgrowth of the SFAS #107 "Disclosures About the Fair Value of Financial Instruments." SFAS #107 requires CRNB to disclose the estimated fair value of its financial instruments; i.e., loans, investments, deposits and debt instruments.

In determining the fair value of financial instruments, SFAS #107 requires the use of quoted market prices, where available. In cases where quoted market prices are not available, fair values are based on CRNB's best estimate of fair values, using techniques that include calculating the present value of future cash flows. Present value is calculated by estimating the future cash flows and discounting them back using a build-up approach to determine the discount rate. Future cash flows are effected by scheduled principal maturities, repricing characteristics, prepayment assumptions, and interest cash flows. The build-up approach starts with a rate from the Treasury yield curve and adds amounts for credit quality, servicing expense, and a prepayment option price to arrive at the discount rate. These techniques are significantly affected by the assumptions used, such as projections of future cash flows and discount rates. Therefore, CRNB's estimates of fair value for certain financial instruments cannot be substantiated by comparison to independent markets, nor may the estimate of fair value represent the amounts that would be actually realized in the sale of the financial instruments.

Cash	The fair value is assumed to be the carrying value.
Short-Term Investments	The fair value is assumed to be the carrying value.
Securities	Fair values are based on quoted market prices, if available. If quoted market prices are not available, fair value is estimated using the quoted market prices for comparable securities. If there are no comparable securities for which market prices are available, fair value is based on a calculated present value.
Loans	The fair value of loans is determined building portfolios of loans with similar characteristics, estimating the future cash flows, then using a built-up discount rate.
Deposits	The fair value of demand deposits, checking and savings accounts, and money market deposit accounts is defined by SFAS #107 to be the amount payable on demand at the reporting date. CRNB has chosen to report the value of its core-deposit intangibles separately as allowed by SFAS #107. The fair value of fixed term certificates of deposit is determined by calculating the present value of the estimated cash flows, using a discount rate that takes into account the possibility of early withdrawal.
Short-Term Borrowings	The fair value is assumed to be the carrying value.

FAIR MARKET VALUE OF ASSETS & LIABILITIES
Dollars in Thousands
December 31, 2002

Figure 2-17

	FAIR MARKET VALUE	NET CARRYING VALUE	DIFFERENCE	PERCENT
FINANCIAL ASSETS:				
CASH, FLOAT & RESERVES	27021	27021	0	0.00
SHORT-TERM TREASURIES	44238	44290	-52	-0.12
LONG-TERM TREASURIES	42192	42200	-8	-0.02
ASSET BACKED SECURITIES	5520	5143	377	7.32
ALL OTHER SECURITIES	6329	6324	5	0.08
TOTAL SECURITIES	98278	97957	321	0.33
SHORT-TERM INVESTMENTS	23529	23529	0	0.00
COMMERCIAL LOANS-FIXED	48132	46946	1186	2.53
COMMERCIAL LOANS-FLOAT	57875	56497	1378	2.44
MORTGAGE LOANS-FIXED	32134	32866	-732	-2.23
MORTGAGE LOANS-ADJ	34466	34501	-36	-0.10
HOME EQUITY LOANS	15601	15294	307	2.01
CONSUMER LOANS	73310	70556	2754	3.90
CREDIT CARD LOANS	30182	29340	842	2.87
AUTO LOANS	2116	2072	44	2.14
TOTAL LOANS	293816	288071	5745	1.99
UNALLOCATED RESERVES		-321	321	-100.00
NET LOANS	293816	287750	6066	2.11
TOTAL FINANCIAL ASSETS	442644	436258	6387	1.46
FINANCIAL LIABILITIES:				
DEMAND DEPOSITS	43591	43591	0	0.00
IBC & SAVINGS	107122	107122	0	0.00
MMDAs	97677	97677	0	0.00
SMALL CDs	29293	28969	324	1.12
LARGE CDs	94528	94416	113	0.12
PUBLIC CDs	37561	37506	55	0.15
OTHER CDs	3227	3217	10	0.31
TOTAL DEPOSITS	412999	412497	502	0.12
SHORT-TERM BOR FUNDS	4913	4913	0	0.00
LONG-TERM DEBT	0	0	0	0.00
TOTAL FINANCIAL LIAB	417912	417410	502	0.12
TOTAL UNRECOGNIZED ITEMS	0	0	0	0.00
CORE DEPOSIT INTANGIBLES:				
CORE DEP INTANG PURCHASED		925	-925	-100.00
DEMAND DEPOSITS	1416		1416	3.25
IBC & SAVINGS	877		877	0.82
MMDAs	-1273		-1273	-1.30
TOTAL CORE DEP INTANG	1021	925	96	0.04
FIXED ASSETS & NET OTHER	5708	5708	0	0.00
NET TOTAL ASSET VALUES	31461	25481	5980	23.47

Figure 2-18

PRICE/EARNINGS RATIO

	12/02 ACTUAL	12/01 ACTUAL	DIFFERENCE
CAPITAL FACTOR	1.18	3.47	-2.29
PROFITABILITY FACTOR	2.05	2.31	-0.26
LIQUIDITY FACTOR	2.64	2.50	0.14
GROWTH FACTOR	2.98	4.00	-1.02
ASSET QUALITY FACTOR	2.00	2.00	0.00
RATE LEVEL FACTOR	-0.01	-0.01	0.00
PRICE/EARNINGS RATIO	10.84	14.26	-3.42
C1 ASSET LEVERAGE	0.66	0.83	-0.17
C2 DEPOSITS TO EQUITY	0.79	1.83	-1.04
C3 LOANS TO EQUITY	0.09	0.96	-0.87
C4 RISK BASED CAPITAL	-0.36	-0.15	-0.21
CAPITAL FACTOR (C1+C2+C3+C4)	1.18	3.47	-2.29
P1 RETURN ON ASSETS	0.83	0.93	-0.09
P2 NET INT MARGIN	1.10	1.12	-0.02
P3 OVERHEAD	0.11	0.26	-0.15
PROFITABILITY FACTOR (P1+P2+P3)	2.05	2.31	-0.26
L1 NET FED FDS TO EQUITY	2.10	1.91	0.19
L2 LOANS TO AVAIL DEP	2.29	2.25	0.04
L3 PURCH FDS TO EA	1.13	1.13	0.00
L4 S-T INV TO ASSETS	2.39	2.21	0.18
LIQUIDITY FACTOR (L1+L2+L3+L4) / 3	2.64	2.50	0.14
G1 DEPOSIT GROWTH	1.23	1.19	0.05
G2 LOAN GROWTH	1.34	1.21	0.13
G3 INCOME GROWTH	0.41	2.01	-1.60
GROWTH FACTOR[*] (G1+G2+G3)	2.98	4.00	-1.02
Q1 INVEST MKT TO BOOK	0.62	0.34	0.28
Q2 LOSS PROV TO LOANS	1.72	1.51	0.22
Q3 LOAN CONCENTRATION	0.78	0.94	-0.16
ASSET QUALITY FACTOR[*] (Q1+Q2+Q3)	2.00	2.00	0.00
RATE LEVEL FACTOR	-0.01	-0.01	0.00
PRICE/EARNINGS RATIO	10.83	14.26	-24.1
EARNINGS PER SHARE(ANN)	1.11	1.06	0.05
STOCK PRICE PER SHARE	12.02	15.12	-3.10

[*] Growth factor has a maximum value of 4.00. Asset Quality factor has a maximum value of 2.00. Refer to Figure 2-21.

The price/earnings (P/E) ratio in this case is intended as a tool to assist in the educational experience. It gives weight to those factors that investors would typically evaluate. The P/E ratio is used to compute the market value of the bank's common stock. To protect against unusual market conditions, an arbitrary market-price floor of $2 per share has been set.

PRICE/EARNINGS RATIO

Figure 2-19

	12/03 FORECAST	12/02 ACTUAL	DIFFERENCE
CAPITAL FACTOR	3.30	1.18	2.12
PROFITABILITY FACTOR	1.67	2.05	-0.37
LIQUIDITY FACTOR	3.14	2.64	0.50
GROWTH FACTOR	4.00	2.98	1.02
ASSET QUALITY FACTOR	2.00	2.00	0.00
RATE LEVEL FACTOR	0.00	-0.01	0.01
PRICE/EARNINGS RATIO	14.11	10.84	3.02
C1 ASSET LEVERAGE	0.75	0.66	0.09
C2 DEPOSITS TO EQUITY	1.25	0.79	0.46
C3 LOANS TO EQUITY	1.28	0.09	1.19
C4 RISK BASED CAPITAL	0.02	-0.36	0.38
CAPITAL FACTOR (C1+C2+C3+C4)	3.30	1.18	2.12
P1 RETURN ON ASSETS	0.67	0.83	-0.17
P2 NET INT MARGIN	1.05	1.10	-0.05
P3 OVERHEAD	-0.04	0.11	-0.15
PROFITABILITY FACTOR (P1+P2+P3)	1.67	2.05	-0.37
L1 NET FED FDS TO EQUITY	2.16	2.10	0.06
L2 LOANS TO AVAIL DEP	3.17	2.29	0.88
L3 PURCH FDS TO EA	1.14	1.13	0.01
L4 S-T INV TO ASSETS	2.94	2.39	0.55
LIQUIDITY FACTOR (L1+L2+L3+L4) / 3	3.14	2.64	0.50
G1 DEPOSIT GROWTH	1.17	1.23	-0.06
G2 LOAN GROWTH	0.90	1.34	-0.44
G3 INCOME GROWTH	2.46	0.41	2.06
GROWTH FACTOR* (G1+G2+G3)	4.00	2.98	1.02
Q1 INVEST MKT TO BOOK	0.53	0.62	-0.10
Q2 LOSS PROV TO LOANS	1.71	1.72	-0.01
Q3 LOAN CONCENTRATION	0.93	0.78	0.16
ASSET QUALITY FACTOR* (Q1+Q2+Q3)	2.00	2.00	-0.00
RATE LEVEL FACTOR	0.00	-0.01	0.01
PRICE/EARNINGS RATIO	14.11	10.83	3.28
EARNINGS PER SHARE(ANN)	1.38	1.11	0.27
STOCK PRICE PER SHARE	19.47	12.02	7.45

* Growth factor has a maximum value of 4.00. Asset Quality factor has a maximum value of 2.00. Refer to Figure 2-21.

The determinants of the P/E ratio are five factors which are directly influenced by management, plus one factor which is external to the bank. The five internal factors are capital adequacy, profitability, liquidity, growth, and asset quality. The external factor is the level of interest rates. Figure 2-18 and 2-19 show the Price/Earnings Ratio Reports.

All commercial banks in the United States are shareholder owned corporations. The objectives of commercial banks are to provide substantial financial returns to their shareholders, and to serve their markets while adhering to regulatory requirements. Modern financial theory generally accepts the maximization of a corporation's stock price as the most important measure of financial returns to shareholders. A bank's stock price at any point in time reflects the financial markets assessment of the bank's present value, and one measure of relative value is the P/E ratio. This ratio measures how much investors are willing to pay, at the present time, for a pro rata share of the bank's earnings (Earnings per share or EPS).

The P/E ratio, in this case, is intended to serve as a tool to enhance the bank management experience. The P/E ratio gives weight to those factors that investors in bank stocks would evaluate when considering the purchase of a share of bank stock.

The first four factors reflect elements of bank performance, which are evaluated by regulators in the bank examination process, and which have given rise to the acronym CAMEL. The level of interest rates is the external factor which influence P/E ratios. As interest rates increase, investments in interest-bearing securities may become relatively more attractive when compared to common stock which does not have a fixed-rate of return.

Other things being equal, bank managers and shareholders prefer a higher P/E ratio to a lower one, since it represents a higher capitalization of the bank's earnings by the financial markets. The market capitalization figure for CRNB, shown below, are substantially smaller than those examples shown in Figure 1-5. Market capitalization figures of CRNB's size would fit a community bank or smaller regional bank as discussed in Chapter One-External Forces. Other things being equal, a bank with a smaller market capitalization is more likely to be subject to a takeover than a bank with a larger market capitalization. In the simulation, a good performance by the bank management team will be recognized by the financial markets and will result in a higher P/E ratio.

Market Capitalization

Figure 2-20

	2000	2001	2002	2003*
Shares Outstanding (000)	3,000	3,000	3,000	3,000
Price/Earnings Ratio	13.90	14.26	10.83	14.11
Stock Price (Year End)	12.37	15.12	12.02	19.47
Market Capitalization(000)	37,110	45,360	36,060	58,410

* Forecast

Price/ Earnings Formula

The formula for calculating the ratio is presented in Figure 2-21. Several scaling constants are used within the price/earnings formula. These constants have been chosen to highlight results created by different decisions. Each of the six factors is constrained within maximum and minimum limits.

All data for the price/earnings formula are derived from information available in the case. Most of the items are taken directly from the Key Ratios Report. A good performance by bank management will result in a corresponding increase in the P/E ratio.

PRICE/EARNINGS RATIO COMPUTATION

Figure 2-21

Price/Earnings Ratio = C + E + L + G + Q + R, where:

$C =$ Capital Factor $G =$ Growth Factor
$E =$ Earnings Factor $Q =$ Quality of Assets Factor
$L =$ Liquidity Factor $R =$ Interest Rate Factor

$C = (C_1 + C_2 + C_3 + C_4)$ with $1 \leq C \leq 4$, where:

$C_1 = $ (Asset Leverage — 5.00)
$C_2 = $ (16.5 — Deposits to Equity Ratio) $\times 2$
$C_3 = $ (11.5 — Loans to Equity Ratio) $\times 2$
$C_4 = $ (Risk-weighted Capital Ratio — 10.00)

$E = (E_1 + E_2 + E_3)$ with $1 \leq E \leq 4$, where:

$E_1 = $ Return on Assets %
$E_2 = $ (Interest Margin on Earning Assets %) $\div 4$
$E_3 = $ (2.5 — Overhead/Earnings Assets)

$L = (L_1 + L_2 + L_3 + L_4) \div 3$ with $1 \leq L \leq 4$, where:

$L_1 = $ (100 — Net Fed Funds to Equity %) $\div 80$
$L_2 = $ (100 — Loans to Available Deposits %) $\div 6$
$L_3 = $ (100 — Purchased Funds to Earning Assets %) $\div 60$
$L_4 = $ (Short-Term Investments to Total Assets %) $\div 6$

$G = (G_1 + G_2 + G_3)$ with $1 \leq G \leq 4$, where:

$G_1 = $ (Total Deposit Growth %) $\div 10$
$G_2 = $ (Total Loan Growth %) $\div 10$
$G_3 = $ (Net Income Growth %) $\div 10$

$Q = (Q_1 + Q_2 + Q_3)$ with $-1 \leq Q \leq 2$, where:

$Q_1 = $ (Investments Market to Book % — 100) $\div 2$
$Q_2 = $ (1 — Loss Provision to Loans %) $\times 4$
$Q_3 = $ (Loan Concentration $\div 10$)

$R = R_1$ with $-1 \leq R \leq 1$, where:

$R_1 = $ (7.47 — 12 month average rate on 3-year governments)

Interest Rates

Interest rates are perhaps the most fundamental concern of bank management. For CRNB, earning assets are forecast to be 93.5% of total assets during 2003. Earning assets are so called because they generate interest income for the bank. Interest income is the largest income source for CRNB and for the banking industry in general. The productivity of a bank's assets is measured by the yield on earning assets which compares interest income to earning assets. CRNB's yield on earning assets for 2003 is forecast to be 10.47% as shown in the Interest Rate Report in Figure 2-10.

Interest-bearing liabilities are forecast to provide 82.3% of CRNB's funds during 2003 and interest expense is the largest expense item. This is also typical of the banking industry. The cost of funds rate is a measure of the bank's efficiency in acquiring funds, and is determined by comparing interest expense with interest-bearing liabilities. The cost of funds rate for 2003 is forecast to be 6.89%.

The basic earning power of a bank results from the difference or spread between the yield on earning assets and the cost of funds rate on interest-bearing liabilities. Net interest spread for 2003 for CRNB is forecast to be 3.57%. The actual spread achieved by each bank management team, during 2003, will depend on the mix and volume of earning assets and interest-bearing liabilities achieved by each bank management team, as well as on the level of interest rates and the yield curve during 2003.

Yield Curve (Bond Equivalent Yield)

The yield curve illustrates the relationship of yields on financial instruments of various maturities at a point in time. Actual yield curves are shown on a monthly basis in the Yield Curve and Market Rates Reports for 2001 and 2002 (Figures 2-22 and 2-23) and a forecast yield curve for 2003 is provided in the Yield Curve and Market Rates Report for 2003 (Figure 2-24).[1] The yield curve, also known as the term structure of interest rates, is charted daily in *The Wall Street Journal* and other business publications.

The yield curves used in this case utilize yields on interest-bearing instruments as they are quoted in the financial markets, and converts market yields on discount instruments to a bond (or interest-bearing) equivalent. An example of this conversion can be observed for 3-month Treasury bills. The interest rate for 3-month Treasury bills in January 2003, which is quoted in the Market Rates section, is calculated on a discount basis and is shown to be 6.81%. A more accurate measure of the return that an investor would earn on this instrument is the bond equivalent yield which converts the yield from a discount basis to the equivalent yield on an interest-bearing basis. This conversion is shown in the Yield Curve section where the bond equivalent yield on the same 3-month Treasury bill is shown to be 7.03% compared to the 6.81% discount yield.

---

[1] The interest rates used in this simulation for 2001 and 2002 are the actual interest rates that were in effect in 1989 and 1990 respectively.

YIELD CURVE AND MARKET RATES
2001 ACTUAL

Figure 2-22

	JAN	FEB	MAR	APR	MAY	JUN	JUL	AUG	SEP	OCT	NOV	DEC
YIELD CURVE: (BOND EQUIVALENT YIELD)												
1-DAY RATE	6.72	7.31	8.27	8.31	8.02	7.85	7.07	7.33	7.63	7.42	6.93	6.63
1-MONTH RATE	7.30	7.95	8.47	8.73	8.10	7.92	7.17	7.40	7.72	7.52	7.25	7.01
3-MONTH RATE	8.59	8.79	9.16	9.02	8.70	8.51	8.19	8.18	7.98	7.85	7.91	7.90
6-MONTH RATE	8.87	9.05	9.42	9.26	8.91	8.45	8.05	8.15	8.17	8.05	7.86	7.85
1-YEAR RATE	9.16	9.32	9.43	9.51	9.15	8.85	8.16	8.01	8.19	7.90	7.69	7.66
2-YEAR RATE	9.18	9.37	9.68	9.45	9.02	8.41	7.82	8.14	8.28	7.98	7.80	7.78
3-YEAR RATE	9.20	9.27	9.61	9.40	9.05	8.37	7.83	8.13	8.26	8.02	7.80	7.77
5-YEAR RATE	9.15	9.27	9.51	9.30	8.91	8.29	7.83	8.09	8.17	7.97	7.81	7.75
7-YEAR RATE	9.14	9.23	9.43	9.24	8.88	8.31	7.94	8.11	8.23	8.03	7.86	7.85
10-YEAR RATE	9.09	9.17	9.36	9.18	8.86	8.28	8.02	8.11	8.19	8.01	7.87	7.84
20-YEAR RATE	9.00	9.05	9.20	9.10	8.84	8.28	8.05	8.12	8.17	8.00	7.88	7.88
30-YEAR RATE	8.93	9.01	9.17	9.03	8.83	8.27	8.08	8.12	8.15	8.00	7.90	7.90
MARKET RATES:												
PRIME RATE (LG BKS)	10.50	10.93	11.50	11.50	11.50	11.07	10.98	10.50	10.50	10.50	10.50	10.50
TREASURY BILL RATE 3 MO	8.29	8.48	8.83	8.70	8.40	8.22	7.92	7.91	7.72	7.59	7.65	7.64
TREASURY BILL RATE 6 MO	8.38	8.54	8.87	8.73	8.41	8.00	7.63	7.72	7.74	7.63	7.46	7.45
TREASURY BILL RATE 1 Y R	8.45	8.59	8.68	8.75	8.44	8.18	7.58	7.45	7.61	7.35	7.17	7.14
90-DAY CD RATE(NATIONAL)	9.20	9.38	10.09	9.94	9.68	9.20	8.76	8.64	8.78	8.60	8.39	8.32
LONDON INTERBANK RATE	9.27	9.39	10.12	10.14	9.77	9.33	8.96	8.59	8.82	8.78	8.42	8.39

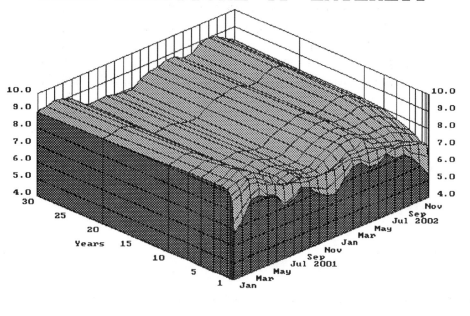

TERM STRUCTURE OF INTEREST

Figure 2-23

YIELD CURVE AND MARKET RATES
2002 ACTUAL

	JAN	FEB	MAR	APR	MAY	JUN	JUL	AUG	SEP	OCT	NOV	DEC
YIELD CURVE: (BOND EQUIVALENT YIELD)												
1-DAY RATE	6.50	7.16	7.67	7.69	7.24	7.24	7.61	7.11	7.12	6.73	6.13	5.31
1-MONTH RATE	7.23	7.57	8.02	7.86	7.48	7.48	7.60	7.63	7.63	7.02	6.76	6.34
3-MONTH RATE	7.90	8.03	8.14	8.05	8.05	8.00	7.92	7.69	7.62	7.42	7.30	7.03
6-MONTH RATE	7.93	8.15	8.27	8.25	8.25	8.06	7.98	7.75	7.72	7.58	7.40	7.10
1-YEAR RATE	7.74	7.98	8.36	8.32	8.70	8.24	8.09	7.92	7.78	7.51	7.28	7.02
2-YEAR RATE	8.09	8.37	8.63	8.72	8.64	8.35	8.16	8.06	8.08	7.88	7.60	7.31
3-YEAR RATE	8.13	8.39	8.63	8.78	8.69	8.40	8.26	8.22	8.27	8.07	7.74	7.47
5-YEAR RATE	8.12	8.42	8.60	8.77	8.74	8.43	8.33	8.44	8.51	8.33	8.02	7.73
7-YEAR RATE	8.20	8.48	8.65	8.81	8.78	8.52	8.46	8.64	8.79	8.59	8.28	8.00
10-YEAR RATE	8.21	8.47	8.59	8.79	8.76	8.48	8.47	8.75	8.89	8.72	8.39	8.08
20-YEAR RATE	8.24	8.48	8.58	8.77	8.74	8.47	8.48	8.80	8.96	8.79	8.46	8.16
30-YEAR RATE	8.26	8.50	8.56	8.76	8.73	8.46	8.50	8.86	9.03	8.86	8.54	8.24
MARKET RATES:												
PRIME RATE (LG BKS)	10.11	10.00	10.00	10.00	10.00	10.00	10.00	10.00	10.00	10.00	10.00	10.00
TREASURY BILL RATE 3 MO	7.64	7.76	7.87	7.78	7.78	7.74	7.66	7.44	7.38	7.19	7.07	6.81
TREASURY BILL RATE 6 MO	7.52	7.72	7.83	7.82	7.82	7.64	7.57	7.36	7.33	7.20	7.04	6.76
TREASURY BILL RATE 1 YR	7.21	7.42	7.76	7.72	8.05	7.65	7.52	7.37	7.25	7.01	6.81	6.58
90-DAY CD RATE(NATIONAL)	8.16	8.22	8.35	8.42	8.35	8.23	8.10	7.97	8.06	8.06	8.03	7.82
LONDON INTERBANK RATE	8.22	8.24	8.37	8.44	8.35	8.23	8.09	7.99	8.07	8.06	8.04	7.87

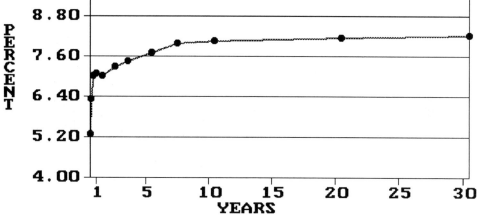

TERM STRUCTURE OF INTEREST
DECEMBER 2002

YIELD CURVE AND MARKET RATES
2003 FORECAST

Figure 2-24

	JAN	FEB	MAR	APR	MAY	JUN	JUL	AUG	SEP	OCT	NOV	DEC
YIELD CURVE: (BOND EQUIVALENT YIELD)												
1-DAY RATE	5.31	5.31	5.31	5.31	5.31	5.31	5.31	5.31	5.31	5.31	5.31	5.31
1-MONTH RATE	6.34	6.34	6.34	6.34	6.34	6.34	6.34	6.34	6.34	6.34	6.34	6.34
3-MONTH RATE	7.03	7.03	7.03	7.03	7.03	7.03	7.03	7.03	7.03	7.03	7.03	7.03
6-MONTH RATE	7.10	7.10	7.10	7.10	7.10	7.10	7.10	7.10	7.10	7.10	7.10	7.10
1-YEAR RATE	7.02	7.02	7.02	7.02	7.02	7.02	7.02	7.02	7.02	7.02	7.02	7.02
2-YEAR RATE	7.31	7.31	7.31	7.31	7.31	7.31	7.31	7.31	7.31	7.31	7.31	7.31
3-YEAR RATE	7.47	7.47	7.47	7.47	7.47	7.47	7.47	7.47	7.47	7.47	7.47	7.47
5-YEAR RATE	7.73	7.73	7.73	7.73	7.73	7.73	7.73	7.73	7.73	7.73	7.73	7.73
7-YEAR RATE	8.00	8.00	8.00	8.00	8.00	8.00	8.00	8.00	8.00	8.00	8.00	8.00
10-YEAR RATE	8.08	8.08	8.08	8.08	8.08	8.08	8.08	8.08	8.08	8.08	8.08	8.08
20-YEAR RATE	8.16	8.16	8.16	8.16	8.16	8.16	8.16	8.16	8.16	8.16	8.16	8.16
30-YEAR RATE	8.24	8.24	8.24	8.24	8.24	8.24	8.24	8.24	8.24	8.24	8.24	8.24
MARKET RATES:												
PRIME RATE (LG BKS)	10.00	10.00	10.00	10.00	10.00	10.00	10.00	10.00	10.00	10.00	10.00	10.00
TREASURY BILL RATE 3 MO	6.81	6.81	6.81	6.81	6.81	6.81	6.81	6.81	6.81	6.81	6.81	6.81
TREASURY BILL RATE 6 MO	6.76	6.76	6.76	6.76	6.76	6.76	6.76	6.76	6.76	6.76	6.76	6.76
TREASURY BILL RATE 1 YR	6.58	6.58	6.58	6.58	6.58	6.58	6.58	6.58	6.58	6.58	6.58	6.58
90-DAY CD RATE(NATIONAL)	7.82	7.82	7.82	7.82	7.82	7.82	7.82	7.82	7.82	7.82	7.82	7.82
LONDON INTERBANK RATE	7.87	7.87	7.87	7.87	7.87	7.87	7.87	7.87	7.87	7.87	7.87	7.87

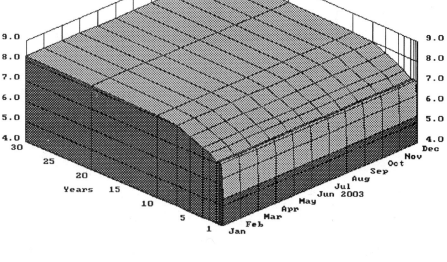

It can be observed from Figures 2-22 through 2-24 that the yield curve has a variety of slopes as well as various levels of interest rates at different times. The yield curve for 2003 is upward sloping with yields on longer term maturities exceeding those on shorter term maturities. Yields on 30-year Treasury bonds are forecast to be 8.24%, while yields on 3-month Treasury bills are forecast to be 7.03%. This results in a difference in yield of 1.21 percentage point (121 basis points).

A number of theories have been advanced to explain the variety of slopes in the yield curve that are observed at different periods of time. The unbiased, or pure expectations theory, holds that the longer term interest rates are the geometric mean of expected shorter term interest rates. Under this theory, an upward sloping yield curve indicates that investors expect shorter term interest rates to fall. The liquidity preference theory indicates that investors prefer shorter term financial instruments to longer term, because of the greater risk inherent in longer term instruments. Longer term instruments are viewed as having more risk because of the greater market price changes that take place in longer term instruments in response to a change in the level of interest rates. Finally, the segmented market theory indicates that different types of financial institutions have preferred investment maturities and tend to invest in securities with those maturities resulting in a yield curve of relatively independent segments.

Figure 2-25

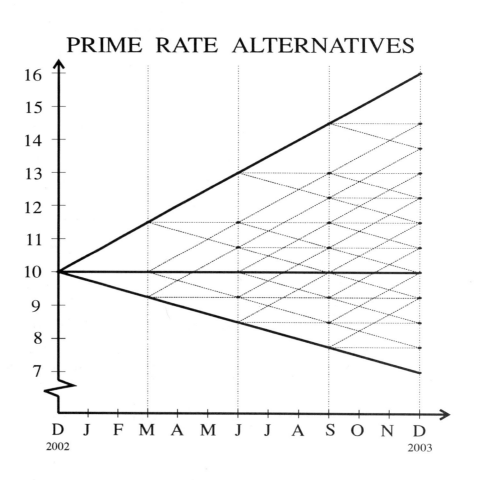

Although interest rate levels are forecast by the bank's economist to be constant for 2003, it is possible that monetary and economic conditions will change, and that interest rates will rise or fall during the year. Each bank management team will be notified of any changes in interest rates prior to making their asset and liability decisions. The process for change is designed to maintain the element of uncertainty for interest rates while providing a sense of the short term outlook for rates.

Market Rates   Market rates are shown in the lower section of the Yield Curve and Market Rates Report in Figures 2-22 through 2-24. The prime rate and London Interbank Offering Rate (LIBOR) are quotes for interest-bearing obligations, as are the rates on 90-day Certificates of Deposit. Market rates for Treasury bills are quoted on a discount basis, as is the custom in the financial markets, and must be converted to a bond equivalent yield basis in order to make meaningful comparisons with interest-bearing instruments. This conversion is shown in the Yield Curve section of the report where all interest rates are shown on a bond equivalent basis.

All market rates are influenced by supply and demand factors in the financial markets as well as by Federal Reserve monetary policy and inflation prospects. Some market rates, such as the rates on Treasury bills, are highly sensitive to these factors and change on a daily basis.

Prime is also influenced by these factors, but it is a bank administered rate and therefore its volatility is somewhat less than for other market rates. The prime rate is probably the most widely quoted and closely followed interest rate in the banking industry. It is closely followed because many commercial loans are floating-rate loans on which the interest rate is tied, in some way, to the prime rate. In this case, the bank management team may make floating-

Examples of Prime Rate Alternatives

Figure 2-26

1Q	Level	Falling	Rising	Level	Rising	Falling
2Q	Level	Falling	Rising	Falling	Rising	Level
3Q	Level	Falling	Rising	Falling	Falling	Level
4Q	Level	Falling	Rising	Rising	Level	Falling
January	10.00%	9.75%	10.50%	10.00%	10.50%	9.75%
February	10.00	9.50	11.00	10.00	11.00	9.75
March	10.00	9.25	11.50	10.00	11.50	9.50
April	10.00	9.00	12.00	9.75	12.00	9.25
May	10.00	8.75	12.50	9.50	12.50	9.25
June	10.00	8.50	13.00	9.25	13.00	9.25
July	10.00	8.25	13.50	9.00	12.75	9.25
August	10.00	8.00	14.00	8.75	12.50	9.25
September	10.00	7.75	14.50	8.50	12.25	9.25
October	10.00	7.50	15.00	9.00	12.25	9.00
November	10.00	7.25	15.50	9.50	12.25	8.75
December	10.00	7.00	16.00	10.00	12.25	8.50

rate commercial loans at the prime rate, or at a differential above or below prime, and the interest rate earned by the bank will change as the prime rate changes. In addition to its role in commercial loans, prime also serves as a base lending rate for pricing other types of loans and bank products, many of which carry variable interest rates that change with the prime rate.

If interest rates should change from the forecast, each bank management team will be notified of such change prior to making any operating decisions. Adjustment to a change in interest rates is estimated as follows: under a rising rate scenario, the base rate moves upward by 50 basis points per month, under falling rates, the base rate declines by 25 basis points per month. Examples of a chart of all possible prime rate alternatives for the year are shown in Figure 2-25 and some prime rate alternatives for 2003 are shown in Figure 2-26.

Changes in Term Structure of Interest

In addition to changes in the level of interest rates, change may occur in the term structure of rates. Short-term rates fully recognize 100% of the change each month, intermediate-term rates recognize almost 75% of the change, and long-term rates recognize almost 50% of the change. Volatile short-term rates generally lead prime changes and for this case, change at a rate of 200% of the change in prime during the first month of each quarter; 100% in the second month of each quarter and 0% in the third month of each quarter. The definitions for changes to the term structure of interest are shown in Figures 2-27 and 2-28.

Changes to Term Structure of Interest

Figure 2-27

Treasury Yield Curve Rates

Volatile Short-Term:	1-Day Rate	200% of change in Base Rates in first month of quarter
Short-Term:	30-Day Rate 3-Month Rate 6-Month Rate	100% of change each month
Intermediate-Term:	1-Year Rate 2-Year Rate	75% of change each month
Long-Term:	3-Year Rate 5-Year Rate 7-Year Rate 10-Year Rate 20-Year Rate 30-Year Rate	50% of change each month

Incremental Yields and Rates

The Incremental Yields and Rates Forecast presented on a monthly basis in Figure 2-29 indicates that the bank's economist is forecasting level interest rates for 2003. Yields that are expected to be earned on new earning assets acquired during the year are shown in the upper part of the forecast, and the rates forecast to be paid on new liabilities acquired during the same time period are shown in the lower part.

Forecast yields on earning assets for 2003 range from a low of 7.03% for short-term Treasuries, through 10.00% on floating-rate commercial loans, to a high of 18.00% on credit card loans. In the case of short-term Treasuries, the bank is a yield taker since it cannot influence yields in this market due to size and international scope of the market. As will be seen later, the yield that the bank earns as a rate taker on short-term Treasuries will be identical to the rate shown in the Market Yield and Rates Forecast. This forecast indicates the prevailing interest rates on a variety of money and capital market instruments

In the case of floating-rate commercial loans, the bank management team administers the rate it offers and has control over the pricing of this product. Rates offered on floating-rate commercial loans range from a low of the prime rate minus 100 basis points to a high of the prime rate plus 200 basis points. The preliminary forecast of the bank's performance for 2003 has been prepared using the prime rate of 10.00%. However, during 2003, the bank management team may wish to attract more loans and will lower interest rates on these loans or they may wish to make fewer of these loans and decide to raise the rate they offer.

Changes to Term Structure of Interest

Market Rates shown on Interest Rate Report

Figure 2-28

Volatile Short-Term:	Federal Funds London Interbank Offering Rate (LIBOR)	200% of change in Base Rates in first month of quarter
Short-Term:	Prime Rate 90-Day CD Rate 3-Month Treasury Bill Rate 6-Month Treasury Bill Rate	100% of change each month
Intermediate-Term:	NONE	
Long-Term:	U.S. Government Yield (3 Yrs) Municipal Bond Yield Conventional Mortgage Rate	50% of change each month

Figure 2-29

INCREMENTAL YIELDS AND RATES
2003 FORECAST

	JAN	FEB	MAR	APR	MAY	JUN	JUL	AUG	SEP	OCT	NOV	DEC
EARNING ASSETS:												
SHORT-TERM TREASURIES	7.03	7.03	7.03	7.03	7.03	7.03	7.03	7.03	7.03	7.03	7.03	7.03
LONG-TERM TREASURIES	7.60	7.60	7.60	7.60	7.60	7.60	7.60	7.60	7.60	7.60	7.60	7.60
US AGENCY SECURITIES	8.58	8.58	8.58	8.58	8.58	8.58	8.58	8.58	8.58	8.58	8.58	8.58
OUR SECURITIZED MTG LNS	8.83	8.83	8.83	8.83	8.83	8.83	8.83	8.83	8.83	8.83	8.83	8.83
FHLB STOCK	6.25	6.25	6.25	6.25	6.25	6.25	6.25	6.25	6.25	6.25	6.25	6.25
TERM FED FUNDS SOLD	7.31	7.31	7.31	7.31	7.31	7.31	7.31	7.31	7.31	7.31	7.31	7.31
OVERNIGHT FED FUNDS SOLD	7.31	7.31	7.31	7.31	7.31	7.31	7.31	7.31	7.31	7.31	7.31	7.31
TRADING ACCOUNT	8.16	8.16	8.16	8.16	8.16	8.16	8.16	8.16	8.16	8.16	8.16	8.16
COM'L PARTIC PURCH-FIXED	10.00	10.00	10.00	10.00	10.00	10.00	10.00	10.00	10.00	10.00	10.00	10.00
DIRECT COM'L LOANS-FIXED	10.00	10.00	10.00	10.00	10.00	10.00	10.00	10.00	10.00	10.00	10.00	10.00
COM'L PARTIC PURCH-FLOAT	10.25	10.25	10.25	10.25	10.25	10.25	10.25	10.25	10.25	10.25	10.25	10.25
DIRECT COM'L LOANS-FLOAT	10.00	10.00	10.00	10.00	10.00	10.00	10.00	10.00	10.00	10.00	10.00	10.00
MORTGAGE LOANS-FIXED	9.76	9.76	9.76	9.76	9.76	9.76	9.76	9.76	9.76	9.76	9.76	9.76
MORTGAGE LOANS-ADJ	8.02	8.02	8.02	8.02	8.02	8.02	8.02	8.02	8.02	8.02	8.02	8.02
HOME EQUITY LOANS	10.58	10.58	10.58	10.58	10.58	10.58	10.58	10.58	10.58	10.58	10.58	10.58
CREDIT CARD LOANS	18.00	18.00	18.00	18.00	18.00	18.00	18.00	18.00	18.00	18.00	18.00	18.00
AUTO LOANS	11.52	11.52	11.52	11.52	11.52	11.52	11.52	11.52	11.52	11.52	11.52	11.52
LIABILITIES:												
INTEREST-BEAR CHECKING	5.00	5.00	5.00	5.00	5.00	5.00	5.00	5.00	5.00	5.00	5.00	5.00
MMDAs	7.03	7.03	7.03	7.03	7.03	7.03	7.03	7.03	7.03	7.03	7.03	7.03
LARGE CDs	7.82	7.82	7.82	7.82	.82	7.82	7.82	7.82	7.82	7.82	7.82	7.82
PUBLIC CDs	8.22	8.22	8.22	8.22	8.22	8.22	8.22	8.22	8.22	8.22	8.22	8.22
REPOS	6.81	6.81	6.81	6.81	6.81	6.81	6.81	6.81	6.81	6.81	6.81	6.81
FED FUNDS PURCHASED	7.56	7.56	7.56	7.5	67.56	7.56	7.56	7.56	7.56	7.56	7.56	7.56
LONG-TERM DEBT	10.25	10.25	10.25	10.25	10.25	10.25	10.25	10.25	10.25	10.25	10.25	10.25
FHLB ADVANCES	9.75	9.75	9.75	9.75	9.75	9.75	9.75	9.75	9.75	9.75	9.75	9.75

Interest rates forecast to be paid on interest-bearing liabilities are shown in the lower part of the Incremental Yields and Rates Forecast. Rates vary from a low of 5.00% forecast to be paid on interest-bearing checking accounts, through 8.22% on public certificates of deposit, up to 10.25% on long-term debt. As with earning assets, the bank management team has more control in some markets than it does in others. For interest-bearing checking accounts, the forecast has been prepared using an interest rate of 5.00%. This is a local and personal market, and the bank management team may vary the rate it pays from 4.00 to 6.00%. In the case of long-term debt, funds must be attracted from a national and impersonal market, and the bank must pay the market rate in order to utilize these borrowings.

Risk Measurement and Management

The major financial risks inherent in the operation of a financial institution are *asset quality, liquidity,* and *interest-rate risk.* Concepts of measurement and management of these risks are important to the notion of Strategic Financial Management.

Dictionaries define risk as the possibility of injury or loss. Bankers, financial managers and analysts define financial risk as the possibility of loss from financial transactions entered into with other parties. Loans, investment securities, deposits, borrowed funds, and off-balance sheet financial instruments are such transactions and the underlying contracts, combined with an uncertain future, create the concept of financial risk.

Measurements of financial risk are stated either in dollars, percentages or ratios. The percentages and ratios represent static relationships and/or rates of change over time. Most techniques for measuring financial risk begin with a definition of the current status of the portfolio. Then, to varying degrees, the measurement techniques attempt to quantify the amount of possible loss, the probability of loss occurring, and the time value of money.

Managing financial risk involves the use of systematic processes for identifying, measuring, reporting, and controlling the various risks; the use of hedges (insurance against possible losses); and the provision of adequate capital (ability to absorb possible losses which have not been hedged).

Identification and Measurement of Risk

Authors have defined and categorized the financial risks inherent in the operation of a financial institution in various ways.[1] For purposes of this chapter, financial risks have been classified as:

Asset Quality Risk The possibility that principal value paid out in the past will not be repaid in the future, or that investable funds will not generate adequate yields.

Liquidity Risk The possibility that cash funds will not be available to meet deposit withdrawals; to accommodate loan requests; to pay operating expenses; or to pay other financial obligations.

Interest-Rate Risk The possibility that interest rates will change unexpectedly in the future and thereby create a loss of net interest income; a loss of net asset value; or both.

Asset Quality Risk

The quality of assets held by a financial institution is determined primarily by three things. First, is the credit quality (credit worthiness) of the person or entity to which funds have been advanced. Second, is the degree of concentration or diversification in the various portfolios. And third, is the level and nature of non-earning assets held.

Credit quality

Credit risk is the possibility that the funds paid or committed to borrowers will not be repaid as agreed upon at the time the contract was made. Generally, at the time a loan is made, credit quality is considered good or at least acceptable. After credit is granted, however, circumstances may change and thereby adversely impact the borrowers ability or willingness to honor obligations, either in whole or in part.

Credit quality is an issue for direct loans made to bank customers; for security investments made in the capital or money markets; and for agreements to loan or invest funds in the future (formal commitments) under circumstances where the bank does not retain an option to withdraw from the contract if the borrower's credit worthiness deteriorates.

To help keep credit risk reasonable at the time loans or investments are made, bankers must perform thorough analysis of credit worthiness; exercise good judgment in the amount of lending or investing relative to the need and capacity of the borrower; and be prudent in the amount of collateral value required to protect the lender in the event of adverse conditions. To keep credit risk reasonable over time, bankers must adhere to comprehensive checklists for documentation; follow a continuous process for updating information files; and perform regular reviews of loan portfolios, selected individual loans, and evolving circumstances.

---

[1] A classification was demonstrated in Chapter One by reference to the publication, *Risk Management*, distributed by the OCC.

Credit quality of security investments. Investments in U. S. Treasury notes and bonds are considered by the financial world to be free of credit risk. For security investments in the money and capital markets other than U. S. Treasury securities, credit quality is reflected in credit ratings published by major credit rating firms. Moody's Investor Services, Standard & Poor's, Fitch Investment Services and others have provided ratings for traded debt securities for many years and have provided good credit information to investors. Moody's bond ratings range in descending order of quality from *AAA* to *A* and on down through *C*. Financial institutions are generally restricted to investments in debt securities which are viewed as being investment grade, that is in the top four rating categories.

The credit quality of a security is reflected in its current market value. Over time, the impact of changes in the credit quality of security investments on the financial performance of a bank will be reported in various ways depending upon accounting rules. Accounting treatment for securities includes three categories — securities held for trading, securities held for sale, which are to be marked-to-market at each period end; and securities held for investment which are carried at amortized historical cost.[2]

In the case of securities held for trading and securities held for sale, changes up or down in market value, caused by credit quality, will be reflected in the carrying amount on the balance sheet. Trading account gains and losses are cleared through an income account, while gains and losses on securities held for sale are cleared through the bank's equity account. In the case of securities held for investment, declines in market value caused by credit quality may represent permanent impairment. If so, such declines will be reflected in a reserve or contra-asset account and the net carrying value will reflect negative changes in credit quality.

Credit quality of loans. Good quality lending by financial institutions is also done under a system of loan grading or rating. The various grade levels reflect financial and other characteristics of the borrower; credit history; the purpose of the loan; the underlying cash flows of the loan and its repayment; the existence, status and value of collateral; the existence and quality of loan documents; nature of the industry; pertinent economic conditions; and relevant circumstances since the time the loan was made. The various grade levels determine the amount and adequacy of loan loss reserves.

The measurement of quality for loan portfolios is stated in negative terms (i.e., what portion of the portfolio represents poor asset quality?). The level and nature of *non-performing assets* is reported internally and in annual reports. Bank regulators identify *classified assets* which are shown in bank examination reports but not reported publicly. The level of non-performing and classified assets reveals significant information about bank performance and is the basis for determining the adequacy of the allowance for loan losses.

---

[2] On April 13, 1993, the FASB adopted a new accounting standard titled *Accounting for Certain Investments in Debt and Equity Securities.* This new standard will change the accounting rules for security investments in financial institutions.

60

Figure 3-1 shows information which identifies the asset quality for CRNB for the three years of history (2000, 2001, and 2002) and a forecast for 2003. Figure 3-2 shows similar information for the actual years of 1988, 1989, 1990, and 1991 as provided by the FFIEC in the UBPR for Peer Group No. 5.[3]

Loan Analysis Report
Community Regional National Bank*

Figure 3-1

	2000	2001	2002	2003**
TOTAL GROSS LOANS ($EOP)	229622	259414	292786	308674
TOTAL GROSS LOANS ($AVG)	217694	244143	276926	301924
CLASSIFIED ASSETS ($EOP):				
NONACCRUING LOANS	2698	2874	3158	3576
RENEGOTIATED LOANS	100	115	115	115
OTHER REAL ESTATE OWNED	398	545	641	525
NONPERFORMING ASSETS	3196	3534	3914	4216
90-DAY PAST DUE	46	52	58	64
OTHER CLASSIFIED ASSETS	15	20	20	20
TOTAL CLASSIFIED	3257	3606	3992	4300
LOAN LOSS RESERVE:				
BEGINNING BALANCE	3540	3933	4462	5036
- LOANS CHARGED OFF	1117	1231	1397	1633
+ LOANS RECOVERED	112	148	140	163
+ CURRENT PROVISION	1399	1612	1831	1633
ENDING BALANCE	3933	4462	5036	5055
RATE COMPOSITION (%):				
FIXED RATE	67.99	68.16	68.43	66.60
FLOATING RATE	32.01	31.84	31.57	33.40
TOTAL LOANS	100.00	100.00	100.00	100.00
LOAN RATIOS:				
LOSS PROVISION/LOANS %	0.64	0.66	0.66	0.49
NET CHARGE-OFFS/LOANS %	0.46	0.44	0.45	0.49
NON-ACCRUAL/LOANS %	1.17	1.11	1.08	1.16
90-DAY P.D./LOANS %	0.02	0.02	0.02	0.02
FORECLOSED/LOANS %	1.17	0.21	0.22	0.17
NONPERFORMING/LNS(EOP) %	1.39	1.36	1.34	1.37
LOSS RESERVE/LOANS %	1.70	1.69	1.69	1.62
CLASSIFIED LNS/EQUITY %	15.18	15.38	15.67	15.18

* The years used to illustrate this simulation case may be compared to the actual years 1988 — 1991.
** Forecast

---

[3] The FFIEC is a federal agency coordinating the supervisory efforts of the OCC, FDIC, FRB, OTS, and NCUA. The UBPR is compiled from the call reports filed by banks with the FDIC each quarter. The UBPR includes twenty-five peer groups classified by asset size, number of banking offices, and location. On December 31, 1991 there were 347 banks in Peer Group No. 5. This group had assets between $300 and $500 million with three or more banking offices.

Non-performing assets include non-accruing loans; loans with contract terms restructured for rate, payments, maturity, principal, or collateral; and assets resulting from collateralized loan defaults such as other real estate owned (OREO) and foreclosed properties. Non-accruing loans are damaging to bank performance because the lack of interest accruing represents a drag on portfolio earnings, even if the principal is eventually collected in full. Restructured loans may be performing currently, but on terms not as desirable as originally intended. OREO and foreclosed properties are carried at current realizable value but represent a drag on performance because income is usually not being earned, future value fluctuations may impair realizable value, and the costs of holding and managing the assets may be substantial.

Classified assets are those assets identified as delinquent, substandard, doubtful, loss or other assets especially mentioned (OAEM). The first four categories are based upon fairly clear facts and are analytical in nature. For example, classified assets would include all items defined above as non-performing assets and depending upon the severity of the impairment, the assets would be classified as delinquent, substandard, doubtful, or loss. Generally, amounts of assets classified as loss will be charged-off against reserves or current earnings. Substandard and doubtful classes will require loss reserves to various degrees. Depending upon the level of existing reserves, the substandard and doubtful classes may increase the expense provision for expected losses, which is a current period expense. Delinquent loans (such as loans 90-days past due) are a warning signal, but will not significantly impact the level of required reserves.

Credit Quality Ratios

Figure 3-2

UBPR PEER GROUP No. 5

Banks with Assets Between $300 and $500 Million

	1988	1989	1990	1991
LOSS PROVISION/LOANS %	0.46	0.53	0.61	0.60
NET CHARGE-OFFS/LOANS %	0.33	0.42	0.48	0.54
NONACCRUAL LOANS/LOANS	0.63	0.80	1.00	1.05
90 DAY PAST DUE/LOANS	0.32	0.33	0.27	0.25
FORECLOSED ASSETS/LOANS	0.16	0.17	0.27	0.48
NONPERFORMING/LOANS %	1.11	1.30	1.55	1.78
LOSS RESERVE/LOANS %	1.20	1.23	1.28	1.35

OAEM have a checklist for review of specific characteristics but are mostly determined by subjective judgment. For example, OAEM may include loans with a bad history of payment, even though, the status may now be current. Inadequate loan documentation, or a lien which has not been properly perfected, may cause the asset to be criticized. Any circumstance which interferes with the bank's ability to monitor or review a loan or its underlying collateral on a regular basis may cause criticism. Economic or general market conditions which are unfavorable (such as the energy problems of the early 1980s, or the real estate problems of the late 1980s and early 1990s) may cause the asset to be criticized.

CRNB compares favorably to the peer group averages for most items and shows an improvement over the years. Since some portion of the non-performing loans can be expected to return to performing status and eventually be paid in full, the reserve does not need to show 100% coverage of non-performing. However, for 2002, CRNB shows a reserve for loan losses of 1.69% which is in excess of the non-performing amount of 1.34% The level of classified assets as a percentage of equity is less than 50% which should be sufficient to keep a regulatory CAMEL rating of 3 or better. Net charge-offs are averaging slightly less than 50 basis points which is near the peer average.

Figure 3-3 shows that a large percentage of the securities portfolio is held in U.S. Treasuries (which have no credit risk) and Figure 3-1 shows that CRNB's loan loss ratios compare quite favorably to peer averages. It is reasonable to conclude, therefore, that CRNB has very good asset quality.

Portfolio concentrations Diversification is one of the principles of managing risk in a portfolio. If all your eggs are in one basket, you lose all your eggs if that basket drops. This old adage will be true forever, and bankers use it as one important guide for portfolio management. Most banks have policies for portfolio mix percentage targets, minimums and/or maximums.

Percentage Asset Composition
Community Regional National Bank*

Figure 3-3

	2000	2001	2002	2003**
CASH, FLOAT & RESERVES	6.9	6.3	6.0	3.6
U.S. TREASURIES	19.5	19.3	19.3	20.7
ASSET BACKED SECURITIES	1.1	1.1	1.1	2.9
ALL OTHER SECURITIES	3.5	3.0	1.7	1.3
TOTAL SECURITIES	24.2	23.5	22.2	25.0
SHORT-TERM INVESTMENTS	2.1	3.0	4.1	4.9
COMMERCIAL LOANS	23.7	23.9	23.5	23.0
REAL ESTATE LOANS	17.0	17.4	18.1	17.5
CONSUMER LOANS	22.4	22.4	23.0	22.8
TOTAL LOANS	63.3	63.8	64.7	63.4
RESERVE FOR LOAN LOSSES	-1.0	-1.0	-1.1	-1.0
NET LOANS	62.2	62.8	63.6	62.3
OTHER ASSETS	4.3	4.1	3.9	3.9
TOTAL ASSETS	100.0	100.0	100.0	100.0
TOTAL EARNING ASSETS	89.7	90.5	91.1	93.5

* The years used to illustrate this simulation case may be compared to the actual years 1988 — 1991.
** Forecast

The subject of portfolio concentrations must now formally be addressed by banking regulators. Section 305 of FDICIA requires that federal banking agencies develop a technique for identification of concentration limits and the implementation of these concentration limits into the definitions of risk-based capital. At the time of publication of this text, the called for federal regulations have not been established.

Guideline targets can be set for the percentage mix of loans, investment securities and non-earning assets to total assets. Figure 3-3 illustrates the percentage mix of total assets for CRNB for the three years of history (2000, 2001, and 2002) and a forecast for 2003. Figure 3-4 shows similar information for the actual years of 1988, 1989, 1990, and 1991 as provided by the FFIEC in the UBPR for Peer Group No. 5.

CRNB has comparable mix percentages for securities, short-term investments, and loans. Within the loan portfolios, CRNB holds more in commercial loans, less in real estate loans and more in consumer loans than the average of banks its size.

Percentage Asset Composition

UBPR PEER GROUP No. 5

Figure 3-4

Banks with Assets Between $300 and $500 Million

	1988	1989	1990	1991
CASH & DUE FROM BANKS	5.7	5.4	5.2	4.8
US TREASURY & AGENCY SEC	15.3	15.1	15.9	18.4
STATE & MUNI SECURITIES	4.1	4.0	4.0	3.5
OTHER SECURITIES	1.5	1.6	1.4	1.3
TOTAL SECURITIES	20.8	20.7	21.2	23.2
SHORT TERM INVESTMENTS	6.2	6.0	5.9	5.2
COMMERCIAL LOANS	19.8	18.9	17.5	15.4
REAL ESTATE LOANS	29.3	31.4	33.4	35.7
CONSUMER LOANS	16.9	16.3	15.3	14.1
TOTAL LOANS & LEASES	64.8	65.5	65.3	64.4
LOAN & LEASE RESERVES	-0.8	-0.8	-0.8	-0.9
NET LOANS & LEASES	64.1	64.7	64.5	63.5
OTHER ASSETS	3.2	3.2	3.2	3.4
TOTAL ASSETS	100.0	100.0	100.0	100.0
TOTAL EARNING ASSETS	91.9	92.3	92.4	92.8

Security investment concentrations. As indicated earlier, most financial institutions are restricted to security investments with relatively high credit quality. Therefore, concentration which would result in large defaults of principal payments is not of great concern. However, liquidity risk and interest-rate risk can be substantially increased, if all security investments are of one or similar types.

When loan growth exploded after World War II, the security portfolios of financial institutions declined to approximately 20 to 25% of total assets. After the transition, a security mix of one-third U.S. Treasuries, one-third U.S. government agencies and one-third state and municipal securities became an industry norm. With the advent of asset-backed securities (mortgage-backed securities in particular) and with the adverse changes in federal tax laws in 1986, a typical bank today is likely to show that municipal securities have dropped to 10 to 20%, Treasuries have dropped to 15 to 25%, U. S. government agencies comprise about 25%, and asset-backed securities comprise 30 to 50%. Within the category of asset-backed securities, there are many different types. Some asset-backed securities are equity types (pass-through securities), and some are debt types (such as Collateralized Mortgage Obligations (CMOs)). Some are backed by mortgage loans, and some are backed by other types of loans receivable, such as credit card receivables, home equity loans, automobile loans, or other receivables. In any event, mix guidelines which limit concentrations will lessen risk exposure.

Maturity concentrations are another type of possible risk with security investment portfolios. For many banks a simple "laddering" approach, which spreads the term-to-maturity evenly over all time periods, is pursued as an investment strategy. A "bar bell" approach which concentrates the portfolio with 40 to 45% in short maturities, 40 to 45% in long maturities, and the remaining 10 to 20% spread over intermediate maturities is sometimes promoted. The maturity distribution of a security portfolio will determine what portion of the "yield curve" will dominate the average yield on the portfolio and have a major impact on liquidity strategy. The maturity concentration issue is complex because the "portfolio" security investments must be analyzed in connection with the asset mix percentages of the short-term investments. Short-term investments include federal funds sold overnight and for a longer term, reverse repo agreements, commercial paper, trading account, CDs in other financial institutions, etc. Decisions to place funds in the "portfolio" versus short-term will be determined by the length of time the funds are forecast to be available; the comparative rate structure; and some new accounting rules which govern the terms held for sale and held for investment.

The rate or yield characteristics of security investments may also create a concern of concentration. Fixed versus adjustable- rate securities create different kinds of interest-rate risk. Within the category of adjustable-rate securities, different indexes for adjustment exist (prime rate, Federal Home Loan Bank (FHLB) cost of funds, short constant maturity Treasury, long constant maturity Treasury, LIBOR, etc.). Other yield impacting characteristics must also be considered for concentration risk assessment such as zero-coupon versus interest paying; purchase at par, discount or premium; tax status; and prepayment speeds.

In summary, within a security investment portfolio, type, maturity, yield, prepayment speeds and other characteristics are of concern because of the potential for excessive concentration. To help managers focus on diversification, a multi-dimensional analytical matrix of the various characteristics would be helpful. In addition, relationships to capital and liquidity measurements are necessary to gain some perspective of the magnitude of the risk.

Loan portfolio concentrations. Several perspectives of portfolio mix concentration in the loan portfolios exist and usually are guarded against or actively managed as a risk position. A percentage mix of loans by type may be set (such as business, consumer, real estate, energy, agriculture, etc.). A percentage mix of loans made by geographic or political region may be set as targets, minimums, or maximums (such as loans to Brazil or Mexico; loans in beach resort areas; or loans in a particular state).

A percentage mix of loans by maturity classification may be set (i.e., one month or one year). A percentage mix of loans by type of rate contract may be set (i.e., fixed-rate loans versus floating-rate loans). Within the category of floating or variable-rate loans, a percentage mix of loans with interest rate caps or floors may be set.

A concentration of loans to one or a few borrowers should also be avoided to control risk. Bankers regularly review specific loans to the ten (or some number) largest borrowers and most banks have policies controlling the level of lending to large borrowers. National banks have a legal lending limit of 15% of capital to any one borrower[4]. Figure 3-5 illustrates the loans outstanding to each of the ten largest borrowers for CRNB. The percentage of total loans represented by the 10 largest borrowers declined from 2001 to 2002. There does not appear to be a problem from undue concentration to any one borrower; in fact, CRNB has never made a loan in excess of $2.5 million to any borrower.

Ten Largest Borrowers
Community Regional National Bank
Dollars in Thousands

Figure 3-5

	Outstanding Balance	Outstanding Balance	Approved Limit
	12/31/01	12/31/02	
1. Rider Machinery Co.	$ 2335	$ 2045	$ 3000
2. Joseph Clarke	2179	1792	2500
3. Ashmont Computer Co.	2070	1448	2200
4. Enterprises, Inc.	2050	1362	2200
5. Cooke Construction Inc.	1930	1330	2000
6. Wagner Fuel Co.	1686	1168	1800
7. United Delivery Services	1671	1154	1800
8. Lincoln Electrical Supply Co.	1095	1127	1500
9. Wilmont Steel Warehouse, Inc.	789	968	1000
10. Toy Manufacturing Co.	660	915	1000
Total Largest Loans	$16,465	$13,309	$19,100
Percent of Total Loans	9.13%	7.38%	

[4] Comptroller of the Currency, Administrator of National Banks, *Comptroller's Handbook for National Bank Examiners*, updated through March 1990.

Usually analysts are concerned about concentrations in the loan portfolios. Annual financial reports contain various degrees of information about percentage mixes such as outlined above.[5] Over time, the concentration of immediate concern has varied with problem circumstance (highly leveraged transactions, energy loans, foreign loans and investments, real estate loans, and some types of mortgage-backed securities are representative of concentration concerns over the past decade).

The measurement and limits for concentration varies with the size and health of the bank. If a portfolio appears to have reasonable credit quality and is actively managed, a larger percentage mix in any one category is acceptable. Alternatively, if the credit quality is suspect, there should be a lower threshold for concentrations.   From the information shown in Figures 3-1 through 3-4 it appears that CRNB actively manages its loan portfolios, has good credit quality, and does not have a problem with concentrations.

Non-earning assets

Non-earning assets consist of till cash, cash reserves, and cash items; foreclosed assets and other real estate owned; premises and equipment; and other assets, such as intangibles, accrued income, deferred expenses, customer liability on acceptances. These assets do not generate interest income and thereby do not contribute to earnings efficiency.

Analysts compute the percentage of earning assets to total assets (see Figure 3-3) and refer to this ratio as the efficiency ratio. For smaller community banks, the efficiency ratio generally is between 92% and 95%. This ratio has been boosted in recent years with lower cash reserve requirements and more efficient collection processes, but it has been hurt by higher levels of foreclosed assets and OREO.

The level of investment in fixed assets is a constant pressure for all banks. In the past, regulators set a maximum target of 50% as the percentage of fixed assets to total capital, but this is not a meaningful measurement today. For bankers, however, the cost of buildings, equipment, and new technology is as much of a concern as it ever was.

Figure 3-3 shows CRNB's efficiency ratio to be 91.1% for 2002. This is slightly lower than the peer average of 92.4% shown in Figure 3-4 for 1990. The lower efficiency ratio is a result of a higher percentage of cash and a higher percentage of fixed assets. Because the trend has been close to peer and slightly improving, the efficiency ratio does not appear to be a problem.

---

[5] The Securities Act Guide 3, *Statistical Disclosure by Bank Holding Companies*, which establishes some of the rules and regulations of the SEC, provides for disclosure of loan concentrations. SEC registrants must disclose any foreign loans or group of foreign loans which exceed 1% of total assets. In addition, any loan or group of loans which exceed 10% of total loans must be separately disclosed.

Other asset Other asset quality issues include foreign exchange contracts, funds in the
quality issues process of transfer and other operating contract risks. These items are of
more concern today, due to the increased dollar amount of financial transactions and the increased speed of communication and transfers. The issues are of greater concern to some banks than others depending upon location and the nature of the bank's business. When a bank has exposure to one or more of these issues, the risks must be identified, measured and managed. These types of risk are not of major concern to CRNB.

Liquidity Liquidity is a requirement for trust between the bank and its customers.
Risk Depositors must believe that deposited funds will be available on demand and borrowers want to be sure that loan commitments will be honored. Liquidity enables a bank to meet the withdrawal needs of depositors and the borrowing needs of its loan customers.

Normally, liquidity obligations can be met through the day-to-day matching of cash inflows and outflows; through the acquisition of additional liabilities; or through the sale of assets. When conditions turn sour, however, growth stops, performance is poor, asset quality declines, depositors withdraw funds, lenders to the bank become reluctant and liquidity can become a significant problem. *Liquidity risk* is the *possibility* that the bank will not have adequate cash funds to meet its needs. The liquidity challenge is to maintain sufficient liquidity to meet the bank's needs without keeping so much liquidity that long-term earnings are adversely impacted.

There are three different analytical concepts which are useful in understanding, measuring and managing liquidity in financial institutions:

Cash flows   The amount and pattern of cash inflows and cash outflows on a periodic basis (daily, weekly, monthly, etc.) from routine operations.

Asset liquidity The amount of liquidity available from assets via their maturity structure and marketability.

Funding liquidity The type and extent of leverage funding (other than capital) with particular emphasis on the amount of core deposits versus purchased funds.

Cash flows Cash inflows and outflows occur on a daily basis in all banks and the management of the cash flows is a significant activity. The goal is to minimize the amount of idle cash and cash reserves held over any night, weekend, or holiday. Generally, the goal is accomplished through the selling and buying of federal funds to or from other financial institutions.

Cash flows in a financial institution result from operations (revenue, expenses or dividends); from financing activities (deposits, borrowing or equity issues); and from investment activities (lending or investing).[6] Transactions resulting in cash inflows and outflows are outlined below:

---

[6] These classifications are consistent with the definitions in *SFAS No. 95* and *SFAS No. 104*, which are pronouncements of the FASB, Norwalk, CT. Formal cash flow reports are shown in Chapter Two, Figures 2-15 and 2-16.

Cash Inflows: Financing Activities
> Checking and savings account deposits
> Certificates of deposit issued
> Short and long-term borrowings
> Issuance of shares of stock

Investment Activities
> Loans maturing, repaid, or prepaid
> Securities maturing or sold

Operations
> Interest earned on loans and investments
> Non-interest income

Cash Outflows: Financing Activities
> Checking and savings account withdrawals
> Certificates of deposit maturing
> Short and long-term borrowings repaid

Investment Activities
> Loans made
> Securities purchased

Operations
> Interest paid on deposits and borrowings
> Non-interest expenses paid
> Income taxes paid
> Dividends paid

Figures 3-6 through 3-9 illustrate Schedules of Cash Flows for CRNB for the year 2002 and a forecast for 2003. The cash flow report classifies the monthly transaction summaries according to whether they result in inflows of cash or outflows of cash. The report shows the amount of the transaction summaries and the month in which they take place. This report is used to help plan and review the timing of transactions.

For the most part, the Schedule of Cash Flows shows gross cash inflows (sources) and gross cash outflows (uses). One exception is the flows in and out of transaction accounts (demand deposits, savings accounts, now accounts, and money market accounts); these are usually reported on a net basis. On the Schedule of Cash Flows in Figures 3-6 and 3-7, the transaction accounts are shown on a net basis.

Outflows of cash for the purchase of securities or for disbursement of loans will result in subsequent inflows of cash according to the contractual maturity of the securities or the terms of the loan. Short-term Treasuries have a maturity of three months. The purchase of $15,456,000 of these securities in November 2002 will result in an outflow of cash in that month, and a corresponding inflow of cash three months later, in February 2003, when these securities mature. The interest earned on these securities is included as cash income from operations.

The bank is also forecast to make $20,800,000 of direct floating-rate commercial loans in January 2003. These loans have a contractual maturity of three months and will mature in April 2003. When they are repaid by the borrowers a corresponding inflow of cash will occur. The interest earned on these loans is included as cash income from operations.

In addition to these short-term investments and loans, the bank is forecast to make longer term investments and loans which will be repaid in a lump sum in future years or be repaid in installments during 2003. The $800,000 investment in long-term Treasuries forecast to be purchased in January 2003 has a maturity of four years and the repayment of principal on these investments will not occur until that time. However, the bank will earn interest on these investments during 2003.

Cash income from operations includes interest received on earning assets such as the loans and investments mentioned above. The bank also earns non-interest income, which includes service charges on checking accounts and commitment fees on loans.

Inflows of cash from deposits and loans with fixed maturities will result in outflows of cash at a predetermined time in the future. Public certificates of deposit have a fixed maturity of three months, and the forecast indicates that the bank will obtain $14,843,000 from this deposit source in January 2003. These deposits will be repaid at maturity three months later, and will result in a corresponding outflow of cash of $14,843,000 in April 2003. Interest paid on these deposits is included as cash expense from operations.

In addition to interest expense on deposits and borrowings, cash expenses from operations includes a number of non-interest expenses. These include salaries and benefits, occupancy expense, promotion expense, furniture and equipment expenses, and hedging expense.

The bank paid dividends on common stock on a quarterly basis during the year 2002. The forecast calls for cash dividends of $330,000 to be paid at the end of each quarter during 2003.

Figure 3-6

SCHEDULE OF CASH FLOWS

2002 ACTUAL
Dollars in Thousands

	JAN	FEB	MAR	APR	MAY	JUN	JUL	AUG	SEP	OCT	NOV	DEC
SOURCES OF CASH:												
SHORT-TERM TREASURIES	13130	13001	13242	13357	12474	13789	12711	12730	13951	14076	13970	14320
LONG-TERM TREASURIES	550	700	750	650	550	600	800	1100	1100	1000	750	1000
US AGENCY SECURITIES	47	47	48	49	50	50	50	51	53	54	54	54
TAX EXEMPTS	300	250	250	200	200	300	400	300	100	250	200	200
MAT/SALE OF SECURITIES	14027	13998	14324	14256	13274	14739	13961	14181	15204	15380	14974	15574
DIRECT COM'L LNS-FIXED	4538	4567	4590	4608	4620	4628	4653	4730	4795	4838	4878	4917
DIRECT COM'L LNS-FLOAT	18654	16776	16846	19096	17222	17296	19550	17679	17756	20014	18147	18228
MORTGAGE LOANS-FIXED	138	139	139	140	141	142	143	144	145	147	148	149
MORTGAGE LOANS-ADJ	29	30	31	32	33	34	34	35	36	37	37	38
HOME EQUITY LOANS	381	387	393	398	404	410	417	423	429	435	441	444
CONSUMER LOANS	2367	2395	2424	2454	2485	2517	2549	2583	2617	2652	2688	2712
CREDIT CARD LOANS	9292	9355	9509	9702	9901	10085	10236	10340	10384	10434	10508	10604
AUTO LOANS	69	70	71	72	73	74	75	75	76	75	76	77
NET LOANS CHARGED OFF	-99	-100	-101	-102	-103	-104	-105	-106	-108	-109	-110	-110
REPAYMENT OF LOANS	35369	33618	33903	36401	34776	35080	37551	35902	36130	38523	36814	37060
SMALL CDs	2527	2368	2371	2374	2376	2379	2382	2385	2388	2391	2394	2635
LARGE CDs	26861	28885	30172	27766	29800	31096	28700	30743	32050	29664	31717	33034
PUBLIC CDs	12228	11953	11231	12495	12222	11502	12768	12497	11779	13047	12580	11879
OTHER CDS	470	503	453	471	507	588	506	540	491	509	545	627
NEW CERTIFICATES	42086	43709	44227	43106	44905	45565	44357	46166	46708	45611	47235	48175
TREASURY, TAX & LOAN	3793	3804	3815	3826	3836	3847	3858	3869	3880	3891	3902	3913
REPOS	0	500	500	500	500	500	0	0	500	500	500	0
FED FUNDS PURCHASED	1000	1000	1000	1000	1000	1000	1000	1000	1000	1000	1000	1000
NEW BORROWING	4793	5304	5315	5326	5336	5347	4858	4869	5380	5391	5402	4913
BUSINESS DEMAND	158	159	160	161	163	164	165	166	168	169	170	172
PUBLIC DEMAND	18	53	53	53	54	54	55	55	55	56	16	20
INTEREST-BEAR CHECKING	649	656	663	670	677	684	692	699	706	714	722	729
REGULAR SAVINGS	331	335	338	341	345	348	351	355	358	362	365	369
MMDAs	1029	1041	1054	1067	1080	1093	1106	1119	1133	1147	1161	1175
NET CHANGE IN TRANS A/C	2185	2243	2268	2293	2318	2343	2369	2395	2421	2448	2435	2465
SALE OF ASSETS	1324	0	0	1237	0	0	1272	0	0	1304	0	0
CASH INC FROM OPERATIONS	3560	3486	3618	3600	3699	3708	3758	3803	3790	3873	3846	3913
TOTAL SOURCES OF CASH	103344	102358	103654	106217	104307	106783	108126	107315	109633	112529	110706	112099

Figure 3-7

SCHEDULE OF CASH FLOWS

2003 FORECAST
Dollars in Thousands

	JAN	FEB	MAR	APR	MAY	JUN	JUL	AUG	SEP	OCT	NOV	DEC
SOURCES OF CASH:												
SHORT-TERM TREASURIES	14445	15456	14389	27386	11380	13789	27445	12432	13456	33474	12711	12357
LONG-TERM TREASURIES	600	650	400	700	650	600	800	800	900	500	600	550
US AGENCY SECURITIES	108	105	111	114	116	119	120	122	119	120	119	121
TAX EXEMPTS	150	50	150	50	150	100	150	150	100	100	50	50
MAT/SALE OF SECURITIES	15303	16857	15050	28250	12821	14608	28515	13504	14575	34194	13580	13078
DIRECT COM'L LNS-FIXED	4272	4558	4861	5031	5084	5133	5183	5229	5261	5288	5312	5338
DIRECT COM'L LNS-FLOAT	20490	18626	18712	20800	19000	19000	21000	19300	19400	21400	19600	19700
MORTGAGE LOANS-FIXED	531	494	525	535	535	544	535	534	498	490	465	457
MORTGAGE LOANS-ADJ	315	299	317	325	329	337	335	338	323	322	312	311
HOME EQUITY LOANS	449	450	453	456	459	461	464	467	469	472	474	476
CONSUMER LOANS	2733	2777	2821	2864	2901	2940	2982	3027	3075	3124	3170	3214
CREDIT CARD LOANS	8375	5424	5938	6459	6986	7520	8060	8608	9162	9724	7900	8001
AUTO LOANS	77	81	84	87	90	93	96	100	103	106	109	113
NET LOANS CHARGED OFF	-262	-118	-120	-122	-123	-124	-124	-125	-124	-124	-124	-125
REPAYMENT OF LOANS	36980	32592	33591	36435	35261	35905	38531	37478	38168	40802	37219	37486
SMALL CDs	2500	2600	2700	2700	2800	2800	2700	2700	2700	2700	2700	2700
LARGE CDs	30160	32116	33536	30665	32724	34046	31177	33239	34564	31698	33763	35090
PUBLIC CDs	14843	14442	14041	15000	14542	14041	15000	14542	14041	15000	14542	14041
OTHER CDS	528	562	513	531	567	650	551	585	536	554	591	673
NEW CERTIFICATES	48031	49720	50790	48896	50633	51536	49428	51066	51841	49952	51596	52504
TREASURY, TAX & LOAN	3934	3954	3975	3996	4017	4038	4059	4081	4102	4124	4145	4167
REPOS	0	1000	1000	1000	0	1000	0	0	1000	1000	500	0
FED FUNDS PURCHASED	1000	1000	1000	1000	1000	1000	1000	1000	1000	1000	1000	1000
NEW BORROWING	4934	5954	5975	5996	5017	6038	5059	5081	6102	6124	5645	5167
BUSINESS DEMAND	324	92	90	84	94	114	124	99	75	83	95	87
PUBLIC DEMAND	359	372	432	31	20	0	0	0	0	0	0	0
INTEREST-BEAR CHECKING	0	500	500	500	500	500	500	500	500	500	500	500
REGULAR SAVINGS	49	51	54	56	59	61	63	66	68	71	73	76
MMDAs	673	650	650	650	650	650	650	650	650	650	650	650
NET CHANGE IN TRANS A/C	1405	1666	1726	1322	1323	1325	1338	1315	1294	1303	1318	1313
SALE OF ASSETS	1186	0	0	1507	0	0	1509	0	0	1612	0	0
CASH INC FROM OPERATIONS	4013	3959	4141	4125	4159	4151	4194	4220	4178	4200	4179	4247
TOTAL SOURCES OF CASH	111851	110749	111273	126530	109214	113563	128574	112663	116158	138188	113537	113795

Figure 3-8

SCHEDULE OF CASH FLOWS

2002 ACTUAL (continued)
Dollars in Thousands

	JAN	FEB	MAR	APR	MAY	JUN	JUL	AUG	SEP	OCT	NOV	DEC
USES OF CASH:												
SHORT-TERM TREASURIES	13357	12474	13789	12711	12730	13951	14076	13970	14320	14445	15456	14389
LONG-TERM TREASURIES	1300	1150	1350	1200	700	950	1000	1050	1200	900	750	800
US AGENCY SECURITIES	0	0	400	0	0	0	0	600	0	0	0	0
PURCHASE OF SECURITIES	14707	13624	15789	14011	13430	14951	15076	15620	15620	15395	16256	15189
DIRECT COM'L LNS-FIXED	4887	4918	4945	4965	4980	4990	5018	5097	5165	5211	5254	5296
DIRECT COM'L LNS-FLOAT	19096	17222	17296	19550	17679	17756	20014	18147	18228	20490	18626	18712
MORTGAGE LOANS-FIXED	832	497	502	507	513	518	524	530	536	542	548	554
MORTGAGE LOANS-ADJ	394	399	405	410	416	421	426	432	437	443	449	54
HOME EQUITY LOANS	578	587	596	605	614	623	632	642	651	660	470	476
CONSUMER LOANS	3137	3174	3213	3253	3293	3335	3377	3421	3465	3511	2938	2862
CREDIT CARD LOANS	9552	9617	9774	9969	10171	10357	10511	10618	10664	10717	10794	10893
AUTO LOANS	92	93	95	96	97	98	99	101	102	101	102	103
NEW LOANS	38568	36507	36824	39354	37762	38098	40602	- 8986	39248	41675	39181	38951
SMALL CDs	2172	2174	2175	2176	2178	2179	2180	2182	2183	2184	2186	2025
LARGE CDs	25984	27999	29276	26861	28885	30172	27766	29800	31096	28700	30743	32050
PUBLIC CDs	12137	11690	10966	12228	11953	11231	12495	12222	11502	12768	12497	11779
OTHER CDS	436	469	419	436	471	552	470	503	453	471	507	588
CERTIFICATE WITHDRAWAL	40729	42331	42836	41701	43486	44134	42911	44706	45234	44123	45933	46443
TREASURY, TAX & LOAN	3782	3793	3804	3815	3826	3836	3847	3858	3869	3880	3891	3902
REPOS	0	0	500	500	500	500	500	0	0	500	500	500
FED FUNDS PURCHASED	1000	1000	1000	1000	1000	1000	1000	1000	1000	1000	1000	1000
REPAYMENT OF BORROWING	4782	4793	5304	5315	5326	5336	5347	4858	4869	5380	5391	5402
PAYMENT OF DIVIDENDS	0	0	325	0	0	325	0	0	325	0	0	325
ACQUISITION OF ASSETS	76	683	715	78	725	718	79	738	733	80	732	739
CASH EXP FROM OPERATIONS	3372	2980	2788	3455	3211	2881	3595	3302	2956	3667	3328	3045
TOTAL USES OF CASH	102235	100919	104580	103913	103940	106443	107611	108210	108986	110321	110822	110093
SUMMARY OF CASH FLOWS:												
TOTAL SOURCES OF CASH	103344	102358	103654	106217	104307	106783	108126	107315	109633	112529	110706	112099
LESS USES OF CASH	-102235	-100919	-104580	-103913	-103940	-106443	-107611	-108210	-108986	-110321	-110822	-110093
NET CASH INFLOW	1109	1439	-926	2304	367	340	515	-895	647	2208	-116	2006

Figure 3-9

SCHEDULE OF CASH FLOWS

2003 FORECAST (continued)
Dollars in Thousands

	JAN	FEB	MAR	APR	MAY	JUN	JUL	AUG	SEP	OCT	NOV	DEC
USES OF CASH:												
SHORT-TERM TREASURIES	27386	11380	13789	27445	12432	13456	33474	12711	12357	32493	13387	12129
LONG-TERM TREASURIES	800	800	800	800	800	800	800	800	800	800	800	800
US AGENCY SECURITIES	700	700	400	200	300	400	200	450	200	500	450	250
PURCHASE OF SECURITIES	36686	13430	14989	28495	13532	14706	35074	14061	13407	33793	14687	13179
DIRECT COM'L LNS-FIXED	4500	4800	5100	5500	5500	5600	5600	5400	5400	5400	5500	5500
DIRECT COM'L LNS-FLOAT	20800	19000	19000	21000	19300	19400	21400	19600	19700	21800	20000	20000
MORTGAGE LOANS-FIXED	0	0	0	0	0	0	0	0	0	0	0	0
MORTGAGE LOANS-ADJ	880	880	880	880	880	880	880	880	880	880	880	880
HOME EQUITY LOANS	500	505	510	515	520	525	530	535	540	545	550	555
CONSUMER LOANS	2900	2950	3000	3100	3200	3300	3450	3600	3650	3550	3500	3400
CREDIT CARD LOANS	7305	7399	7494	7591	7688	7787	7887	7987	8090	8193	8297	8403
AUTO LOANS	206	206	206	208	206	208	210	212	216	218	220	222
NEW LOANS	37091	35740	36190	38794	37294	37700	39957	38214	38476	40586	38947	38960
SMALL CDs	2082	2082	2082	2082	2082	2082	1733	1748	1763	1763	1778	1778
LARGE CDs	29664	31717	33034	30160	32116	33536	30665	32724	34046	31177	33239	34564
PUBLIC CDs	13047	12580	11879	14843	14442	14041	15000	14542	14041	15000	14542	14041
OTHER CDS	627	545	509	491	540	506	528	562	513	531	567	650
CERTIFICATE WITHDRAWAL	45420	46924	47504	47576	49180	50165	47926	49576	50363	48471	50126	51032
TREASURY, TAX & LOAN	3913	3934	3954	3975	3996	4017	4038	4059	4081	4102	4124	4145
REPOS	0	0	1000	1000	1000	0	1000	0	0	1000	1000	500
FED FUNDS PURCHASED	1000	1000	1000	1000	1000	1000	1000	1000	1000	1000	1000	1000
REPAYMENT OF BORROWING	4913	4934	5954	5975	5996	5017	6038	5059	5081	6102	6124	5645
PAYMENT OF DIVIDENDS	0	0	330	0	0	330	0	0	330	0	0	330
ACQUISITION OF ASSETS	137	911	938	144	944	939	146	991	977	147	975	989
CASH EXP FROM OPERATIONS	5697	2424	2332	5798	2708	2339	5856	2717	2352	6068	2757	2519
TOTAL USES OF CASH	129944	104362	108237	126782	109654	111196	134997	110619	110984	135167	113616	112655
SUMMARY OF CASH FLOWS:												
TOTAL SOURCES OF CASH	111851	110749	111273	126530	109214	113563	128574	112663	116158	138188	113537	113795
LESS USES OF CASH	-129944	-104362	-108237	-126782	-109654	-111196	-134997	-110619	-110984	-135167	-113616	-112655
NET CASH INFLOW	18093	6387	3036	-252	-440	-2367	-6423	2044	5174	3021	-79	1140

74

Asset liquidity Financial institutions enter into contracts when they acquire assets or assume liabilities. Among the contract terms is a date when the contract will terminate or mature. Maturity dates may be on demand or on some specified or determinable date. Some final maturities are bullet or one-time maturities, and some are amortizing or periodic payment maturities.

Security investments provide liquidity through careful structuring of the final maturities and through marketability in the financial markets. Loan portfolios can absorb liquidity or provide liquidity, depending upon bank opportunities, strategy and policies. Loan mix, maturities, quality, and pricing all play a role in the determination of the impact of the lending function on liquidity.

Figure 3-10

Schedule of Investment Securities

Community Regional National Bank

December 31, 2002   Dollars in Thousands

	Under 1 Year	1-3 Years	Over 3 Years	Book Value	Mix Portfolio	Mix Assets
Short-Term Treasuries	$44,290	$ 0	$ 0	$44,290	45.3%	9.7%
Long-Term Treasuries	7,750	22,100	12,350	42,200	43.1	9.3
US Agency Securities	1,276	1,643	2,224	5,143	5.3	1.1
Tax Exempts	1,250	1,550	400	3,200	3.2	.7
Other Securities	100	750	2,274	3,124	3.1	.7
Total Portfolio	$54,936	$26,043	$17,248	$97,957	100.0%	21.5%
Fed Funds Sold	23,529	0	0	23,529		5.2%
Totals	$78,195	$26,043	$17,248	$121,486		26.0%

	Months to Maturity	Market Value	Pledged	Book Value	Yield New	Yield Average
Short-Term Treasuries	1.4	$44,211	$ 59	$44,290	7.20%	7.00%
Long-Term Treasuries	25.8	43,176	43,176	42,200	7.60	8.28
US Agency Securities	35.9	5,684	5,684	5,143	8.58	13.44
Tax Exempts	17.0	3,224		3,200	7.09	7.57
Other Securities	80.3	3,340		3,124	10.38	10.93
Total Portfolio	17.1	$99,635	$48,919	97,957		
Fed Funds Sold	.1	23,529	0	23,529	7.31%	7.17%
Total		$123,164	$48,919	$121,486		7.87%

Liquidity from security investments. Security investments are generally held by commercial banks specifically to provide secondary liquidity. If depositors withdraw more cash than is provided by loan cash inflows, the bank can sell some securities to meet the cash needs. In this regard, banks have traditionally held a majority of their security investments in government agencies (U.S. Treasuries, U.S. government agencies, and state and municipal securities). Over the past two decades, however, many alternatives have evolved. On the short end, overnight federal funds, term fed funds, commercial paper, bankers' acceptances, and repurchase agreements have become important investment vehicles. On the long end, mortgage-backed securities, asset-backed securities, and other corporate securities have become increasingly important components of bank investment portfolios.

Bank investment policy is guided by three major factors. One, banks have limited capacity to sustain loss of principal; two, the accounting rules which classify securities as trading, held for sale, or held for investment; and, three, liquidity needs may require liquidation of the securities on short notice.

Liquidation on short notice requires either a short term-to-maturity or the ability to sell the security in a secondary market. The ability to sell the security is dependent upon three things. First, a secondary market must exist with relative ease of access, which means that the securities must be of high quality. Second, the securities must not be pledged as security to a depositor or a creditor. Third, the market value must be relatively close to, or above, book value in order to avoid large losses.

Figure 3-10 is a Schedule of Investment Securities for December 31, 2002. At that time, 21.5% of the bank's assets were invested in the security portfolio and 5.2% of total assets were in overnight federal funds sold. These percentages compare favorably to the percentages shown for UBPR Peer Group No. 5 shown in Figure 3-4. The average maturity of the security portfolio is 17.1 months. This means that 56% of the security portfolio matures in one year. The schedule also shows that $78,195,000 of non-loan earning assets will mature in one year which is nearly two-thirds (64%) of all non-loan earning assets.

The Schedule of Investment Securities shows that $48,919,000 of the market value of securities is pledged to depositors or borrowers, which is 50% of the security portfolio. This means that the ability to shrink the portfolio is somewhat constrained. However, since the total portfolio as a percentage of assets is about the norm for banks of this size (see Figure 3-4), it is unlikely that CRNB will significantly shrink the size of the portfolio in the near future. The level of pledging suggests that pledged borrowing, as a source of liquidity, has already been used, but can be further used to the extent of about $45 million.

The average yield on most items in the portfolio is higher than the new or marginal yield. This explains why the market value of most items is above book value on December 31. The exception is the short-term Treasury securities. Apparently the short-term rates have risen during the last several months of 2002, and this fact has caused a decline in the market value of the short-term Treasury securities. Since these securities will mature within a short period of time, it is unlikely that the bank will sell the securities prior to maturity.

Liquidity from loans. Generally, loans provide liquidity cash flows from interest receipts; principal payments; the ability to sell whole or partial loans (loan participations); or the ability to sell a block of similar loans (loan sales or securitizations). Consumer installment loans, business term loans, credit card loans, residential mortgage loans, and commercial mortgage loans are illustrations of loans which provide periodic payments of principal amounts. The shortest single pay loans are on call loans made to brokers who provide the bank with marketable securities as collateral. For the most part, broker call loans can provide instant liquidity if needed.

Other short-term single payment loans represent a significant amount of commercial bank lending. While these loans have a definite term, such as 30, 60, or 90 days, roll over or renewal is quite common; and in such case, they provide no cash inflow. The renewals are generally made under positive conditions. This means at the bank's option, the balance could be collected, if needed, for liquidity. However, if the bank gets trapped into continual renewals caused by the borrower's inability to pay, the defined legal maturity does not provide liquidity.

Mortgage loans provide their own special kind of liquidity considerations. Most mortgage loans are long term - 15, 20, 25, and 30 years - according to the original term-to-maturity. However, since the customer can prepay at any time without penalty, many mortgage loans do not remain on the books until final maturity. While some prepayments are due to people moving, changing jobs, etc., many prepayments are a result of interest rate swings. When interest rates drop, mortgage loans tend to be refinanced and the average age of mortgage portfolios shorten. When interest rates rise, the average age of mortgage portfolios tend to lengthen dramatically.

Good credit judgment and good documentation were discussed above as necessary for the maintenance of good asset quality in loan portfolios. These factors become very important if liquidity is tight and a bank must sell some of its loans for liquidity purposes. Over the past several decades the use of loan portfolios to generate liquidity by sale (in whole or in part) to other parties has become a normal part of banking activities. Loan participations and asset securitizations have provided bankers with the ability to fund rapid loan growth when deposit funding was not available or when capital leverage ratios were under pressure.

The securitization process in which a unique corporate entity is formed to purchase a pool of loans (credit card loans, mortgage loans, automobile receivables, etc.) requires very high credit standards and high quality documentation. The development of the concept of conforming mortgage loans by several Federal agencies has set standards for credit judgment and loan documentation to be used when selling loans. In addition to good credit quality the special purpose corporate entities are formed to protect the investor against the sponsor becoming bankrupt. The investor protections may also include overcollateralization, a financial guarantee from an insurance agency, a letter of credit issued by an independent bank, or some other technique. The existence of the credit enhancement means the securities should be readily marketable and thus the technique of securitization provides good liquidity to many loan portfolios.

Funding liquidity   A major turning point in bank management philosophy occurred in 1961 when New York City banks introduced negotiable-rate certificates of deposit. The new instruments signaled a shift towards purchased funds as a means of increasing asset growth. Bankers realized that it was not necessary to sit back passively and wait for deposits.

In addition to negotiable certificates of deposit, banks actively began purchasing federal funds, using repurchase agreements, and buying Eurocurrency (borrowing from foreign branches). Banks also found they could replace liquidity on the asset side of the balance sheet with liquidity on the liability side, by reducing reserves and short-term Treasury issues and by using purchased funds, as needed, for liquidity.

The capital or equity of a financial institution provides some amount of funding for assets. The amount can vary from lows of 3 or 4% to highs of 12 or 13% for surviving banks (some more extreme cases may surface once in a while). Leverage funding (other than capital) for a bank is provided by core deposits, large market-rate-sensitive deposits, short-term borrowed money or long-term debt. The percentage funding for CRNB is shown in Figure 3-11 and comparable figures are shown for UBPR Peer Group No. 5 are shown in Figure 3-12.

Figure 3-13 illustrates some additional measures of liquidity for the past several years (2000, 2001, and 2002) and a forecast for 2003. Figure 3-14 shows similar information for the actual years of 1988, 1989, 1990, and 1991 as provided by the FFIEC in the UBPR for Peer Group No. 5.

The ratio of cash to deposits compares a bank's cash (including vault cash, reserves, and items in process of collection) with total deposits. Deposits represent funds which may be withdrawn by depositors, either upon demand or when they mature. Comparing cash to deposits indicates the portion of deposits that has not been committed to earning assets and is viewed, therefore, as providing liquidity. Since regulatory authorities establish reserve requirements which specify the minimum level of assets that must be kept in the form of cash, the cash figures usually represent liquid assets, if and when the deposits underlying these assets are withdrawn.

The ratio of interest-bearing deposits to total deposits measures the proportion of total deposits that are not demand deposits. A higher ratio indicates that the bank has more deposits which have known maturities. To the extent that maturities are known, uncertainty is reduced, and the bank can plan better for the possible outflow of cash.

The ratio of purchased funds to earning assets indicates how much reliance the bank has placed on buying funds from interest-sensitive sources as opposed to funding earning assets with core deposits. The purchased funds percentage to earning assets suggests the extent the bank has relied upon short-term funding.

Figure 3-11

Percentage Funding Composition
*Community Regional National Bank**

	2000	2001	2002	2003[**]
DEMAND DEPOSITS	10.9	10.4	9.9	9.7
IBC & SAVINGS	22.8	23.3	23.5	23.1
MMDAs	19.8	20.5	21.2	21.3
CONSUMER & OTHER CDs	7.3	7.2	7.1	7.6
LARGE & PUBLIC CDs	29.1	29.1	29.2	29.4
TOTAL DEPOSITS	90.1	90.7	91.0	91.3
SHORT-TERM BORROWINGS	1.1	0.8	0.7	0.7
OTHER LIABILITIES	2.6	2.6	2.5	2.2
EQUITY	6.0	5.8	5.7	5.7
TOTAL LIAB & EQUITY	100.0	100.0	100.0	100.0
TOTAL INTEREST-BEARING LIAB	80.4	81.1	81.8	82.3

[*] The years used to illustrate this simulation case may be compared to the actual years 1988 — 1991.
[**] Forecast

Figure 3-12

Percentage Funding Composition
UBPR PEER GROUP No. 5
Banks with Assets Between $300 and $500 Million

	1988	1989	1990	1991
DEMAND DEPOSITS	14.8	13.9	12.9	11.7
IBC & SAVINGS	17.6	17.7	17.3	18.3
MMDAs	16.2	14.3	13.1	13.3
CONSUMER & OTHER CDs	24.0	28.0	31.4	34.4
LARGE & PUBLIC CDs	9.8	10.5	10.7	10.0
FOREIGN INT BRG DEPOSITS	6.5	4.2	3.2	1.4
TOTAL DEPOSITS	88.9	88.7	88.6	89.1
SHORT-TERM BORROWINGS	3.2	3.3	3.2	2.8
OTHER LIABILITIES	1.0	1.0	1.0	0.9
EQUITY	6.9	7.0	7.2	7.2
TOTAL LIAB & EQUITY	100.0	100.0	100.0	100.0
TOTAL INTEREST-BEARING LIAB	77.3	78.0	78.9	80.2

Compared to the peer group, CRNB has apparently funded its earning assets with a greater proportion of large CDs. This is shown in Figures 3-11 and 3-12. CRNB has substantially less funding from consumer certificates of deposit. In Figures 3-13 and 3-14, CRNB, when compared to the peer group, is shown to have more funding from interest-bearing accounts, which means less from non-interest demand deposits.

Liquidity Ratios
Community Regional National Bank*

Figure 3-13

	2000	2001	2002	2003**
LOANS/TOTAL DEPOSITS %	70.25	70.43	71.12	69.43
LOANS TO EARNING ASSETS %	70.55	70.57	71.06	67.86
CASH/TOTAL DEPOSITS %	7.73	7.00	6.64	4.01
PURCHASED FUNDS/E.A. %	32.85	32.48	32.32	31.73
NET FED FUNDS/E. A. %	3.24	2.89	2.56	2.24
PUBLIC/TOTAL DEPOSITS %	12.13	11.46	11.16	11.86
INT BEAR/TOTAL DEPOSITS %	87.89	88.50	89.12	89.33

* The years used to illustrate this simulation case may be compared to the actual years 1988 — 1991.
** Forecast

Liquidity Ratios
UBPR PEER GROUP No. 5
Banks with Assets Between $300 and $500 Million

Figure 3-14

	1988	1989	1990	1991
LOANS/TOTAL DEPOSITS %	72.96	73.87	73.70	72.23
LOANS TO EARNING ASSETS%	70.54	71.03	70.67	69.38
CASH/TOTAL DEPOSITS %	6.42	6.09	5.83	5.34
PURCHASED FUNDS/E.A. %	14.17	14.98	15.06	13.78
NET FED FUNDS/E.A. %	-3.24	-2.97	-2.88	-2.56
INT BEAR/TOTAL DEPOSITS %	83.32	84.29	85.42	86.87

Interest-Rate Risk

Since future interest rates are always uncertain, a bank is exposed to interest-rate risk because it owns financial assets. A bank is also exposed to interest-rate risk because it owes financial liabilities. *Interest-rate risk* is defined as the possibility that future changes of interest rates will result in less net interest income; in a lower market value of net assets; or both.

A comprehensive discussion of interest-rate risk could fill many volumes. The objective of the discussion of interest-rate risk in this text is to summarize the practical concepts and demonstrate how the issues impact CRNB. For more details, the reader will need to study materials on the subjects of economic theory, financial accounting standards, interest-rate mathematics, portfolio management principles, and interest-rate forecasting.

Net interest income risk

Accountants define *net interest income* as gross interest income less interest expense. It is the primary source of earning power shown on the statement of income for a financial institution (see Figures 2-5 and 2-6). It provides the means for absorbing loan losses, covering overhead expenses, honoring tax liabilities, paying dividends, and building capital needed for growth.

Given the current level of interest rates; the current term structure of interest rates and a bank's existing asset and liability positions (loans, securities, deposits, and borrowed funds); what will happen if interest rates change in the future? Will the net interest income change? If so, what is the down side possibility? Can the bank afford to earn this much less net interest income?

The above questions suggest the presence of *risk* to future accounting *net interest income*. Beyond the identification of risk, the question is how do you measure it? In the past, many analysts used a measurement technique referred to as *Gap Analysis*. But since the early 1980s, analysts have begun to favor a technique called *Interest Rate Shock Simulation*. This "new" technique is a variation on the use of financial forecasting models which dates back to the early 1960s.

Gap analysis. Gap analysis or balance sheet sensitivity analysis shows when book amounts will be repriced or mature. As such, it is designed to indicate what will happen to net interest income within each future time period if interest rates change. For example, if rates rise by 100 basis points during the first year, the Balance Sheet Gap Analysis (Figure 3-15) suggests that CRNB will experience a drop in accounting net interest income because more liabilities will reprice than assets. The accuracy of this suggestion, however, depends on many factors. These factors include such items as the recent direction of interest rates, the length of time the current maturities have been on the books, how closely the assumptions about core deposit decay reflect cash flows or repricing characteristics, lead/lag definitions in adjustable-rate contracts, the timing pattern of rate movements within the quarter, and others.

Gap analysis is a technique which evolved simultaneously in many banks during the early 1970s. An early published discussion appeared in 1975.[7] Clifford's so-called "gap analysis" provided a conceptual balance sheet classification which identified the mix of assets and liabilities by type of interest-rate characteristics — fixed or variable. It is a useful concept in that it gives a general understanding of maturity and repricing patterns. However, in today's world, balance sheet gap analysis is waning in importance for serious

[7] Clifford, John T., "A Perspective on Asset/Liability Management," *The Magazine for Bank Administration*, March 1975, p. 36-52.

Figure 3-15

BALANCE SHEET GAP ANALYSIS

Community Regional National Bank

December 31, 2002   Dollars in Thousands

	3 MONTHS	3-12 MONTHS	1-5 YEARS	OVER 5 YEARS	TOTAL
ASSETS:					
CASH	27021	0	0	0	27021
SHORT-TERM TREASURIES	44290	0	0	0	44290
LONG-TERM TREASURIES	1650	6100	34450	0	42200
US AGENCY SECURITIES	319	957	2409	1458	5143
TAX EXEMPTS	350	900	1950	0	3200
OTHER SECURITIES	0	100	820	2204	3124
TOTAL SECURITIES	46609	8057	39629	3662	97957
SHORT-TERM INVESTMENTS	23529	0	0	0	23529
DIRECT COM'L LNS-FIXED	12926	28648	6477	0	48051
DIRECT COM'L LNS-FLOAT	57828	0	0	0	57828
MORTGAGE LOANS-FIXED	1550	4593	11576	15239	32958
MORTGAGE LOANS-ADJ	9345	25255	0	0	34600
HOME EQUITY LOANS	1326	3655	10356	0	15338
CONSUMER LOANS	8089	21745	42150	0	71984
CREDIT CARD LOANS	13161	16750	0	0	29911
AUTO LOANS	229	624	1263	0	2116
TOTAL LOANS	104453	101272	71822	15239	292786
RESERVE FOR LOAN LOSSES	0	0	0	-5036	-5036
NET LOANS	104453	101272	71822	10203	287750
OTHER ASSETS	0	0	0	18071	18071
TOTAL ASSETS	201613	109329	111451	31936	454329
LIABILITIES & CAPITAL:					
BUSINESS DEMAND	15724	12672	7693	0	36090
PUBLIC DEMAND	7501	0	0	0	7501
INTEREST BEAR CHECKING	12203	36608	20338	0	69148
REGULAR SAVINGS	2234	6701	29038	0	37973
MMDAs	17237	51711	28729	0	97677
SMALL CDs	6246	14394	8329	0	28969
LARGE CDs	94416	0	0	0	94416
PUBLIC CDs	37506	0	0	0	37506
OTHER CDS	1680	1537	0	0	3217
TOTAL DEPOSITS	194747	123624	94126	0	412497
SHORT-TERM BORROWINGS	4913	0	0	0	4913
OTHER LIABILITIES	0	0	0	11438	11438
EQUITY	0	0	0	25481	25481
TOTAL LIAB & CAPITAL	199660	123624	94126	36919	454329
GAP	1953	-14295	17325	-4982	0
CUMULATIVE GAP	1953	-12342	4982	0	0

interest-rate risk analysts. It does not provide consistently a good prediction of what will happen to net interest income. The cash flows underlying a gap report provide a foundation for and have a logical linkage to forecasts and interest rate shock simulations. However, the analysis presented in a gap report stops short of calculating net interest income changes which is an important step for good risk measurement. For this reason, analysts are shifting back to financial simulation models.

Interest rate shock simulation. Financial simulation models, which forecast net income in financial institutions, were introduced in the early 1960s.[8] The objectives of the models were to provide the capability to forecast a bank's balance sheet, to calculate future net income, and to illustrate alternative possible results in response to what-if questions.

Some of the early models were based upon the linear programming and some were accounting-based. The complexity of the early models and a general lack of understanding caused many to try simple techniques, such as Clifford's gap analysis for measuring interest-rate risk.

By definition and tradition, interest rate shock simulation is a process which:

1) produces the calculation of a base scenario of financial performance results using assumptions about the next twelve months; then,

2) produces one or more alternative scenarios for the same twelve future months, by holding the balance sheet assumptions the same as the base scenario, but changing the underlying assumptions about the level and/or term structure of market interest rates; then,

3) compares the net interest income between the base scenario and each separate alternative scenario; and then,

4) produces a report which shows the net interest income for the base scenario; the net interest income for the alternative scenarios; the dollar amount of change in net interest income between the base and the alternatives; and the percentage change in net interest income between the base and the alternatives. Such a report is illustrated in Figure 3-16 for CRNB.

The scenario simulations are based upon calculation models which reflect the characteristics of the institution's assets, liabilities, and off-balance sheet contracts. The calculations must first use the maturity cash flows within the current book of business. Then, embedded options (such as prepayments, early withdrawals, and others) must be estimated. Next, all interest-rate implications must be identified (such as market indexes; embedded portfolio yields; repricing spreads, caps, floors and timing; and maturing amounts, rates and timing). Then, the model must deal effectively with off-balance sheet contracts, either as embedded calculations representing micro hedges, or as stand alone calculations for macro type hedges. Finally, the model must

---

[8] Cohen, Kalman J., and Hammer, Frederick S. *Analytical Methods in Banking*, Homewood, Il, Richard D. Irwin, 1966.

Figure 3-16

INTEREST RATE SHOCK SIMULATION REPORT
Community Regional National Bank

Constant Rate, Balance, Mix Assumptions
December 31, 2002   Dollars in Thousands

NET INTEREST INCOME - EARNING POWER FOR 12 MONTHS

	PRIOR YEAR	WHAT-IF	PAR'L +200	PAR'L -200	SHIFT UP	SHIFT DOWN
NET INTEREST MARGIN ON E.A.	4.32	4.32	4.25	4.39	4.28	4.37
NET INTEREST INCOME	16563	17833	17500	18109	17640	18015
AMOUNT CHANGE IN NII			-333	276	-193	182
PERCENT CHANGE IN NII			-1.87	1.55	-1.08	1.02

NET INCOME - EARNING POWER FOR 12 MONTHS

	PRIOR YEAR	WHAT-IF	PAR'L +200	PAR'L -200	SHIFT UP	SHIFT DOWN
NET INTEREST INCOME	16563	17833	17500	18109	17640	18015
LOAN LOSS PROVISION	1831	1154	1154	1154	1154	1154
NET NON-INTEREST EXPENSE	9585	11038	11038	11038	11038	11038
NET INCOME BEFORE TAXES	5147	5642	5309	5917	5449	5823
TAXES	1807	2023	1894	2130	1949	2092
NET INCOME	3340	3619	3415	3787	3500	3731
AMOUNT CHANGE IN NET INCOME			-204	168	-119	112
PERCENT CHANGE IN NET INCOME			-5.65	4.65	-3.30	3.10

reflect how internal rates, balances, and cash flows relate to the financial market rates as reflected by the Treasury yield curve.[9] In summary, the calculations are long and complex, with few short cuts. If decisions are to be made as a result of the measurement process, risk managers must have the confidence that the calculations have incorporated all important characteristics. The forecasts and the simulations for CRNB in this case have incorporated all of the above characteristics.

As shown in Figure 3-16, the base scenario (What-if) for interest rate shock simulation is based upon a set of *constant* rate, balance, and mix assumptions. The underlying market yield curve, the balance sheet totals, and the mixes of assets and liabilities are held constant from the last date of historical perfor-

---

[9] For a discussion of the Treasury yield curve, see Chapter Two.

mance. Maturities and repricing characteristics assume that the maturing cash flows will be reinvested into the balance sheet mix, maturity, and rate characteristics that existed on the last day of the historical period.

Conceptually, interest rate shock simulation would be better if a set of executive forecast assumptions were used for the base scenario, instead of the constant rate, balance and mix assumptions. The process would give information for understanding the question: What will happen to the bank's net interest income if the executive forecast of interest rates is wrong, and the operating managers pursue the targets of performance represented by the forecast balance sheet?

Many regulators and other outside analysts have shown a preference for the constant balance sheet assumption method. The constant balance sheet method seeks a solution to an extreme set of circumstances (i.e., what if interest rates change and bank management does nothing?). The notion has been suggested to be conservative in terms of risk. In addition, not all banks have good forecasts upon which to base a comparative rate shock analysis.

An Interest Rate Shock Simulation Report is shown in Figure 3-16. The base scenarios (What-if) shows the results attained during a 12- month period if the balances, mixes, interest rates and term structure of interest, which prevailed on the last day of history, continued for the twelve future months.

The Par'l +200 and Par'l -200 scenarios assume a parallel movement of all points along the Treasury yield curve by the amount of 200 basis points. The scenarios are recalculations of the base (What-if) scenario using all the assumptions of the base, except the underlying market interest rates. The results of these two scenarios indicate the results attained if the yield curve moved up or down, instantaneously on the first future day and remained at that new level through the twelve future months.

The Shift Up and the Shift Down scenarios assume that the movements of the various points along the Treasury yield curve are not parallel (i. e., the short rates will move differently from long rates). An examination of the actual movements of rates over some defined historical period will provide information about the nature and probability of future interest rate changes. The changes used in the "Shift" scenarios reflect two standard deviations of quarterly absolute changes in rates over the five years 1988 thru 1992.[10] The two "Shift" scenarios used the following adjustments to various points along the yield curve:

Maturity	Rate Adjustment in Basis Points
0 - 3 Months	115
3 - 12 Months	120
1 - 3 Years	130
3 - 5 Years	125
5 - 10 Years	110
10 - 20 Years	100
Over 20 Years	80

---

[10] Staff of Board of Governors of the Federal Reserve System, *Notice of Proposed Rulemaking: Risk-Based Capital Standards to Account for Interest Rate Risk,* March 26,1993.

Of the four shock scenarios, the parallel +200 scenario shows the largest decline in net interest income (1.87%). The Shift Up scenario shows a smaller decline in net interest income (1.08%) which suggests that CRNB's net interest income is less susceptible to decline when short rates are more volatile than long rates.

The question now is: What is the likelihood that such extreme cases may occur? If the bank officers believe that the rising rate scenario is somewhat likely, either the bank must be able to suffer this deterioration to net interest income; changes should be made to the balance sheet structure before the rates rise; or some transaction should be entered into to hedge the risk.

From the report, the conclusion is that the risk to net interest income ranges from 1.08% - 1.87% of the net interest income. The most important conclusion is that very little of CRNB's net interest income is at risk.

Market value risk Traditionally, bankers, analysts, and regulators have been focused on the risk to net interest income from changes in interest rates (as discussed above). During the past decade, however, many have realized that a narrowed focus on earnings impact misses part of the risk. When interest rates change, future earnings may be impacted but in addition, the value or immediate economic worth of the financial instrument contracts held by the bank also may be impacted. Accounting standards for financial instruments are currently undergoing dramatic changes,[11] but still are based fundamentally upon the historical cost principle. This means that the impact of interest rate changes may become buried in accounting system rules and may not be immediately reflected on the income statement or the balance sheet. To overcome the analytical problem, analysts have now turned their attention to market values and the risk of economic loss caused by changes in interest rates.

The vast majority of a bank's activities are transactions involving financial instruments. The amount of the exchange price (market value) for any financial transaction is determined either directly or indirectly by conditions or events in the financial markets. When conditions change in the markets, the market values of financial instruments change. When a bank holds financial instruments, the bank is subject to the *risk* that *market values* will move and thereby cause an economic loss.

Figures 2-3 and 2-4 in Chapter Two show that CRNB holds over 95% of its assets in financial assets (cash, investment securities, and loans) and that over 91% of the bank's liabilities are financial liabilities (deposits and borrowed funds). Figures 1-1 and 1-2 in Chapter One show that these same percentages are approximately the same for most banks. In addition, some banks hold off-balance sheet contracts (loan commitments, financial futures, options, swap and other contracts) which are financial instruments representing future assets or liabilities.

---

[11] The FASB added a project on financial instruments and off-balance sheet financing to its agenda in May 1986. The project is expected to develop broad standards to aid in resolving existing financial accounting and reporting issues and other issues that will likely arise in the future about various financial instruments and transactions. Through April 1993 several new accounting standards have resulted from the financial instruments project and substantial efforts have been expanded on new disclosure, recognition, and reporting standards which will be finalized during the next several years.

The concept of market value of financial instruments is applicable to financial assets, financial liabilities and off-balance sheet financial instrument contracts. Therefore, by reason of economic and accounting definitions, the concept of market value of financial instruments is applicable to the net asset or net equity position of the bank. Analysts use the term "market value of portfolio equity" to distinguish between the concepts of market value of net assets and the market value of the bank's outstanding capital stock (sometimes also referred to as market capitalization).

The market value of portfolio equity is equal to the present value of the bank's net assets (present value of financial assets, less the present value of financial liabilities, adjusted for the net present value of off-balance sheet financial contracts). Present value of any financial instrument is either equal to book value, equal to the quoted market values of actively traded financial instruments, or an estimate of fair value based upon a mathematical calculation. In contrast, the market value of a bank's stock is a function of many things including the franchise value of the bank's operating area, the earnings capabilities of its non-financial services, the current value of its fixed assets, the relative prospects for bank stocks, and many other stock valuation factors.

Estimating market values of financial instruments. When a buyer purchases a bond or other type of debtor created financial contract, an initial price (market value) is paid in exchange for future interest payments; for repayment of par value (principal) at maturity; or both. A universal technique used by the financial world to determine financial asset prices is to compute the present value of future cash flows. Variations, such as option pricing calculations, have evolved for asset pricing, but no matter how complex the mathematics, discounted cash flow is always at the heart of the analysis.

In the simplest of cases, such as with a fixed-rate, interest paying debt instrument with no options, the stream of interest payments is defined and the par value is known. If the investor is satisfied with a rate of return provided by the interest rate stated within the contract, then the purchase price (market value) will be at par. Market value is equal to par value when the discount rate applied to the future cash flows is the same as the "earnings" rate used to determine the periodic interest payments.

Unfortunately, the world is more complex than the simple case above. Traditionally, the financial markets have been divided into debt markets and equity markets, but such distinction has been blurred and new financial products have evolved which defy the traditional debt/equity classification. Also, the financial markets are generally divided into the money markets (short maturities) and the capital markets (long maturities), and the specific techniques for calculation of value differs between the two. Some financial instruments are coupon bonds (providing periodic interest payments) and some are discount notes or zero-coupon bonds. Some contracts provide for interest rates which are fixed for the full term, and some have interest payments which move with market rates at definable dates prior to the final maturity. Some are subject to early termination via call provisions, prepayments, or early withdrawals. Some have optional transactions in the future. There are financial instruments held by banks which are products of customer markets which involve "eye to eye" negotiations to set prices. But, many are standardized products of the financial markets which involve impersonal bidding and asking within "organized" exchanges or third party brokers.

The complexities, cited above, simply mean that measurement and analysis of market value is complex. Financial engineers have developed computer models to explain and rationally deal with these issues, and the measurement of market value risk from changes in interest rates. Many efforts have been undertaken by the SEC, bank regulators, FASB, Congress, and others to develop an effective means of measuring and reporting market values within the accounting reports produced by all companies. New financial accounting standards and bank regulations are evolving from these efforts.

Figure 3-17 shows the Present Value and Duration Report for CRNB. The bottom line of the report shows the present value and the book value of equity. The book value of equity is the same as on the statement of condition shown in Figure 2-1 in Chapter Two and the net carrying value for net total asset values shown on the Fair Market Value of Assets and Liabilities for CRNB (Figure 3-18).[12]

Three fundamental points of reference are available for the estimates of present value or market values — book value (carrying value), quoted market prices, and calculated values. These points of reference are used for present value and duration analysis as well as the basis of preparation of the footnote disclosure required by SFAS #107 in most cases. These values are also the basis for measurement of interest-rate risk through the calculation technique of modified duration or interest-rate elasticity.

Book value is used as the basis for estimating the present value (or fair market value) of cash and short-term investments. Cash and cash items have no future cash flows and are available for immediate transaction exchange. Therefore, the book value is present value, fair market value, and net carrying value. Short-term investments and short-term borrowings have maturities ranging from one day to several months (almost always under one year and the largest percentage will be overnight). Even though these financial instruments have future cash flows, the time frame is so short (usually shorter than the time to gather the data and perform present value computations) it is acceptable to estimate the present value (and fair market value) as equal to book or carrying value.

Quoted market prices are used as the basis for estimating the present value (and fair market value) of investment securities. The investment securities held by banks are mostly debt securities which are actively traded in organized financial markets. A few exceptions include some small amount of equities and local government bonds or loans. For the traded securities, quoted market values are available every business day. For the few that do not trade actively, the use of market prices of similar securities, as points

---

[12] The report shown in Figure 3-18 has been created to assist CRNB in the prepartion of its footnote disclosure required by SFAS #107. Net carrying value, in the case of loans, is the book value less the amount of reserve for loan loss allocated to the specific loan account. Fair market value, in the case of deposits with no stated maturity, is set equal to net carrying value by definition. Any core deposit intangibles may be optionally disclosed in a separate section. FDICIA also calls for the disclosure of "...the fair market value of assets and liabilities in all reports required by federal regulatory agencies..." (Section 121).

Figure 3-17

PRESENT VALUE AND DURATION REPORT
Community Regional National Bank
December 31, 2002   Dollars in Thousands

	BOOK VALUE	PRESENT VALUE	DURATION (MONTHS)	INT. RATE ELASTICITY	DISC. CASH FLOW YIELD
ASSETS:					
CASH	27021	27021	0.0	0.00	0.00
SHORT-TERM TREASURIES	44290	44238	1.5	-0.12	8.02
LONG-TERM TREASURIES	42200	42192	23.1	-1.82	8.56
US AGENCY SECURITIES	5143	5520	32.1	-2.59	9.62
TAX EXEMPTS	3200	3179	15.7	-1.24	8.15
OTHER SECURITIES	3124	3150	52.0	-3.96	11.19
TOTAL SECURITIES	97957	98278	14.6	-1.15	8.95
SHORT-TERM INVESTMENTS	23529	23529	0.0	0.00	0.00
DIRECT COM'L LNS-FIXED	48051	48132	6.2	-0.51	9.75
DIRECT COM'L LNS-FLOAT	57828	57875	0.5	-0.04	8.51
MORTGAGE LOANS-FIXED	32958	32134	44.6	-3.55	11.06
MORTGAGE LOANS-ADJ	34600	34466	5.6	-0.46	10.29
HOME EQUITY LOANS	15338	15601	18.9	-1.54	10.39
CONSUMER LOANS	71984	73310	14.9	-1.22	11.74
CREDIT CARD LOANS	29911	30182	3.9	-0.32	14.78
AUTO LOANS	2116	2116	15.1	-1.23	12.49
TOTAL LOANS	292786	293816	11.9	-0.96	11.18
RESERVE FOR LOAN LOSSES	-5036	0	0.0	0.00	0.00
NET LOANS	287750	293816	11.9	-0.96	11.18
OTHER ASSETS	18071	17146	0.0	0.00	0.00
TOTAL ASSETS	454329	459791	10.7	-0.86	10.53
LIABILITIES:					
BUSINESS DEMAND	36090	34754	6.5	-0.54	6.86
PUBLIC DEMAND	7501	7421	1.9	-0.16	6.61
INTEREST-BEAR CHECKING	69148	68987	8.3	-0.69	5.33
REGULAR SAVINGS	37973	37258	24.0	-1.97	6.43
MMDAs	97677	98950	8.2	-0.68	5.40
SMALL CDs	28969	29293	10.3	-0.85	6.73
LARGE CDs	94416	94528	1.5	-0.12	6.99
PUBLIC CDs	37506	37561	1.4	-0.12	6.82
OTHER CDS	3217	3227	2.8	-0.24	5.97
TOTAL CERTIFICATES	164108	164610	3.1	-0.26	6.79
TOTAL DEPOSITS	412497	411979	7.4	-0.61	6.04
SHORT-TERM BORROWINGS	4913	4913	0.0	0.00	0.00
OTHER LIABILITIES	11438	11438	0.0	0.00	0.00
TOTAL LIABILITIES	428848	428330	7.1	-0.58	6.04
TOTAL EQUITY	25481	31461	60.3	-4.61	

Figure 3-18

FAIR MARKET VALUE OF ASSETS & LIABILITIES
Community Regional National Bank
December 31, 2002   Dollars in Thousands

	FAIR MARKET VALUE	NET CARRYING VALUE	DIFFERENCE	PERCENT
FINANCIAL ASSETS:				
CASH, FLOAT & RESERVES	27021	27021	0	0.00
SHORT-TERM TREASURIES	44238	44290	-52	-0.12
LONG-TERM TREASURIES	42192	42200	-8	-0.02
ASSET BACKED SECURITIES	5520	5143	377	7.32
ALL OTHER SECURITIES	6329	6324	5	0.08
TOTAL SECURITIES	98278	97957	321	0.33
SHORT-TERM INVESTMENTS	23529	23529	0	0.00
COMMERCIAL LOANS-FIXED	48132	46946	1186	2.53
COMMERCIAL LOANS-FLOAT	57875	56497	1378	2.44
MORTGAGE LOANS-FIXED	32134	32866	-732	-2.23
MORTGAGE LOANS-ADJ	34466	34501	-36	-0.10
HOME EQUITY LOANS	15601	15294	307	2.01
CONSUMER LOANS	73310	70556	2754	3.90
CREDIT CARD LOANS	30182	29340	842	2.87
AUTO LOANS	2116	2072	44	2.14
TOTAL LOANS	293816	288071	5745	1.99
UNALLOCATED RESERVES		-321	321	-100.00
NET LOANS	293816	287750	6066	2.11
TOTAL FINANCIAL ASSETS	442644	436258	6387	1.46
FINANCIAL LIABILITIES:				
DEMAND DEPOSITS	43591	43591	0	0.00
IBC & SAVINGS	107122	107122	0	0.00
MMDAs	97677	97677	0	0.00
SMALL CDs	29293	28969	324	1.12
LARGE CDs	94528	94416	113	0.12
PUBLIC CDs	37561	37506	55	0.15
OTHER CDs	3227	3217	10	0.31
TOTAL DEPOSITS	412999	412497	502	0.12
SHORT-TERM BOR FUNDS	4913	4913	0	0.00
LONG-TERM DEBT	0	0	0	0.00
TOTAL FINANCIAL LIAB	417912	417410	502	0.12
TOTAL UNRECOGNIZED ITEMS	0	0	0	0.00
CORE DEPOSIT INTANGIBLES:				
CORE DEPOSIT INTANGIBLES		925	-925	-100.00
DEMAND DEPOSITS	1416	0	1416	3.25
IBC & SAVINGS	877	0	877	0.82
MMDAs	-1273	0	-1273	-1.30
TOTAL CORE DEP INTANG	1021	925	96	0.04
FIXED ASSETS & NET OTHER	5708	5708	0	0.00
NET TOTAL ASSET VALUES	31461	25481	5980	23.47

of reference, will provide reasonable estimates of market value. For the Present Value and Duration Report (Figure 3-17), and Fair Market Value of Assets and Liabilities for CRNB (Figure 3-18) quoted market prices for the financial instruments in the securities portfolio were used for the present value and fair market value.

Quoted market prices are sometimes used as the basis for some liabilities and off-balance sheet contracts. In some instances, the bank's time certificates of deposit, holding company commercial paper, and/or long-term debt issues are publicly traded. For such, quoted market prices may be available as the estimate of present value and fair market value. To the extent the bank has acquired any off-balance sheet financial instruments, quoted market values may also be available. For the Present Value and Duration Report (Figure 3-17), and Fair Market Value of Assets and Liabilities for CRNB (Figure 3-18) no quoted market prices were available for any financial liabilities and no off-balance sheet contracts were in existence on December 31, 2002.

Calculated values are used as the basis for estimating the present value and fair market value for most loan and deposit contracts. Such contracts are not actively traded with quoted market prices. Calculated values will also be used for other financial instruments which have no market price quote. For the calculations, the expected future cash flows must be discounted to obtain a present value. For the Present Value and Duration Report (Figure 3-17), and Fair Market Value of Assets and Liabilities for CRNB (Figure 3-18) the present values and fair market values for all loans and deposits were calculated by means of the discounted cash flow method.

Calculation of present value requires cash flow data and a discount rate, both of which may be difficult to obtain. The cash flows of interest and maturity of principal will generally be specified by the terms of the financial instrument, but some contracts may be uncertain, optional, or variable. Estimates will be required.

The discount rate should be the reinvestment rate associated with the cash flows, but this depends upon expectations and future reinvestment decisions. Sometimes the future uncertainty is reflected in adjusted cash flows and sometimes the future uncertainty is reflected in an adjusted discount rate. Calculation at the portfolio level, rather than for thousands of individual contracts, presents another level of complexity. The choices of alternatives in the calculation process are difficult because no absolute rules exist. However, judgment and consistency are required to measure interest rate exposure to market value changes. Recent developments in the reporting and regulatory process (FASB and FDICIA in particular), mean that in most cases, not performing the present value calculations is no longer an alternative.

Some loan and deposit contracts have embedded customer options for prepayment (or early withdrawal) of principal. For embedded customer options, option contracts contained in the investment portfolio, as well as option provisions of exchange traded off-balance sheet contracts, it may be desirable to go beyond the simple present value technique and make use of option pricing calculations. Option pricing models which use Monte Carlo techniques (generating random numbers to simulate the "luck of the draw" or probabilities) for generating interest rate paths may add more precision to the calculations.

Core deposits, or deposits with no specified maturity, represent a special challenge when calculating present value. The mathematical equation requires a schedule of maturing cash flows. For legally defined maturities, there is no problem. However, in the case of no legally defined maturities for core deposits, estimates of cash flow (sometimes referred to as decay) must be developed, just as is the case for estimating loan prepayments. Various methods for estimating core deposit decay have been used, but most methods incorporate the concept of historical volatility, just as is the case for estimating loan prepayments. For purposes of FDICIA, the federal regulators are in the process of defining maximum limits on the period over which bankers may "decay" core deposit balances when calculating interest-rate risk. Most analysts recognize that interest-rate risk within the balance sheet of a financial institution cannot be effectively measured unless a concept of decay is associated with core deposits. To estimate fair market value for purposes of disclosure under SFAS #107, deposits with no stated maturity are to be shown at book (carrying) value. However, SFAS #107 does not prohibit the calculation of core deposit fair market value and the subsequent disclosure of the difference between fair market value and net carrying value as "core deposit intangible" (an asset by definition).

The discount rate (discounted cash flow yield) is the current market price or rate used for new customers. However, since the portfolios being evaluated are already on the books, the discount rate may need to be modified to reflect the current credit quality status and current prepayment patterns. As an alternative, the discount rates used for the development of the present value amounts for loans and deposits in Figure 3-17 reflect a current risk free rate (Treasury yield curve), a current credit quality assessment, current prepayment assumptions, and a cost for servicing. This built-up rate should approximate the new rate offered to customers except for credit quality and prepayment differences between new business and business which has been on the books for some time. The Present Value and Duration Report (Figure 3-17) shows the present value of the principal and interest cash flows expected from each loan and deposit account, discounted by an appropriate rate. The present value amount serves as an estimate of current market value for comparison with book value for each account. For example, for consumer loans, the present value of $73.3 million compares favorably with the book value of $71.9 million.

Duration: estimating market value risk. An estimate of current market values becomes a foundation for starting the interest-rate risk analysis. Risk is identified by calculating the potential change in market value which may be caused by movement in market interest rates. Duration analysis identifies how rapidly the present value will change if the discount rate is changed.

For CRNB, as shown in Figure 3-17, the present values of security investments are quoted market values. The duration numbers and the discount rate for the securities are implied from the book balance, the market values, and the maturity information (implied internal rate of return).

For CRNB (Figure 3-17) the present values of all loans, deposits, and borrowed funds are calculated estimates of market values using discounted cash flow. Off-balance sheet contracts (if any) were embedded into the present value calculations of specific asset or liability accounts. The duration numbers were derived by calculation after the present values were determined.

Figure 3-17 shows two types of duration. Macaulay's duration (third column) expressed in months, is a time concept and expresses the weighted average months to reprice half the estimated future cash flows from each account (after a change in market rates). For example, the duration of consumer loans account is 14.9 months. Looking at the entire balance sheet, the duration of total assets is 10.7 months and of total liabilities is 7.1 months. This means that liabilities will reprice more quickly than assets. Since the duration of assets is longer than the duration of total liabilities, an increase in current market rates would result in the change in the present value of total assets greater than the offsetting change in present value of total liabilities; as a result the present value of equity will decrease with rising rates and increase with falling rates.

Interest-rate elasticity (sometimes called modified duration)[13] is an estimate of the percentage change of present value of an account given a 100 basis point increase in market rates. The logic of the concept is that the higher the interest-rate elasticity statistic, the larger the expected change in present value from a change in market interest rates; the larger the expected change in present value, the higher the risk of financial loss. For example, if the discount rate were increased from 11.74% to 12.74% (+100 basis points), the present value of consumer loans would drop $894 thousand from $73.3 million to $72.4 million (-1.22%). In contrast, if rates increased 100 basis points, the present value of fixed-rate mortgage loans would drop $1.1 million from $32.1 million to $31.0 million (-3.55%). For CRNB, mortgage loans have more interest-rate risk than consumer loans and the interest-rate elasticity statistic shows an estimate of the amount of risk.

The adoption of modified duration for measuring interest-rate risk in commercial banks assumes that all assets, liabilities, and off-balance sheet financial instruments can be blended and netted into the concept of a single portfolio. Further, modified duration assumes that a single (netted) calculated number for a bank represents the magnitude of change in capital which will occur if a specific change (100 basis points) in the level of market interest rates occurs.

The amount of potential loss of asset value can be translated to a potential loss of net asset value which is equal to the potential loss of market value of portfolio equity. Figure 3-17 shows an interest-rate elasticity statistic of equity of -4.61%. This means that if interest rates rise by 100 basis points, the present value of equity will drop by 4.61% or $1.45 million. The questions for bank management are twofold. How much interest-rate risk is too much? Can the bank handle a 4.6% drop in the value of the equity?

---

[13] See Appendix G for more discussion on these topics.

Some analysts have divided the amount of equity at risk by the book value of assets to express the dollar risk to market value changes as a percentage of total assets. The market value risk as a percentage of total book assets is 0.32%, in the case of CRNB. The Federal regulators are presently writing regulations to measure the amount of risk exposure as a percentage of assets.[14] Although the new regulations will have unique definitions for calculation and assumption, the 0.32% is well within the 1% guideline which has been proposed.

Modified duration, as a measurement of interest-rate risk in a financial institution, has been criticized for many reasons. Some of the reasons are the lack of homogeneity of financial instruments within the portfolios; the 100 basis points assumed rate movements; the linearity assumption (both in rate movements and in the impact upon the present values); the issue of no maturities for core deposits; divergent opinions about how to predict and analyze prepayments; and the issue of data collection are a few of the "practical problems."

For most of the past two decades, financial engineers have been effectively working toward solutions for the problems. New data collection and estimation techniques have been employed to identify homogeneous groupings of financial instruments and to answer practical and theoretical objections. Computer models reduce calculation times to an acceptable level. Training and education programs help everyone understand the concepts.

In short, the result of a risk measurement technique is an estimate which requires judgmental benchmarks for implementation. Modified duration is a technique originally developed for measuring interest-rate risk within homogeneous fixed-rate portfolios. With reasonable care and attention, it can be extended to the not so homogeneous portfolio called the bank's balance sheet.

Interest rate shock simulation: estimating market value risk. Interest rate shock simulation (discussed above) was originally developed to calculate the risk to net interest income from interest rate changes. A second dimension to interest rate shock simulation is the incorporation of present value calculations, as illustrated in Figure 3-19. Given a base, the present value of equity under alternative interest rate assumptions will provide information about the change in market value of portfolio equity, which will occur with an assumed change in market rates. This technique helps overcome some of the objections to modified duration, namely, the 100 basis points limitation and the assumption of linearity of change.

Figure 3-16 shows that CRNB's net interest income is at risk if interest rates rise. Figure 3-19 shows that the market value of portfolio equity (MVPE) is also at risk to rising rates. The magnitude of the risk to equity is much greater, however. If interest rates rise, MVPE could drop over 19% if the 200 basis point increase were parallel and the drop could be almost 10% if the term structure of rates were to shift as the rate increases occurred.

---

[14] Staff of Board of Governors of the Federal Reserve System, *Notice of Proposed Rulemaking: Risk-Based Capital Standards to Account for Interest Rate Risk*, March 26, 1993.

Figure 3-19

INTEREST RATE SHOCK SIMULATION REPORT
Community Regional National Bank

Constant Rate, Balance, Mix Assumptions
December 31, 2002   Dollars in Thousands

MARKET VALUE OF PORTFOLIO EQUITY

	PRIOR YEAR	WHAT-IF	PAR'L +200	PAR'L -200	SHIFT UP	SHIFT DOWN
BOOK EQUITY (EOP)	25481	25481	25481	25481	25481	25481
MVPE (EOP)	31461	31461	25410	36828	28358	34484
AMOUNT CHANGE IN MVPE			-6050	5368	-3102	3023
PERCENT CHANGE IN MVPE			-19.23	17.06	- 9.86	9.61

ECONOMIC RATE OF RETURN

	WHAT-IF	PAR'L +200	PAR'L -200	SHIFT UP	SHIFT DOWN
AMOUNT CHANGE IN MVPE	0	-6050	5368	-3102	3023
NET INCOME BEFORE TAXES	5642	5309	5917	5449	5823
TOTAL ECONOMIC RETURN ($)	5642	-741	11285	2347	8846
PRETAX ECONOMIC RATE OF RETURN	17.93	-2.36	35.87	7.46	28.12

The drop in MVPE is significant beyond just the fact that it drops. For the parallel rising rate scenario, the MVPE drops to an amount which is less than the book value of equity. Now that FASB, FDICIA, and the SEC are all imposing new financial disclosure and reporting requirements, management will need to pay greater attention to portfolio positions and interest-rate risk.

This loss of economic value plus the earning power of net income before taxes can be translated into a pretax economic rate of return on equity. Figure 3-19 shows that the rates of return are negative when interest rates rise by the assumed amounts. Thus, CRNB is exposed to rising rates. If management continues the current asset and liability positions, the bank will earn a 17.93% pretax economic rate of return on equity if interest rates remain the same as current; the bank will earn a large economic rate of return if interest rates decline; and the bank will experience a much lower economic rate of return if interest rates rise in some manner close to the assumptions of the interest rate changes used in the rate shock simulations.

In conclusion, CRNB appears to have long fixed-rate maturities (repricing) on the asset side of the balance sheet and shorter maturities on the liability side. If rates fall, changes in both net interest income and market value will be positive. If rates rise, changes in both net interest income and market values will be negative.

Management of Financial Risk

Managing the relationship between risk and return is key to success in banking. The identification, recognition, and measurement of financial risk, as described above, is the first step. Next is the decision to avoid or accept the measured risks. While some risks can be and should be avoided, to earn a profit, bankers normally accept reasonable amounts of financial risk. Once a banker embraces the notion that some amount of risk is inevitable, four things must be recognized as fundamental elements of the process of risk management.

The first is a *risk management culture*, which determines and helps explain how people act and react in acknowledgement of risk.

The second is *balance sheet management* which is a process of disciplined decision-making and control.

The third is *hedging financial risk* which is an insurance concept, whereby others help protect the risk taker against possible loss.

And the fourth is *capital adequacy* which protects the shareholders and the banking system against those risks which have been accepted by the bank and its management team, but not hedged.

Risk Management Culture
Culture is generally represented by informal and unwritten rules of conduct which guide how people interact. These things are seldom written down or discussed; rather, they are learned by living in an organization and becoming part of it. Risk management culture is a subset of the broader corporate culture, but in the world of financial institutions, risk management culture may well be the major part of bank-wide culture and, due to its overwhelming importance, probably sets the tone for the total corporate culture.

Does everyone in the bank understand the corporate goals and risk management profile? Can everyone in the bank describe the bank's risk management philosophy in the same terms? Is there a clear message? For a bank to have an effective risk management system, everyone must be on the same wave length and effective communications must take place on a regular basis.

Risk management culture can be described in several different ways. It will include reference to leadership emphasis; key corporate priorities; risk attitudes; and the basis for rewards. Although all four parts will rarely be crystal clear and distinguishable, each will be present and help to determine how risks are managed.

Leadership emphasis. All organizations have a leader who is either chosen, evolves, or takes control by unilateral actions. The leader generally identifies the rally focus or driving force to which everyone will march. Things like a clear long-range vision; a major corporate problem (possibly life threatening); a heavy dedication to customer service; the search for a defined quality of corporate life; or a desire to build market share illustrate possible alternatives for a leadership emphasis.

The more singular and focused the leadership emphasis, the sharper the rally and march. However, a highly focused organization carries implications for risk management. In some cases the leadership focus makes the management team blind to the realities of risk. Alternatively, good risk management may help assure the pursuit of the leader's goals.

Key corporate priorities. Goals, targets, rewards, or corporate priorities are all names to describe the basis upon which many corporate decisions are made. Asset growth, current earnings, rate of return on assets or equity, net interest margin, net overhead burden, dividends, and stock price are all illustrations.

Decisions are usually explained in terms of impact on current priorities and risk management decisions are no exception. However, risk control decisions usually adversely impact corporate goals because of the risk/return tradeoff. The priority of goals and the stretch required to attain those goals will have a significant impact on the nature and strength of the risk management process.

Risk attitudes. Corporate attitudes toward risk are usually visible after a period of performance and an analysis of that performance. Low charge-offs, large percentages of collateralized loans, low loan to deposit ratios, the absence of borrowed funds, short security investments, etc. suggest a strong risk avoidance attitude. A strong risk avoidance philosophy normally would be accompanied by low earnings.

Except for an occasional visit by lady luck, if a financial institution exhibits strong and increased earnings along with characteristics of risk avoidance, a managerial discipline of risk management and/or hedging positions are probably playing important roles. Strategy selection, policy guidelines, disciplined decision-making, and control systems will keep risks within acceptable limits and provide a rate of return consistent with the amount of risk assumed. Hedging positions provide the opportunity to have others assume some of a bank's risk in exchange for a price.

Many other attitudes can be important to the risk management culture. The encouragement of experimentation rather than strict adherence to previously defined rules and operating procedures gives employees latitude, but can be risky unless limited to acceptable levels. The pursuit only of business activities, which have been defined as acceptable versus the encouragement to explore and seize new opportunities, will impact a bank's risk profile. "Do it now" rather than in due process is an attitude. Lead versus follow is an attitude. Learn from training versus on the job is an attitude. All of these "attitudes" help form a risk management culture.

Basis for rewards. People generally work hard to attain performance goals in exchange for rewards. If the reward is high, the pursuit will be aggressive, and vice versa. High rewards for targeted performance probably will encourage the assumption of more risk. The higher the rewards, relative to the performance goals, the more important the process of risk control.

In addition to magnitude of reward incentives, the focus or direction of the incentive system is important. If the bank provides good incentives for targeted performance, a good risk control system will be important. Alternatively, if the bank provides good incentives for risk avoidance or control, a technique to assure minimum levels of acceptable performance will be needed.

Balance Sheet Management

All risks (asset quality, liquidity, interest rate, and others) must be managed on a regular and recurring basis through an active balance sheet management process. The lack of a managerial process to monitor, continually evaluate, and decisively control risk will lead to almost certain problems.

A strong focus on strategic plans and goals; adherence to policy guidelines and the ALCO process; flexibility to make continual adjustments to the marketing mix; and, at any moment, a willingness to participate in financial market transactions (to counter-balance a risk position in the customer markets) are all part of an ongoing process. Contrary to popular myth, the more disciplined the managerial processes, the more capabilities the organization will have to take advantage of real opportunities.

During the 1970s and 1980s many referred to Asset/Liability Management (A/LM) or ALCO as a managerial process designed to plan and control the balance sheet. Unfortunately, some viewed "A/LM" in more narrow terms (gap reporting, A/L models, interest-rate risk, the investment and short funding portfolios, or other narrow concepts). As a result of the differing perspectives, no consensus about a definition evolved. The definitional void created confusion as well as problems of learning and education about this newly evolved subject. In its broadest sense, A/LM is what the authors refer to as balance sheet management.

Strategic plans and goals. The first principle of balance sheet management is to know who you are and what you want to do. Chapter One discussed the subject of strategic financial planning, including the selection of a basic strategy and the setting of financial goals. Some of the alternatives for strategic focus are to serve the middle market business needs; to provide credit to a new and growing community and find the funding from outside the market; to provide depository services and actively manage financial instruments in the capital markets to absorb the related liquidity; to grow across a major economic region by merger and acquisition; and to trade actively in the wholesale financial markets. The balance sheet characteristics are very different for each of the various strategies. CRNB appears to be ready for a transition. It has been a community bank in the past, providing many different services to many different markets. Currently, it has a good position in the business markets and is poised for a new emphasis as a regional bank if the management team so decides. As the case is set (see

Chapter Five), the management team has four fundamental strategic alternatives from which to choose.

Financial goals include rates of return on assets and equity; targets for net interest margin percent, net overhead and loan loss provisions; dividends; share price; asset growth rates; and other specific and measurable goals. Sometimes the goals are ranges to be attained on the average over a long time period and at times the targets are set to be time specific. In the case of CRNB, the rate of return on assets appears to be sluggish (see Figures 2-7 and 2-8 in Chapter Two) at less than 1%. The rate of return on equity, however, is close to a target of 15% because the bank's capital leverage is higher than many banks of this size (approximately 5.7% rather than approximately 7% as the percentage of equity to total assets).

The low rate of return on assets and the low percentage of equity are both consistent with the low levels of risk observed earlier in this chapter. CRNB has a low level of credit risk as evidenced by low charge-offs and low levels of non-performing assets. CRNB's low liquidity risk is evidenced by an almost constant net funds sold position and short maturities in the investment portfolio. CRNB also has a low level of interest-rate risk as evidenced by a large amount of variable-rate lending, short maturities for fixed-rate instruments and a low interest-rate elasticity of equity. CRNB has paid out about 39% of its earnings as dividends and has a P/E ratio of approximately eleven (Figure 2-20 in Chapter Two). Goals for the future need to be set.

Another element in the planning and control process is the need for forecasts, net income simulations and budgets or profit plans for specific time periods. Before strategic plans are finalized, they must be visualized. The potential financial results from implementation of the strategies must be estimated to give decision-makers the comfort that the goals are achievable and the efforts required to attain the goals are desirable. A complete strategic plan includes a financial forecast for the next three to five years with some indication of how next year's profit plan or budget will fit the overall strategy.

Imagine how dangerous it would be to drive an automobile that has its windshield completely blacked out, but has a huge rear-view mirror that shows perfectly the route the car has just traveled. No sane person would try to drive under conditions like these, but thousands of bankers routinely practice balance sheet management under similar conditions. Many bankers develop techniques that describe, with considerable accuracy, where they have been and where they are, but do little to develop a picture of where they are going.

Forecasting, net income simulation and profit planning have similarities to driving a car. All require a forward looking approach; all require regular surveillance and assessment of what is ahead; all work best when alternatives are available; and all require discipline and concentration to achieve the desired result. The driver wants to reach the destination safely. The banker wants to achieve a set of planned goals.

Forecasting, within the context of balance sheet management, is the managerial practice of making assumptions about the future (customer behavior, competition, regulators, interest rates, financial resources, and other variables), and estimating the performance characteristics which would result from those assumptions. Simulation is a computerized process using mathematical expressions of economic relationships, accounting principles, banking laws, statistical techniques, and managerial assumptions. Simulation models produce expected performance results using forecast assumptions.

The forecast included in the case study (Chapter Two) has been prepared for CRNB on the assumption of the status quo for another year. In other words, the momentum of the past several years will carry the bank forward and no great change in the structure of the balance sheet or earnings formulas will occur. The strategy is to continue as a large community bank while taking a few steps toward changing into a regional bank. The expected financial results are demonstrated for the year 2003 as a forecast. Each operating decision in Chapter Four can be evaluated by "what-if" simulation, and a subsequent comparison of the "what-if" results against the base forecast results.

Policies, guidelines, and ALCO process. In every bank (large or small) managerial tasks are carried out by more than one person. Therefore, written formal policies and procedures are necessary to facilitate communication, co-ordination, and delegation. Balance sheet management (asset/liability management) policies are no exception to the rule. Written policies and measurable guidelines, in addition to being good business practice, are required by bank regulators.

Asset/Liability Management Policies Reference[15]

Figure 3-20

A. Asset Quality

1. Cash and Float Management
2. Portfolio Concentration
3. Loan Concentration
4. Loan Quality

B. Liquidity

1. Asset Liquidity
2. Funding Liquidity
3. Public Deposits
4. Purchased Funds
5. Brokered Deposits
6. Off-Balance Sheet Liquidity
7. Contingency Funding

C. Interest-Rate Risk

1. Gap Position
2. Interest-Rate Shock Simulation

Most banks have formalized their balance sheet management activities into a process generally referred to as the "ALCO Process". The ALCO process includes a formally constituted managerial committee (in smaller banks may include members of the board of directors); a designated analytical support staff (may be a part-time function in smaller banks); and a formally scheduled time cycle (monthly, quarterly and annual planning and control process).

ALCO policies are management's formal basis for financial decision-making. Written policies coordinate various divisions and departments within the bank, help control performance to targets or benchmarks for desired results,

---

[15] Figures 3-20 and 3-21 are excerpts from the *Community Bank Guide to Asset/Liability Management Policies*, prepared by Olson Research Associates, Inc. for the American Bankers Association, Washington, D.C., 1991, pp. 151 and 170-171.

Figure 3-21

Liquidity: Purchased Funds[15]

Policy Statement

The bank's primary source of funds is deposits by customers in the local market place. Additional liability funding is provided by purchased funds, which include CDs over $100,000 (large and public), federal funds purchased (see the policy on short-term investments), and brokered deposits (see the policy on brokered deposits).

Although some of the bank's primary sources of funds are sensitive to money-market rates, they are considered reliable. Purchased funds, however, are not considered reliable because of the likelihood that the deposit holders will withdraw their funds to earn a higher rate elsewhere. Also, in the event of poor earnings trends, severe loan losses, or excessive capital leverage, the bank could be limited in (or even prohibited from) obtaining these purchased funds, even if it were willing to pay competitive rates.

It is the bank's policy to minimize its reliance on purchased funds. The bank usually will accept Large CDs from customers outside the local market, but these funds will not be solicited. The bank will purchase federal funds from its primary correspondents as documented in the policies on off-balance-sheet liquidity and short-term investments. The potential use of brokered deposits is documented in the policy on brokered deposits.

Guideline

The bank controls its reliance on purchased funds by the following ratios:

> Purchased funds to earning assets
> Net federal funds to equity

where,

> Purchased funds equals the sum of large CDs, public CDs, and federal funds purchased;
> Earning assets are gross before deduction for loan-loss reserve, and
> Net federal funds equals federal funds purchased less federal funds sold.

---

and help educate line managers and junior executives who will someday become part of the senior management team. ALCO policies are needed for each of the primary risks (asset quality, liquidity, and interest-rate risk); for capital adequacy; and for the return elements of profitability and growth. Figure 3-20 illustrates policies of the primary risks for a bank.

Each policy should have a routine format. It should include a general policy statement; a defined and quantifiable guideline; a set of reference numbers; and it should define how the policy is to be monitored on a regular basis. Figure 3-21 is an illustration of a specific policy on liquidity as it pertains to purchased funds.

Chapter Five, *Management Simulation: Policies and Procedures* contains some of the Asset/Liability policies for CRNB. The loan to deposit ratios, limits on long-term securities, minimum capital ratios, limits on public deposits, limits on mortgage-backed securities, etc.; all represent control limits designed to keep risk within bounds. Some limits (loan to deposit ratios, for example) are different for different types of banks. This is because different opportunities, different control systems, and different managerial philosophies exist.

---

[15] Figures 3-20 and 3-21 are excerpts from the *Community Bank Guide to Asset/Liability Management Policies*, prepared by Olson Research Associates, Inc. for the American Bankers Association, Washington, D.C., 1991, pp. 151 and 170-171.

Liquidity: Purchased Funds

Figure 3-21
(Continued)

Reference

Historically, the bank has been above its peer groups for purchased funds to earning assets. Its net federal funds to equity indicates the bank has been a net seller of funds for the past three years. Both average ratios are found in the Key Ratios Report.

	19XX	19XX	19XX	19XX
Purchased Funds to Earning Assets %				
FCB	33.8	33.0	33.4	33.2
Banks $100 - $500 million	20.1	17.3	16.2	14.3
UBPR Peer Group 5	20.1	19.0	18.1	18.1
Net Federal Funds to Equity % *				
FCB	12.8	-9.6	-5.7	-7.5
UBPR Peer Group 5	18.0	1.4	-7.0	-3.0

* A negative sign indicates a net funds sold position.

Guide Target

Purchased funds to earning assets	Maximum 30%
Net federal funds to equity	As close to zero % as possible

Monitoring

The cashier manages the bank's purchased funds and reports the status of the purchased funds position to the ALCO monthly. If the purchased funds ratio shows trends above 30% on the quarterly simulation runs, the cashier will perform further analysis and, with recommendations from the president, will make suggestions to correct the potential problem.

Due to seasonal borrowing patterns, the net federal funds to equity ratio occasionally is positive. This is tolerated, but management expects this ratio to be negative (a net sold position) over time. If the 12-month forecast varies from this expectation, the executive vice president will perform an analysis and recommend action to return to a net sold position.

Marketing mix. Chapter Four, *Management Simulation: Operating Decisions*, describes many different asset and liability management decisions. The asset decisions are separated into loan decisions and capital market decisions. The liability decisions are separated into deposit and capital market decisions. The loan and deposit decisions address the bank's customer markets. It is within these customer markets that most banks acquire and use the majority of the funds shown on their balance sheets. The types and mix of asset and liability contracts with the bank's customers will determine primarily the risk and return characteristics of the balance sheet.

To a major extent, customers determine what type of deposit and loan services are needed or desired. Customers, through market actions, determine what rate, maturity and prepayment characteristics will be part of the offerings by financial institutions. If customers want to borrow money for thirty years to buy homes and a bank does not make thirty year home mortgage loans, the home buyer will go elsewhere. If the customer wants a 5-year fixed-rate CD, the bank will need such a product if the bank wants to acquire the customer's deposit.

A bank management team can influence customer behavior by its decisions on the marketing mix. The decisions described in Chapter Four are all about serving the customer. The authors have selected a set of decisions which represent a spectrum of loan and deposit products offered by many banks. In this case, many elements of the total decision-making process have been "frozen" in order to focus the student's attention.

The marketing mix includes at least three distinct elements. The type and nature of products and services offered; the prices (interest rates in many instances) set for each product or service; and the promotional activities and delivery systems are all important parts to a bank's marketing program.

Together these three elements will determine the volume of funds generated and invested as well as the collective set of risk/return characteristics. The products and services available to CRNB are addressed in Chapter Four. The bank has the opportunity to make or not make mortgage loans; to buy or not buy the installment paper from auto dealers; to offer or not offer a new consumer CD; to bid or not bid for public deposits; and to introduce or not introduce a new fee generating service: home telephone banking. CRNB has an opportunity to observe pricing actions on commercial loans, public CDs, interest-bearing checking accounts, and Money Market Deposit Accounts (MMDAs). CRNB's decisions on promotions and delivery systems include interest-bearing checking, consumer CDs, and consumer loans. The bank may also buy or sell several branches which will impact the bank's ability to deliver its services conveniently to all its customers.

In summary, a bank's marketing mix will have a significant impact on its risk/return profile. This profile can be directly influenced by customer behavior and customer behavior can be directly influenced by marketing decisions.

Financial market transactions. Transactions in the financial markets can be conveniently divided into current or cash market transactions and future or forward market transactions. A cash market transaction is one in which the parties currently exchange financial instrument contracts and each party recognizes those contract values within its accounting records and reports. A future or forward transaction usually involves an agreement to exchange financial contracts in the future and, except for nominal fees, no transaction is recognized in the formal books of account. Banks utilize both markets.

When financial market transactions are entered into as part of the normal activities of the bank, with profitability, fundamental balance sheet structure, and customer service as the underlying basis, the banker will need to analyze the transaction characteristics of risk and return in much the same manner that customer market transactions are analyzed as discussed above. On the other hand, if the financial markets transaction is entered into as a technique to counterbalance a risk position, the transaction needs to be analyzed as a hedge transaction as discussed below.

Although exceptions exist, most financial market transactions are entered into via established channels of brokers, dealers and agent intermediaries within organized markets, procedural traditions, or governmental controlled processes. Bond dealers, financial agents, investment bankers, regulatory agencies, and formal security exchanges all play key roles.

The traditional "bond account" for most banks has included U. S. Treasury securities, U. S. government agencies, and state and municipal securities. During the past twenty-five years, asset-backed securities (mostly in the form of mortgage-backed securities), swap contracts, and mutual funds (institutional offerings of large professional asset management firms; i.e., Federated Investors of Pittsburgh) have become a major part of many bank investment management activities. In some banks, additional security investments in other futures products and various derivative financial instruments are also acceptable. Regulators, however, prefer caution and on-board expertise when banks step away from traditional investment activities.

In addition to the asset side of the balance sheet, most banks view the liability side as part of overall balance sheet management activities. Borrowings in the form of Fed Funds purchased, Security Repurchase Agreements (REPOS), Commercial Paper (in the case of bank holding companies), and other funding transactions (such as FHLB Advances) are now part of normal banking.

In Chapter Four, CRNB is presented with many financial market transaction decisions. Short and long maturities of U. S. Treasury securities, U. S. government agencies, state and municipal securities, mortgage-backed securities, and interest rate swap and option contracts; all present investment opportunities. On the borrowing side, federal funds, repos, long-term debt and advances from FHLB are available to help manage the funding side of the balance sheet.

For the most part, the financial markets are large, impersonal, reasonably efficient, and driven by price, supply and demand. Single participants in the financial markets usually have little influence over instrument characteristics or price.

Hedging Financial Risk

Dictionaries define hedging in the following manner: "to counterbalance one transaction with other transactions so as to limit risk (the possibility of injury or loss)". Hedging is an insurance concept which means, for a fee, a banker can ask another party to share the risk exposure.

If a bank were to acquire an advance from the FHLB in the amount of $1 million with a fixed-interest-cost rate of 8.00% and a maturity of one year and simultaneously invest in a U. S. Treasury security in the amount of $1 million with a fixed-interest yield of 8.00% and a maturity of one year, the bank would have no risk from these transactions. There is no credit risk (in our world as we know it today); no liquidity risk as the investment is perfectly match funded with like maturity dates and no prepayment options outside of the bank's control; and no interest-rate risk because both "offsetting" contracts are fixed-rate contracts for identical time periods. In this hypothetical financial markets transaction, the bank is not providing a service to a customer and is not taking any financial risk; therefore, there is no gain. Commercial banks must provide a service and/or assume some risk to earn a profit. If every risk is hedged, profits from customer service must be adequate to provide a return to the shareholders.

Depending on the philosophy of the management team, risks may be hedged on the opposite side of the balance sheet or off the balance sheet with synthetic assets or liabilities. For those decisions which result in balance sheet contracts, the discussion above about marketing mix and financial market transactions represent the actions to be taken. Generally, balance sheet positions change due to changes in customer demand or managerial policy and transaction decisions. Hedging in this section refers to off-balance sheet protection against financial risks inherent in any given balance sheet.

Borrowers can be asked to pledge collateral to help hedge credit quality risk. Financial markets in general and other financial institutions in particular can be asked to stand-by to help hedge liquidity risk. Off-balance sheet contracts such as options, swap and futures contracts are available to help hedge interest-rate risk.

It is important to understand that the risk is created by the original transaction or set of transactions entered into by the financial institution. The hedge transaction is constructed to provide a reverse or mirror image (whole or partial) of the risk. The goal is that the hedge transaction will yield a gain if the initial transaction realizes the possible loss (whether or not the reverse is true depends on the characteristics of the hedge transaction).

From an economic and financial decision perspective, after the initial and hedge transactions have been entered into, the transactions have become one, and subsequent analysis of the transactions separately is inappropriate. The cost of the hedge transaction is the expense of designing and executing the hedge contract, not the value of the hedge or the value of the original transaction. The independent value of the hedge reflects the risks inherent in the original position.

Risks may be hedged on a transaction basis; on a portfolio basis; or on an entity basis. If the amount of any one transaction (loan, security investment, deposit, or borrowed funds) is very large and a loss related to that very large transaction represents a significant percentage of the bank's capital account, it may warrant a special hedge contract to offset the possible loss.

Alternatively, if the risk concentrated within one portfolio is large compared to capital even though the value of any one transaction is small relative to capital, the risk exposure may warrant a hedge transaction to protect against the concentrated risk. The concept of hedging on an entity basis recognizes the existence of portfolios with internal offsetting risks and the fact that a bank may have some natural hedges between its asset portfolios and its liability portfolios.

Hedging credit quality risk. The largest financial risk generally assumed by a financial institution is credit quality risk. Lenders, after examining the cash flow characteristics of a loan application, may request that the borrower pledge some assets as collateral for the specific loan. Collateral, with proper documentation, gives the lender protection from loss in the event the borrower defaults.

Credit quality risks can also be hedged with the use of third party insurance contracts. For example, some banks have purchased "pledging bonds" to provide state and municipal entities with collateral pledges in exchange for the public entity making deposits in the bank. Any depositor can now purchase deposit insurance for deposits in excess of the amounts for which deposit insurance is provided by the FDIC. Credit enhancement contracts or standby letters of credit are a technique often used to provide credit enhancement to asset securitization transactions.

For CRNB, "normal" collateral is assumed for loans, such as mortgages, and not assumed for others. The credit culture of CRNB has been such that high quality cash flow and income standards have been set for its lending function, and the importance of collateral is less than banks with more lax analysis and credit standards. The fixed-rate commercial loans require compensating balances, which may serve as some type of collateral and this requirement may be lowered or raised. Such action, while in fact is a hedge against credit risk, is most often viewed simply as an adjustment to the effective borrowing cost rate or yield.

Hedging liquidity risk. The liquidity risk of a bank can be hedged by means of contingent plans and standby contracts or procedures. Conceptually, contingency funding is an integral part of a good liquidity management system.

The primary technique for management of liquidity is the planning and scheduling of cash inflows and cash outflows. If a banker plans for a mismatch of cash flows in such a way as to always have an excess of cash inflows or always holds very liquid and marketable assets, the liquidity risk is low. The risk is high when the planned match between outflows and inflows is tight and the assets held are not marketable nor very liquid (i.e., the asset maturities are not short).

To provide for a short-term mismatch of cash flows, the bank must be prepared to orderly liquidate assets or acquire funding from standby sources. Standby lines of credit from upstream correspondent banks or other financial institutions are essential if a bank maintains non-liquid loans and investments as a high percentage of deposits. Since short maturity assets are low yielding and standby lines of credit incur a fee, contingency liquidity also incurs a cost and must be kept in perspective.

Beyond potential short-term negative mismatches in cash flows, a liquidity crisis can occur. Liquidity crises are usually surprises to bank management and directors. These, most often, arise from a sudden event which undermines the confidence of customers and causes a major drain of the bank's liquid assets (natural disasters and unanticipated losses are illustrations). Contingency planning is the most effective technique for hedging both anticipated liquidity shortages and unanticipated crises.

The first step in a contingency plan is to have a process for notification of all key bank personnel that a problem exists. In addition, other employees, key regulatory officials, potential lenders, investment bankers, large investors, and possibly the financial press will need to be contacted in an orderly fashion.

Next, in a calm but decisive manner, marketable securities will need to be liquidated, cash reserves in branches strengthened, liabilities of all types should be lengthened as much as possible, and all standby lines should be called into play. In short, the first step in a potential liquidity crisis is to create as much liquidity as possible, before the full magnitude of the crisis is known. If a full crisis does happen, an initial display of strength will be important. If it subsides, the expenses incurred during the early stages of the potential crisis are the cost of the liquidity hedge.

In CRNB, the decision to join the FHLB represents a decision to increase the standby relationships for liquidity contingency purposes. The securitization of the mortgage loans, the sale of the credit card loan portfolio, loan participations sold, the use of repurchase agreements as a source of funds, etc. all represent the direct management of the bank's balance sheet and use some of the bank's contingency funding sources. The need for liquidity hedges in the past have not been of much importance to the bank's management team due to the conservative management of cash flows, the relatively high percentage of short maturity assets, and the low utilization of purchased funds to expand the earning assets.

Many bankers discuss liquidity contingency plans such as the ability to increase rates paid on deposit accounts, the ability to acquire funds from federal funds or otherwise borrow from upstream correspondents, the ability to sell loans or securitize portfolios, the ability to use the Federal Reserve Discount window, etc. Most seasoned analysts and bankers know, however, that talking doesn't mean a thing when liquidity is needed. It's demonstrated action that counts. Going through the process of exercising contingency plans on a test basis is what is important. Therefore, to demonstrate that a bank does, in fact, have a contingent source of funding, the bank must have gone through with one or more actual transactions in the past and, as time passes, repeat the test on a regular basis.

Hedging interest-rate risk. The subject of measuring interest-rate risk above covered the impact of market interest rate movements on future net interest income and on the market value of portfolio equity. Both impacts can be managed on the balance sheet by restructuring the maturity and repricing characteristics of the loan and deposit portfolios or by buying and selling financial instruments in the money or capital markets. In addition, a variety of off-balance sheet instruments are available to hedge interest-rate risk. These off-balance sheet contracts include financial futures contracts, interest rate swap agreements, option contracts and other custom designed forward rate agreements.

Financial futures contracts are standardized commitments to make or take delivery of a specified quantity and quality of a particular financial instrument, at a designated time in the future, at a predetermined price established in a central marketplace. Financial futures contracts are generally written in denominations of $1 million. U. S. Treasury bonds, notes, or bills are some of the types of contracts. They are traded primarily on the Chicago Board of Trade (CBT) and the Chicago Mercantile Exchange (CME). Generally, a futures contract is purchased to directly offset the risk of holding a balance sheet or cash position in the same or similar financial instrument. Gains or losses in the futures contract are expected to offset losses or gains from holding the cash position.

In most instances, when financial futures contracts are used by banks, the contracts are specifically linked to balance sheet positions in order to qualify for hedge accounting. This means that gains and losses on the futures contracts are not reported through current earnings, but rather deferred until the designated asset or liability position is closed out. The success or effectiveness of hedging with financial futures contracts depends on the similarities of the characteristics (timing, rate base, embedded options, the movements of the yield curve) of the cash position and the futures position.

An interest rate swap is an agreement between two parties to exchange interest payments related to a specific type and amount of principal or notional value. On a micro level, a swap contract can be use to change a particular loan, deposit or borrowing contract from a fixed-rate financial instrument into a variable-rate instrument. Alternatively, on a macro level, a swap contract can be used to acquire more fixed or variable rate contracts to offset an "excess" position on the balance sheet in the aggregate.

In Chapter Four, CRNB is confronted with decisions about interest rate swap contracts at the micro level for loan participations purchased, for brokered CDs, and for long-term debt; and at the macro level, a swap contract can be purchased in several different denominations. If interest rates change, swap contracts can have a significant impact on future net income and on the market value of portfolio equity.

An option contract represents the right (but not the obligation) to buy or sell a financial asset by a specific date at a specific price. The assets that underlie options include stocks, stock indices, foreign currencies, interest-rate future contracts, debt instruments and others. The difference between an options contract and a futures contract is the delivery requirement: options are rights to buy/sell, while futures contracts are obligations. Thus, with a futures contract, future movements in market value must be absorbed while in an options contract, "losses" of future movements in market value will not be realized beyond the original price paid for the option contract.

In Chapter Four, CRNB is presented with an opportunity to enter into an option contract to hedge a large fixed-rate loan commitment. If the hedge contract is entered into, and if rates remain relatively flat or falls, the cost of the option represents the cost of "insurance". Alternatively, if rates rise, the payoff on the option will offset the negative impact of the fixed-rate loan commitment.

Illustrations of customized forward rate agreements are market rate caps and floors. As the names imply, these contracts give the buyer the ability to set how high or low rates will be permitted to go without providing protection against loss. The counterparty to either contract agrees to payments beyond a strike price or rate level. A bank would use a cap contract if rates were anticipated to rise and the bank wanted to fix the cost of funding. Alternatively, if the bank held a large amount of variable-rate loans and wanted to protect against market rates falling, a floor contract would be purchased.

In Chapter Four, CRNB has the opportunity to enter into a market cap or a market floor contract in various denominations and at various strike prices. The bank's interest-rate forecast, the nature of the bank's rate exposure, and the need to protect capital will all be part of the decision.

Capital Adequacy

Capital is the final part of the risk management equation. For all the risks a bank accepts with the various financial transactions, a bank may or may not hedge these risks. For all the risks which are not hedged, the question is: Can the bank afford the exposure? If the potential loss(es) occur, will the future existence of the bank be threatened?

The answer is capital. Capital is necessary to protect the bank and all interested parties against the possibility of loss from risks which are accepted, but not hedged. There are three perspectives of capital as protection against financial risks: adequacy of balance sheet reserves; regulatory capital requirements; and the amount of capital leverage.

Capital adequacy is usually expressed as ratios of capital to other balance sheet amounts, such as assets. Figure 3-22 shows the capital ratios for CRNB for the years 2000, 2001, 2002 and a forecast for the year 2003. Figure 3-23 shows those same ratios for the UBPR peer group No. 5. For all measures, CRNB shows less capital than the peer group. This lower capital is consistent with the low risk profile shown by each measurement of risk discussed above. In addition, the lower amount of capital (greater capital leverage) accounts for the relatively higher rate of return on equity observed on the Key Ratio Reports.

Leverage & Capital Adequacy Ratios

Community Regional National Bank*

Figure 3-22

	2000	2001	2002	2003**
TIER 1 RISK-WEIGHTED %	8.77	8.59	8.38	8.77
TOTAL RISK-WEIGHTED %	10.03	9.85	9.64	10.02
ASSET LEVERAGE %	5.98	5.91	5.75	5.76
EQUITY TO ASSETS %	6.05	5.87	5.74	5.70
DIVIDEND PAYOUT %	44.15	38.01	38.92	31.71

* The years used to illustrate this simulation case may be compared to the actual years 1988 — 1991.
** Forecast

Leverage & Capital Adequacy Ratios

UBPR PEER GROUP No. 5

Banks with Assets Between $300 and $500 Million

Figure 3-23

	1988	1989	1990	1991
TIER 1 RISK-WEIGHTED %	10.47	10.70	11.23	11.74
TOTAL RISK-WEIGHTED %	11.65	11.94	12.55	13.18
ASSET LEVERAGE %	7.53	7.67	7.71	7.69
EQUITY TO ASSETS %	6.93	7.03	7.16	7.16
DIVIDEND PAYOUT %	38.25	46.09	48.85	44.59

Adequacy of balance sheet reserves. A balance sheet reserve is an accounting concept; it is a negative asset value. The purpose of a reserve is to record losses which have been recognized with a charge against earnings, either in the current period or in prior periods. Reserves are created when there is reasonable certainty that the asset account value is less than the gross book value amount, but it is not practical to identify the portion of the asset account which no longer has value.

The idea behind balance sheet reserves is to adjust the gross asset values to a net carrying value equal to a net realizable value. The theory is that if the net carrying value is realizable, upon liquidation of the net asset values, all liabilities can be paid in full. Banks operate with a large amount of leverage. Usually less than 10% of assets is funded by capital funds. The other 90% is provided by depositors or creditors, who expect to have their funds returned at some time. If a bank loses more than 10% of its assets, it cannot repay its liabilities unless the net carrying value adequately reflects the realizable value. This depends on the adequacy of the balance sheet reserves. Therefore, depositors and creditors are interested in adequacy of balance sheet reserves as well as the adequacy of a bank's capital to assure the repayment of their funds.

Examples of balance sheet reserves are allowance for depreciation of fixed assets; allowance for loan losses; allowance for declines on investment in securities; and OREO reserves. By far, the most important reserve issue in financial institutions is the allowance for loan losses (reserve). In the peer group numbers shown in Figure 3-2, the reserve, as a percentage of loans, is approximately 1.35% and in Figure 3-4 the reserve is nearly 1% of total assets. The reserve for CRNB is larger than peer group numbers, both as a percentage of total loans and as a percentage of total assets.

Since the reserve represents past losses on loans, as opposed to future losses, the primary evaluation is historical. A review of the original loan grading analysis, a review of events and conditions since the time of the original approval, a reexamination of the future cash flow assumptions, and an assessment of the current status of the collateral, all provide information for the analysts in evaluating current adequacy of reserves. The focus is to recognize the portion of the loan accounts which represents losses already incurred.

The credit culture in financial institutions underwent a major shock in the 1980s. Analytical techniques used prior to that time failed to keep pace with the credit problems of energy and real estate created from the robust expansion of the economy during the late 1970s and the early 1980s. Prior to that time, the reserve was estimated on average percentages of loan portfolios. During the economic problems and emerging into the 1990s, more detailed analysis and specific identification of problems has become an accepted technique. Both for regulatory examination purposes and for SEC reporting organizations, the reserves are allocated to the specific loan portfolios for purposes of judging the adequacy of the reserves. The proper accounting treatment of reserve has been guided by SFAS No. 5, *Accounting for Contingencies* (and subsequent ammendments).

Currently the FASB is in the process of setting a new standard for the Accounting for Impaired Loans. This new standard is expected to be applicable by the end of 1993. It will require determination of the adequacy of the reserve based upon a discounted cash flow technique. Still, the focus is on historical fact; not the recognition of future losses. The assets will be carried at net realizable value in order to assure that liabilities can be repaid at face value, if need be without impairing capital. The adequacy of reserves is of great concern to creditors, depositors, regulators and investors.

Regulatory capital requirements. Bank regulators are charged with the responsibility to assure the safety and soundness of the financial system. Regulators are interested in capital adequacy to protect the "public depository institution" from the potential failures of individuals or management teams.

In early 1989, Federal banking regulators established new capital guideline definitions which went into final effect on December 31, 1992. The new guidelines are referred to as Risk-Based Capital (RBC). The keys to the current system are (1) the definitions of capital and (2) the assignment of risk weights to assets and off-balance sheet contracts representing credit quality assessments.

Risk-based capital reports for CRNB are included in Appendixes A, B and C. The ratios for risk-based capital (sometime referred to as risk-weighted capital) are included on the Key Ratios Reports. Total risk-based capital has been averaging about 10% and the asset leverage ratio has been averaging just above 5%.

The new capital definitions identify Tier 1 and total capital. Tier 1 is essentially the amount of shareholder's equity with some adjustments for intangible assets. Reserves for loan loss (up to certain limits) and some types of preferred stock are included in the total capital definition but not in Tier 1. For purposes of computing the asset leverage ratio, only Tier 1 capital is used.

The new capital regulations assign different risk weights to various assets depending on credit risk. There are four classes of risk weights: 0, 20, 50 and 100%. A risk weight of 50% means that 50% of the book value of an asset portfolio must be supported by some amount of capital and the other 50% requires no capital support. This is significantly different than the previous method of determining capital adequacy which treated all assets the same, and 100% of all assets required capital support. In addition, the new RBC regulation requires that off-balance sheet contracts be assigned credit-equivalent asset values and those equivalent values require some amount of capital support as well.

The 0% risk-weighted assets include Treasury securities and Government National Mortgage Association (GNMA) mortgage-backed securities. The 20% risk-weighted assets include the Federal National Mortgage Association (FNMA) and the Federal Home Loan Mortgage Corporation (FHLMC) mortgage-backed securities, CMO tranches with agency collateral and municipal securities. The 50% risk-weighted assets include municipal revenue bonds, residential and rental mortgages on one to four family dwellings, and other qualifying mortgage securities. The 100% risk-weighted assets include commercial, foreign, agriculture, consumer loans and commercial mortgages. In Chapter Four, many decisions can be made about asset allocations. Should the bank make more real estate loans, buy Treasury bonds, invest in mortgage-backed securities? The amount of risk weighted assets is directly determined by the decisions.

The RBC regulations only cover credit risk. Interest-rate risk, concentration risk and the risks inherent in some other types of transactions were excluded. Because of these exclusions, the asset leverage ratio is still a part of the regulatory definition of capital adequacy. The 1991 FDICIA legislation requires that these other risks be measured and included for capital determination. New regulations covering these risks will be developed over the next several years.

Figure 3-24 shows the new categories of capital, as defined in FDICIA, and the values for Tier 1 RBC, total RBC, and leverage which are required by each category.

Capital Adequacy[16]

Figure 3-24

Capital Category	Total Risk-Based Capital - %	Tier I Risk-Based Capital - %	Leverage Ratio %
Well Capitalized	10	6	5
Adequately Capitalized	8	4	4
Undercapitalized	less than 8	less than 4	less than 4
Significantly Undercapitalized	less than 6	less than 3	less than 3
Critically Undercapitalized			2% or less tangible equity

The well capitalized category of 10% RBC and 5% leverage is very significant. For most banks, this well capitalized category is becoming the minimum target for capital adequacy. Legislatively defined restrictions come into action if a bank falls below the adequately capitalized categories. It is important to note that if a bank fails to meet the criteria in any category, the bank is automatically classified at the next lower level.

The various categories of capital adequacy are extremely important. The new FDIC insurance premium assessments are higher for lower capitalized banks. In addition, restrictions on undercapitalized banks apply with respect to brokered deposits, interbank borrowings, pass-throughs of FDIC insurance coverage on large deposits from retirement plans, dividend payments, executive compensation, and other matters. These restrictions are not at the discretion of an examination staff, but are imposed automatically by legislative edict.

In Chapter Five, CRNB is expected to maintain the total RBC ratio at 10% and the asset leverage ratio at 5%. The reason for these minimums is the desire to remain well above the undercapitalized categories. In the simulation case, if a management team violates these minimums, the bank will be forced to issue stock.

Amount of capital leverage. Investors are interested in generating the best possible rate of return by maximizing the amount of earning assets which are leveraged by the bank's capital. They are also interested in capital adequacy

[16] This table was complied from information in the new FDICIA legislation. Paul Allan Schoot, of the firm Brown & Wood of Washington, D.C., presented the information during his speech, Prompt Corrective Action, on May 19, 1993.

leveraged by the bank's capital. They are also interested in capital adequacy to maintain everyone's confidence in the success of the bank.

In attempts to provide a better return to shareholders, some banks have entered into financial market transactions referred to as risk controlled arbitrages or structured arbitrage transactions. These transactions create purchased assets and are funded by borrowings collateralized by the assets. The financial instruments of the structured arbitrage transactions are usually hedged with off-balance sheet contracts to minimize the amount of risk exposure but to give the shareholders some extra return on equity.

Even without the heavy structure of arbitrage, banks can acquire funds through brokered CDs, repos, term fed funds purchased, FHLB advances, and other sources. These funds can be then invested to approximate an asset's term, prepayment, and interest characteristics. The amount of asset growth available in an underleveraged bank can be calculated. If the management team has set some specific targets for growth and earnings, the "optimum" amount of capital can be determined.

CRNB is well capitalized as measured by the new Federal bank regulatory RBC standards. However, the bank is operating just above the minimum standards (established in FDICIA) in the category of "well capitalized." Excessive growth, low earnings, losses from high risk positions could all impair capital. The simulation exercise is designed to give the student an opportunity to explore different asset and liability decisions and to observe the impact of day-to-day operations on capital adequacy.

Conclusions and Summary

Financial management is a concept which includes planning for strategic resource allocation and the control of financial risk. A bank's strategies will reflect management's perceptions and analysis of market opportunities. Success will depend on management's ability to identify and pursue these opportunities while controlling financial risk.

Techniques for the measurement and management of financial risk such as those presented in this chapter have evolved over the past several decades. These techniques are now an ordinary part of day-to-day management in many financial institutions.

PART II

Bank
Management
Simulation

Chapter FOUR

Management Simulation:
Operating Decisions

This bank management simulation case places four bank management teams in direct competition for sources and uses of funds in a financial service market. The objective of the simulation is to provide participants the opportunity to determine a strategic managerial philosophy, to engage in financial analysis, to make operating decisions, and to experience competition. Each management team selects specific goals for its bank and the team's efforts should be directed toward achieving these goals within the guidelines established for the simulation.

The simulation operates on the performance data of the commercial bank presented in Chapter Two and is set in the year 2003. All four banks start with the same historical and forecast data and have equal access to market and economic data. Historical financial data for the bank for the years 2001 and 2002 is provided, along with a preliminary forecast for the year 2003.

The operating decisions which each team makes for the year 2003 are discussed in detail in this chapter. The guidelines and ground rules under which the decisions are made are presented in Chapter Five along with a discussion of strategic managerial philosophy and specific management goals.

Sequence of Events An overview of the sequence of simulation events is helpful in identifying the timing of the key elements of the case.

Team organization meeting Team members meet and develop an organizational structure to address required managerial tasks. Each team determines its strategic managerial philosophy and establishes specific bank goals for the simulated year 2003. Strategic managerial philosophies and goals are discussed in Chapter Five.

Periodic decisions Each team makes the operating decisions, discussed in this chapter, incorporating the latest forecast of interest rates for the time period involved. Decisions may be made quarterly, semi-annually, or annually.

Period results	The simulation is executed based on each team's decisions and financial reports are prepared and distributed to each team. Financial reports that will be distributed to each team include periodic reports for the individual team and comparative reports for all four banks in the simulation.
Presentation Preparation	At the end of the simulated year 2003, each team prepares an analysis of its bank's performance for the year including its financial results and its goal achievement.
Annual meeting	Each team presents a report on its overall performance at an annual shareholders' meeting.
Performance evaluation	An evaluation of each team's performance is based on measures of strategic managerial philosophy, management goals, peer comparisons, regulatory assessment, and investor relations.

It is the intent of the case to simulate a real-world banking situation and to have participants operate as a management team. Team work and competition are the case mechanisms used to emphasize the importance of financial management. Gamesmanship which runs counter to reasonable bank management will not be rewarded in the final performance evaluation.

Operating Decisions

After selecting a strategic managerial philosophy and management goals, the team turns its attention to the operating decisions involved in managing CRNB. The decision items are classified according to the primary nature of the decision: rate, volume, or various other issues. There are twenty-six decision items of which eight are liability or equity management decisions, fourteen are asset management decisions, two are off-balance sheet decisions, and two involve other areas. All decisions must be made considering market conditions, and some are made in direct competition with the other bank management teams. Not all decisions pertain to all banks. Depending on the strategic managerial philosophy (i.e., community, regional, superregional, or money center) of the bank, some of the operating decisions are limited. Figure 4-1 provides an overview of the operating decisions.

The operating decisions reflect different types and levels of competition, growth potential, overhead expenses, yields or rates, and a variety of other factors. While many issues must be considered in managing a bank, this simulation case highlights a few for simplicity, and this allows participants to observe the impact of specific decisions on financial results.

Overview of Decisions

Figure 4-1

	Direct Competition	Rate	Volume		Other Decision Issues
LIABILITIES:					
IBCs	Yes	x		x	Service Charge
MMDAs	Yes	x			
Small CDs	No			x	Maturity Mix, New Product
Large CDs	No		x	x	Brokered CDs, Swaps[1]
Public CDs	Yes	x	x	x	Maximum Volume
Repos	No		x		
Long-Term Debt	No			x	Issue, Swap[1], FHLB
Common Stock	No			x	New Issue
ASSETS:					
S/T Treasuries	No		x		
L/T Treasuries	No		x	x	Sales from Portfolio
Trading Account[1]	No		x		
Asset-Backed Securities	No		x		
Term Fed Funds	No		x	x	Credit Standards
Coml - Fixed	No		x	x	Compensating Balance, Commit[1], Hedge[1]
Coml - Floating	Yes	x			
Loan Participations	No		x	x	Swaps[1]
Mortgages	No		x	x	Fixed vs Adjustable, CMO[1]
Home Equity Loans	Yes			x	Maturity
Consumer Loans	Yes			x	Maturity, Promotion $
Credit Cards	No			x	Portfolio Sale
Auto Loans	No		x	x	Indirect Loans via Dealers
Reserve for Loan Loss	No			x	Ability to Increase
OFF-BALANCE SHEET:					
Loan Commitments[1]	No		x		
Interest Rate Contract[1]	No		x	x	Market Cap/ Floor, Swap
OTHER:					
Non-Interest Income and Expense	No			x	New Service, Buy[2]/Sell Branches[2], Decrease/Increase Credit Dept. Staff, General Staff Reduction
Interest Rate Scenarios	No	x			

[1] Decisions not available for the Community bank.

[2] Decisions not available for the Money Center bank.

The interaction of decisions and its impact on performance adds significantly to the complexity of the exercise. Decision alternatives should be evaluated with this interaction in mind and not in isolation. Furthermore, the conflicting long and short term objectives of shareholders, regulators, and members of the management team along with competition from peer banks may lead to different conclusions regarding decision alternatives.

Liability Management Decisions

Each liability decision item involves a bank source of funds. Some markets have limited growth potential, where depositors or lenders exhibit a degree of bank loyalty. Others reflect significant growth that is extremely competitive and rate sensitive. Decision alternatives must be considered with respect to maturity and cost considerations.

Deposit Items

Interest-Bearing Checking

Interest-Bearing Checking (IBC) accounts represent an important source of bank funding with balances of $69,148,000 at year-end 2002. Pricing of IBCs includes not only the offered interest rate on balances, but also a monthly service charge based on a minimum balance..

The current pricing package of 5% interest and $8 service charge has garnered a 25% market share for the bank and each of its competitors with an average account balance of $1,000. A change in the pricing package affects average account balances, the number of accounts, and the proportion of accounts paying the minimum balance service charge. There is also a $2 per account/month data processing charge. Figure 4-2 illustrates the results of pricing packages including interest rate alternatives of 4.0%, 5.0%, and 6.0% and service charge alternatives of $7, $8, and $9.

Interest-Bearing Checking
Price Alternatives and Account Information

Figure 4-2

Rate	Service Charge	Average Balance	Number of Accounts / Jan 2003	% Under Min Bal
4.0%	$9	$1,300	53,191	10%
4.0	8	1,200	57,623	15
4.0	7	1,100	62,862	20
5.0	9	1,100	62,862	20
5.0	**8**	**1,000**	**69,148**	**25**
5.0	7	900	76,831	30
6.0	9	900	76,831	30
6.0	8	800	86,435	35
6.0	7	700	98,783	40

An increase in the IBC interest rate attracts highly rate sensitive depositors with a tendency towards minimizing balances held in transaction accounts. Accordingly, a higher proportion of these accounts violate the minimum balance requirement and incur the monthly service charge. Conversely, lower rates attract depositors who are less rate sensitive and tend to avoid the minimum balance requirement by holding larger average balances.

The distribution of all pricing packages in the market determines the market's average account balance. In turn, this average determines the total size of the market. If all institutions indicate a desire to serve the retail market by offering high interest rates and low service charges, the average balance decreases and additional funds are attracted from other institutions and markets. This approach increases the total size of the market. Conversely, low rates and high service charges decrease the total market.

The change in market size is stated in terms of a market adjustment factor by dividing the "normal" average account balance ($1,000) by the actual average account balance. The adjustment factor for the maximum market is 1.42 (= 4,000/2,800) and the minimum market adjustment factor is 0.77 (= 4,000/5,200); the resultant market balances are shown in Figure 4-3.

Interest-Bearing Checking

Forecast Balances for Total Market (000s)

Figure 4-3

	Normal Market	Loyalty Factor		Normal Market	Loyalty Factor
January	$276,592	100	July	$288,592	70
February	278,592	100	August	290,592	60
March	280,592	100	September	292,592	60
April	282,592	80	October	294,592	50
May	284,592	80	November	296,592	50
June	286,592	70	December	298,592	50

The bank's share of the total market of IBCs is a positive function of the relative competitiveness of its pricing package. If all institutions offer the same pricing package, each garners 25% market share. The allocation of market share, given different pricing of IBC's by local institutions, is illustrated in Figure 4-4 where two banks have moved to opposite endpoints of the pricing scheme for IBCs (6.0% and $7, 4.0% and $9).

Interest-Bearing Checking

Example of Market Share Allocation

Figure 4-4

Bank	Interest Rate	Service Charge	Number of Accounts	Market Share	Average Balance	Market Adjustment Factor
A	6.0%	$7	98,783	32.12%	700	
B	6.0	8	86,435	28.10	800	
C	5.0	8	69,148	22.48	1,000	
D	4.0	9	53,191	17.29	1,300	
			307,557	100.00		4,000/3,800 = 1.05

The final calculation of each bank's share of competitive balances under this scenario is shown in Figure 4-5. (e. g., Bank A = 98,783 * 700 * 1.05)

Figure 4-5

Interest-Bearing Checking

Allocation of Competitive Balances (000s)

	Adjusted Market Total Balances	Share of Competitive Market			
		Bank A	Bank B	Bank C	Bank D
April	$297,465	$78,601	$76,213	$72,869	$69,782
May	299,571	79,158	76,752	73,385	70,276
June	301,675	81,861	78,228	73,141	68,445

The bank management team must decide on the pricing of the IBCs beginning with the second quarter and enter the option as Items 1a (as a 4, 5, or 6) & 1b (as a 7, 8, or 9) on the Decision Form. The new pricing will operate for the rest of the year.

Money Market Deposit Accounts

Money Market Deposit Accounts (MMDAs) are an important source of bank funding with balances of $97,677,000 at year-end 2002. Depositors may write 3 checks per month, and they receive an interest rate competitive with that of money market mutual funds. The current and forecast rate on MMDAs floats at the 1-year Treasury bill rate. In the past, the rate has sometimes been above and sometimes been below the 1-year T-bill rate.

The bank's market share of these accounts is entirely rate dependent. The aggressive pricing through high rates is indicative of a desire to serve the retail market. Pricing alternatives include a fixed-rate account or one floating with the 1-year Treasury bill (T-bill) Bond Equivalent Yield (BEY). A fixed-rate at 6% yields five percent less in MMDA market balances than pricing at the 1-year T-bill; furthermore, differentials of 100 basis points above/below the T-bill rate increase/decrease market balances by 10%. The calculation for the percentage of the market for each bank is shown in Figure 4-6.

Money Market Deposit Accounts

Example of Market Share Allocation

Figure 4-6

Bank	Pricing Decision	Rate	Computations	Percent of Market Share
A	Fixed	6.00%	6.00 / 27.06	22.17
B	Float - 1.00	6.02	6.02 / 27.06	22.25
C	Float + 0.00	7.02	7.02 / 27.06	25.94
D	Float + 1.00	8.02	8.02 / 27.06	29.64
Total		27.06		100.00

Figure 4-7 shows the balances associated with the different rate options. Thus, for Bank A in January, fixed at 6.00%; ($373,732,000 * .2217 = $82,856,384.40).

Figure 4-7

Money Market Deposit Accounts

Forecast Balances (000s) - Total Market

Fixed/Float	Fixed	Float	**Float**	Float
Index	6.00%	1-yr T-bill	**1-yr T-bill**	1-yr T-bill
Differential	+0.00%	+1.00%	**+0.00%**	-1.00%
January	$373,732	$432,740	**$393,400**	$354,060
February	376,200	435,600	**396,000**	356,400
March	378,672	438,460	**398,600**	358,740
April	381,140	441,320	**401,200**	361,080
May	383,612	444,180	**403,800**	363,420
June	386,080	447,040	**406,400**	365,760
July	388,522	449,900	**409,000**	368,100
August	391,020	452,760	**411,600**	370,440
September	393,492	455,620	**414,200**	372,780
October	395,960	458,480	**416,800**	375,120
November	398,432	461,340	**419,400**	377,460
December	400,900	464,200	**422,000**	379,800

*Forecast Interest Rates**

Fixed/Float	Fixed	Float	**Float**	Float
Index	6.00%	1-yr T-bill	**1-yr T-bill**	1-yr T-bill
Differential	+0.00%	+1.00%	**+0.00%**	-1.00%
January	6.00%	8.02%	**7.02%**	6.02%
February	6.00	8.02	**7.02**	6.02
March	6.00	8.02	**7.02**	6.02

* For the interest rates for the months of April through December use the 1-year T-bill BEY rate shown in the Yield Curve section of the Yield Curve and Market Rates Report in Figure 2-24.

> The bank must decide on the pricing of the MMDAs at the beginning of the second quarter and enter the option as Item 2 (either as a fixed-rate (6.0%) or a differential from 1-year T-bill (-1.0, 0.0, +1.0)) on the Decision Form.

Small Certificates of Deposit

At year-end 2002, the balance of small certificates of deposit stands at $28,969,000 with a concentration in 12-month maturities. The bank offers a range of maturities from 6 months to four years to attract these time deposits of under $100,000. Currently, the bank spends $5,000 a month promoting this account. It channels deposits into the maturity it desires by promoting a specific term and offering a slightly higher rate on that term.

Pricing of small CDs is expressed as a differential from the Treasury yield curve for comparable maturities. Currently, small CD maturities are priced 25 basis points below the Treasury yield curve with the exception of the 12-month maturity which is priced 25 basis points above the Treasury yield

122

curve. The Treasury yield curve is made up of the 1-day rate, the 30-day rate, the 3-month rate, the 6-month rate and the 1, 2, 3, 5, 7, 10, 15, 20, and 30-year rates.

The bank must emphasize one maturity out of a selection of 6-months, 1, 2, 3, or 4-years (Figure 4-8) by pricing the selected maturity term 25 basis points above the Treasury yield curve. Emphasis of the maturity will be reflected in a concentration of 40% of new dollar volume with all other maturities spread evenly among the remaining 60%. The remaining maturities will be priced at 25 basis points below the Treasury yield curve. Then, based on rate expectations (the current period's rate), the market will be allocated as in Figure 4-9, with any remaining funds being allocated to 3-month CDs.

Small Certificates of Deposit

Figure 4-8

Forecast New Dollar Volumes (000s) - Each Bank

	New Dollars		New Dollars
January	$2,500	July	$2,700
February	2,600	August	2,700
March	2,700	September	2,700
April	2,700	October	2,700
May	2,800	November	2,700
June	2,800	December	2,700

Forecast Interest Rates*

	6 Mo	**12 Mo**	24 Mo	36 Mo	48 Mo
January	6.85%	**7.27%**	7.06%	7.22%	7.35%
February	6.85	**7.27**	7.06	7.22	7.35
March	6.85	**7.27**	7.06	7.22	7.35

* For the interest rates for the months of April through December use the appropriate maturity on the yield curve in the Yield Curve and Market Rates Report. The 48-month rate is the midpoint between the 3 and 5-year rates in Figure 2-24.

The bank's liquidity position and weighted average rate on small CDs change in accordance with the maturity and rate implications of the decision alternatives. The bank may change the emphasized maturity based upon the alternatives outlined in Figure 4-8, then adjusted as in Figure 4-9.

Figure 4-9

Small Certificates of Deposit
Consumer Preference Matrix - Per Bank

	6 Mo	12 Mo	24 Mo	36 Mo	48 Mo
Level	95%	100%	95%	85%	75%
Rising	115	105	95	85	75
Falling	65	75	85	95	105

> The bank's decision on the emphasized maturity for each quarter should be entered as Item 3a (as a 6, 12, 24, 36, or 48) on the Decision Form.

Small CDs
New Product

In addition to the above small CD alternatives, the bank is considering the introduction of a new product called: *'Option CDs'*. These CDs have a maturity of 60 months, are priced 50 basis points below the Treasury yield curve and have an option to reprice to a rate 50 basis points above the Treasury yield curve on December 31, 2003. If the bank elects to begin issuing these CDs, 30% of the new dollar volume will go to this new product and 30% to the emphasized maturity. This is shown in Figure 4-10. The balance of maturities, not including the maturities for small certificates of deposit, above, will split up the 40% remainder.

Small Certificates of Deposit - 'Option CDs'
Forecast New Dollar Volumes (000s) - Each Bank

Figure 4-10

	New Dollars		New Dollars
January	$750	July	$810
February	780	August	810
March	810	September	810
April	810	October	810
May	840	November	810
June	840	December	810

Forecast Interest Rates*

	Option CD Rate
January	7.23%
February	7.23
March	7.23

* For the interest rates for the months of April through December use the 60-month maturity on the yield curve in the Yield Curve and Market Rates Report in Figure 2-24.

> The decision to issue *'Option CDs'* for the first quarter should be entered as Item 3b (as a Y for Yes or N for No) on the Decision Form.

**Large
Certificates
of Deposit**

The bank uses large certificates of deposit as another major source of funding with balances of $94,416,000 at year-end 2002. These CDs are obtained locally and regionally in denominations of $100,000 or more, and are issued in 3-month maturities that pay the 90-day CD rate. At any point in time, the balance of large CDs is the sum of the inflows for the previous three months. From a cash flow perspective, inflows for October 2002 will result in outflows in January 2003; inflows for November 2002 will result in outflows in February 2003; and inflows for December 2002 will result in outflows in March 2003. The monthly net inflows of funds required to maintain current balances of these short maturities is substantial.

The forecast calls for new volumes in the $30,000,000 per month range as shown in Figure 4-11 with interest rates for the level, consistently falling, and consistently rising rate forecasts. Funds in excess of $40,000,000 can be acquired only by paying 25 basis points above the market rate; funds of $50,000,000 or more require 50 basis points over 90-day CD rate. These higher rates are applied to the entire balance of large CDs originated during a given month. If the bank chooses to attract funds from this market, the minimum purchase is $1 million.

Large Certificates of Deposit

Figure 4-11

Forecast New Dollar Volumes(000s) - Each Bank

	Volume		Volume
January	**$30,160**	July	**$31,177**
February	**32,116**	August	**33,239**
March	**33,536**	September	**34,564**
April	**30,665**	October	**31,698**
May	**32,724**	November	**33,763**
June	**34,046**	December	**35,090**

Forecast Interest Rates[*]

	Falling	Level	Rising
January	7.57%	7.82%	8.32%
February	7.32	7.82	8.82
March	7.07	7.82	9.32

[*] For the interest rates for the months of April through December use the 90-day CD rate in the Market Rate section of the Yield Curve and Market Rates Report in Figure 2-24.

The decision on the desired monthly new dollar volume should be entered in thousands as Item 4a (e.g., 40 million is input as 40000) on the Decision Form.

Large CDs
Brokered Funds

In addition to obtaining funds directly in the CD market, the bank has been offered the opportunity to obtain up to $12,000,000 in brokered CDs. The funds are through a broker, who pools investors' funds, and places them with selected banks. The specifics of this contract are: $4,000,000 blocks in July, August, and September; 2-year maturities; and a floating-rate 25 basis points above the 90-day CD rate with a quarterly reset.

Since these brokered certificates carry a floating-rate and have a 2-year maturity, they subject the bank to greater risk from rising interest rates than do the fixed-rate, 90-day maturity certificates of deposit sold directly by the bank. It is possible to reduce this risk by entering into an interest rate swap transaction.

An interest rate swap is an agreement between two parties to exchange interest payments related to a specific type and amount of principal on their respective balance sheets. In this instance, the bank can swap its floating-interest payments for fixed-interest payments. The broker can swap the floating-rate CDs, as they become available, for a fixed-rate of 50 basis points above LIBOR. If the swap contract is accepted, the bank will receive the 90-day CD rate plus 25 basis points with a quarterly reset, and pay a fixed-rate of LIBOR plus 50 basis points for the two-year term of the certificates.

> The decision to accept this offer should be entered in Item 4b (as a Y for Yes or N for No) on the Decision Form. If any brokered CDs are accepted, then the decision to swap these funds must be entered for each month of the third quarter as Item 4c (as a Y for Yes or a N for No) on the Decision Form.

Public Certificates of Deposit

The balance of public certificates of deposit is $37,506,000 at year-end 2002. These funds have a maturity of three months and are obtained from state governments, municipal organizations, school districts, and other public agencies that normally have funds for deposit. The majority of the bank's public CDs are generated from local organizations that have a policy of using local institutions for their banking needs.

Currently, the bank is bidding 8.22%, 10 basis points below the maximum rate bid allowed by bank policy. This rate bid will attract one quarter of the market, except that the bank may put a forecast ceiling, not to be less than $1 million, on the public CDs it will accept in any month. If the bank desires no new public CDs, bid at the minimum rate and enter zero as the dollar maximum volume.

The competition for public CDs is strong and on a bid-rate basis. Allowable bids range from a bank policy maximum of 50 basis points above the 90-day CD rate to a minimum of 25 basis points below the 3-month T-bill BEY. It is well known that the minimum rate bid in the city will attract only a very small amount of public CDs for the bank. Figure 4-12 shows the forecast market of new funds and bid ranges given level, consistently falling, and consistently rising rates.

Figure 4-12

Public Certificates of Deposit

Forecast New Certificates for Total Market(000s)

	Market		Market
January	$59,400	July	$60,000
February	57,800	August	58,200
March	56,200	September	56,200
April	60,000	October	60,000
May	58,200	November	58,200
June	56,200	December	56,200

*Forecast Interest Rates**

	Falling Rates Min	Max	Level Rates Min	Max	Rising Rates Min	Max
January	6.53%	8.07%	6.78%	8.32%	7.28%	8.82%
February	6.28	7.82	6.78	8.32	7.78	9.32
March	6.03	7.57	6.78	8.32	8.28	9.82

* For the interest rates for the months of April through December use the 90-Day CD rate for the maximum and the 3-Month Treasury bill BEY for the minimum from the Yield Curve and Market Rates Report in Figure 2-24.

Figure 4-13 provides an example of market share allocation based on bid rates throughout the allowable range for level rates.

Public Certificates of Deposit

Figure 4-13

Example of Market Share Allocation

Bank	Rate	Minimum Bid	Differential Above Minimum	Market Share
A	7.29%	6.78%	0.51	60.00%
B	7.06	6.78	0.28	32.95
C	6.84	6.78	0.06	7.05
D	6.78	6.78	0.00	0.00
Total			0.85	100.00

The bank's market share of new public CDs is related to the differential it offers over the minimum rate bid in the city (e.g., 0.51/0.85 = 60.00%).

The level of public CDs affects other balances. Historically, public demand deposits have been approximately 20% of the public CD balance and this relationship is expected to continue in the future. Also, all public balances are subject to the pledging requirements of the state and must be matched on a dollar-for-dollar basis by the bank's holdings of marketable securities. Short-term Treasuries, long-term Treasuries and trading accounts securities are satisfactory for meeting pledging requirements.

> The decision regarding the bid rate for public CDs should be entered as Item 5a (e.g., 7.15 bid is input as a 7.15) on the Decision Form.

> In addition to generating new funds based on monthly bid rate and resultant market share, the bank may specify the maximum desired new volume of public CDs for each month of the decision time frame. This maximum should be entered as Item 5b (e.g., 1 million is input as a 1000) on the Decision Form.

Capital Market Decisions

Repurchase Agreements

Repurchase agreements, also known as repos, RPs, and buybacks, are essentially borrowed funds collateralized by securities. More specifically, a buyer (lender) and seller (borrower) enter into an agreement whereby the borrower sells securities and simultaneously agrees to repurchase, usually at a stated time, the same securities at the same price plus an agreed upon rate of interest. Under this agreement, the seller incurs a liability equal to the purchase price of the security while the buyer acquires title to the securities for the term of the agreement. The underlying securities are most often U.S. Treasuries and government agencies, but agreements have also been structured using mortgage-backed securities and high-quality money market instruments (i.e., negotiable bank certificates of deposit, prime bankers acceptances, and commercial paper). During the term of the repo, the interest earned on these securities accrues to the lender of the securities.

When a bank enters into this type of agreement as the borrower (supplier of the securities), the transaction is called a repo. Banks are considered "natural borrowers" since they usually hold large inventories of the underlying securities in their investment/trading portfolios. In order to assume the role of the investor, a bank must enter into the agreement as the lender (purchaser of the securities). In this situation, a "reverse repo" or a matched sale-purchase agreement is created. A bank will most often enter into this type of agreement as an alternative to entering into a series of one-day sales of federal funds.

Since the market value of the underlying securities will fluctuate with changes in interest rates, both parties in a repo are exposed to risk. The lender of funds (buyer of securities) is subject to the risk that interest rates will rise and the value of the securities will fall, resulting in undercollateralization of the funds lent. Conversely, the borrower of the funds (seller of securities) is subject to the risk that interest rates will fall and the value of the securities will rise, resulting in overcollateralization of the funds borrowed. In order to protect the lender against risk of undercollateralization, repos are usually priced at a discount from the current market price of the underlying securities. This discount, also called a "margin" or "haircut," is negotiated by the parties, with the lender desiring a greater margin and the borrower seeking a smaller margin.

This bank frequently holds a balance of overnight repurchase agreements (repos), effectively borrowing funds against its inventory of marketable securities. Pursuant to these agreements, the bank sells securities with the commitment to repurchase them the following day at the original price plus interest at a stated rate. Reflective of the pledge of high quality collateral, the rate on repos is 50 basis points below the Fed Funds (Sold) rate. The forecast new dollar volumes and rates are shown in Figure 4-14.

Figure 4-14

Repurchase Agreements
Forecast New Dollar Volumes (000's) - Each Bank

	Volume			Volume
January	$ 0	July		$ 0
February	1,000	August		0
March	1,000	September		1,000
April	1,000	October		1,000
May	0	November		500
June	1,000	December		0

*Forecast Interest Rates**

	Falling	Level	Rising
January	6.56%	6.81%	7.31%
February	6.31	6.81	7.81
March	6.06	6.81	8.31

* For the interest rates for the months of April through December use the repos rate on the Incremental Yields and Rates Report in Figure 2-29.

An excess of repos over the sum of unpledged Treasury securities (including the trading account) and asset-backed securities results in the purchase of short-term Treasuries to offset the shortage.

The decision of the desired monthly volume of repos should be entered as Item 6 (e.g., 1 million is input as a 1000) on the Decision Form.

Long-Term Debt
Federal Home Loan Bank Advances

The FHLB is a system of twelve regional banks currently providing credit to entities that own FHLB stock. FHLB stock shares offer the following advantages: (1) they are acceptable as security for public deposits, including Treasury tax and loan accounts; (2) national banks may freely invest in them without restriction; and (3) their dividends are generally exempt from state and local taxes.

The bank's Board of Directors has approved the purchase of the $1,000,000 of FHLB stock required to take down an Advance. The stock pays a dividend of 6.25% annually. The bank would receive a $5,000,000, 5-year FHLB loan if it chooses to go along with this option. The ALCO must decide if the Advance is to be fixed or variable. The fixed-rate Advance is priced at 150 basis points below prime, the variable-rate Advance floats semi-annually on the 5-year Treasury yield curve plus 75 basis points.

> The decision to acquire funds with a FHLB Advance can be made in any quarter, but only once for the year. Enter the decision as item 7a (as a Y for Yes to accept and N for No). If item 7a is Yes, a decision between a fixed or variable-rate must be entered as decision 7b (as a F for Fixed or V for Variable).

New Issue The bank has been contemplating the issuance of long-term debt. To this end, it has completed all necessary filings and is prepared to issue $10,000,000 of 10-year balloon notes in April. The expense involved in issuing this debt is $100,000 and will be accounted for in other expenses. This debt issue will qualify as Tier 2 capital under the risk-based capital regulations.

The issue resets on a quarterly basis with the rate floating at prime rate minus 150 basis points. Forecast rates for prime minus 150 basis points under the level, falling, and rising rate scenarios are shown in Figure 4-15. Principal repayment occurs at the end of 10 years.

Long-Term Debt - New Issue

Figure 4-15

Forecasts

Prime minus 150 basis points*

	Falling Rates	Level Rates	Rising Rates
January	8.25%	8.50%	9.00%
February	8.00	8.50	9.50
March	7.50	8.50	10.00

* For the interest rates for the months of April through December use the prime rate in the Market Rate Section of the Yield Curve and Market Rates Report in Figure 2-24.

Interest Rate Swap Agreement Concern within the bank over a floating coupon rate has prompted discussions of hedging the issue of long-term debt through an interest rate swap agreement with a national broker. Such agreements allow banks to tailor the rate characteristics of their debt to maximize spreads given their asset structures. A broker facilitates the transaction whereby the floating-rate debt payments of the bank are exchanged for the fixed-rate debt payments of another institution.

A swap will convert the floating debt to fixed debt with quarterly interest payments at LIBOR plus 50 basis points. Under the swap contract terms, the bank will pay LIBOR plus 50 basis points fixed for the 10 years, and receive prime minus 150 basis points, reset on a quarterly basis. Forecast rates for LIBOR plus 50 basis points under level, falling and rising rate scenarios are shown in Figure 4-16. The bank may enter the swap agreement at the beginning of any decision period at the time of, or after, the issuance of the debt.

Long-Term Debt - Interest Rate Swap Agreement

*Forecast LIBOR plus 50 basis points**

Figure 4-16

	Falling Rates	Level Rates	Rising Rates
January	7.87%	8.37%	9.37%
February	7.62	8.37	9.87
March	7.62	8.37	9.87

* For the interest rates for the months of April through December use the London Interbank Offering Rate in the Market Rate Section of the Yield Curve and Market Rates Report in Figure 2-24.

The decision regarding the issuance of long-term debt in April should be entered as Item 7c (as a Y for Yes and N for No) on the Decision Form.

The decision regarding the swap agreement is entered as Item 7d (as a Y for Yes and N for No) on the Decision Form.

Common Stock

At year-end 2002, the bank's capital consists of $25,481,000 of common stock and retained earnings. In 2002 the bank's stock traded at a high price of $16.62 and a low of $11.66, closing out the year at $12.02. This capital position is adequate to support the existing asset and liability structure.

The bank may generate additional capital with the issuance of new shares of common stock if retained earnings are insufficient to fund desired expansion. The required SEC registration may be obtained for the issuance of $5,000,000 of common stock by July. The number of shares to be issued is determined by the market price of the existing shares at the previous month-end. The price at which the stock will be sold will be five percent below the market. This reflects the underpricing necessary to sell the increased supply of stock. Net proceeds of the issue reflect the investment banker's fee of $200,000 to underwrite the sale of all shares at the issue price.

Management should also consider the potential opposition of existing shareholders, who may be concerned that future earnings from the additional capital might not offset its dilutive effect.

The decision regarding the issuance of new shares of common stock in July should be entered as Item 8 (as a Y for Yes and N for No) on the Decision Form.

Asset Management Decisions

Each asset decision item involves a use of funds. Some markets are extremely competitive and the growth of bank market share in these markets is very rate sensitive. Other markets exhibit strong growth potential that is not price sensitive. All asset decisions must be considered with respect to maturity and yield considerations.

Capital Market Items

Short-Term Treasury Securities

At year-end 2002, the bank holds $44,290,000 of short-term U.S. Treasury securities in the form of 3-month T-bills. Accordingly, securities purchased in October 2002 will mature in January 2003; November 2002 purchases will mature in February 2003; and December 2002 purchases will mature in March 2003.

There is no upward limit on the purchase of 3-month T-bills, however, the bank maintains a policy of purchasing a minimum of $1,000,000 in new short-term Treasuries per month. Forecast new volumes is shown in Figure 4-17 along with yields under the level, consistently falling, and consistently rising rate scenarios.

Figure 4-17

Short-Term Treasury Securities
Forecast Purchases (000s) - Each Bank

	Volume		Volume
January	$27,386	July	$33,474
February	11,380	August	12,711
March	13,789	September	12,357
April	27,445	October	32,493
May	12,432	November	13,387
June	13,456	December	12,129

Forecast Yields*

	Falling	Level	Rising
January	6.78%	7.03%	7.53%
February	6.53	7.03	8.03
March	6.28	7.03	8.53

* For the yields for the months of April through December use the 3-month T-bill BEY rate in the Yield Curve and Market Rates Report in Figure 2-24.

Short-term Treasuries are used in conjunction with other marketable securities to satisfy the bank's pledging requirements on public deposits, Treasury, Tax and Loan (TT&L), and repos. As stipulated by state banking law, the bank must protect public deposits by pledging marketable securities as collateral on a dollar-for-dollar basis. If the bank attracts public funds in excess of these securities, 3-month T-bills are purchased to cover the deficiency.

> The decision on the desired monthly purchase of short-term Treasury securities should be entered in thousands as Item 9 (e.g., 10 million is input as a 10000) on the Decision Form.

Long-Term Treasury Securities

Long-term Treasury securities are a long term use of funds and also may be used to satisfy pledging requirements. The bank has a balance of $42,200,000 at year-end 2002 with purchase dates, amounts and yields as shown in Figure 4-18. These investments have a fixed yield over their maturity of four years and were purchased at par value.

Long-Term Treasury Securities

Figure 4-18

Composition of Maturities ($000s) and Yields at Year-End 2002

	1999		2000		2001		2002	
	$Pur	Yield	$Pur	Yield	$Pur	Yield	$Pur	Yield
January	$600	6.41%	$750	7.87%	$950	9.20%	$1,300	8.13%
February	650	6.56	1,000	7.38	1,000	9.27	1,150	8.39
March	400	6.58	1,200	7.50	600	9.61	1,350	8.63
April	700	7.32	900	7.83	750	9.40	1,200	8.78
May	650	8.02	800	8.24	900	9.05	700	8.69
June	600	7.82	1,000	8.22	1,100	8.37	950	8.40
July	800	7.74	1,050	8.44	800	7.83	1,000	8.26
August	800	8.03	950	8.77	1,050	8.13	1,050	8.22
September	900	8.67	800	8.57	1,150	8.26	1,200	8.27
October	500	8.75	600	8.43	750	8.02	900	8.07
November	600	7.99	1,300	8.72	700	7.80	750	7.74
December	550	8.13	1,100	9.11	900	7.77	800	7.47

Security purchases for portfolio are made at the prevailing rate on 4-year bonds on the Treasury yield curve and are bound by bank policy limiting the balance of holdings to 30% of the prior month's ending total deposits. Forecast purchases of $800,000 of long-term Treasury securities represent a decrease from the previous year's activity and are shown in Figure 4-19 with yields given the level, consistently falling, and consistently rising rate scenarios.

Long-Term Treasury Securities Purchases

Forecast Purchases (000s)

Figure 4-19

	Purchases		Purchases
January	$800	July	$800
February	800	August	800
March	800	September	800
April	800	October	800
May	800	November	800
June	800	December	800

*Forecast Yields**

	Falling	Level	Rising
January	7.35%	7.60%	8.10%
February	7.10	7.60	8.60
March	6.85	7.60	9.10

* For the yields for the months of April through December use the Yield Curve and Market Rates Report. The 4-year rate is the midpoint between the 3 and 5-year rates shown on the yield curve in Figure 2-24.

In addition to the purchase of new long-term Treasuries, the bank may also sell securities from its portfolio which were originally purchased between 1999 and 2002. All purchases are made at par value and prevailing market yields will determine the gain or loss on the sale of any security. If the security's coupon rate exceeds the current market rate of similar securities, its future cash flows will exceed those available in the marketplace and the security will sell for a gain. Conversely, if market yields exceed the security's coupon rate, future cash flows of the security will be less than those available in the market and the security can be sold only for a loss. The composition of the maturities is shown in Figure 4-18, and one sale per month is permitted.

The desired monthly volume of long-term Treasury purchases should be entered in thousands as Item 10a (e.g., 1 million is input as a 1000) on the Decision Form.

Any sale of a long-term Treasury security should be entered one month at a time as Item 10b (as shown in Figure 4-18) and the purchase date of this security as Item 10c (e.g., March 2002 as a 03 02) on the Decision Form.

Trading Account

In the past, the bank has utilized its trading account from time to time. In December, the bank decided to reactivate the trading account beginning in January 2003. Bank policy limits the trading account to a maximum dollar amount invested in U.S. government bonds with an average maturity of 20 years. This account earns interest at the 20-year rate from the Treasury yield curve. These rates are shown in Figure 4-20. The bank has used the trading account to speculate on long-term interest rate movements. The account will be marked-to-market on a monthly basis and any gains or losses will be shown on the income statement.

If in the first quarter the bank decides to run the trading account to zero, then the balance will be zero by March 31st.

Trading Account
*Forecast Yields**

Figure 4-20

	Falling	Level	Rising
January	7.91%	8.16%	8.66%
February	7.66	8.16	9.16
March	7.41	8.16	9.66

* For the yields for the months of April through December use the 20-year bond rate on the yield curve in the Yield Curve and Market Rates Report in Figure 2-24

The management team can make one of four decisions: 0 for no utilization; 5 to limit the trading account to an ending balance of $5,000,000; 10 to limit the account to $10,000,000; or 15 to maximize the account at $15,000,000. Enter this number as Item 11 on the Decision Form.

Asset-Backed Securities

Asset-backed securities are those backed by assets, such as mortgages, auto loans, and other bank receivables. An integral concept is that of "securitization," which is the process of converting loans and other assets that are not readily marketable or tradeable into securities that can be placed and traded on the securities markets.

Asset-backed securities include, but are not limited to, pass-throughs and CMOs. These pertain to the mortgage market and hence are different forms of "mortgage-backed securities." The allure of mortgage-backed securities as bank investments stems primarily from their attractive yields. In addition, these securities offer credit quality, since many of them carry either the federal guarantee or the backing of a federal agency. To their disadvantage, mortgage-backed securities are characterized by volatile average lives and are also not as liquid as U.S. Treasury and government agency securities.

Through its Mortgage-Backed Securities Program, GNMA guarantees the pass-through securities privately issued by other institutions, such as banks and thrifts. Pass-through securities are a form of mortgage-backed securities; that is, they are backed or supported by pools of mortgages. They are so named since the monthly payments of principal and interest "pass" from the homeowner (mortgagor) "through" the issuer (mortgage servicer) to the security holder. Note the pass-throughs are not debt securities of the issuer;

instead, they represent an ownership interest in the underlying mortgage pool.

Pass-throughs marked the beginning of the development of the secondary mortgage market. The three major issuers of these securities, in order of precedence, are GNMA, FHLMC, and FNMA. Of these, only GNMA pass-throughs carry the Federal guarantee; i.e., the backing of the full faith and credit of the U.S. government. GNMA pass-throughs are also referred to as "fully modified" since they guarantee the timely payment of interest and principal. This means that investors will receive scheduled interest and principal repayments even if the mortgagors fail to make such payments.

The bank has balances of U.S. government agency asset-backed securities of $5,143,000 at year-end 2002, which are primarily GNMA securities. These high quality securities represent proportional ownership interest in pools of residential mortgages and offer relatively high yields given the backing of GNMA. As a holder of these securities, the bank receives the principal and interest payments of the underlying mortgages. The bank also receives any prepayments made by mortgagers and faces added volatility of yield and maturity as a result.

The expected yields of available issues are dependent upon the interest rate scenario. These issues are affected by prepayments; which are estimated by the Public Securities Association (PSA) method, and dependent on changes in interest rates. Given the level, consistently falling, and consistently rising rate scenarios, market price and yields of the forecast purchases are shown in Figure 4-21. Because of the prepayment risk of these issues, the bank's Board of Directors has limited purchases of asset-backed securities to a maximum of $10,000,000 per month.

Asset-Backed Securities

Figure 4-21

Forecast Purchases (000s) - Per Bank

	Purchases		Purchases
January	$700	July	$200
February	700	August	450
March	400	September	200
April	200	October	500
May	300	November	450
June	400	December	250

Forecast Yields*

	Falling	Level	Rising
January	8.33%	8.58%	9.08%
February	8.08	8.58	9.58
March	7.83	8.58	10.08

* For the yields for the months of April through December use the Incremental Yields and Rates Report for U.S. agency securities in Figure 2-29.

136

Term Fed Funds

In the months of April through September, the bank has an opportunity to place Term Fed Funds sold with various other banks. The bank may place contracts of $3,000,000 per month with institutions the bank deems to be credit-worthy. The term is for one year and the yields are based on the credit rating of the borrowing institution. The yield calculations are shown in Figure 4-22. In December, the banks will be re-rated A through E by the rating agencies.

Term Fed Funds*

Figure 4-22

Available Contracts and Yields each Month (Apr - Sep) - Per Bank

Rating	Contracts	*Term Fed Funds Yield* + BP
A	0	- 25
B	1	+ 50
C	1	+ 100
D	1	+ 200
E	0	+ 300

* Yields for Term Fed Funds are shown in the Incremental Yields and Rates Report in Figure 2-29.

The rating analysts currently believe that on average there is a 40% chance that any given bank's credit rating will change in December. However, they do not expect that any bank's credit rating will change by more than two rating levels. The discount rate used to compute year-end present value will change to reflect either more or less risk.

Loan Items

Commercial Loans
Fixed Rate

At year-end 2002, the bank has fixed-rate commercial loan balances in the amount of $48,051,000. These loans are 18-month maturities priced at the prime rate at the time of origination and require compensating deposit balances of 10%. The prime rate can be found in the Yield Curve and Market Rates Report in Figure 2-24.

The forecast calls for the compensating balance requirement to remain at 10%; however, the management team may decide to change the requirement within the range of 5% to 15%. The bank's market share of total new loan volume is linearly related to its compensating balance requirement. Given the compensating balance requirements of 5%, 10%, and 15%, resultant loan volumes are shown in Figure 4-23.

Commercial Loans - Fixed Rate

Figure 4-23

Forecast New Dollars by Compensating Balance Requirement (000s) - Per Bank

	5%	10%	15%
January	$6,750	**$4,500**	$2,250
February	7,200	**4,800**	2,400
March	7,650	**5,100**	2,550
April	8,250	**5,500**	2,750
May	8,250	**5,500**	2,750
June	8,400	**5,600**	2,800
July	8,400	**5,600**	2,800
August	8,100	**5,400**	2,700
September	8,100	**5,400**	2,700
October	8,100	**5,400**	2,700
November	8,250	**5,500**	2,750
December	8,250	**5,500**	2,750

> The bank's decision regarding the compensating balance requirement (between 5% and 15%) on fixed-rate commercial loans should be entered as Item 14a (e.g., input 7% as a 7) on the Decision Form.

Commercial Loans

Large Loan Commitment

In addition to the new loan growth shown above, the bank has the opportunity to commit to an 18-month fixed-rate commercial loan of $4,000,000 to a national manufacturing firm. Terms of the commitment fix the rate at the January 2 prime of 10%, although the loan will not close for twelve months. The bank has negotiated a $30,000 commitment fee from the borrower, if the commitment is made. If the commitment is made and not hedged, the $30,000 commitment fee will be credited to the other income account monthly on a pro rata basis.

The company has a credit rating of AAA, and is interested in expansion of its local production facilities. If the commitment is made, prospects for future business with the manufacturer will be positive where past attempts to generate a relationship have failed. By making the commitment the bank is indicating its willingness to accept the loan terms and inherent rate risk.

If the loan commitment is made, the bank can either assume the risk of committing to a fixed-rate loan at an interest rate set twelve months in advance or to hedge its position by engaging in an offsetting transaction. A financial instrument available to hedge the commitment is an exchange traded 12-month call option on the prime rate. If the prime rate increases between January and December, the bank will experience a gain on the *call option*. This will offset any economic loss incurred by the bank if the company exercises its option to take down the loan under the terms of the fixed commitment.

The price of one option contract has been quoted at $2,200 by a broker. This contract is based upon a notional principal of $1,000,000 and provides a return of $25 for each basis point that the prime rate of December 2003 is in excess of 10% .

The total exposure for purposes of this option is on $4 million for a period of 18 months. To calculate the number of standardized contracts necessary to cover this exposure, the interest rate exposure (per basis point) over the term of the loan is determined. For this loan the interest rate exposure is $600 per basis point ($4,000,000 * .0001 * ((18*30)/360) = 600). This exposure is then divided by the contract'sreturn of $25 per basis point. Twenty-four contracts (600/25 = 24) at $2,200 each, result in a total cost of $52,800 for the exchange traded option contract.

Each month the value of the option contracts will be marked-to-market. The market value of the option contracts is debited to an asset account called option contracts and last month's entry is reversed out. This debit is offset by a credit to the liability account deferred gain/loss. The financing and hedging expense account is debited for a pro rata (1/12) portion of the net expense ($52,800-30,000). If the prime rate of December 2003 is not in excess of the prime rate of December 2002, the $52,800 of cost will have served as an "insurance" premium on a contract which expired without a payoff.

> The bank's decisions regarding the loan commitment and possible hedging should be entered as Item 14b (as a N for None, C for Commit, or H for Commit and Hedge) on the Decision Form.

Commercial Loans
Floating Rate

Floating-rate commercial loans represent a major use of the bank's funds with 2002 year-end balances of $57,828,000. The bank offers these loans in the form of 3-month maturities priced from 100 basis points below prime to 200 basis points above prime. The forecast is for new loans to have an average price of prime rate as shown in the Incremental Yields and Rates Report in Figure 2-29. New loan volume has two components: new loans to existing borrowers and loans to new borrowers.

Existing borrowers exhibit a degree of loyalty which represents approximately 25% of total new loan volume as shown in Figure 4-24. However, market demand from new borrowers is extremely rate sensitive: a small increase in rates sends borrowers to other markets, contracting loan volume, while lower rates will attract borrowers from other markets, expanding loan volume. The relationship between pricing and new loan demand for the market has been estimated as follows: market demand will remain stable for the range of 0 to 99 basis points over prime, 100 to 200 basis points over prime will reduce market demand by 25%, and 1 to 100 basis points under prime will increase market demand by 50%. The resultant volumes are shown in Figure 4-24.

Commercial Loans - Floating Rate

Forecast New Dollar Volumes (000s)

Figure 4-24

	Loyal Per Bank	Competitive Market		
		-100 BP to -1 BP	0 BP to +99 BP	+100 BP to +200 BP
January	$5,200	$93,600	$62,400	$46,800
February	4,750	85,500	57,000	42,750
March	4,750	85,500	57,000	42,750
April	5,250	94,500	63,000	47,250
May	4,825	86,850	57,900	43,425
June	4,850	87,300	58,200	43,650
July	5,350	96,300	64,200	48,150
August	4,900	88,200	58,800	44,100
September	4,925	88,650	59,100	44,325
October	5,450	98,100	65,400	49,050
November	5,000	90,000	60,000	45,000
December	5,000	90,000	60,000	45,000

The bank's share of the total new loan volume is inversely related to the interest rate it charges on these loans. If all institutions offer the same pricing, each garners 25% market share. The allocation of market share given different emphasis on floating-rate commercial loans by local institutions is illustrated in Figure 4-25. This example shows two banks moving to opposite endpoints of pricing (-100 basis points and +200 basis points).

Commercial Loans - Floating Rate

Example of Market Share Allocation

Figure 4-25

Bank	Rate Differential	Difference From High Endpoint / 300 BP	Market Share
A	-100	400	44.44%
B	+100	200	22.22
C	+100	200	22.22
D	+200	100	11.12
Total		900	100.00%

The bank's pricing decision and subsequent new loan volume affects the loan loss provision. Lowering the rate differential to increase loan demand affords the bank greater selectivity in credit decisions and correspondingly lower default risk and loss provisions.

Loan Losses

In addition to influencing the amount of floating-rate commercial loans that a bank obtains, the level of interest rates charged by that bank also affects loan losses. If low rates are offered by a bank, it will experience relatively greater demand for loans and will be able to select better credit risks from the increased volume of loan requests. These better credit risks are more likely to repay their loans and therefore the probability of loan losses will be reduced. If a bank offers high rates, it will experience relatively lower loan demand, may not be as selective in extending loans, and will have to accept lower credit risks that will have a higher probability of default.

Compensating Balances

Demand deposits maintained by the bank's business or commercial customers are also influenced by the commercial lending activity of the bank. Business demand deposits include a constant balance of approximately $20,000,000, plus a percentage of both the floating and fixed-rate commercial loans. Twenty percent of the floating-rate commercial loans will be maintained as business demand deposits during 2003. The compensating balance on fixed-rate commercial loans is set by the bank management team.

> The decision regarding the pricing of floating-rate commercial loans should be entered as Item 15 (as a differential (-100 through +200)) on the Decision Form.

Commercial Loans
Participations

The bank has one other option with commercial loans. It has been offered the opportunity to participate in a round of loan syndications. These loans are all of superior credit quality. Fixed-rate participations have 2-year terms fixed at the prime rate plus 50 basis points. The floating-rate participations have 1-year terms and float monthly at 25 basis points over prime rate. These participations come in $2,500,000 blocks. Bank policy will allow participation in these loan syndications (fixed and floating) each quarter beginning with the second quarter.

If the bank wants to extend the maturity of its commercial loan portfolio by accepting the 2-year loan participations, but not accept the attendant risk of the fixed-rate on the participations, it can engage in an interest rate swap. Under the terms of the interest rate swap, the bank can exchange the fixed-interest income it receives on the participations for variable-interest income reset monthly at LIBOR plus 220 basis points.

> The bank management team should enter the desired number of total participation blocks as Item 16a (as a number between 0 and 100) on the Decision Form. The bank management team should then enter the desired number of fixed-rate participation blocks as Item 16b (as a number between 0 and not to exceed 16a) on the Decision Form.

> If the bank decides to swap any or all of their fixed-rate participations, enter the number of blocks to be swapped in Item 16c (as a number between 1 and not to exceed the amount input in 16b) on the Decision Form. If the bank decides not to swap any of these participations, this should be entered in Item 16c (as a 0) on the Decision Form.

Mortgage Loans

The bank currently originates and holds both fixed-rate and adjustable-rate mortgages (ARMs) in its portfolio. The year-end 2002 balance of fixed-rate loans is $32,958,000 and the balance of ARMs is $34,600,000.

New mortgages, both fixed and adjustable-rate, are originated with an average balance of $80,000 per loan and are amortized over a 30-year term. Fixed-rate mortgages are priced at the national conventional mortgage rate, plus 2 points for origination. In the past, ARMs were priced 200 basis points above the 1-year T-bill rate plus 2 points and adjusted every twelve months. The bank has a policy of not offering teaser rates.

The bank is currently embarking on a new program to increase its mortgage loan originations over the next year with a increased proportion of them being adjustables. This is due to a heightened desire for increased market share on the part of the bank. The bank will switch to pricing its adjustable-rate mortgages 100 basis points above the 1-year T-bill BEY plus 2 points and offering 6-month instead of 12-month adjustables. The bank can originate mortgages in any combination of fixed or ARM up to the maximum outlined in Figure 4-26.

The forecast shows eleven mortgage originations for each month. All new loans are forecast to be ARMs. Market analysis, however, shows that up to one hundred new loans could be made each month.

It is possible for the bank to securitize some of its assets by packaging $30,000,000 of its fixed-rate mortgage portfolio as a CMO which can be sold to the FHLMC.

CMOs are simply defined as "collateralized debt backed by mortgage receivables." They were introduced in 1983 by the FHMLC to overcome some of the disadvantages inherent in pass-throughs. Essentially, pass-throughs are undesirable since their cash flows, and hence their maturity, are unpredictable due to the prepayment features of the underlying mortgages. Under the CMO structure, specific maturities are provided for by splitting the cash flow from the mortgage pool into different classes or tranches. These tranches can be structured in many different ways.

CMOs differ from pass-throughs in several significant ways aside from the existence of different classes. First, CMOs are debt instruments, representing collateralized debt of the issuer; pass-throughs represent a sale of mortgages by the issuer, with ownership interests transferred to security holders. This difference results from the Sears Rule, which is a tax law restricting pass-throughs to only one pro rata class of ownership interests. As a result, investors often require a higher yield from CMOs since they are not owners but secured creditors. Since CMOs are debt instruments, the issuer must record income received from the mortgages, then deduct the interest paid on the CMOs. In pass-throughs, the issuer is relieved from this recordkeeping since income is merely passed from the mortgagor to the security holder.

Second, a CMO requires the issuer to maintain some equity to support the debt structure. This equity (or residual) is usually generated through the overcollateralization of the CMO by an amount up to 2% of the CMO principal. Third, although CMOs collect monthly mortgage payments from the mortgage pool, they remit these payments to investors only on a quarterly basis.

Sale of the CMO enables the bank to acquire $30,000,000 (par, no premium or discount) in cash, which can be used to make other loans or investments. The bank can also choose to repurchase the FHLMC CMO, which allows the bank to hold effectively the fixed-rate mortgages in its investment portfolio through the securitization of the mortgages. If the bank securitizes the mortgages it will retain the servicing of the mortgages, earning 62.5 basis points on the portfolio or approximately $13,000 in servicing fees per month. If the bank repurchases the CMO it will be carried on its books in the investment portfolio with a weighting of 20% for the calculation of risk-based capital requirements.

Mortgages

Figure 4-26

Maximum New Dollar Volumes and Originations - Per Bank (000s)

	Volume	# Orig		Volume	# Orig
January	$8,000	100	July	$8,000	100
February	8,000	100	August	8,000	100
March	8,000	100	September	8,000	100
April	8,000	100	October	8,000	100
May	8,000	100	November	8,000	100
June	8,000	100	December	8,000	100

Mortgages

Forecast Interest Rates[*]

	Falling Rates		Level Rates		Rising Rates	
	Fixed	ARM	Fixed	ARM	Fixed	ARM
January	9.51%	7.17%	9.76%	8.02%	10.26%	8.52%
February	9.26	7.52	9.76	8.02	10.76	9.02
March	9.01	7.27	9.76	8.02	11.26	9.52

[*] For the interest rates for the months of April through December use the Incremental Yields and Rates Report in Figure 2-29.

The current yield on the $30 million package is 10.39%. Securitization costs and credit guarantees combine to produce a net yield to the securities held of 8.83% after securitization.

The bank's decision regarding the total number of mortgages it will originate should be entered as Item 17a (as a number between 0 and 100) on the Decision Form. The number of fixed-rate originations is entered as Items 17b (as a number between 0 and the total number of mortgage originations entered in 17a) on the Decision Form. The number of adjustable-rate originations the bank will make is the difference between 17a and 17b.

The decision to sell and/or repurchase the securitized mortgage loans should be entered as Item 17c (as a N for None, S to Sell, or H to Hold) on the Decision Form.

Home Equity Loans

The bank's portfolio of home equity loans has a balance of $15,338,000 at year-end 2002. The current home equity loan offered in the market is a 5-year maturity and each competitor holds a 25% share of the market. Loans are priced at a fixed-rate 285 basis points above the 5-year Treasury yield curve. The bank has a policy of not offering teaser rates. The forecast market demand and rates are shown in Figure 4-27.

Figure 4-27

Home Equity Loans
Forecast Market Demand - Total Market (000s)

	Market		Market
January	$2,000	July	$2,120
February	2,020	August	2,140
March	2,040	September	2,160
April	2,060	October	2,180
May	2,080	November	2,200
June	2,100	December	2,220

Forecast Interest Rates on 5 Year Loans[*]

	Falling	Level	Rising
January	10.46%	10.58%	12.10%
February	10.33	10.58	12.35
March	10.21	10.58	12.60

[*] For the yields for the months of April through December use the Incremental Yields and Rates Report for Home Equity Loans in Figure 2-29.

The bank is considering a change in the term for home equity loans. Other maturity alternatives include 3, 7, and 10-year loans priced in accordance with the bank's assumption of risk as shown in Figure 4-28.

Figure 4-28

Home Equity Loans
Alternative Maturity Terms and Rates[*]

	Falling Rates			Level Rates			Rising Rates		
	3 Yr	7 Yr	10 Yr	3 Yr	7 Yr	10 Yr	3 Yr	7 Yr	10 Yr
Rate Differential	2.35%	3.85%	4.85%	2.35%	3.85%	4.85%	2.35%	3.85%	4.85%
January	9.57%	11.60%	12.68%	9.82%	11.85%	12.93%	10.32%	12.35%	13.43%
February	9.32	11.35	12.43	9.82	11.85	12.93	10.82	12.85	13.93
March	9.07	11.10	12.18	9.82	11.85	12.93	11.32	13.35	14.43

[*] For the yields for the months of April through December apply the indicated rate differential to the appropriate maturity on the yield curve in the Yield Curve and Market Rates Report in Figure 2-24.

A bank's market share of new loan volume is directly related to the term it offers relative to its competitors. By extending the maturity, the bank expands market share while increasing the expected rate of loans charge-off. By decreasing the maturity, the bank experiences a contraction of market share and can expect a lower rate of charge-offs. An example of market share allocation and the charge-off rates by maturity are shown in Figure 4-29.

Home Equity Loans
Example of Market Share Allocation and Charge-Off Rates

Figure 4-29

Bank	Term	Market Share	Charge-Off Rate
A	3	12.00%	0.10%
B	5	20.00	0.46
C	7	28.00	0.56
D	10	40.00	0.65
Total	25	100.00	

> The decision regarding the maturity of new home equity loans should be entered as Item 18 (as a 3, 5, 7, or 10) on the Decision Form.

Consumer Loans

Consumer loans represent the single largest component of the bank's loan portfolio with balances of $71,984,000 at year-end 2002. These installment loans are offered in maturities of 24, 36, 48, and 60 months all priced 400 basis points above the Treasury yield curve for the appropriate maturity. The banks in the city currently offer loans with 36-month maturities and each bank has a 25% market share. Forecast growth in market demand is strong but highly competitive. Demand and rates for consumer loans are shown in Figure 4-30.

Consumer Loans
Forecast Total Market Loan Volume (000s)
For 36-month Maturities, $2,500 Promotional Expense

Figure 4-30

	Volume		Volume
January	$11,600	July	$13,800
February	11,800	August	14,400
March	12,000	September	14,600
April	12,400	October	14,200
May	12,800	November	14,000
June	13,200	December	13,600

Forecast Interest Rates - 36-month Loans[*]

	Falling	Level	Rising
January	11.35%	11.47%	11.72%
February	11.22	11.47	11.97
March	11.10	11.47	12.22

[*] For the interest rates for the months of April through December use appropriate maturity on the yield curve in the Yield Curve and Market Rates Report in Figure 2-24.

Substantial market pressures have reduced rates to very competitive levels and a further reduction in pricing to attract new loan volume is not considered a viable alternative. Offering of longer term loans and promotional expenditures to expand awareness increases market demand since consumers prefer smaller monthly payments.

The bank is forecasting expenditures of $2,500 per month for promotion of consumer loans and expenditures of over $5,000 are considered excessive and ineffective in generating additional loans. The effect of maturity term and promotion expense on market share is shown in Figure 4-31. Expenditures between the illustrated midpoint and endpoints require interpolation of market share percentages. If more than one bank selects the same maturity, the promotional dollars will directly compete and additional market share will be awarded proportionally.

Consumer Loans

Figure 4-31

Market Share Impact of Maturity Term and Promotion Expense - Per Bank

Promotional Dollars	Maturity			
	24 Month	36 Month	48 Month	60 Month
$5,000	20%	30%	40%	50%
2,500	15	25	35	45
0	10	20	30	40

The decisions regarding the offered term and promotion expenditure for consumer loans should be entered for each decision period as Items 19a (as a 24, 36, 48, or 60) & 19b, promotion dollars (e.g., 5 thousand is input as a 5) on the Decision Form.

Credit Card Loans

Credit card loans represent the riskiest component of the bank's loan portfolio from the standpoint of default risk. The high fixed yield of these loans at 18.00% is designed to compensate for a high charge-off rate which averages 1.08% of loans. At year-end 2002, the bank holds a balance of $29,911,000 in credit card loans. Forecast balances reflecting substantial growth expectations are shown in Figure 4-32.

Figure 4-32

Credit Card Loans

Forecast Balances (000s) - Per Bank

	Volume		Volume
January	$28,841	July	$34,299
February	30,816	August	33,678
March	32,372	September	32,605
April	33,503	October	31,074
May	34,206	November	31,472
June	34,473	December	31,874

The bank has been approached by a large regional bank offering to purchase the card operations for $34,645,000 in April. This selling price represents a premium of $754,000. Sale of the portfolio would affect net interest income, the provision for loan losses, and operating expenses. For the year, the forecast loan loss provision related to the credit card portfolio is $400,000 and expenses to service the credit cards are forecast at $1,200,000.

If the management is operating a money center or superregional bank, and the credit card portfolio is sold, a small balance of credit card loans will still remain with the bank.

> The decision regarding the sale of credit card operations should be entered as Item 20 (as a Y for Yes or N for No) on the Decision Form.

Automobile Loans

The bank's balance of automobile loans at year-end 2002 is $2,116,000 and the forecast reflects growth of 10%. These are 4-year loans and are priced at the 1-year T-bill BEY plus 450 basis points.

To increase auto loan activity, the bank is considering the purchase of indirect auto loan paper from dealers. The bank would indirectly make credit available to consumers by purchasing dealer installment contracts and providing funds for the generation of auto loans at the dealer level. The desirability of this increased loan volume would be tempered by the increased default risk associated with dealer credit decisions. If the bank decides to issue indirect paper, it must determine the extent to which it would enter the market and assume risk. Alternatives, outlined in Figure 4-33, are none, cautious, and aggressive.

Automobile Loans
Forecast Growth Alternatives (000s) - Monthly Per Bank

Growth (Approx.) Indirect Paper	**10%** **None**	15% Cautious	20% Aggressive
January	$206	$309	$412
February	206	309	412
March	206	309	412
April	208	312	416
May	206	309	412
June	208	312	416
July	210	315	420
August	212	318	424
September	216	324	432
October	218	327	436
November	220	330	440
December	222	333	444

Automobile Loans
Forecast Interest Rates[*]

	Falling	Level	Rising
January	11.27%	11.52%	12.02%
February	11.02	11.52	12.52
March	10.77	11.52	13.02

[*] For the interest rates for the months of April through December use the Incremental Yields and Rates Report in Figure 2-29.

> The decision regarding auto loans and the issuance of indirect paper should be entered as Item 21, (as a N for None, C for Cautious, or A for Aggressive) on the Decision Form.

Reserve for Loan Losses

The bank management team may decide to boost the reserve for loan losses account at year end by $500,000. Since the reserve for loan losses qualifies as Tier 2 capital for calculating risk based capital, an addition to the reserve would improve the bank's capital position.

> The decision to add/or not add $500,000 to the bank's reserve is a decision item for each run of the simulation. Enter the decision in item 22 only one time, for December (as a Y for Yes or N for No) on the Decision Form.

Figure 4-33

Off-Balance Sheet and Other Decisions

Loan Commitments

Currently the bank is forecast to make loan commitments under 2 years (Figure 4-34, first column), most of which are 6-months. The bank earns a fee of 5 basis points on these commitments. The bank's Board of Directors has given its permission for the bank to begin making 2-year loan commitments. The bank believes it can earn 25 basis points on these commitments. The 25 basis points will be amortized over 2 years. It also realizes these 2-year loan commitments will impact risk-based capital calculations (there is no impact with 6-month loan commitments). The expected volumes for 2-year loan commitments are also shown in Figure 4-34 in the second column.

Loan Commitments

Forecast Volumes (000s) - Per Bank

Figure 4-34

	Less than Two-Years 5 bp	Greater than Two-Years 25 bp	Total Forecast Volume
January	$3,300	$4,300	$ 7,600
February	3,400	3,200	6,600
March	3,400	4,500	7,900
April	3,200	5,400	8,600
May	3,300	4,800	8,100
June	4,400	4,900	9,300
July	4,200	5,100	9,300
August	5,500	4,200	9,700
September	6,900	5,600	12,500
October	5,800	6,300	12,100
November	4,600	5,900	10,500
December	3,500	5,400	8,900

The decision to make two-year loan commitments should be entered as Item 23 (as a Y for Yes or N for No) on the Decision Form.

Interest Rates
Rate Contracts

As an additional asset/liability management tool, the Bank has established relationships with the trading department of several money center banks and investment bankers. The agreements provide various interest rate contracts which can give the bank interest margin protection from interest rate movements. The three types of contracts are market caps, market floors and macro swap contracts. For this case, the contracts have been constructed on prime rate with a two-year time horizon.

The cap/floor contracts carry notional values of principal of $10, $20, $40, or $100 million. The market cap contracts carry a strike rate of 100 or 200 basis points over prime. The market floor contracts carry a strike rate of 100 or 200 basis points below prime. The swap contract converts a fixed-rate stream of payments or receipts into a variable-rate stream of payments or receipts or vice-versa.

The prices of the contracts reflect the probabilities of the strike rates occurring. The market cap and floor contract prices are as follows:

Market Caps
      100 bp over prime   .00500 of notional principal
      200 bp over prime   .00250 of notional principal

Market Floors
      200 bp under prime   .00125 of notional principal
      100 bp under prime   .00250 of notional principal

If the strike rates are hit, the money center bank will pay an amount determined by multiplying positive only differences between the actual prime rate and the strike prices by the notional amount. Payments occur each month the contract is "in the money," and are credited to the "Interest Rate Contracts - Options" account on the income statement.

A simple example of a macro interest rate swap contract is when one party agrees to pay an amount of interest, generated by a defined principal amount at one type of interest rate and the other party agrees to pay an amount of interest generated by another interest rate off the same principal amount. The two interest payments off the same principal amount or *notional* amount are swapped.

The bank has the choice of swapping interest payments on $10, $20, $40 or $100 million worth of principal at prime rate. It can pay fixed prime and receive floating-rate starting at prime minus 50 basis points, repricing every quarter. The bank's second choice is to pay floating-rate prime plus 50 basis points, repricing every quarter and receive fixed-rate prime. The expense related to swaps will be debited to the "Interest Rate Contracts - Swaps" account on the income statement, which is a net interest income/expense account.

The market cap or market floor, or the swap contract decision can be made in any quarter, but only once for the year. Enter the decision of either a cap contract or a floor contract as item 24a (as a N for None, C for Cap, F for Floor or S for Swap). Enter the dollar amount as item 24b (i.e., 10 million, 20 million, 40 million or $100 million as a 10, 20, 40 or 100). Enter the strike levels for the interest rate contracts as item 24c (if Cap was chosen in item 24a enter a 100 for +100 bp or 200 for +200 bp; if Floor was chosen enter a -100 for -100 bp or -200 for -200 bp). If a Swap Contract is chosen in item 24a, enter the type of interest rate payment your bank will make to the counterparty using a V for paying variable-rate and receiving Fixed-rate or a F for paying fixed-rate and receiving variable-rate.

Non-Interest Income and Expense

The Board of Directors has recently been reviewing various proposals to reduce net overhead burden and enter new markets. While continuing the review of more proposals, the Board has given management the latitude to move ahead on one or more of the following major decisions: 1) enter into a new fee generating service; 2) buy or sell branches; 3) change in the Credit Department staff; and 4) general staff reduction. These four proposals are described in detail below.

New Service

In an effort to increase non-interest income the bank is searching for new services to sell to customers. One new service that is being considered is home banking by telephone. The success of this new business will be related to how competitive the market will be as evidenced by the number of banks in the city which enter the market.

If the Bank enters this new market, the associated net income before taxes is projected as follows:

Number of Banks Entering the New Market	Each Bank earns	
1	$ 30,000	per month
2	20,000	per month
3	-10,000	per month
4	-15,000	per month

Buy/Sell Branches

In the month of January, the bank has the opportunity to buy three additional branches or sell three of its existing branches. This opportunity is available to all banks except the money center bank. There will be no premium associated with the purchase or either sale. However, there will be a one-time charge associated with the purchase or sale: $20,000 for the purchase, $30,000 for the sale of 3 branches. This charge will be recorded in other operating expense in January.

For example, if CRNB purchased the branches, the consolidated balance sheet would show an increase of $100 thousand in home equity loans for the month of January and in each succeeding month.

Figure 4-35

Purchase/Sale of Three Branches*

Name	Purchase Jan. $[1]	Sell Jan. $[1]	Sell Dec. Balance[2]
Mortgage Loans-ADJ	—	—	—
Home Equity Loans	+100	-100	-20 %
Consumer Loans	+250	-500	-35 %
Auto Loans	+25	-50	-20 %
Interest Bearing Checking	+10,500	-10,500	—
Regular Savings	+5,000	-5,000	—
MMDA	+20,000	-20,000	—
Small CDs	+400	-400	-20 %
Other CDs	+50	-50	-20 %

* All numbers approximate

1 Adjustment to January's forecast, also each month

2 Adjustment to December, 2002's balance

Credit Department Staff

The credit department staff may be large, normal, or small; the overall effectiveness of the department will be a function of its size. A large credit department is able to engage in a more thorough credit investigation and analysis of loan applications and subsequent servicing (administration) of the loans extended. The additional salary expense (six people) involved in maintaining a large credit department is $12,000 per month more than the normal department's salaries. A small credit department (six fewer people) will result in a salary expense of $12,000 per month less than the normal expense, but this department will be less effective in credit investigation, analysis, and servicing of loans. The present salary expense forecast for 2003 is adequate to support the normal credit administration that the bank has employed in the past.

General Staff Reduction

Management may undertake a staff reduction of about twenty-five employees. This will be bankwide and not be concentrated in any single department. The benefits of this action will be a decrease in salary and benefits, occupancy expenses, and other miscellaneous expenses related to personnel. Such expenses are estimated at $600,000 on an annualized basis.

There are several costs and risks associated with this decision. There is a $50,000 charge associated with employee severance. This decision may impact loan quality and be reflected in higher charge-offs. With fewer people, the operating risk profile of the bank will be increased, increased risk will change the discount rates used to compute the present value of assets (higher discount rates) and liabilities (lower discount rates).

Each quarter, only one net overhead decision can be made.

The net overhead decision regarding the buying or selling of the bank's branches can only be made in the first quarter. Enter the decision as item 25 in January (as a B to buy 3 branches, or a S to sell 3 branches on the Decision form. If the decision to buy or sell branches is made, no other net overhead decision can be made in the first quarter.

The remaining net overhead decisions can be made for any quarter of the year:

If the bank decides to embark on the new service, this is marked in item 25 (as an A for Add New Service) on the Decision Form

The decision regarding the Credit Department Staff can be entered as item 25 (as an I for Increasing or a D for Decreasing) on the Decision Form.

The decision to reduce the general staff is chosen in item 25 (as a G for General Staff Reduction) on the Decision Form.

In any quarter the decision to do none of the above can be entered as item 25 (an N for None) on the Decision Form.

Interest Rates
Scenarios

An interest rate scenario is necessary for analysis of decision alternatives as well as to forecast earnings. The simulation case predicts interest rates as either level, falling, or rising and the forecast may be revised quarterly at the instructor's discretion.

> The level of interest rates may be specified by the instructor or may be a decision item for each run of the simulation. The decision to change the interest rates can only be made in the future quarters of the simulation. If interest rates are an available decision enter the decisions in item 26 for each future quarter (as a R for Rising, L for Level, or F for Falling) on the Decision Form.

Decision Form

Operating decisions should be entered in the Decision Form on a quarterly or semi-annual basis as designated by the instructor. A sample Decision Form is shown in Figure 4-36. Following each decision set, financial reports reflecting operations during the decision time frame will be distributed to the teams.

Figure 4-36

DECISION FORM
Deposit Items (Liabilities)

Interest-Bearing Checking
Item 1a: Rate Paid (4.0, 5.0, 6.0 %)

| 5.0 |
APRIL

Item 1b: Service Charges ($7, 8, 9 per account, per month)

| 8 |
APRIL

Money Market Deposit Accounts
Item 2:   Interest-Rate Differential from 1-year T-bill (-1.0, 0.0, 1.0,) or Fixed at 6.0%

| 0.0 |
APRIL

Small Certificates of Deposit
Item 3a: Emphasized Maturity (6, 12, 24, 36, or 48 months)

| 12 | | 12 | | 12 | | 12 |
| JAN | | APR | | JULY | | OCT |

Item 3b: Issue Option CDs (Y = Yes, N = No)

| N |
JAN

Large Certificates of Deposit
Item 4a: New Dollar Volume ($000's)

JAN	FEB	MAR	APR	MAY	JUNE	JULY	AUG	SEPT	OCT	NOV	DEC
30160	32116	33536	30665	32724	34046	31177	33239	34564	31698	33763	35090

Item 4b: Accept Brokered CDs (Y = Yes, N = No)

| N | N | N |
| JULY | AUG | SEPT |

Item 4c: Swap Brokered CDs (Y = Yes, N = No)

| | | |
| JULY | AUG | SEPT |

Public Certificates of Deposit
Item 5a: Bid Rate (%)

JAN	FEB	MAR	APR	MAY	JUNE	JULY	AUG	SEPT	OCT	NOV	DEC
8.22	8.22	8.22	8.22	8.22	8.22	8.22	8.22	8.22	8.22	8.22	8.22

Item 5b: Maximum New Dollar Volume per month ($000's)

| 15000 | | 15000 | | 15000 | | 15000 |
| JAN | | APRIL | | JULY | | OCT |

(Page 1)

Figure 4-36

DECISION FORM
Capital Market Items (Assets & Liabilities)

Repurchase Agreements
Item 6:   New Dollar Volume per month ($000's)

JAN	FEB	MAR	APR	MAY	JUNE	JULY	AUG	SEPT	OCT	NOV	DEC
0	1000	1000	1000	0	1000	0	0	1000	1000	500	0

Long-Term Debt
Item 7a: FHLB Advance Accept (Y = Yes, N = No)

JAN	APRIL	JULY	OCT
N	N	N	N

Item 7b: FHLB Interest Rate (F = Fixed, V = Variable)

JAN	APRIL	JULY	OCT

Item 7c: Issuance of Long-Term Debt (Y = Yes, N = No)

APRIL
N

Item 7d: Swap Agreement (Y = Yes, N = No)

APRIL	JULY	OCT

Common Stock
Item 8:   Issuance of New Common Stock (Y = Yes, N = No)

JULY
N

Short-Term Treasury Securities
Item 9:   Purchases ($000's)

JAN	FEB	MAR	APR	MAY	JUNE	JULY	AUG	SEPT	OCT	NOV	DEC
27386	11380	13789	27445	12432	13456	33474	12711	12357	32493	13387	12129

Long-Term Treasury Securities
Item 10a: Purchases ($000's)

JAN	FEB	MAR	APR	MAY	JUNE	JULY	AUG	SEPT	OCT	NOV	DEC
800	800	800	800	800	800	800	800	800	800	800	800

Item 10b: Sales ($000's)

JAN	FEB	MAR	APR	MAY	JUNE	JULY	AUG	SEPT	OCT	NOV	DEC
0	0	0	0	0	0	0	0	0	0	0	0

Item 10c: Date Purchased (mm/yy)

JAN	FEB	MAR	APR	MAY	JUNE	JULY	AUG	SEPT	OCT	NOV	DEC

Trading Account
Item 11:   Ending Balance ($0, 5, 10, 15 million)

JAN	APRIL	JULY	OCT
5	5	5	5

Asset-Backed Securities
Item 12:   Purchases ($000's, Maximum $10 million per month)

JAN	FEB	MAR	APR	MAY	JUNE	JULY	AUG	SEPT	OCT	NOV	DEC
700	700	400	200	300	400	200	450	200	500	450	250

Term Fed Funds
Item 13:   Placement (B, C, D, or N for None)

APR	MAY	JUNE	JULY	AUG	SEPT
N	N	N	N	N	N

(Page 2)

Figure 4-36

DECISION FORM
Loan Items (Assets)

Commercial Loans - Fixed
Item 14a: Compensating Balance Requirement (5-15% range)

JAN	FEB	MAR	APR	MAY	JUNE	JULY	AUG	SEPT	OCT	NOV	DEC
10.0	10.0	10.0	10.0	10.0	10.0	10.0	10.0	10.0	10.0	10.0	10.0

Item 14b: Commitment (N = None, C = Commit, H = Commit & Hedge)

JAN
N

Commercial Loans - Floating
Item 15:   Interest-Rate Differential from prime (-100 bp to +200 bp)

JAN	FEB	MAR	APR	MAY	JUNE	JULY	AUG	SEPT	OCT	NOV	DEC
0	0	0	0	0	0	0	0	0	0	0	0

Commercial Loan - Participations
Item 16a: Total Number of Participations (0 to 100)

APRIL	JULY	OCT
0	0	0

Item 16b: Number of Fixed-Rate Participations (0 to a number not exceeding 16a)

APRIL	JULY	OCT
0	0	0

Item 16c: Number of Fixed-Rate Participation Swap Contracts (0 to a number not exceeding 16b)

APRIL	JULY	OCT
0	0	0

Mortgages
Item 17a: Total Mortgage Originations (0 to 100)

JAN	FEB	MAR	APR	MAY	JUNE	JULY	AUG	SEPT	OCT	NOV	DEC
11	11	11	11	11	11	11	11	11	11	11	11

Item 17b: Fixed-Rate Originations (0 to a number not exceeding 17a)

JAN	FEB	MAR	APR	MAY	JUNE	JULY	AUG	SEPT	OCT	NOV	DEC
0	0	0	0	0	0	0	0	0	0	0	0

Item 17c: Sell or Securitize Mortgage Loans (N = None, S = Sell, H = Hold)

APRIL
N

Home Equity Loans
Item 18:   Maturity (3, 5, 7, or 10 years)

JAN	APRIL	JULY	OCT
5	5	5	5

Consumer Loans
Item 19a: Maturity (24, 36, 48, or 60 Months)

JAN	APRIL	JULY	OCT
36	36	36	36

Item 19b: Promotion Expense ($000's per month)

JAN	APRIL	JULY	ocT
2.5	2.5	2.5	2.5

Credit Card Loans
Item 20:   Sale of Card Portfolio (Y = Yes, N = No)

APRIL
N

Automobile Loans
Item 21:   Issuance of Indirect Paper (N = None, C = Cautious, or A = Aggressive)

JAN	APRIL	JULY	OCT
N	N	N	N

Reserve for Loan Losses
Item 22:   Add $500,000 to Reserve (Y = Yes, N = No)

DEC
N

Figure 4-36

DECISION FORM
Off-Balance Sheet and Other Decisions

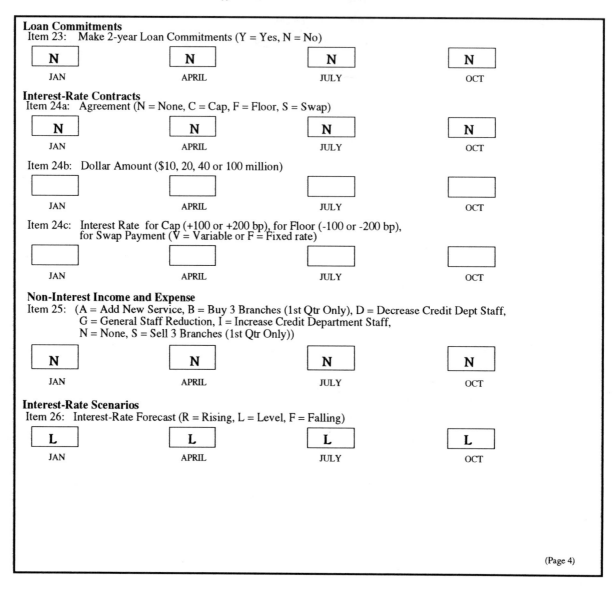

Loan Commitments
Item 23:   Make 2-year Loan Commitments (Y = Yes, N = No)

N	N	N	N
JAN	APRIL	JULY	OCT

Interest-Rate Contracts
Item 24a: Agreement (N = None, C = Cap, F = Floor, S = Swap)

N	N	N	N
JAN	APRIL	JULY	OCT

Item 24b: Dollar Amount ($10, 20, 40 or 100 million)

JAN	APRIL	JULY	OCT

Item 24c: Interest Rate for Cap (+100 or +200 bp), for Floor (-100 or -200 bp),
for Swap Payment (V = Variable or F = Fixed rate)

JAN	APRIL	JULY	OCT

Non-Interest Income and Expense
Item 25:   (A = Add New Service, B = Buy 3 Branches (1st Qtr Only), D = Decrease Credit Dept Staff,
G = General Staff Reduction, I = Increase Credit Department Staff,
N = None, S = Sell 3 Branches (1st Qtr Only))

N	N	N	N
JAN	APRIL	JULY	OCT

Interest-Rate Scenarios
Item 26:   Interest-Rate Forecast (R = Rising, L = Level, F = Falling)

L	L	L	L
JAN	APRIL	JULY	OCT

(Page 4)

Chapter FIVE

Management Simulation:
Policies and Procedures

Commercial banks operate in an increasingly complex and competitive environment when compared to most other businesses. They also continue to be heavily regulated by both federal and state regulatory authorities despite the fact that there has been a recent policy shift toward deregulation. The individual asset/liability operating decisions facing each bank management team have been discussed in Chapter Four.

This chapter discusses the operating procedures or ground rules to which each bank management team will be subject. The simulation is designed to be conducted on a "level playing field" with all participants subject to the same rules and having equal access to information. Topics covered in this chapter include team organization, strategic managerial philosophy, and goal determination along with the operating policies and procedures employed in the simulation. Operating policies and procedures deal with loans, investments, regulation, capital position and dividend policy, federal funds, overhead expenses, non-interest income, and other asset and liability accounts. The final section of the chapter explains how each bank management team's performance will be evaluated.

The simulation case is designed for groups of four bank management teams to compete against each other in managing their individual banks. Each group simulates four banks in a market that interact according to the competitive decisions that have been detailed previously. This section describes procedures for each team and criteria for team performance evaluation.

Organization   The first team meeting should focus on delegation of tasks and analyses and to the selection of the officers described below:

President   chief executive officer with primary responsibility for all decisions and the final report

Vice President, Secretary   coordinates staff, assists President, delivers decision forms, and picks up reports

Vice President, Lending   recommends goals, strategies, and decisions regarding business, real estate and consumer loans

Vice President, Investments & Funds Management   recommends goals, strategies, and decisions regarding deposits, borrowed funds, investment securities

Vice President, Controller   performs financial analysis and provides interpretation of financial data

Vice President, Marketing   performs analysis of market conditions, competition and economic trends

A Bank Personnel Form is provided for each team to record the assignment of officers as shown in Figure 5-1. Additional assignments may be created and existing functions consolidated to accommodate team size. The Bank Personnel Form is turned in with the first decision set.

Bank Personnel Form

Figure 5-1

BANK PERSONNEL
President
VP, Secretary
VP, Lending
VP, Investments & Funds Management
VP, Controller
VP, Marketing
BANK NAME _____ CITY NUMBER ____

Strategic Decisions and Goals

The case simulation requires participants to make two types of decisions: strategic and operating. The strategic decisions encompass the identification of marketing targets and goals, while operating decisions guide the bank to these goals. Operating decisions have been discussed in Chapter Four.

Strategic Managerial Philosophy

Strategic financial planning has been discussed in detail in Chapter One and different types of banks have been identified and defined. CRNB has traditionally been a community bank. In this exercise, the first task facing each bank management team is the decision as to what strategy they wish to follow and what type of strategic plan will result. For the year 2003 the bank management team may choose from four options: (a) community bank, (b) regional bank, (c) superregional bank, and (d) money center bank.

Community Bank

If the bank management team decides that its strategy will be to serve a specific geographic area and to provide basic retail and business banking services; it will be a community bank. Community banks generally rely on core deposits which they gather in the geographic market which they serve. Consequently, they plan to grow along with their community. They do not experience the more dramatic growth that a bank which purchases funds might. Community banks typically do not engage in off-balance sheet financial contracts, trade securities, or securitize loans for resale. In the simulation, a community bank would not make the following operating decisions: Swaps (Items 4-c, 7-d, 16-c); Trading Accounts (Item 11); Loan Commitments (Items 14-b, 23); Securitize Mortgages (Item 17-c); or Interest Rate Contracts (Item 24).

Regional Bank

The bank management team can also develop a strategic plan which includes providing a full range of banking services to a number of communities in a particular region. A regional bank typically operates an extensive branch system. Regional banks would be expected to grow faster than community banks since they serve a number of communities and can also purchase funds to enhance their growth. Off-balance sheet contracts are employed by regional banks for a variety of purposes including limiting risk exposure and enhancing profitability. The only interest rate swap not available to the regional bank is the $100 million contract.

Superregional Bank

A superregional bank serves a wider geographic area than a regional bank and is very likely to be organized as a multi-bank holding company. Superregionals provide a complete line of banking services and often utilize capital market instruments to support their growth strategy. If the bank management team makes a strategic decision to become a superregional bank, the amount of long term financing that it raises in the form of Common Stock (Item 8) and from FHLB Advances and Long-Term Debt (Items 7a,b,and c) will be twice that available to a regional bank.

Money Center Bank

Money Center banks are relatively few in number and are characterized by the fact that they raise funds in large blocks with relatively short maturities. Because funds are procured in this manner, there is no need for an extensive branch system. As a result, they make few consumer and real estate loans. If the bank management team decides that it wants to become a money center bank, the bulk of its current branch system, 17 branches, will be sold in January (Figure 5-2). There will be a one-time charge of $70,000 associated with this sale. The amount of long term financing that it raises in the form of common stock (Item 8) and FHLB Advances and Long-Term Debt (Items 7a,b,c) will be twice that available to a regional bank. The bank would also not purchase branches (Item 25).

Sale of 17 Branches*

Figure 5-2

	January $[1]	December Balance[2]
Mortgage Loans-ADJ	—	-80 %
Home Equity Loans	-400	-80 %
Consumer Loans	-1,100	-97 %
Auto Loans	-200	-80 %
Interest-Bearing Checking	-42,000	—
Regular Savings	-20,000	—
MMDA	-80,000	—
Small CDs	-1,200	-80 %
Other CDs	-200	-80 %

* All numbers approximate

1 Adjustment to January's forecast, also each month

2 Adjustment to December, 2002's balance

Selection of a marketing target incorporates a particular risk/return trade-off. At one end of the spectrum, a community bank orientation provides predictable, steady growth, higher operating expense, and higher spread. The other end of the spectrum, a wholesale money center bank orientation is a high risk, low spread, but higher volume alternative. The higher risk of a wholesale money center bank is accompanied by the potential for greater profitability. Each team must select a marketing strategy based on its risk/return orientation and enter their selection in the first section of the Strategic Decision Form shown in Figure 5-3.

Strategic Decision

Figure 5-3

STRATEGIC DECISION FORM

STRATEGIC MANAGERIAL PHILOSOPHY
(Select one)

[ ] A. Community Bank
[ ] B. Regional Bank
[ ] C. Superregional Bank
[ ] D. Money Center Bank

Goals   As shown in the Statement of Goals Form in Figure 5-4, each team must select one goal within each category and indicate an overall priority of its goals by ranking them from first through sixth. General categories include asset quality, liquidity, interest rate exposure, capital adequacy, earnings, and growth. The selection of goals will be incorporated in evaluation of the team's performance.

Figure 5-4   **Statement of Goals for 2003**

Select one goal from each category and indicate its overall priority 1 through 6 with 1 being the highest

ASSET QUALITY

[   ]   A. Most balanced percentage mix within the loan portfolio (AVG)
[   ]   B. Highest ratio of reserves to non-performing assets (EOP)
[   ]   C. Lowest net loans charged-off, net of recoveries (AVG)
[   ]   D. Highest market/book value percentage for investments (EOP)

LIQUIDITY (All Average ratios)

[   ]   A. Highest percentage of short-term assets to total assets
[   ]   B. Lowest percentage of purchased funds to earning assets
[   ]   C. Lowest percentage of net short borrowed funds to total assets
[   ]   D. Lowest percentage of total loans to net available deposits

INTEREST RATE EXPOSURE (All EOP ratios)

[   ]   A. Lowest negative percentage change in present value of equity due to high or low
          interest-rate shock for December 31, 2003
[   ]   B. Lowest percentage change in net interest income ($) due to high or low interest-
          rate shock for 2003
[   ]   C. Highest percentage present value of equity to book value on December 31, 2003
[   ]   D. Highest percentage of assets and liabilities which reprice
          or mature within one year of December 31, 2003

CAPITAL ADEQUACY (All EOP ratios)

[   ]   A. Highest ratio of equity to total assets
[   ]   B. Highest market capitalization
[   ]   C. Highest ratio of total capital to risk weighted assets (RBC)
[   ]   D. Highest multiple of price to earnings for common stock

EARNINGS (All Average ratios)

[   ]   A. Highest percentage of net interest margin to earning assets
[   ]   B. Lowest percentage of net overhead to earning assets
[   ]   C. Highest yield on earning assets
[   ]   D. Highest total dollars of net income

GROWTH

[   ]   A. Most balanced growth of loans, deposits and equity (YTD AVG)
[   ]   B. Highest composite growth of loans, deposits and equity (YTD AVG)
[   ]   C. Highest total assets on December 31, 2003 (EOP)
[   ]   D. Highest growth in total deposits (YTD AVG)

Operating Policies and Procedures

Loans

Loan Policy

The Board of Directors has indicated a desire for the bank to be active in lending, either direct or indirect. At the same time the board is also interested in protecting liquidity through lending controls and has established an acceptable range for the end of period loans to deposits ratio as follows:

	Low	-	High
Community Bank	50	-	75%
Regional Bank	60	-	90%
Superregional Bank	60	-	80%
Money Center Bank	40	-	80%

Loan participations will be sold or purchased to avoid violation of this criteria. Such participations are 9-month maturities of fixed-rate commercial loans priced at the current prime rate.

Reserve for Loan Losses

All loan charge-offs are debited against the reserve account and this account is further adjusted to target a balance of 1.70% of average gross loans based on the current loan mix. The loan loss reserve for each type of loan is:

Commercial	
Fixed	2.35%
Float	1.05
Real Estate	0.70
Consumer	1.72
Unspecified	0.23

The adjustment to the reserve is reflected as an expense in the loan loss provision.

The economy can deviate from the forecast and cause loan losses to escalate. loan loss escalation can occur in the following loan categories: commercial, real estate and consumer. Each sector of the economy can deviate at different rates.

Charge-offs and Loan Administration

As discussed in the section on floating-rate commercial loans, the level of interest rates charged by the bank will impact loan losses. Loan loss rates on other loans may vary from the expected loss rates by a small amount based upon economic conditions as shown in Figure 5-5. The expected annualized loss rates on loans are as follows:

Commercial	- Fixed	.75%
	- Floating	.48%
Mortgage	- Fixed	.12%
	- Adjustable	.09%
Home Equity		.12%
Consumer		.72%
Credit Cards		1.08%
Auto Loans		.24%

Charge-offs

Change per month from BASE

Figure 5-5

	Rising Rates	Level Rates	Falling Rates
Floating	Unchanged	Unchanged	Unchanged
Fixed*	Down 5.0%	Unchanged	Up 2.5%

* The following accounts are classified as fixed for charge-offs: Commercial Loans - Fixed, Mortgage - Fixed, Home Equity, Consumer, Auto, Credit Cards.

Recoveries run at about 10% of normalized charge-offs and it is possible to be in a position of net recoveries during a particular month.

Investments

Investment Policy

Investment policy has been established within the ALCO process and has been reviewed and approved by the bank's Board of Directors. Three issues are important to the management of the bank's investment portfolio:

- Minimum purchase of short-term Treasuries
- Maximum level of long-term Treasuries, and
- Maximum level of asset-backed securities

Short-term Treasuries: Minimum purchase

The volatility of interest rates in past years has prompted the institution of a policy requiring a minimum monthly purchase of $1,000,000 in short-term Treasury securities. If short-term rates rise rapidly, the bank forfeits higher interest income for 90 days in exchange for the guarantee of 90 days worth of relatively higher interest income in times of rapid decline in short-term rates.

Long-term Treasuries: Maximum level

To minimize the risk of market value deterioration of the long-term portfolio and to prevent speculation on short-term changes in rates, the investment in long-term Treasuries and U.S. agency securities is limited to 30% of the prior month's end of period deposits. This policy does not apply to long-term maturities purchased for the trading account.

The bank's investment policy stresses an intent to hold the long-term maturities until maturity. On several occasions in the past, the bank has sold some securities prior to maturity in order to manage liquidity and interest-rate exposure. The bank's auditors have warned against selling securities prior to maturity to take profits created from falling interest rates. If a judgment is reached that the management team is actively "gains trading", the long-term Treasuries may be classified as investments held for sale and would be marked to market value. Any resulting write down to market value will be shown as gain or loss being reflected in equity.

Asset-backed securities:
Maximum level

To minimize the liquidity and interest-rate risks of the asset-backed portfolio, monthly purchases for this account are limited to a maximum of $10,000,000 subject to the 30% long-term treasury limitation. Additionally, with ALCO and Board approval, a special purchase of a Class B tranche of a CMO was made in December and is scheduled for delivery on January 2. This will not be included in the $10,000,000 maximum.

The CMO Class B tranche was purchased via one of the bank's approved security dealers. It is a secondary trade at par plus accrued interest. Beginning in February and every three months following thereafter, the bank will receive interest on the outstanding balance plus a payment of principal of 7.55%. The amount of principal payments will be affected by the amount of loan prepayments on the underlying mortgages. The amount of loan prepayments falls when interest rates rise and increase when interest rates fall.

The Class B tranche was scheduled to begin principal paydown in February 2003 and has an expected maturity of August 1, 2006, assuming no change in interest rates. The yield to maturity on this investment at the time of delivery is 9.08%.

The Board has also approved the securitization of the $30 million of mortgage loans in April, if the ALCO decides to go ahead with it. The Board has also given special approval to the holding of the securitized mortgages as an investment, but, the final decision will be made by the bank's ALCO. This $30 million does not impact the $10,000,000 maximum purchases of asset-backed securities.

Regulatory Considerations

Reserve Requirements

The bank is required to hold reserves as required by the Federal Reserve Board of Governors. The current reserve requirement on demand deposits and interest-bearing checking account deposits, net of float and due from bank balances is 10%. Reserve requirements may be met by holding vault cash or deposits at the regional Federal Reserve Bank.

Public Deposits:
Pledging requirements

State banking law requires protection for the deposits of public agencies through the pledge of marketable securities as collateral on a dollar-for-dollar basis. Securities satisfying the pledging requirement include all Treasury securities, asset-backed securities and any securities issued by the state or its political subdivisions. If these marketable securities fail to meet the pledging requirement during any month, short-term Treasury securities will be purchased to make up the difference.

Capital Position and Dividend Policy

The capital position of the bank is adequate to support its existing asset and liability structure and additional capital will be generated by retained earnings net of any dividends paid. The bank can voluntarily issue new shares of common stock as explained in the *Common Stock* section of *Capital Market Items* in Chapter Four.

Required Capital Infusions

The bank may be required to add new common equity if its growth in assets is rapid or changed to a higher risk profile. Issuance of new shares will automatically take place if there is a violation of capital adequacy policies including minimum equity to assets of 5.5%, and minimum risk-based capital of 10% on an end-of-quarter basis. If the bank violates either of these measures by more than 10%, or if it violates both measures, issuance of new common stock will be required by the bank's principal regulator, and will be issued the beginning of the following quarter.

The price at which the stock will be sold will be 10% below the market price in order to reflect the underpricing and floatation expense necessary to sell the increased supply of stock.

Dividend Policy

The bank's dividend policy stipulates the declaration of quarterly dividends of $.11 per share at each quarter's end. Payment of the dividend occurs during the last month of each quarter as reflected in the Cash Flow Report.

Federal Funds

The bank uses the federal funds market to balance daily sources and uses of funds. Funds in excess of the Federal Reserve Board's reserve requirement are sold to other banks to earn the overnight Fed Funds rate. Conversely, banks with insufficient funding on a given day may borrow funds at the Fed Funds borrowing rate. The bank also buys Fed Funds from "downstream" respondents for resale "upstream" to money market banks. As a result of these activities, a daily minimum of $1,000,000 in Fed Funds is purchased and sold in each month. The rate applied to purchases of Fed Funds exceeds the Fed Funds sold rate by 25 basis points as shown in Figure 5-6.

Federal Funds

Forecast Interest Rates*

Figure 5-6

	Falling Rates		Level Rates		Rising Rates	
	Sold	Purchased	Sold	Purchased	Sold	Purchased
January	7.06%	7.31%	7.31%	7.56%	7.81%	8.06%
February	6.81	7.06	7.31	7.56	8.31	8.56
March	6.56	6.81	7.31	7.56	8.81	9.06

* For interest rates for the months of April through December use the Fed Funds purchased rate in the Incremental Yields and Rates Report in Figure 2-29.

Overhead *(Non-Interest Expenses)*

Number of Employees

On December 31, 2002 the bank employed 245.6 employees (full-time equivalent). The average total assets for the month of December 2002 was $450,073,000 This means that there was one employee for each $1.83 million dollars in average assets.

The number of employees each month in the year 2003 will be dependent upon the total level of bank assets as well as the mix of assets and liabilities. Loan and deposit products require more employees for operations, while capital market transactions, such as investments and purchased funds, require fewer employees. The number of people employed by each bank in the year 2003 will be determined by the type of loans and the type of deposits. The dollar balances in the following loan categories will add or subtract people accordingly: securitized mortgage loans, direct commercial loans-fixed, direct commercial loans-floating, mortgage loans-fixed, mortgage loans-adjustable, home equity loans, consumer loans, credit card loans, and auto loans. The dollar balances in the following deposit accounts will add or subtract people accordingly: demand deposits, IBC and savings, MMDAs, and public CDs. Total number of full-time equivalent employees for each month will be determined by the total average balances in each of the above accounts divided by approximately 2.33 million. The forecast for January 2003 generates the need for 248.7 employees (FTE).

In the text discussion concerning credit card loans, it is indicated that the bank has the option of selling its entire credit card portfolio. If the decision is made to sell the credit card portfolio, the bank will eliminate 17 full-time equivalent positions from its staff.

Salaries and Benefits

The average salary and benefits per employee for the month of December 2002 was $29,221. This average will grow during the forecast year by the rate of inflation which is approximately 6% per year. The total salaries and benefits for the bank will be a result of the average salaries and benefits per employee times the number of full-time equivalent employees.

Occupancy Expense

The occupancy expense of the bank (which includes office rental, utilities, and related expenses) increase and decrease with the number of employees. For the year 2003, occupancy expense will be 9.5% of the total salaries and benefits expense.

Promotion Expense

Includes a minimum of $50,000 per month plus the amount spent in order to attract consumer loans.

Property and Equipment

New expenditures for property and equipment are added to this account each month and the entire balance is subject to a monthly depreciation charge.

Furniture and Fixtures

The furniture and equipment expense of the bank (which includes equipment rentals, supplies, and depreciation) increase and decrease with the number of employees. For the year 2003, furniture and equipment expense will be 15% of the total salaries and benefits expense.

Data Processing Expense

Fixed expense of $15,000 per month plus a variable expense of $2.00 per IBC account per month. The number of IBC accounts each bank attracts is based on the interest rate and service charge decisions.

Finances and Hedging Expense

If the bank decides to hedge the large commercial loan commitment, the net cost of $22,800 ($52,800 cost less $30,000 commitment fee income) is amortized over the 12 month life, or $1,900 per month.

Other Operating Expenses

Includes an average of $120,000 per month plus expenses resulting from operating decisions. Expenses will result from operating decisions concerning issuing long term debt, general staff reduction, purchase or sale of branches, change in credit department staff, and offering telephone home banking services.

Overhead *(Non-Interest Income)*

Non-interest income will be affected by the decisions regarding the following:

Service Charges

Service charges are determined by the number of interest-bearing checking accounts, i.e., the percentage falling below the minimum balance multiplied by the service charge.

Other Income

Other income is determined by loan commitment fees; possible gain on the sale of credit cards; mortgage service income on mortgage loans sold; income from the new service (Home Telephone Banking); and $100,000 per month of normal other income.

Securities Gains or Losses

Gains or losses on securities are generated from sales of the long-term Treasury portfolio. The portfolio will be marked-to-market and the resultant gains and losses will be reflected in equity.

Other Accounts

Cash, Reserves and Due From

The cash position of a commercial bank is comprised of cash reserves, items in process of collection, due from bank deposits, and cash in excess of required reserves. More specifically, cash reserves include till and vault cash as well as required deposits at the Federal Reserve Bank. The current reserve requirement on demand and IBC deposits net of float and due from bank balances is 10%.

Due from bank balances are deposits maintained with other banks in exchange for services. Items in process of collection are generated from the daily processing of customer transactions (float). Average float balances are generated from these transactions. The amount of float averages 20% for business and public demand deposit balances and 10% for IBC balances.

Other Assets This account will change only to reflect monthly accrual of interest income. Collection of interest occurs monthly for amortized loans, at maturity for single-payment loans and short-term investments, and semi-annually for long-term investments.

Regular Savings The forecast reflects a slight increase for the balance of this account and additional growth is largely outside management control.

Other Liabilities The balance in this account fluctuates with accrued income taxes, accrued dividends, and accrued interest expense.

Performance Evaluation

Overall operating performance is measured by a composite evaluation in five categories: strategic managerial philosophy, management goals, peer comparison, regulatory assessment, and investor relations. Within each category, scoring reflects the sum of both relative scoring and absolute scoring. The relative portion of the evaluation process measures results in comparison to the performance of other teams in the same market. The absolute portion measures performance against established standards. The five categories and proportionate weights for relative and absolute scoring are shown in Figure 5-7. The maximum composite score is 100 points.

Performance Evaluation
Point Allocations

Figure 5-7

	Relative	Absolute	Total
Strategic Managerial Philosophy	0	10	10
Management Goals	25	0	25
Peer Comparison	5	10	15
Regulatory Assessment	5	20	25
Investor Relations	10	15	25
Total	45	55	100

Management Goals The management goals category measures only relative performance and includes no absolute performance evaluation. The performance of each bank is compared with the goals established by the team and points are awarded accordingly. If a bank achieves all of its goals, it will receive the maximum of 25 points (63/63*25=25). Achievement of the highest priority goal will garner 18 points for the team, 15 points for the second priority goal, 12 points for the third priority goal, 9 points for the fourth priority goal, 6 points for the fifth priority goal, and 3 points for the lowest priority goal. The schedule of points awarded by priority and performance is shown in Figure 5-8.

Management Goals

Point Allocations

Figure 5-8

Goal Priority	Relative Performance			
	First	Second	Third	Fourth
Highest	18	12	6	0
Second	15	10	5	0
Third	12	8	4	0
Fourth	9	6	3	0
Fifth	6	4	2	0
Sixth	3	2	1	0
Total	63	42	21	0

Peer Comparison

Peer group comparison is both relative and absolute in evaluation. Relative scoring is based on a ranking of the average asset growth rates in the market. The relative scoring is reflected as follows: 5 points for the team with the highest growth, 4 points for the second highest growth, 3 points for the third highest growth, and 2 points for the lowest growth in the market.

Absolute scoring is a linear function of return on assets as shown in Figure 5-9. Point values are interpolated and rounded to two decimal places, if necessary.

Peer Comparison

Absolute Point Allocations

Figure 5-9

ROA (%)			Points		
1.20	and	above	10.00		
1.15	to	1.20	9.00	to	10.00
1.10	to	1.15	8.00	to	9.00
1.05	to	1.10	7.00	to	8.00
1.00	to	1.05	6.00	to	7.00
0.95	to	1.00	5.00	to	6.00
0.90	to	0.95	4.00	to	5.00
0.85	to	0.90	3.00	to	4.00
0.80	to	0.85	2.00	to	3.00
0.75	to	0.80	1.00	to	2.00
0.70	to	0.75	0.00	to	1.00
	below	0.70	0.00		

Regulatory Assessment

Regulatory assessment has both relative and absolute scoring components. Relative scoring is based on the ratio of net loan charge-offs to average loan balances. The bank with the lowest ratio earns 5 points, the second lowest earns 4 points, the third lowest earns 3 points, and the highest ratio earns 2 points.

The absolute score is awarded on the bank's performance on four ratios: balanced growth, purchased funds to earning assets, risk-based capital, and interest margin. These ratios appear on the Interbank Key Ratio Report distributed at the end of each simulation run. A maximum of five points is awarded for each ratio as shown in Figure 5-10. Point values are interpolated and rounded to two decimal places, if necessary.

Regulatory Assessment

Absolute Point Allocations

Figure 5-10

Points	Balanced Growth %	Pur Funds/ Earn Assets %	Risk-Based Capital %	Interest Margin %
0	6 & above	55 & above	below 8.00	below 2.50
0 to 1	6 to 5	55 to 50	8.00 to 8.75	2.50 to 3.00
1 to 2	5 to 4	50 to 45	8.75 to 9.50	3.00 to 3.50
2 to 3	4 to 3	45 to 40	9.50 to 10.25	3.50 to 4.00
3 to 4	3 to 2	40 to 35	10.25 to 11.00	4.00 to 4.50
4 to 5	2 to 1	35 to 30	11.00 to 11.75	4.50 to 5.00
5	below 1	below 30	11.75 & above	5.00 & above

Investor Relations

Evaluation under investor relations measures both relative and absolute performance. Evaluation is designed to recognize that investors buy bank stocks for various reasons, including expected dividend income and expected appreciation in the market value of shares. The share price is determined by earnings per share and the price/earnings multiple and is shown on the Interbank P/E Ratio Report distributed following each simulation run. The relative scoring in investor relations is based on the ranking of share price. The team with the highest share price receives 10 points, the second highest receives 8 points, the third highest receives 6 points, and the lowest receives 4 points.

The absolute scoring of investor relations is based on the growth in total deposits and total loans. A maximum of five points is awarded for each ratio as shown in Figure 5-11. Point values are interpolated and rounded to two decimal places, if necessary.

Investor Relations

Absolute Point Allocations

Figure 5-11

Points	Deposit Growth (%)
0	below 7.00
0 to 1	7.00 to 7.99
1 to 2	8.00 to 8.99
2 to 3	9.00 to 9.99
3 to 4	10.00 to 10.99
4 to 5	11.00 to 11.99
5	12.00 & above

Investor Relations

Absolute Point Allocations

Points	Loan Growth (%)
0	below 7.00
0 to 2	7.00 to 7.99
2 to 4	8.00 to 8.99
4 to 6	9.00 to 9.99
6 to 8	10.00 to 10.99
8 to 10	11.00 to 11.99
10	12.00 & above

Annual Meeting

An annual shareholders' meeting is held at the conclusion of the simulated year 2003. Each management team presents a report on the simulated year's performance to the body of shareholders comprised of all other simulation participants and the instructor. The report should include discussions on strategy, goal selection, summary of decisions, goal attainment, peer group comparisons, and the bank's position as it enters 2004. Figure 5-12 is an outline to use as a guide by the bank management team when presenting its report to the stockholders. Following each presentation shareholder questions are directed to the management team.

Shareholders' Report

Figure 5-12

Outline

1. Describe your bank's strategic managerial philosphy.

2. Present your goals and the priority of importance. How well did your bank succeed in achieving these goals?

3. Describe the strategies employed during each quarter of the year 2003.

4. Compare your performance for 2003 with your competitors in terms of:

    - Asset quality
    - Liquidity
    - Interest rate exposure
    - Capital adequacy
    - Earnings
    - Growth

5. As rates change, discuss how the bank is positioned for the future in terms of:

    - Liquidity
    - Interest rate exposure
    - Market value

6. Prepare questions for the other banks regarding their performance.

PART III

Comparative Financial Reports

ENDING STATEMENT OF CONDITION
Dollars in Thousands

	12/02 ACTUAL	12/01 ACTUAL	DIFFERENCE	PERCENT
ASSETS:				
CASH, FLOAT & RESERVES	27021	25188	1834	7.3
SHORT-TERM TREASURIES	44290	39373	4917	12.5
LONG-TERM TREASURIES	42200	39400	2800	7.1
ASSET BACKED SECURITIES	5143	4750	393	8.3
ALL OTHER SECURITIES	6324	8658	-2334	-27.0
TOTAL SECURITIES	97957	92181	5776	6.3
SHORT-TERM INVESTMENTS	23529	16363	7166	43.8
COMMERCIAL LOANS-FIXED	48051	43688	4363	10.0
COMMERCIAL LOANS-FLOAT	57828	52276	5552	10.6
MORTGAGE LOANS-FIXED	32958	28072	4886	17.4
MORTGAGE LOANS-ADJ	34600	30320	4280	14.1
HOME EQUITY LOANS	15338	13165	2173	16.5
CONSUMER LOANS	71984	63450	8534	13.5
CREDIT CARD LOANS	29911	26625	3286	12.3
AUTO LOANS	2116	1819	297	16.3
TOTAL LOANS	292786	259414	33372	12.9
RESERVE FOR LOAN LOSSES	-5036	-4462	-574	12.9
NET LOANS	287750	254952	32798	12.9
PROPERTY & EQUIPMENT	9769	9170	598	6.5
OREO & FORECLOSED ASSETS	830	715	115	16.0
OTHER ASSETS	7472	7226	246	3.4
TOTAL OTHER ASSETS	18071	17112	959	5.6
TOTAL ASSETS	454329	405796	48533	12.0
LIABILITIES & CAPITAL:				
DEMAND DEPOSITS	43591	41073	2518	6.1
IBC & SAVINGS	107122	94662	12460	13.2
MMDAs	97677	84474	13203	15.6
SMALL CDs	28969	25993	2976	11.4
LARGE CDs	94416	83259	11157	13.4
PUBLIC CDs	37506	34792	2714	7.8
OTHER CDs	3217	2783	434	15.6
TOTAL CERTIFICATES	164108	146827	17280	11.8
TOTAL DEPOSITS	412497	367036	45461	12.4
SHORT-TERM BOR FUNDS	4913	4782	131	2.7
OTHER LIABILITIES	11438	10537	901	8.6
COMMON STOCK & SURPLUS	5000	5000	0	0.0
RETAINED EARNINGS	20481	18441	2040	11.1
TOTAL EQUITY	25481	23441	2040	8.7
TOTAL LIAB & EQUITY	454329	405796	48533	12.0
TOTAL EARNING ASSETS	414272	367958	46314	12.6
TOTAL INT-BEAR LIAB	373819	330746	43074	13.0

ENDING STATEMENT OF CONDITION
Dollars in Thousands

	12/03 FORECAST	12/02 ACTUAL	DIFFERENCE	PERCENT
ASSETS:				
CASH, FLOAT & RESERVES	17615	27021	-9406	-34.8
SHORT-TERM TREASURIES	58009	44290	13719	31.0
LONG-TERM TREASURIES	44050	42200	1850	4.4
ASSET BACKED SECURITIES	15129	5143	9986	194.2
ALL OTHER SECURITIES	6474	6324	150	2.4
TOTAL SECURITIES	123662	97957	25705	26.2
SHORT-TERM INVESTMENTS	30911	23529	7382	31.4
COMMERCIAL LOANS-FIXED	51299	48051	3248	6.8
COMMERCIAL LOANS-FLOAT	61800	57828	3972	6.9
MORTGAGE LOANS-FIXED	26815	32958	-6143	-18.6
MORTGAGE LOANS-ADJ	41297	34600	6697	19.4
HOME EQUITY LOANS	16118	15338	780	5.1
CONSUMER LOANS	75956	71984	3972	5.5
CREDIT CARD LOANS	31874	29911	1963	6.6
AUTO LOANS	3515	2116	1399	66.1
TOTAL LOANS	308674	292786	15887	5.4
RESERVE FOR LOAN LOSSES	-5055	-5036	-19	0.4
NET LOANS	303619	287750	15868	5.5
PROPERTY & EQUIPMENT	10101	9769	332	3.4
OREO & FORECLOSED ASSETS	2170	830	1339	161.3
OTHER ASSETS	8224	7472	752	10.1
TOTAL OTHER ASSETS	20494	18071	2423	13.4
TOTAL ASSETS	496301	454329	41972	9.2
LIABILITIES & CAPITAL:				
DEMAND DEPOSITS	46168	43591	2578	5.9
IBC & SAVINGS	113369	07122	6248	5.8
MMDAs	105500	97677	7823	8.0
SMALL CDs	38214	28969	9245	31.9
LARGE CDs	100551	94416	6135	6.5
PUBLIC CDs	43583	37506	6077	16.2
OTHER CDs	3491	3217	273	8.5
TOTAL CERTIFICATES	185838	164108	21730	13.2
TOTAL DEPOSITS	450876	412497	38379	9.3
SHORT-TERM BOR FUNDS	5167	4913	254	5.2
OTHER LIABILITIES	11934	11438	496	4.3
COMMON STOCK & SURPLUS	5000	5000	0	0.0
RETAINED EARNINGS	23324	20481	2843	13.9
TOTAL EQUITY	28324	25481	2843	11.2
TOTAL LIAB & EQUITY	496301	454329	41972	9.2
TOTAL EARNING ASSETS	463247	414272	48974	11.8
TOTAL INT-BEAR LIAB	409874	373819	36055	9.6

AVERAGE STATEMENT OF CONDITION
Percentage Composition

	1/02 - 12/02 ACTUAL	1/01 - 12/01 ACTUAL	DIFFERENCE
ASSETS:			
CASH, FLOAT & RESERVES	6.0	6.3	-0.3
SHORT-TERM TREASURIES	9.5	9.4	0.2
LONG-TERM TREASURIES	9.8	10.0	-0.2
ASSET BACKED SECURITIES	1.2	1.2	0.0
ALL OTHER SECURITIES	1.7	3.0	-1.3
TOTAL SECURITIES	22.2	23.6	-1.4
SHORT-TERM INVESTMENTS	4.1	3.1	1.1
COMMERCIAL LOANS-FIXED	10.7	10.9	-0.2
COMMERCIAL LOANS-FLOAT	12.9	13.0	-0.2
MORTGAGE LOANS-FIXED	7.2	6.9	0.2
MORTGAGE LOANS-ADJ	7.6	7.4	0.2
HOME EQUITY LOANS	3.4	3.2	0.2
CONSUMER LOANS	15.9	15.5	0.5
CREDIT CARD LOANS	6.6	6.6	0.0
AUTO LOANS	0.5	0.4	0.0
TOTAL LOANS	64.7	63.9	0.8
RESERVE FOR LOAN LOSSES	-1.1	-1.1	0.0
NET LOANS	63.6	62.8	0.8
PROPERTY & EQUIPMENT	2.2	2.3	-0.1
OREO & FORECLOSED ASSETS	0.2	0.2	0.0
OTHER ASSETS	1.6	1.7	-0.1
TOTAL OTHER ASSETS	4.0	4.2	-0.2
TOTAL ASSETS	100.0	100.0	0.0
LIABILITIES & CAPITAL:			
DEMAND DEPOSITS	9.9	10.4	-0.5
IBC & SAVINGS	23.6	23.3	0.3
MMDAs	21.3	20.6	0.7
SMALL CDs	6.4	6.6	-0.2
LARGE CDs	20.7	20.5	0.3
PUBLIC CDs	8.5	8.7	-0.2
OTHER CDs	0.7	0.7	0.0
TOTAL CERTIFICATES	36.3	36.4	-0.1
TOTAL DEPOSITS	91.0	90.7	0.3
SHORT-TERM BOR FUNDS	0.7	0.8	-0.1
OTHER LIABILITIES	2.5	2.6	-0.1
COMMON STOCK & SURPLUS	1.2	1.3	-0.1
RETAINED EARNINGS	4.6	4.6	0.0
TOTAL EQUITY	5.7	5.9	-0.1
TOTAL LIAB & EQUITY	100.0	100.0	0.0
TOTAL EARNING ASSETS	91.1	90.5	0.6
TOTAL INT-BEAR LIAB	81.8	81.1	0.8

AVERAGE STATEMENT OF CONDITION
Percentage Composition

	1/03 - 12/03 FORECAST	1/02 - 12/02 ACTUAL	DIFFERENCE
ASSETS:			
CASH, FLOAT & RESERVES	3.7	6.0	-2.4
SHORT-TERM TREASURIES	11.7	9.5	2.1
LONG-TERM TREASURIES	9.1	9.8	-0.7
ASSET BACKED SECURITIES	2.9	1.2	1.8
ALL OTHER SECURITIES	1.4	1.7	-0.4
TOTAL SECURITIES	25.1	22.2	2.8
SHORT-TERM INVESTMENTS	5.0	4.1	0.8
COMMERCIAL LOANS-FIXED	10.5	10.7	-0.2
COMMERCIAL LOANS-FLOAT	12.6	12.9	-0.3
MORTGAGE LOANS-FIXED	6.3	7.2	-0.9
MORTGAGE LOANS-ADJ	8.0	7.6	0.4
HOME EQUITY LOANS	3.3	3.4	-0.1
CONSUMER LOANS	15.5	15.9	-0.5
CREDIT CARD LOANS	6.8	6.6	0.2
AUTO LOANS	0.6	0.5	0.1
TOTAL LOANS	63.4	64.7	-1.3
RESERVE FOR LOAN LOSSES	-1.0	-1.1	0.1
NET LOANS	62.4	63.6	-1.3
PROPERTY & EQUIPMENT	2.1	2.2	-0.1
OREO & FORECLOSED ASSETS	0.3	0.2	0.1
OTHER ASSETS	1.5	1.6	0.0
TOTAL OTHER ASSETS	3.9	4.0	0.0
TOTAL ASSETS	100.0	100.0	100.0
LIABILITIES & CAPITAL:			
DEMAND DEPOSITS	9.7	9.9	-0.2
IBC & SAVINGS	23.2	23.6	-0.4
MMDAs	21.3	21.3	0.1
SMALL CDs	6.9	6.4	0.5
LARGE CDs	20.5	20.7	-0.3
PUBLIC CDs	9.0	8.5	0.5
OTHER CDs	0.7	0.7	0.0
TOTAL CERTIFICATES	37.1	36.3	0.8
TOTAL DEPOSITS	91.3	91.0	0.3
SHORT-TERM BOR FUNDS	0.7	0.7	0.0
OTHER LIABILITIES	2.2	2.5	-0.3
COMMON STOCK & SURPLUS	1.0	1.2	-0.1
RETAINED EARNINGS	4.7	4.6	0.1
TOTAL EQUITY	5.7	5.7	0.0
TOTAL LIAB & EQUITY	100.0	100.0	0.0
TOTAL EARNING ASSETS	93.5	91.1	2.4
TOTAL INT-BEAR LIAB	82.3	81.8	0.5

STATEMENT OF INCOME
Dollars in Thousands

	1/02 - 12/02 ACTUAL	1/01 - 12/01 ACTUAL	DIFFERENCE	PERCENT
INTEREST INCOME:				
SHORT-TERM TREASURIES	3098	2916	181	6.2
LONG-TERM TREASURIES	3363	3062	300	9.8
ASSET BACKED SECURITIES	606	578	28	4.9
ALL OTHER SECURITIES	664	1244	-580	-46.6
TOTAL SECURITIES	7730	7800	-70	-0.9
SHORT-TERM INVESTMENTS	1432	1072	360	33.6
COMMERCIAL LOANS-FIXED	4540	4352	189	4.3
COMMERCIAL LOANS-FLOAT	5728	5586	142	2.5
MORTGAGE LOANS-FIXED	3198	2787	411	14.7
MORTGAGE LOANS-ADJ	3118	2765	353	12.8
HOME EQUITY LOANS	1664	1401	263	18.8
CONSUMER LOANS	8686	6850	1836	26.8
CREDIT CARD LOANS	5213	4640	573	12.3
AUTO LOANS	248	210	38	17.9
TOTAL LOANS	32396	28591	3805	13.3
TOTAL INTEREST INCOME	41558	37463	4095	10.9
INTEREST EXPENSE:				
IBC & SAVINGS	5219	4613	606	13.1
MMDAs	6815	5606	1210	21.6
SMALL CDs	2241	1931	311	16.1
LARGE CDs	7277	7161	116	1.6
PUBLIC CDs	2970	3029	-59	-2.0
OTHER CDs	223	214	10	4.6
TOTAL CERTIFICATES	12712	12335	377	3.1
SHORT-TERM BOR FUNDS	248	281	-32	-11.6
TOTAL INTEREST EXPENSE	24994	22834	2160	9.5
NET INTEREST INCOME	16563	14629	1935	13.2
PROVISION FOR LOAN LOSS	1831	1612	219	13.6
NET INT INCOME AFTER PROV	14732	13016	1716	13.2
SERVICE CHARGES	1558	1372	186	13.6
OTHER INCOME	1537	1492	45	3.0
GAIN(LOSS) ON SECURITIES	0	0	0	0.0
TOTAL NON-INTEREST INC	3095	2864	231	8.1
SALARIES & BENEFITS	6636	5724	912	15.9
OCCUPANCY, FURN & EQUIP	1752	1495	256	17.1
PROMOTION EXPENSE	636	575	61	10.5
FDIC INSURANCE EXPENSE	0	0	0	0.0
DATA PROCESSING EXPENSE	1786	1584	202	12.8
FINANCING & HEDGING EXP	0	0	0	0.0
OTHER OPERATING EXPENSE	1871	1676	195	11.6
TOTAL NON-INTEREST EXP	12681	11055	1626	14.7
NET INCOME BEFORE TAXES	5147	4826	321	6.6
INCOME TAXES	1807	1617	190	11.8
NET INCOME	3340	3209	13	4.1

STATEMENT OF INCOME
Dollars in Thousands

	1/03 - 12/03 FORECAST	1/02 - 12/02 ACTUAL	DIFFERENCE	PERCENT
INTEREST INCOME:				
SHORT-TERM TREASURIES	3901	3098	803	25.9
LONG-TERM TREASURIES	3574	3363	211	6.3
ASSET BACKED SECURITIES	1465	606	859	141.7
ALL OTHER SECURITIES	620	664	-44	-6.6
TOTAL SECURITIES	9560	7730	1830	23.7
SHORT-TERM INVESTMENTS	1778	1432	347	24.2
COMMERCIAL LOANS-FIXED	4992	4540	451	9.9
COMMERCIAL LOANS-FLOAT	5917	5728	189	3.3
MORTGAGE LOANS-FIXED	3097	3198	-101	-3.1
MORTGAGE LOANS-ADJ	3273	3118	155	5.0
HOME EQUITY LOANS	1778	1664	114	6.9
CONSUMER LOANS	9399	8686	713	8.2
CREDIT CARD LOANS	6250	5213	1037	19.9
AUTO LOANS	344	248	96	38.6
TOTAL LOANS	35050	32396	2654	8.2
TOTAL INTEREST INCOME	46389	41558	4831	11.6
INTEREST EXPENSE:				
IBC & SAVINGS	5711	5219	492	9.4
MMDAs	7160	6815	345	5.1
SMALL CDs	2526	2241	285	12.7
LARGE CDs	7631	7277	354	4.9
PUBLIC CDs	3505	2970	535	18.0
OTHER CDs	246	223	23	10.3
TOTAL CERTIFICATES	13908	12712	1196	9.4
SHORT-TERM BOR FUNDS	250	248	2	0.9
TOTAL INTEREST EXPENSE	27030	24994	2036	8.1
NET INTEREST INCOME	19359	16563	2788	16.9
PROVISION FOR LOAN LOSS	1489	1831	-342	-18.7
NET INT INCOME AFTER PROV	17870	14732	3138	21.3
SERVICE CHARGES	1726	1558	167	10.7
OTHER INCOME	1658	1537	121	7.9
GAIN(LOSS) ON SECURITIES	0	0	0	0.0
TOTAL NON-INTEREST INC	3384	3095	288	9.3
SALARIES & BENEFITS	7782	6636	1146	17.3
OCCUPANCY, FURN & EQUIP	1907	1752	155	8.8
PROMOTION EXPENSE	630	636	-6	-0.9
FDIC INSURANCE EXPENSE	842	0	842	0.0
DATA PROCESSING EXPENSE	1906	1786	119	6.7
FINANCING & HEDGING EXP	0	0	0	0.0
OTHER OPERATING EXPENSE	1662	1871	-209	-11.2
TOTAL NON-INTEREST EXP	14728	12681	2047	16.1
NET INCOME BEFORE TAXES	6525	5147	1379	26.8
INCOME TAXES	2362	1807	555	30.7
NET INCOME	4163	3340	823	24.6

KEY RATIOS REPORT - DETAIL

	1/02 - 12/02 ACTUAL	1/01 - 12/01 ACTUAL	DIFFERENCE
ASSET QUALITY:			
MOST BAL LOAN MIX (AVG)	8.38	10.10	-1.72
RES/NON PERFORM (EOP)	1.23	1.21	0.02
NET CH-OFFS/LOANS(AVG)	0.45	0.44	0.01
INV MKT TO BOOK (EOP)	101.25	100.69	0.56
LIQUIDITY (AVG):			
LOANS/DEPOSITS (EOP)	71.08	70.43	0.65
S-T INVEST TO ASSETS	13.69	12.88	0.80
PURCHASED FUNDS/E.A.	32.32	32.48	-0.16
NET BOR FUNDS/ASSETS	-3.42	-2.26	-1.16
TOTAL LNS/AVAIL DEP	86.52	86.38	0.14
CAPITAL ADEQUACY:			
EQUITY/ASSETS (EOP)	5.61	5.78	-0.17
MARKET CAPITALIZATION	36060	45360	-9300
RISK BASED CAPITAL (EOP)	9.64	9.85	-0.21
PE RATIO (EOP)	10.83	14.26	-3.43
PROFITABILITY / EARNINGS (AVG):			
EARNINGS PER SHARE(ANN)	1.11	1.06	0.05
RETURN ON EQUITY	13.61	14.31	-0.69
RETURN ON ASSETS	0.78	0.84	-0.06
INT MARGIN ON E.A.	4.32	4.36	-0.04
NET OVERHEAD TO E.A.	2.46	2.37	0.09
YIELD ON EARNING ASSETS	10.74	10.96	-0.23
NET INCOME ($000)	3339.83	3209.41	130.42
GROWTH (%):			
TOTAL LOANS (YTD AVG)	13.43	12.15	1.28
TOTAL DEPOSITS(YTD AVG)	12.33	11.86	0.47
TOTAL EQUITY (YTD AVG)	9.37	7.77	1.60
BAL GROWTH (YTD AVG)	4.20	4.40	-0.20
COMP GROWTH (YTD AVG)	34.00	31.90	2.10
TOTAL ASSETS ($EOP)	454329	405796	48533
MEMO ITEMS:			
MKT VALUE OF INVST($MIL)	99	93	6
OUTSTANDING SHARES(000)	3000	3000	0
SAL & BENEFITS/EMP($)	28325	26275	2050
ASSETS (AVG)/EMP($ MIL)	1.83	1.75	0.07
STOCK PRICE ($EOP)	12.02	15.12	-3.10
BK VALUE PER SHARE ($EOP)	8.49	7.81	0.68

KEY RATIOS REPORT - DETAIL

	1/03 - 12/03 FORECAST	1/02 - 12/02 ACTUAL	DIFFERENCE
ASSET QUALITY:			
MOST BAL LOAN MIX (AVG)	8.67	8.38	0.29
RES/NON PERFORM (EOP)	1.16	1.23	-0.06
NET CH-OFFS/LOANS(AVG)	0.49	0.45	0.03
INV MKT TO BOOK (EOP)	101.06	101.25	-0.19
LIQUIDITY (AVG):			
LOANS/DEPOSITS (EOP)	69.67	71.08	-1.41
S-T INVEST TO ASSETS	15.61	13.69	1.93
PURCHASED FUNDS/E.A	31.73	32.32	-0.59
NET BOR FUNDS/ASSETS	-3.19	-3.42	0.23
TOTAL LNS/AVAIL DEP	82.53	86.52	-3.99
CAPITAL ADEQUACY:			
EQUITY/ASSETS (EOP)	5.71	5.61	0.10
MARKET CAPITALIZATION	58410	36060	22350
RISK BASED CAPITAL (EOP)	10.02	9.64	0.38
PE RATIO (EOP)	14.11	10.83	3.28
PROFITABILITY / EARNINGS (AVG):			
EARNINGS PER SHARE(ANN)	1.38	1.11	0.27
RETURN ON EQUITY	15.33	13.61	1.72
RETURN ON ASSETS	0.87	0.78	0.09
INT MARGIN ON E.A.	4.39	4.32	0.07
NET OVERHEAD TO E.A.	2.55	2.46	0.09
YIELD ON EARNING ASSETS	10.47	10.74	-0.27
NET INCOME ($000)	4163.07	3339.83	823.24
GROWTH (%):			
TOTAL LOANS (YTD AVG)	9.03	13.43	-4.40
TOTAL DEPOSITS(YTD AVG)	11.68	12.33	-0.64
TOTAL EQUITY (YTD AVG)	10.68	9.37	1.31
BAL GROWTH (YTD AVG)	2.66	4.20	-1.54
COMP GROWTH (YTD AVG)	31.39	34.00	-2.61
TOTAL ASSETS ($EOP)	496301	454329	41972
MEMO ITEMS:			
MKT VALUE OF INVST($MIL)	125	99	26
OUTSTANDING SHARES(000)	3000	3000	0
SAL & BENEFITS/EMP($)	30527	28325	2202
ASSETS (AVG)/EMP($ MIL)	1.87	1.83	0.04
STOCK PRICE ($EOP)	19.47	12.02	7.45
BK VALUE PER SHARE ($EOP)	9.44	8.49	0.95

INTEREST RATE REPORT

	1/02 - 12/02 ACTUAL	1/01 - 12/01 ACTUAL	DIFFERENCE
EARNING ASSET YIELDS:			
SHORT-TERM TREASURIES	7.59	8.14	-0.55
LONG-TERM TREASURIES	8.06	8.03	0.03
ASSET BACKED SECURITIES	12.08	12.73	-0.65
ALL OTHER SECURITIES	12.75	14.78	-2.03
TOTAL SECURITIES	8.44	9.18	-0.74
SHORT-TERM INVESTMENTS	8.08	9.16	-1.09
COMMERCIAL LOANS-FIXED	9.90	10.43	-0.53
COMMERCIAL LOANS-FLOAT	10.41	11.23	-0.82
MORTGAGE LOANS-FIXED	10.42	10.53	-0.11
MORTGAGE LOANS-ADJ	9.57	9.79	-0.22
HOME EQUITY LOANS	11.57	11.62	-0.05
CONSUMER LOANS	12.74	11.59	1.15
CREDIT CARD LOANS	18.46	18.46	0.00
AUTO LOANS	12.62	12.45	0.17
TOTAL LOANS	11.70	11.71	-0.01
TOTAL EARNING ASSETS	10.74	10.96	-0.23
COST OF FUNDS RATES:			
IBC & SAVINGS	5.18	5.18	0.00
MMDAs	7.49	7.13	0.37
SMALL CDs	8.19	7.71	0.48
LARGE CDs	8.20	9.15	-0.95
PUBLIC CDs	8.20	9.15	-0.95
OTHER CDs	7.46	7.96	-0.50
TOTAL CERTIFICATES	8.18	8.87	-0.68
SHORT-TERM BOR FUNDS	8.03	9.15	-1.12
TOTAL INT-BEAR LIAB	7.14	7.37	-0.23
NET INTEREST SPREAD	3.60	3.60	0.00
NET INTEREST INCOME	4.32	4.36	-0.04
MARKET RATES:			
PRIME RATE (LG BKS)	10.01	10.87	-0.86
FED FUNDS RATE(NATIONAL)	8.10	9.22	-1.12
TREASURY BILL RATE 3 MO	7.51	8.11	-0.60
TREASURY BILL RATE 6 MO	7.47	8.04	-0.58
US GOVT YIELD (3YRS)	8.25	8.55	-0.30
MUNICIPAL BOND YIELD	7.27	7.23	0.05
CONV MTG RATE (NEW)	10.01	10.06	-0.05
90-DAY CD RATE(NATIONAL)	8.15	9.08	-0.93
LONDON INTERBANK RATE	8.16	9.16	-1.00

INTEREST RATE REPORT

	1/03 - 12/03 FORECAST	1/02 - 12/02 ACTUAL	DIFFERENCE
EARNING ASSET YIELDS:			
SHORT-TERM TREASURIES	7.02	7.59	-0.57
LONG-TERM TREASURIES	8.28	8.06	0.22
ASSET BACKED SECURITIES	10.46	12.08	-1.62
ALL OTHER SECURITIES	12.24	12.75	-0.51
TOTAL SECURITIES	8.16	8.44	-0.27
SHORT-TERM INVESTMENTS	7.49	8.08	-0.59
COMMERCIAL LOANS-FIXED	10.01	9.90	0.11
COMMERCIAL LOANS-FLOAT	9.90	10.41	-0.51
MORTGAGE LOANS-FIXED	10.39	10.42	-0.03
MORTGAGE LOANS-ADJ	8.62	9.57	-0.95
HOME EQUITY LOANS	11.34	11.57	-0.23
CONSUMER LOANS	12.77	12.74	0.03
CREDIT CARD LOANS	19.31	18.46	0.85
AUTO LOANS	12.12	12.62	-0.50
TOTAL LOANS	11.61	11.70	-0.09
TOTAL EARNING ASSETS	10.47	10.74	-0.27
COST OF FUNDS RATES:			
IBC & SAVINGS	5.18	5.18	0.00
MMDAs	7.05	7.49	-0.45
SMALL CDs	7.65	8.19	-0.54
LARGE CDs	7.83	8.20	-0.37
PUBLIC CDs	8.20	8.20	0.00
OTHER CDs	7.47	7.46	0.01
TOTAL CERTIFICATES	7.88	8.18	-0.31
SHORT-TERM BOR FUNDS	7.02	8.03	-1.01
TOTAL INT-BEAR LIAB	6.89	7.14	-0.24
NET INTEREST SPREAD	3.57	3.60	-0.03
NET INTEREST INCOME	4.39	4.32	0.07
MARKET RATES:			
PRIME RATE (LG BKS)	10.00	10.01	-0.01
FED FUNDS RATE(NATIONAL)	7.31	8.10	-0.79
TREASURY BILL RATE 3 MO	6.81	7.51	-0.70
TREASURY BILL RATE 6 MO	6.76	7.47	-0.71
US GOVT YIELD (3YRS)	7.47	8.25	-0.78
MUNICIPAL BOND YIELD	7.09	7.27	-0.18
CONV MTG RATE (NEW)	9.76	10.01	-0.25
90-DAY CD RATE(NATIONAL)	7.82	8.15	-0.33
LONDON INTERBANK RATE	7.87	8.16	-0.29

LINE OF BUSINESS REPORT - DETAIL
Dollars in Thousands

	1/02 - 12/02 ACTUAL	1/01 - 12/01 ACTUAL	DIFFERENCE	PERCENT
TOTAL DEPOSITS	389383	346657	42726	12.3
LESS CASH & DUE FROM	25858	24264	1595	6.6
NET DEPOSITS	363525	322393	41132	12.8
CAPITAL - NET	23084	20499	2585	12.6
SHORT TERM BORROWINGS	3092	3068	24	0.8
LONG-TERM DEBT	0	0	0	0.0
TOTAL BANK SOURCES	389701	345960	43741	12.6
SHORT-TERM INVESTMENTS	17718	11693	6025	51.5
TOTAL SECURITIES	95056	90123	4933	5.5
GROSS LOANS	276926	244143	32783	13.4
TOTAL BANK USES	389701	345960	43741	12.6
IBC & SAVINGS	100791	89069	11722	13.2
MMDAs	90945	78652	12293	15.6
SMALL CDs	27360	25032	2328	9.3
TOTAL RETAIL DEPOSITS	219096	192752	26344	13.7
LESS CASH	14550	13491	1058	7.8
TOTAL RETAIL SOURCES	204546	179261	25285	14.1
MORTGAGE LOANS-FIXED	30684	26474	4210	15.9
MORTGAGE LOANS-ADJ	32597	28253	4344	15.4
HOME EQUITY LOANS	14385	12062	2324	19.3
CONSUMER LOANS	68185	59090	9095	15.4
CREDIT CARD LOANS	28243	25140	3103	12.3
AUTO LOANS	1964	1688	276	16.3
TOTAL RETAIL USES	176060	152708	23352	15.3
BUSINESS DEMAND	35091	33216	1875	5.6
LARGE CDs	44373	39129	5243	13.4
OTHER CDS	2996	2685	312	11.6
TOTAL BUSINESS DEPOSITS	82460	75030	7430	9.9
LESS CASH	5476	5252	224	4.3
TOTAL BUSINESS SOURCES	76984	69778	7205	10.3
DIRECT COM'L LOANS-FIXED	45847	41708	4139	9.9
COMMERCIAL LOANS-FLOAT	55019	49727	5292	10.6
TOTAL BUSINESS USES	100866	91435	9431	10.3
PUBLIC DEMAND	7242	6624	618	9.3
LARGE CDs	44373	39129	5243	13.4
PUBLIC CDs	36212	33121	3091	9.3
TOTAL WHOLESALE DEPOSIT	87827	78874	8953	11.4
LESS CASH	5832	5521	312	5.6
NET WHOLESALE DEPOSITS	81995	73354	8641	11.8
SHORT-TERM BORROWINGS	3092	3068	24	0.8
CAPITAL - NET	23084	20499	2585	12.6
TOTAL WHOLESALE SOURCES	108171	96920	11250	11.6
SHORT-TERM INVESTMENTS	17718	11693	6025	51.5
TOTAL SECURITIES	95056	90123	4933	5.5
TOTAL INVESTMENT USES	112775	101816	10958	10.8

LINE OF BUSINESS REPORT - DETAIL
Dollars in Thousands

	1/03 - 12/03 FORECAST	1/02 - 12/02 ACTUAL	DIFFERENCE	PERCENT
TOTAL DEPOSITS	434880	389383	45497	11.7
LESS CASH & DUE FROM	17437	25858	-8422	-32.6
NET DEPOSITS	417444	363525	53919	14.8
CAPITAL - NET	24015	23084	930	4.0
SHORT TERM BORROWINGS	3565	3092	474	15.3
LONG-TERM DEB	0	0	0	0.0
TOTAL BANK SOURCES	445024	389701	55323	14.2
SHORT-TERM INVESTMENTS	23757	17718	6039	34.1
TOTAL SECURITIES	119343	95056	24286	25.5
GROSS LOANS	301924	276926	24998	9.0
TOTAL BANK USES	445024	389701	55323	14.2
IBC & SAVINGS	110350	100791	9559	9.5
MMDAs	101616	90945	10671	11.7
SMALL CDs	33029	27360	5670	20.7
TOTAL RETAIL DEPOSITS	244995	219096	25899	11.8
LESS CASH	9823	14550	-4727	-32.5
TOTAL RETAIL SOURCES	235172	204546	30626	15.0
MORTGAGE LOANS-FIXED	29810	30684	-875	-2.9
MORTGAGE LOANS-ADJ	37968	32597	5371	16.5
HOME EQUITY LOANS	15683	14385	1298	9.0
CONSUMER LOANS	73624	68185	5439	8.0
CREDIT CARD LOANS	32367	28243	4124	14.6
AUTO LOANS	2835	1964	871	44.3
TOTAL RETAIL USES	192288	176060	16228	9.2
BUSINESS DEMAND	37554	35091	2463	7.0
LARGE CDs	48720	44373	4347	9.8
OTHER CDS	3301	2996	304	10.2
TOTAL BUSINESS DEPOSITS	89574	82460	7114	8.6
LESS CASH	3591	5476	-1884	-34.4
TOTAL BUSINESS SOURCES	85982	76984	8999	11.7
DIRECT COM'L LOANS-FIXED	49873	45847	4026	8.8
COMMERCIAL LOANS-FLOAT	59764	55019	4745	8.6
TOTAL BUSINESS USES	109636	100866	8770	8.7
PUBLIC DEMAND	8838	7242	1596	22.0
LARGE CDs	48720	44373	4347	9.8
PUBLIC CDs	42753	36212	6541	18.1
TOTAL WHOLESALE DEPOSIT	100311	87827	12484	14.2
LESS CASH	4022	5832	-1810	-31.0
NET WHOLESALE DEPOSITS	96289	81995	14294	17.4
SHORT-TERM BORROWINGS	3565	3092	474	15.3
CAPITAL - NET	24015	23084	930	4.0
TOTAL WHOLESALE SOURCES	123869	108171	15698	14.5
SHORT-TERM INVESTMENTS	23757	17718	6039	34.1
TOTAL SECURITIES	119343	95056	24286	25.5
TOTAL INVESTMENT USES	143099	112775	30325	26.9

ENDING STATEMENT OF CONDITION - DETAIL
Dollars in Thousands

	12/02 ACTUAL	12/01 ACTUAL	DIFFERENCE	PERCENT
ASSETS:				
CASH, RESERVES & DUE FROM	11388	10884	504	4.6
ITEMS IN PROCESS	15633	14303	1330	9.3
CASH, FLOAT & RESERVES	27021	25188	1834	7.3
SHORT-TERM TREASURIES	44290	39373	4917	12.5
LONG-TERM TREASURIES	42200	39400	2800	7.1
US AGENCY SECURITIES	5143	4750	393	8.3
CMO CLASS B	0	0	0	0.0
OUR SECURITIZED MTG LOANS	0	0	0	0.0
ASSET BACKED SECURITIES	5143	4750	393	8.3
TAX EXEMPTS	3200	5750	-2550	-44.3
OTHER SECURITIES	3124	2908	216	7.4
FHLB STOCK	0	0	0	0.0
INT RTE CONTRACTS-SWAPS	0	0	0	0.0
INT RTE CONTRACTS-OPTIONS	0	0	0	0.0
ALL OTHER SECURITIES	6324	8658	-2334	-27.0
TOTAL SECURITIES	97957	92181	5776	6.3
TERM FED FUNDS SOLD	0	0	0	0.0
OVERNIGHT FED FUNDS SOLD	23529	16363	7166	43.8
TRADING ACCOUNT	0	0	0	0.0
SHORT-TERM INVESTMENTS	23529	16363	7166	43.8
COM'L PARTIC PURCH-FIXED	0	0	0	0.0
DIRECT COM'L LOANS-FIXED	48051	43688	4363	10.0
PART PUR - REQ'D-FIXED	0	0	0	0.0
PART SOLD - REQ'D-FIXED	0	0	0	0.0
COM'L LOANS-OPTION CONTRACT	0	0	0	0.0
COMMERCIAL LOANS-FIXED	48051	43688	4363	10.0
COM'L PARTIC PURCH-FLOAT	0	0	0	0.0
DIRECT COM'L LOANS-FLOAT	57828	52276	5552	10.6
COMMERCIAL LOANS-FLOAT	57828	52276	5552	10.6
MORTGAGE LOANS-FIXED	32958	28072	4886	17.4
MORTGAGE LOANS-ADJ	34600	30320	4280	14.1
HOME EQUITY LOANS	15338	13165	2173	16.5
CONSUMER LOANS	71984	63450	8534	13.5
CREDIT CARD LOANS	29911	26625	3286	12.3
AUTO LOANS	2116	1819	297	16.3
TOTAL LOANS	292786	259414	33372	12.9
RESERVE FOR LOAN LOSSES	-5036	-4462	-574	12.9
NET LOANS	287750	254952	32798	12.9
PROPERTY & EQUIPMENT	9769	9170	598	6.5
OREO & FORECLOSED ASSETS	830	715	115	16.0
OTHER ASSETS	7472	7226	246	3.4
TOTAL OTHER ASSETS	18071	17112	959	5.6
TOTAL ASSETS	454329	405796	48533	12.0

ENDING STATEMENT OF CONDITION - DETAIL
Dollars in Thousands

	12/03 FORECAST	12/02 ACTUAL	DIFFERENCE	PERCENT
ASSETS:				
CASH, RESERVES & DUE FROM	9266	11388	-2122	-18.6
ITEMS IN PROCESS	8349	15633	-7284	-46.6
CASH, FLOAT & RESERVES	17615	27021	-9406	-34.8
SHORT-TERM TREASURIES	58009	44290	13719	31.0
LONG-TERM TREASURIES	44050	42200	1850	4.4
US AGENCY SECURITIES	8501	5143	3358	65.3
CMO CLASS B	6628	0	6628	0.0
OUR SECURITIZED MTG LOANS	0	0	0	0.0
ASSET BACKED SECURITIES	15129	5143	9986	194.2
TAX EXEMPTS	2400	3200	-800	-25.0
OTHER SECURITIES	4074	3124	950	30.4
FHLB STOCK	0	0	0	0.0
INT RTE CONTRACTS-SWAPS	0	0	0	0.0
INT RTE CONTRACTS-OPTIONS	0	0	0	0.0
ALL OTHER SECURITIES	6474	6324	150	2.4
TOTAL SECURITIES	123662	97957	25705	26.2
TERM FED FUNDS SOLD	0	0	0	0.0
OVERNIGHT FED FUNDS SOLD	25911	23529	2382	10.1
TRADING ACCOUNT	5000	0	5000	0.0
SHORT-TERM INVESTMENTS	30911	23529	7382	31.4
COM'L PARTIC PURCH-FIXED	0	0	0	0.0
DIRECT COM'L LOANS-FIXED	51299	48051	3248	6.8
PART PUR - REQ'D-FIXED	0	0	0	0.0
PART SOLD - REQ'D-FIXED	0	0	0	0.0
COM'L LOANS-OPTION CONTRACT	0	0	0	0.0
COMMERCIAL LOANS-FIXED	51299	48051	3248	6.8
COM'L PARTIC PURCH-FLOAT	0	0	0	0.0
DIRECT COM'L LOANS-FLOAT	61800	57828	3972	6.9
COMMERCIAL LOANS-FLOAT	61800	57828	3972	6.9
MORTGAGE LOANS-FIXED	26815	32958	-6143	-18.6
MORTGAGE LOANS-ADJ	41297	34600	6697	19.4
HOME EQUITY LOANS	16118	15338	780	5.1
CONSUMER LOANS	75956	71984	3972	5.5
CREDIT CARD LOANS	31874	29911	1963	6.6
AUTO LOANS	3515	2116	1399	66.1
TOTAL LOANS	308674	292786	15887	5.4
RESERVE FOR LOAN LOSSES	-5055	-5036	-19	0.4
NET LOANS	303619	287750	15868	5.5
PROPERTY & EQUIPMENT	10101	9769	332	3.4
OREO & FORECLOSED ASSETS	2170	830	1339	161.3
OTHER ASSETS	8224	7472	752	10.1
TOTAL OTHER ASSETS	20494	18071	2423	13.4
TOTAL ASSETS	496301	454329	41972	9.2

ENDING STATEMENT OF CONDITION - DETAIL
Dollars in Thousands

	12/02 ACTUAL	12/01 ACTUAL	DIFFERENCE	PERCENT
LIABILITIES & CAPITAL:				
BUSINESS DEMAND	36090	34114	1975	5.8
PUBLIC DEMAND	7501	6958	543	7.8
DEMAND DEPOSITS	43591	41073	2518	6.1
INTEREST-BEAR CHECKING	69148	60888	8260	13.6
REGULAR SAVINGS	37973	33774	4199	12.4
IBC & SAVINGS	107122	94662	12460	13.2
MMDAs	97677	84474	13203	15.6
SMALL CDs	28969	25993	2976	11.4
LARGE CDs	94416	83259	11157	13.4
PUBLIC CDs	37506	34792	2714	7.8
OTHER CDS	3217	2783	434	15.6
INT RTE CONTRACTS-SWAPS	0	0	0	0.0
OTHER CDs	3217	2783	434	15.6
TOTAL CERTIFICATES	164108	146827	17280	11.8
TOTAL DEPOSITS	412497	367036	45461	12.4
TREASURY, TAX & LOAN	3913	3782	131	3.5
REPOS	0	0	0	0.0
FED FUNDS PURCHASED	1000	1000	0	0.0
SHORT-TERM BOR FUNDS	4913	4782	131	2.7
LONG-TERM DEBT	0	0	0	0.0
FHLB ADVANCES	0	0	0	0.0
LONG-TERM DEBT	0	0	0	0.0
OTH LIAB:ACCR INC TAXES	2481	2481	0	0.0
OTH LIAB:ACCR DIVID PAY	325	305	20	6.6
OTH LIAB:ACCR INT PAY	277	264	14	5.2
OTH LIAB:DEFER'D I/E-OBS	0	0	0	0.0
OTH LIAB:ALL OTHER	8355	7487	868	11.6
OTHER LIABILITIES	11438	10537	901	8.6
COMMON STOCK & SURPLUS	5000	5000	0	0.0
RETAINED EARNINGS	20481	18441	2040	11.1
TOTAL EQUITY	25481	23441	2040	8.7
TOTAL LIAB & EQUITY	454329	405796	48533	12.0
TOTAL EARNING ASSETS	414272	367958	46314	12.6
TOTAL INT-BEAR LIAB	373819	330746	43074	13.0

ENDING STATEMENT OF CONDITION
Dollars in Thousands

	12/03 FORECAST	12/02 ACTUAL	DIFFERENCE	PERCENT
LIABILITIES & CAPITAL:				
BUSINESS DEMAND	37452	36090	1362	3.8
PUBLIC DEMAND	8717	7501	1215	16.2
DEMAND DEPOSITS	46168	43591	2578	5.9
INTEREST-BEAR CHECKING	74648	69148	5500	8.0
REGULAR SAVINGS	38721	37973	748	2.0
IBC & SAVINGS	113369	107122	6248	5.8
MMDAs	105500	97677	7823	8.0
SMALL CDs	38214	28969	9245	31.9
LARGE CDs	100551	94416	6135	6.5
PUBLIC CDs	43583	37506	6077	16.2
OTHER CDS	3491	3217	273	8.5
INT RTE CONTRACTS-SWAPS	0	0	0	0.0
OTHER CDs	3491	3217	273	8.5
TOTAL CERTIFICATES	185838	164108	21730	13.2
TOTAL DEPOSITS	450876	412497	38379	9.3
TREASURY, TAX & LOAN	4167	3913	254	6.5
REPOS	0	0	0	0.0
FED FUNDS PURCHASED	1000	1000	0	0.0
SHORT-TERM BOR FUNDS	5167	4913	254	5.2
LONG-TERM DEBT	0	0	0	0.0
FHLB ADVANCES	0	0	0	0.0
LONG-TERM DEBT	0	0	0	0.0
OTH LIAB:ACCR INC TAXES	352	2481	-2129	-85.8
OTH LIAB:ACCR DIVID PAY	330	325	5	1.5
OTH LIAB:ACCR INT PAY	2461	277	2184	787.5
OTH LIAB:DEFER'D I/E-OBS	0	0	0	0.0
OTH LIAB:ALL OTHER	8792	8355	437	5.2
OTHER LIABILITIES	11934	11438	496	4.3
COMMON STOCK & SURPLUS	5000	5000	0	0.0
RETAINED EARNINGS	23324	20481	2843	13.9
TOTAL EQUITY	28324	25481	2843	11.2
TOTAL LIAB & EQUITY	496301	454329	41972	9.2
TOTAL EARNING ASSETS	463247	414272	48974	11.8
TOTAL INT-BEAR LIAB	409874	373819	36055	9.6

STATEMENT OF INCOME - DETAIL
Dollars in Thousands

	1/02 - 12/02 ACTUAL	1/01 - 12/01 ACTUAL	DIFFERENCE	PERCENT
INTEREST INCOME:				
SHORT-TERM TREASURIES	3098	2916	181	6.2
LONG-TERM TREASURIES	3363	3062	300	9.8
US AGENCY SECURITIES	606	578	28	4.9
CMO CLASS B	0	0	0	0.0
OUR SECURITIZED MTG LOANS	0	0	0	0.0
ASSET BACKED SECURITIES	606	578	28	4.9
TAX EXEMPTS	332	540	-208	-38.5
OTHER SECURITIES	332	308	24	7.8
FHLB STOCK	0	396	-396	-100.0
INT RTE CONTRACTS-SWAPS	0	0	0	0.0
INT RTE CONTRACTS-OPTIONS	0	0	0	0.0
ALL OTHER SECURITIES	664	1244	-580	-46.6
TOTAL SECURITIES	7730	7800	-70	-0.9
TERM FED FUNDS SOLD	0	0	0	0.0
OVERNIGHT FED FUNDS SOLD	1432	1072	360	33.6
TRADING ACCOUNT	0	0	0	0.0
SHORT-TERM INVESTMENTS	1432	1072	360	33.6
COM'L PARTIC PURCH-FIXED	0	0	0	0.0
DIRECT COM'L LOANS-FIXED	4540	4352	189	4.3
PART PUR - REQ'D-FIXED	0	0	0	0.0
PART SOLD - REQ'D-FIXED	0	0	0	0.0
COMML LOANS-FIXED OPTION	0	0	0	0.0
COMMERCIAL LOANS-FIXED	4540	4352	189	4.3
COM'L PARTIC PURCH-FLOAT	0	0	0	0.0
COMMERCIAL LOANS-FLOAT	5728	5586	142	2.5
COMMERCIAL LOANS-FLOAT	5728	5586	142	2.5
MORTGAGE LOANS-FIXED	3198	2787	411	14.7
MORTGAGE LOANS-ADJ	3118	2765	353	12.8
HOME EQUITY LOANS	1664	1401	263	18.8
CONSUMER LOANS	8686	6850	1836	26.8
CREDIT CARD LOANS	5213	4640	573	12.3
AUTO LOANS	248	210	38	17.9
TOTAL LOANS	32396	28591	3805	13.3
TOTAL INTEREST INCOME	41558	37463	4095	10.9

STATEMENT OF INCOME - DETAIL
Dollars in Thousands

	1/03 - 12/03 FORECAST	1/02 - 12/02 ACTUAL	DIFFERENCE	PERCENT
INTEREST INCOME:				
SHORT-TERM TREASURIES	3901	3098	803	25.9
LONG-TERM TREASURIES	3574	3363	211	6.3
US AGENCY SECURITIES	843	606	237	39.1
CMO CLASS B	622	0	622	0.0
OUR SECURITIZED MTG LOANS	0	0	0	0.0
ASSET BACKED SECURITIES	1465	606	859	141.7
TAX EXEMPTS	211	332	-121	-36.5
OTHER SECURITIES	410	332	78	23.4
FHLB STOCK	0	0	0	0.0
INT RTE CONTRACTS-SWAPS	0	0	0	0.0
INT RTE CONTRACTS-OPTIONS	0	0	0	0.0
ALL OTHER SECURITIES	620	664	-44	-6.6
TOTAL SECURITIES	9560	7730	1830	23.7
TERM FED FUNDS SOLD	0	0	0	0.0
OVERNIGHT FED FUNDS SOLD	1370	1432	-61	-4.3
TRADING ACCOUNT	408	0	408	0.0
SHORT-TERM INVESTMENTS	1778	1432	347	24.2
COM'L PARTIC PURCH-FIXED	0	0	0	0.0
DIRECT COM'L LOANS-FIXED	4992	4540	451	9.9
PART PUR - REQ'D-FIXED	0	0	0	0.0
PART SOLD - REQ'D-FIXED	0	0	0	0.0
COMML LOANS-FIXED OPTION	0	0	0	0.0
COMMERCIAL LOANS-FIXED	4992	4540	451	9.9
COM'L PARTIC PURCH-FLOAT	0	0	0	0.0
COMMERCIAL LOANS-FLOAT	5917	5728	189	3.3
COMMERCIAL LOANS-FLOAT	5917	5728	189	3.3
MORTGAGE LOANS-FIXED	3097	3198	-101	-3.1
MORTGAGE LOANS-ADJ	3273	3118	155	5.0
HOME EQUITY LOANS	1778	1664	114	6.9
CONSUMER LOANS	9399	8686	713	8.2
CREDIT CARD LOANS	6250	5213	1037	19.9
AUTO LOANS	344	248	96	38.6
TOTAL LOANS	35050	32396	2654	8.2
TOTAL INTEREST INCOME	46389	41558	4831	11.6

STATEMENT OF INCOME - DETAIL
Dollars in Thousands

	1/02 - 12/02 ACTUAL	1/01 - 12/01 ACTUAL	DIFFERENCE	PERCENT
INTEREST EXPENSE:				
INTEREST-BEAR CHECKING	3247	2860	388	13.6
REGULAR SAVINGS	1971	1753	218	12.4
IBC & SAVINGS	5219	4613	606	13.1
MMDAs	6815	5606	1210	21.6
SMALL CDs	2241	1931	311	16.1
LARGE CDs	7277	7161	116	1.6
PUBLIC CDs	2970	3029	-59	-2.0
OTHER CDS	223	214	10	4.6
INT RTE CONTRACTS-SWAPS	0	0	0	0.0
OTHER CDs	223	214	10	4.6
TOTAL CERTIFICATES	12712	12335	377	3.1
TREASURY, TAX & LOAN	151	167	-16	-9.4
REPOS	13	19	-6	29.1
FED FUNDS PURCHASE	83	95	-11	11.8
SHORT-TERM BOR FUNDS	248	281	-32	11.6
LONG-TERM DEBT	0	0	0	0.0
FHLB ADVANCES	0	0	0	0.0
LONG-TERM DEBT	0	0	0	0.0
TOTAL INTEREST EXPENSE	24994	22834	2160	9.5
NET INTEREST INCOME	16563	14629	1935	13.2
PROVISION FOR LOAN LOSS	1831	1612	219	13.6
NET INT INCOME AFTER PROV	14732	13016	1716	13.2
SERVICE CHARGES	1558	1372	186	13.6
OTHER INCOME	1537	1492	45	3.0
GAIN(LOSS) ON SECURITIES	0	0	0	0.0
TOTAL NON-INTEREST INC	3095	2864	231	8.1
SALARIES & BENEFITS	6636	5724	912	15.9
OCCUPANCY, FURN & EQUIP	1752	1495	256	17.1
PROMOTION EXPENSE	636	575	61	10.5
FDIC INSURANCE EXPENSE	0	0	0	0.0
DATA PROCESSING EXPENSE	1786	1584	202	12.8
FINANCING & HEDGING EXP	0	0	0	0.0
OTHER OPERATING EXPENSE	1871	1676	195	11.6
TOTAL NON-INTEREST EXP	12681	11055	1626	14.7
NET INCOME BEFORE TAXES	5147	4826	321	6.6
STATE TAXES	257	241	16	6.6
FEDERAL TAXES	1550	1375	174	12.7
INCOME TAXES	1807	1617	190	11.8
NET INCOME	3340	3209	130	4.1

STATEMENT OF INCOME - DETAIL
Dollars in Thousands

	1/03 - 12/03 FORECAST	1/02 - 12/02 ACTUAL	DIFFERENCE	PERCENT
INTEREST EXPENSE:				
INTEREST-BEAR CHECKING	3584	3247	337	10.4
REGULAR SAVINGS	2127	1971	155	7.9
IBC & SAVINGS	5711	5219	492	9.4
MMDAs	7160	6815	345	5.1
SMALL CDs	2526	2241	285	12.7
LARGE CDs	7631	7277	354	4.9
PUBLIC CDs	3505	2970	335	18.0
OTHER CDS	246	223	23	10.3
INT RTE CONTRACTS-SWAPS	0	0	0	0.0
OTHER CDs	246	223	23	10.3
TOTAL CERTIFICATES	13908	12712	1196	9.4
TREASURY, TAX & LOAN	138	151	-13	-8.8
REPOS	37	13	23	172.9
FED FUNDS PURCHASED	76	83	-8	-9.5
SHORT-TERM BOR FUNDS	250	248	2	0.9
LONG-TERM DEBT	0	0	0	0.0
FHLB ADVANCES	0	0	0	0.0
LONG-TERM DEBT	0	0	0	0.0
TOTAL INTEREST EXPENSE	27030	24994	2036	8.1
NET INTEREST INCOME	19359	16563	2795	16.9
PROVISION FOR LOAN LOSS	1489	1831	-342	-18.7
NET INT INCOME AFTER PROV	17870	14732	3138	21.3
SERVICE CHARGES	1726	1558	167	10.7
OTHER INCOME	1658	1537	121	7.9
GAIN(LOSS) ON SECURITIES	0	0	0	0.0
TOTAL NON-INTEREST INC	3384	3095	288	9.3
SALARIES & BENEFITS	7782	6636	1146	17.3
OCCUPANCY, FURN & EQUIP	1907	1752	155	8.8
PROMOTION EXPENSE	630	636	-6	-0.9
FDIC INSURANCE EXPENSE	842	0	842	0.0
DATA PROCESSING EXPENSE	1906	1786	119	6.7
FINANCING & HEDGING EXP	0	0	0	0.0
OTHER OPERATING EXPENSE	1662	1871	-209	-11.2
TOTAL NON-INTEREST EXP	14728	12681	2047	16.1
NET INCOME BEFORE TAXES	6525	514	1379	26.8
STATE TAXES	326	257	69	26.8
FEDERAL TAXES	2036	1550	487	31.4
INCOME TAXES	2362	1807	555	30.7
NET INCOME	4163	3340	823	24.6

Appendix B

Monthly Financial Reports
for Years
2000 and 2001

Page

ENDING STATEMENT OF CONDITION - DETAIL
2000 ACTUAL

	JAN	FEB	MAR	APR	MAY	JUN	JUL	AUG	SEP	OCT	NOV	DEC
ASSETS:												
CASH, RESERVES & DUE FROM	11977	18056	6944	13096	12053	18208	12136	13319	12278	13434	7395	13557
ITEMS IN PROCESS	12477	11784	12652	11951	12834	12135	13019	12325	13211	12518	13407	12714
CASH, FLOAT & RESERVES	24454	29840	19596	25048	24887	30344	25155	25644	25490	25951	20801	26271
SHORT-TERM TREASURIES	30673	31037	31406	31779	32157	32539	32926	33317	33712	34112	34517	34927
LONG-TERM TREASURIES	32800	33100	33550	33800	34325	34775	35325	35850	35950	36075	36700	37050
US AGENCY SECURITIES	4063	4020	3977	3933	3889	3845	3800	3755	4210	4164	4117	4070
CMO CLASS B	0	0	0	0		0	0	0	0	0	0	0
OUR SECURITIZED MTG LOANS	0	0	0	0	0	0	0	0	0	0	0	0
ASSET BACKED SECURITIES	4063	4020	3977	3933	3889	3845	3800	3755	4210	4164	4117	4070
TAX EXEMPTS	10300	9950	9900	9900	9750	9800	9600	9550	9500	9100	8950	8650
OTHER SECURITIES	2108	2408	2408	2408	2408	2408	2408	2608	2608	2608	2608	2608
FHLB STOCK	0	0	0	0	0	0	0	0	0	0	0	0
INT RTE CONTRACTS-SWAPS	0	0	0	0	0	0	0	0	0	0	0	0
INT RTE CONTRACTS-OPTIONS	0	0	0	0	0	0	0	0	0	0	0	0
ALL OTHER SECURITIES	12408	12358	12308	12308	12158	12208	12008	12158	12108	11708	11558	11258
TOTAL SECURITIES	79944	80515	81241	81820	82529	83367	84059	85080	85980	86059	86892	87305
TERM FED FUNDS SOLD	0	0	0	0	0	0	0	0	0	0	0	0
OVERNIGHT FED FUNDS SOLD	12460	5475	11837	10223	9599	2193	6636	5656	9471	11098	14965	10220
TRADING ACCOUNT	0	0	0	0	0	0	0	0	0	0	0	0
SHORT-TERM INVESTMENTS	12460	5475	11837	10223	9599	2193	6636	5656	9471	11098	14965	10220
COM'L PARTIC PURCH-FIXED	0	0	0	0	0	0	0	0	0	0	0	0
DIRECT COM'L LOANS-FIXED	35414	35854	36299	36749	37205	37666	38133	38605	39082	39565	40054	40153
PART PUR - REQ'D-FIXED	0	0	0	0	0	0	0	0	0	0	0	0
PART SOLD - REQ'D-FIXED	0	0	0	0	0	0	0	0	0	0	0	0
COM'L LNS-OPTION CONTRACT	0	0	0	0	0	0	0	0	0	0	0	0
COMMERCIAL LOANS-FIXED	35414	35854	36299	36749	37205	37666	38133	38605	39082	39565	40054	40153
COM'L PARTIC PURCH-FLOAT	0	0	0	0	0	0	0	0	0	0	0	0
DIRECT COM'L LNS-FLOAT	41506	1999	2497	3000	3509	4024	4545	5072	5604	6143	6688	7239
COMMERCIAL LOANS-FLOAT	41506	1999	2497	3000	3509	4024	4545	5072	5604	6143	6688	7239
MORTGAGE LOANS-FIXED	22716	2897	3080	3264	3449	3636	3825	4015	4206	4399	4594	4790
MORTGAGE LOANS-ADJ	22990	3271	3554	3841	4132	4426	4723	5024	5329	5638	5950	6266
HOME EQUITY LOANS	10142	0218	0295	0372	0450	0529	0608	0688	0768	0849	0930	1013
CONSUMER LOANS	50709	1410	2119	2836	3562	4297	4441	4594	4656	4728	4809	4899
CREDIT CARD LOANS	21302	509	1719	1930	2144	2360	2578	2798	3020	3244	3471	3700
AUTO LOANS	1361	1378	1396	1413	1431	1449	1468	1486	1505	1524	1544	1563
TOTAL LOANS	206140	8535	0958	3407	5884	8388	0321	2282	4171	6090	8039	9622
RESERVE FOR LOAN LOSSES	-3575	3618	3647	3683	3720	3758	3791	3820	3849	3878	3907	3933
NET LOANS	202565	4917	7311	9723	2163	4630	6530	8461	0322	2213	4132	5688
PROPERTY & EQUIPMENT	8247	8279	8311	8344	8377	8409	8442	8475	8509	8542	8575	8609
OREO & FORECLOSED ASSETS	496	507	518	530	541	553	565	577	589	601	614	619
OTHER ASSETS	5416	6031	6638	5441	6055	6689	5569	6213	6862	5648	6311	6989
TOTAL OTHER ASSETS	14158	4817	5468	4315	4972	5651	4576	5265	5960	4792	5500	6217
TOTAL ASSETS	333582	335564	335452	341129	344151	346185	346956	350107	357223	360113	362291	365702

ENDING STATEMENT OF CONDITION - DETAIL
2001 ACTUAL

	JAN	FEB	MAR	APR	MAY	JUN	JUL	AUG	SEP	OCT	NOV	DEC
ASSETS:												
CASH, RESERVES & DUE FROM	10079	10152	10223	10293	10365	10437	10510	10583	10658	10733	10810	10884
ITEMS IN PROCESS	13199	3286	3379	3477	3576	3676	3777	3879	3982	4086	4191	4303
CASH, FLOAT & RESERVES	23277	3437	3602	3770	3941	4113	4287	4462	4640	4819	5000	5188
SHORT-TERM TREASURIES	35456	4943	5408	5917	5248	4572	4707	6810	6186	6638	7076	9373
LONG-TERM TREASURIES	37350	7600	7700	7550	7550	8150	8350	8750	8800	8700	8900	9400
US AGENCY SECURITIES	4030	3989	4649	4606	4563	4520	4477	4433	4889	4843	4796	4750
CMO CLASS B	0	0	0	0	0	0	0	0	0	0	0	0
OUR SECURITIZED MTG LOANS	0	0	0	0	0	0	0	0	0	0	0	0
ASSET BACKED SECURITIES	4030	3989	4649	4606	4563	4520	4477	4433	4889	4843	4796	4750
TAX EXEMPTS	8450	8050	7800	7350	7100	7050	6850	6750	6500	6450	6050	5750
OTHER SECURITIES	2608	2708	2708	2708	2708	2708	2908	2908	2908	2908	2908	2908
FHLB STOCK	5000	0	0	5000	5044	5098	5093	0	5000	5031	5035	0
INT RTE CONTRACTS-SWAPS	0	0	0	0	0	0	0	0	0	0	0	0
INT RTE CONTRACTS-OPTIONS	0	0	0	0	0	0	0	0	0	0	0	0
ALL OTHER SECURITIES	16058	10758	10508	15058	14852	14856	14851	9658	14408	14389	13993	8658
TOTAL SECURITIES	92893	87290	88265	93131	92213	92098	92385	89651	94282	94569	94766	92181
TERM FED FUNDS SOLD	0	0	0	0	0	0	0	0	0	0	0	0
OVERNIGHT FED FUNDS SOLD	8156	14207	12461	9868	10969	11297	12535	15574	11779	13397	13522	16363
TRADING ACCOUNT	0	0	0	0	0	0	0	0	0	0	0	0
SHORT-TERM INVESTMENTS	8156	14207	12461	9868	10969	11297	12535	15574	11779	13397	13522	16363
COM'L PARTIC PURCH-FIXED	0	0	0	0	0	0	0	0	0	0	0	0
DIRECT COM'L LOANS-FIXED	40217	40339	40662	40989	41317	41649	41982	42318	42657	42998	43342	43688
PART PUR - REQ'D-FIXED	0	0	0	0	0	0	0	0	0	0	0	0
PART SOLD - REQ'D-FIXED	0	0	0	0	0	0	0	0	0	0	0	0
COM'L LNS-OPTION CONTRACT	0	0	0	0	0	0	0	0	0	0	0	0
COMMERCIAL LOANS-FIXED	40217	40339	40662	40989	41317	41649	41982	42318	42657	42998	43342	43688
COM'L PARTIC PURCH-FLOAT	0	0	0	0	0	0	0	0	0	0	0	0
DIRECT COM'L LNS-FLOAT	47640	48044	48452	48863	49278	49696	50117	50542	50970	51402	51837	52276
COMMERCIAL LOANS-FLOAT	47640	48044	48452	48863	49278	49696	50117	50542	50970	51402	51837	52276
MORTGAGE LOANS-FIXED	24798	25107	25419	25736	26056	26380	26708	27041	27377	27718	28063	28072
MORTGAGE LOANS-ADJ	26582	26902	27225	27553	27884	28220	28560	28903	29251	29603	29959	30320
HOME EQUITY LOANS	11178	11345	11515	11688	11863	12041	12221	12404	12590	12779	12970	13165
CONSUMER LOANS	55565	56239	56922	57613	58312	59020	59736	60461	61195	61937	62689	63450
CREDIT CARD LOANS	23931	24164	24399	24637	24877	25120	25365	25612	25861	26113	26368	26625
AUTO LOANS	1583	1603	1624	1644	1665	1686	1708	1729	1751	1774	1796	1819
TOTAL LOANS	231493	33743	36219	38723	41253	43811	46397	49011	51653	54324	57025	59414
RESERVE FOR LOAN LOSSES	-3982	-4020	-4063	-4106	-4150	-4194	-4238	-4283	-4328	-4374	-4421	-4462
NET LOANS	227512	29723	32156	34617	37103	39617	42159	44728	47325	49950	52604	54952
PROPERTY & EQUIPMENT	8654	8700	8746	8792	8839	8885	8932	8979	9027	9074	9122	9170
OREO & FORECLOSED ASSETS	623	628	636	645	653	662	671	680	688	697	706	715
OTHER ASSETS	5701	6313	6958	5774	6513	7246	5836	6474	7126	5920	6588	7226
TOTAL OTHER ASSETS	14978	15641	16341	15211	16005	16794	15439	16133	16841	15692	16416	17112
TOTAL ASSETS	366817	370298	372824	376597	380232	383919	386804	390548	394867	398428	402309	405796

ENDING STATEMENT OF CONDITION - DETAIL
2000 ACTUAL

	JAN	FEB	MAR	APR	MAY	JUN	JUL	AUG	SEP	OCT	NOV	DEC
LIABILITIES & CAPITAL:												
BUSINESS DEMAND	30292	30538	30665	30855	31046	31240	31437	31635	31836	32039	32245	32413
PUBLIC DEMAND	6241	6249	6249	6252	6256	6258	6260	6271	6276	6281	6287	6327
DEMAND DEPOSITS	36532	36787	36914	37107	37302	37498	37697	37906	38112	38320	38532	38741
INTEREST-BEAR CHECKING	47713	48221	48735	49254	49779	50310	50846	51388	51936	52489	53049	53614
REGULAR SAVINGS	26980	27244	27512	27782	28054	28330	28608	28889	29172	29458	29747	30039
IBC & SAVINGS	74692	75466	76247	77036	77834	78640	79454	80277	81108	81948	82796	83653
MMDAs	63949	64728	65516	66314	67121	67939	68766	69603	70450	71308	72176	73055
SMALL CDs	22070	22235	22400	22567	22734	22904	23074	23246	23418	23593	23768	23945
LARGE CDs	65427	66116	66812	67516	68228	68946	69673	70407	71148	71898	72655	73421
PUBLIC CDs	31203	31244	31245	31262	31279	31289	31302	31355	31378	31403	31435	31637
OTHER CDS	2200	2218	2237	2255	2274	2292	2311	2330	2349	2369	2388	2408
INT RTE CONTRACTS-SWAPS	0	0	0	0	0	0	0	0	0	0	0	0
OTHER CDs	2200	2218	2237	2255	2274	2292	2311	2330	2349	2369	2388	2408
TOTAL CERTIFICATES	120900	21813	22694	23599	24514	25431	26360	27337	28294	29262	30247	31410
TOTAL DEPOSITS	296074	98793	01371	04056	06772	09508	12277	15123	17964	20837	23751	26860
TREASURY, TAX & LOAN	3456	3474	3491	3509	3527	3545	3564	3582	3600	3619	3638	3656
REPOS	4000	3000	0	3000	3000	2000	0	0	4000	4000	3000	3000
FED FUNDS PURCHASED	1000	1000	1000	1000	1000	1000	1000	1000	1000	1000	1000	1000
SHORT-TERM BOR FUNDS	8456	7474	4491	7509	7527	6545	4564	4582	8600	8619	7638	7656
LONG-TERM DEBT	0	0	0	0	0	0	0	0	0	0	0	0
FHLB ADVANCES	0	0	0	0	0	0	0	0	0	0	0	0
LONG-TERM DEBT	0	0	0	0	0	0	0	0	0	0	0	0
OTH LIAB:ACCR INC TAXES	2481	2481	2481	2481	2481	2481	2481	2481	2481	2481	2481	2481
OTH LIAB:ACCR DIVID PAY	0	0	295	0	0	295	0	0	295	0	0	295
OTH LIAB:ACCR INT PAY	182	167	173	165	174	175	189	198	200	212	210	224
OTH LIAB:DEFER'D I/E-OBS	0	0	0	0	0	0	0	0	0	0	0	0
OTH LIAB:ALL OTHER	6209	6256	6304	6352	6400	6447	6495	6543	6591	6639	6687	6735
OTHER LIABILITIES	8871	8904	9253	8997	9054	9398	9165	9222	9566	9332	9377	9735
COMMON STOCK & SURPLUS	5000	5000	5000	5000	5000	5000	5000	5000	5000	5000	5000	5000
RETAINED EARNINGS	15181	15394	15337	15565	15798	15734	15951	16180	16092	16325	16524	16452
TOTAL EQUITY	20181	20394	20337	20565	20798	20734	20951	21180	21092	21325	21524	21452
TOTAL LIAB & EQUITY	333582	335564	335452	341129	344151	346185	346956	350107	357223	360113	362291	365702
TOTAL EARNING ASSETS	298545	294526	304035	305450	308012	303948	311016	313018	319623	323248	329896	327147
TOTAL INT-BEAR LIAB	267998	269480	268949	274459	276997	278555	279143	281799	288453	291136	292857	295775

ENDING STATEMENT OF CONDITION - DETAIL
2001 ACTUAL

	JAN	FEB	MAR	APR	MAY	JUN	JUL	AUG	SEP	OCT	NOV	DEC
LIABILITIES & CAPITAL:												
BUSINESS DEMAND	32525	32624	32750	32897	33045	33194	33344	33496	33649	33803	33958	34114
PUBLIC DEMAND	6375	6423	6472	6520	6570	6619	6669	6719	6770	6821	6873	6958
DEMAND DEPOSITS	38900	39047	39221	39417	39614	39813	40013	40215	40419	40624	40830	41073
INTEREST-BEAR CHECKING	54186	54763	55347	55937	56533	57135	57744	58360	58982	59610	60246	60888
REGULAR SAVINGS	30334	30632	30932	31236	31543	31852	32165	32480	32799	33121	33446	33774
IBC & SAVINGS	84520	85395	86279	87173	88075	88987	89909	90840	91781	92731	93692	94662
MMDAs	73945	74845	75756	76679	77612	78557	79514	80482	81462	82454	83458	84474
SMALL CDs	24122	24300	24479	24660	24842	25026	25210	25396	25584	25773	25963	25993
LARGE CDs	74194	74976	75765	76563	77370	78185	79009	79841	80682	81532	82391	83259
PUBLIC CDs	31876	32116	32358	32602	32848	33096	33346	33597	33850	34106	34363	34792
OTHER CDS	2437	2467	2497	2527	2558	2589	2620	2652	2684	2717	2750	2783
INT RTE CONTRACTS-SWAPS	0	0	0	0	0	0	0	0	0	0	0	0
OTHER CDs	2437	2467	2497	2527	2558	2589	2620	2652	2684	2717	2750	2783
TOTAL CERTIFICATES	132628	133858	135099	136353	137618	138895	140185	141487	142801	144128	145467	146827
TOTAL DEPOSITS	329993	333145	336356	339621	342920	346253	349621	353024	356462	359936	363447	367036
TREASURY, TAX & LOAN	3667	3677	3687	3698	3708	3719	3729	3740	3751	3761	3772	3782
REPOS	1000	1000	0	500	500	500	0	0	500	500	500	0
FED FUNDS PURCHASED	1000	1000	1000	1000	1000	1000	1000	1000	1000	1000	1000	1000
SHORT-TERM BOR FUNDS	5667	5677	4687	5198	5208	5219	4729	4740	5251	5261	5272	4782
LONG-TERM DEBT	0	0	0	0	0	0	0	0	0	0	0	0
FHLB ADVANCES	0	0	0	0	0	0	0	0	0	0	0	0
LONG-TERM DEBT	0	0	0	0	0	0	0	0	0	0	0	0
OTH LIAB:ACCR INC TAXES	2481	2481	2481	2481	2481	2481	2481	2481	2481	2481	2481	2481
OTH LIAB:ACCR DIVID PAY	0	0	305	0	0	305	0	0	305	0	0	305
OTH LIAB:ACCR INT PAY	237	222	256	257	274	267	271	265	254	263	255	264
OTH LIAB:DEFER'D I/E-OBS	0	0	0	0	0	0	0	0	0	0	0	0
OTH LIAB:ALL OTHER	6797	6859	6922	6984	7047	7109	7172	7235	7298	7361	7424	7487
OTHER LIABILITIES	9514	9562	9963	9723	9802	10162	9924	9981	10337	10105	10160	10537
COMMON STOCK & SURPLUS	5000	5000	5000	5000	5000	5000	5000	5000	5000	5000	5000	5000
RETAINED EARNINGS	16643	16913	16817	17055	17302	17286	17531	17803	17817	18126	18430	18441
TOTAL EQUITY	21643	21913	21817	22055	22302	22286	22531	22803	22817	23126	23430	23441
TOTAL LIAB & EQUITY	366817	370298	372824	376597	380232	383919	386804	390548	394867	398428	402309	405796
TOTAL EARNING ASSETS	332543	335240	336945	341721	344435	347207	351317	354235	357715	362291	365313	367958
TOTAL INT-BEAR LIAB	296759	299775	301822	305402	308514	311659	314337	317548	321294	324574	327888	330746

AVERAGE STATEMENT OF CONDITION - DETAIL
PERCENTAGE COMPOSITION
2000 ACTUAL

	JAN	FEB	MAR	APR	MAY	JUN	JUL	AUG	SEP	OCT	NOV	DEC
ASSETS:												
CASH, RESERVES & DUE FROM	3.8	3.8	3.0	3.0	3.7	3.7	3.7	3.0	3.6	2.9	2.9	2.9
ITEMS IN PROCESS	3.7	3.6	3.7	3.7	3.7	3.7	3.7	3.7	3.6	3.6	3.6	3.6
CASH, FLOAT & RESERVES	7.4	7.4	6.7	6.6	7.4	7.3	7.3	6.6	7.3	6.5	6.5	6.5
SHORT-TERM TREASURIES	9.3	9.3	9.4	9.4	9.4	9.5	9.5	9.6	9.5	9.6	9.6	9.6
LONG-TERM TREASURIES	10.0	9.9	10.0	10.0	10.0	10.1	10.2	10.3	10.2	10.1	10.2	10.2
US AGENCY SECURITIES	1.2	1.2	1.2	1.2	1.2	1.1	1.1	1.1	1.1	1.2	1.2	1.1
CMO CLASS B	0.0	0.0	0.0	0.0	0.0	0.0	0.0	0.0	0.0	0.0	0.0	0.0
OUR SECURITIZED MTG LOANS	0.0	0.0	0.0	0.0	0.0	0.0	0.0	0.0	0.0	0.0	0.0	0.0
ASSET BACKED SECURITIES	1.2	1.2	1.2	1.2	1.2	1.1	1.1	1.1	1.1	1.2	1.2	1.1
TAX EXEMPTS	3.1	3.0	3.0	2.9	2.9	2.9	2.8	2.8	2.7	2.6	2.5	2.4
OTHER SECURITIES	0.6	0.7	0.7	0.7	0.7	0.7	0.7	0.7	0.7	0.7	0.7	0.7
FHLB STOCK	0.0	0.0	0.0	0.0	0.0	0.0	0.0	0.0	0.0	0.0	0.0	0.0
INT RTE CONTRACTS-SWAPS	0.0	0.0	0.0	0.0	0.0	0.0	0.0	0.0	0.0	0.0	0.0	0.0
INT RTE CONTRACTS-OPTIONS	0.0	0.0	0.0	0.0	0.0	0.0	0.0	0.0	0.0	0.0	0.0	0.0
ALL OTHER SECURITIES	3.8	3.7	3.7	3.7	3.6	3.6	3.5	3.5	3.4	3.4	3.3	3.2
TOTAL SECURITIES	24.2	24.2	24.3	24.2	24.2	24.3	24.4	24.4	24.3	24.2	24.2	24.2
TERM FED FUNDS SOLD	0.0	0.0	0.0	0.0	0.0	0.0	0.0	0.0	0.0	0.0	0.0	0.0
OVERNIGHT FED FUNDS SOLD	2.6	2.6	2.4	2.7	1.9	1.5	1.2	1.9	1.6	2.5	2.5	2.5
TRADING ACCOUNT	0.0	0.0	0.0	0.0	0.0	0.0	0.0	0.0	0.0	0.0	0.0	0.0
SHORT-TERM INVESTMENTS	2.6	2.6	2.4	2.7	1.9	1.5	1.2	1.9	1.6	2.5	2.5	2.5
COM'L PARTIC PURCH-FIXED	0.0	0.0	0.0	0.0	0.0	0.0	0.0	0.0	0.0	0.0	0.0	0.0
DIRECT COM'L LOANS-FIXED	10.7	10.7	10.9	10.9	10.9	10.9	11.0	11.1	11.0	11.1	11.1	11.1
PART PUR - REQ'D-FIXED	0.0	0.0	0.0	0.0	0.0	0.0	0.0	0.0	0.0	0.0	0.0	0.0
PART SOLD - REQ'D-FIXED	0.0	0.0	0.0	0.0	0.0	0.0	0.0	0.0	0.0	0.0	0.0	0.0
COM'L LNS-OPTION CONTRACT	0.0	0.0	0.0	0.0	0.0	0.0	0.0	0.0	0.0	0.0	0.0	0.0
COMMERCIAL LOANS-FIXED	10.7	10.7	10.9	10.9	10.9	10.9	11.0	11.1	11.0	11.1	11.1	11.1
COM'L PARTIC PURCH-FLOAT	0.0	0.0	0.0	0.0	0.0	0.0	0.0	0.0	0.0	0.0	0.0	0.0
DIRECT COM'L LNS-FLOAT	12.6	12.6	12.7	12.7	12.7	12.8	12.9	12.9	12.9	12.9	13.0	13.0
COMMERCIAL LOANS-FLOAT	12.6	12.6	12.7	12.7	12.7	12.8	12.9	12.9	12.9	12.9	13.0	13.0
MORTGAGE LOANS-FIXED	6.9	6.9	6.9	6.9	6.9	6.9	6.9	6.9	6.9	6.9	6.9	6.9
MORTGAGE LOANS-ADJ	7.0	7.0	7.0	7.0	7.1	7.1	7.1	7.2	7.2	7.2	7.2	7.2
HOME EQUITY LOANS	3.1	3.1	3.1	3.1	3.1	3.1	3.1	3.1	3.0	3.0	3.0	3.0
CONSUMER LOANS	15.3	15.4	15.6	15.6	15.7	15.8	15.8	15.7	15.5	15.4	15.3	15.2
CREDIT CARD LOANS	6.5	6.5	6.5	6.5	6.5	6.5	6.5	6.5	6.5	6.5	6.5	6.5
AUTO LOANS	0.4	0.4	0.4	0.4	0.4	0.4	0.4	0.4	0.4	0.4	0.4	0.4
TOTAL LOANS	62.4	62.5	63.1	63.1	63.3	63.5	63.8	63.8	63.5	63.5	63.5	63.5
RESERVE FOR LOAN LOSSES	-1.1	-1.1	-1.1	-1.1	-1.1	-1.1	-1.1	-1.1	-1.1	-1.1	-1.1	-1.1
NET LOANS	61.3	61.4	62.1	62.0	62.2	62.4	62.7	62.8	62.4	62.4	62.5	62.4
PROPERTY & EQUIPMENT	2.5	2.5	2.5	2.5	2.5	2.5	2.5	2.4	2.4	2.4	2.4	2.4
OREO & FORECLOSED ASSETS	0.1	0.2	0.2	0.2	0.2	0.2	0.2	0.2	0.2	0.2	0.2	0.2
OTHER ASSETS	1.8	1.7	1.9	1.8	1.7	1.9	1.8	1.7	1.9	1.8	1.7	1.8
TOTAL OTHER ASSETS	4.5	4.4	4.6	4.4	4.3	4.5	4.4	4.3	4.4	4.3	4.2	4.4
TOTAL ASSETS	100.0	100.0	100.0	100.0	100.0	100.0	100.0	100.0	100.0	100.0	100.0	100.0

AVERAGE STATEMENT OF CONDITION - DETAIL
PERCENTAGE COMPOSITION
2001 ACTUAL

	JAN	FEB	MAR	APR	MAY	JUN	JUL	AUG	SEP	OCT	NOV	DEC
ASSETS:												
CASH, RESERVES & DUE FROM	3.3	2.8	2.8	2.7	2.7	2.7	2.7	2.7	2.7	2.7	2.7	2.7
ITEMS IN PROCESS	3.6	3.6	3.6	3.6	3.6	3.6	3.6	3.6	3.6	3.6	3.6	3.5
CASH, FLOAT & RESERVES	6.8	6.4	6.4	6.3	6.3	6.3	6.3	6.3	6.3	6.3	6.3	6.2
SHORT-TERM TREASURIES	9.7	9.6	9.5	9.6	9.5	9.2	9.0	9.2	9.3	9.2	9.3	9.5
LONG-TERM TREASURIES	10.2	10.2	10.2	10.1	10.0	10.0	10.0	10.0	9.9	9.8	9.7	9.7
US AGENCY SECURITIES	1.1	1.1	1.2	1.2	1.2	1.2	1.2	1.2	1.2	1.2	1.2	1.2
CMO CLASS B	0.0	0.0	0.0	0.0	0.0	0.0	0.0	0.0	0.0	0.0	0.0	0.0
OUR SECURITIZED MTG LOANS	0.0	0.0	0.0	0.0	0.0	0.0	0.0	0.0	0.0	0.0	0.0	0.0
ASSET BACKED SECURITIES	1.1	1.1	1.2	1.2	1.2	1.2	1.2	1.2	1.2	1.2	1.2	1.2
TAX EXEMPTS	2.4	2.3	2.1	2.0	1.9	1.9	1.8	1.8	1.7	1.6	1.6	1.5
OTHER SECURITIES	0.7	0.7	0.7	0.7	0.7	0.7	0.7	0.8	0.7	0.7	0.7	0.7
FHLB STOCK	0.7	0.0	0.0	0.7	0.7	0.7	0.7	0.0	0.6	0.6	0.6	0.0
INT RTE CONTRACTS-SWAPS	0.0	0.0	0.0	0.0	0.0	0.0	0.0	0.0	0.0	0.0	0.0	0.0
INT RTE CONTRACTS-OPTIONS	0.0	0.0	0.0	0.0	0.0	0.0	0.0	0.0	0.0	0.0	0.0	0.0
ALL OTHER SECURITIES	3.8	3.0	2.9	3.4	3.3	3.2	3.2	2.5	3.1	3.0	2.9	2.2
TOTAL SECURITIES	24.8	23.9	23.8	24.3	24.0	23.6	23.4	22.9	23.5	23.3	23.1	22.6
TERM FED FUNDS SOLD	0.0	0.0	0.0	0.0	0.0	0.0	0.0	0.0	0.0	0.0	0.0	0.0
OVERNIGHT FED FUNDS SOLD	1.6	3.1	3.0	2.5	2.9	3.1	3.2	3.8	3.0	3.2	3.4	3.8
TRADING ACCOUNT	0.0	0.0	0.0	0.0	0.0	0.0	0.0	0.0	0.0	0.0	0.0	0.0
SHORT-TERM INVESTMENTS	1.6	3.1	3.0	2.5	2.9	3.1	3.2	3.8	3.0	3.2	3.4	3.8
COM'L PARTIC PURCH-FIXED	0.0	0.0	0.0	0.0	0.0	0.0	0.0	0.0	0.0	0.0	0.0	0.0
DIRECT COM'L LOANS-FIXED	11.1	11.0	11.0	10.9	10.9	10.9	10.9	10.9	10.9	10.9	10.8	10.8
PART PUR - REQ'D-FIXED	0.0	0.0	0.0	0.0	0.0	0.0	0.0	0.0	0.0	0.0	0.0	0.0
PART SOLD - REQ'D-FIXED	0.0	0.0	0.0	0.0	0.0	0.0	0.0	0.0	0.0	0.0	0.0	0.0
COM'L LNS-OPTION CONTRACT	0.0	0.0	0.0	0.0	0.0	0.0	0.0	0.0	0.0	0.0	0.0	0.0
COMMERCIAL LOANS-FIXED	11.1	11.0	11.0	10.9	10.9	10.9	10.9	10.9	10.9	10.9	10.8	10.8
COM'L PARTIC PURCH-FLOAT	0.0	0.0	0.0	0.0	0.0	0.0	0.0	0.0	0.0	0.0	0.0	0.0
DIRECT COM'L LOANS-FLOAT	13.1	13.1	13.1	13.0	13.0	13.0	13.0	13.0	13.0	13.0	13.0	13.0
COMMERCIAL LOANS-FLOAT	13.1	13.1	13.1	13.0	13.0	13.0	13.0	13.0	13.0	13.0	13.0	13.0
MORTGAGE LOANS-FIXED	6.8	6.8	6.9	6.9	6.9	6.9	6.9	7.0	7.0	7.0	7.0	7.0
MORTGAGE LOANS-ADJ	7.3	7.3	7.3	7.3	7.4	7.4	7.4	7.4	7.4	7.5	7.5	7.5
HOME EQUITY LOANS	3.1	3.1	3.1	3.1	3.1	3.1	3.2	3.2	3.2	3.2	3.2	3.3
CONSUMER LOANS	15.2	15.3	15.3	15.4	15.4	15.4	15.5	15.5	15.6	15.6	15.6	15.7
CREDIT CARD LOANS	6.6	6.6	6.6	6.6	6.6	6.6	6.6	6.6	6.6	6.6	6.6	6.6
AUTO LOANS	0.4	0.4	0.4	0.4	0.4	0.4	0.4	0.4	0.4	0.4	0.4	0.4
TOTAL LOANS	63.5	63.5	63.6	63.7	63.8	63.8	64.0	64.1	64.1	64.1	64.2	64.3
RESERVE FOR LOAN LOSSES	-1.1	-1.1	-1.1	-1.1	-1.1	-1.1	-1.1	-1.1	-1.1	-1.1	-1.1	-1.1
NET LOANS	62.4	62.4	62.6	62.6	62.7	62.7	62.9	63.0	63.0	63.1	63.1	63.2
PROPERTY & EQUIPMENT	2.4	2.4	2.4	2.4	2.3	2.3	2.3	2.3	2.3	2.3	2.3	2.3
OREO & FORECLOSED ASSETS	0.2	0.2	0.2	0.2	0.2	0.2	0.2	0.2	0.2	0.2	0.2	0.2
OTHER ASSETS	1.7	1.6	1.8	1.7	1.6	1.8	1.7	1.6	1.7	1.7	1.6	1.7
TOTAL OTHER ASSETS	4.3	4.2	4.3	4.2	4.1	4.3	4.2	4.1	4.2	4.1	4.0	4.2
TOTAL ASSETS	100.0	100.0	100.0	100.0	100.0	100.0	100.0	100.0	100.0	100.0	100.0	100.0

AVERAGE STATEMENT OF CONDITION - DETAIL
PERCENTAGE COMPOSITION
2000 ACTUAL

	JAN	FEB	MAR	APR	MAY	JUN	JUL	AUG	SEP	OCT	NOV	DEC
LIABILITIES & CAPITAL:												
BUSINESS DEMAND	9.2	9.1	9.2	9.1	9.1	9.1	9.1	9.1	9.0	9.0	9.0	9.0
PUBLIC DEMAND	1.9	1.9	1.9	1.9	1.8	1.8	1.8	1.8	1.8	1.8	1.8	1.7
DEMAND DEPOSITS	11.1	11.0	11.1	11.0	11.0	10.9	10.9	10.9	10.8	10.8	10.8	10.7
INTEREST-BEAR CHECKING	14.4	14.4	14.6	14.6	14.6	14.6	14.7	14.7	14.7	14.7	14.8	14.8
REGULAR SAVINGS	8.2	8.1	8.2	8.2	8.2	8.2	8.3	8.3	8.3	8.3	8.3	8.3
IBC & SAVINGS	22.6	22.6	22.8	22.8	22.8	22.9	23.0	23.0	22.9	23.0	23.0	23.1
MMDAs	19.3	19.7	19.6	19.6	19.7	19.8	19.9	20.0	19.9	20.0	20.1	20.1
SMALL CDs	6.7	6.7	6.7	6.7	6.7	6.7	6.7	6.7	6.6	6.6	6.6	6.6
LARGE CDs	19.8	19.9	20.0	20.0	20.0	20.1	20.2	20.2	20.1	20.2	20.2	20.3
PUBLIC CDs	9.5	9.4	9.4	9.3	9.2	9.1	9.1	9.0	8.9	8.8	8.8	8.7
OTHER CDS	0.7	0.7	0.7	0.7	0.7	0.7	0.7	0.7	0.7	0.7	0.7	0.7
INT RTE CONTRCTS-SWAPS	0.0	0.0	0.0	0.0	0.0	0.0	0.0	0.0	0.0	0.0	0.0	0.0
OTHER CDs	0.7	0.7	0.7	0.7	0.7	0.7	0.7	0.7	0.7	0.7	0.7	0.7
TOTAL CERTIFICATES	36.7	36.7	36.8	36.6	36.6	36.6	36.6	36.6	36.3	36.3	36.3	36.3
TOTAL DEPOSITS	89.7	89.9	90.3	89.9	90.0	90.1	90.4	90.5	90.0	90.0	90.2	90.2
TREASURY, TAX & LOAN	0.5	0.5	0.5	0.5	0.5	0.5	0.5	0.5	0.5	0.5	0.5	0.5
REPOS	0.6	0.5	0.0	0.4	0.4	0.3	0.0	0.0	0.6	0.6	0.4	0.4
FED FUNDS PURCHASED	0.3	0.3	0.3	0.3	0.3	0.3	0.3	0.3	0.3	0.3	0.3	0.3
SHORT-TERM BOR FUNDS	1.4	1.3	0.8	1.3	1.3	1.1	0.8	0.8	1.4	1.4	1.2	1.2
LONG-TERM DEBT	0.0	0.0	0.0	0.0	0.0	0.0	0.0	0.0	0.0	0.0	0.0	0.0
FHLB ADVANCES	0.0	0.0	0.0	0.0	0.0	0.0	0.0	0.0	0.0	0.0	0.0	0.0
LONG-TERM DEBT	0.0	0.0	0.0	0.0	0.0	0.0	0.0	0.0	0.0	0.0	0.0	0.0
OTH LIAB:ACCR INC TAXES	0.8	0.7	0.7	0.7	0.7	0.7	0.7	0.7	0.7	0.7	0.7	0.7
OTH LIAB:ACCR DIVID PAY	0.0	0.0	0.0	0.0	0.0	0.0	0.0	0.0	0.0	0.0	0.0	0.0
OTH LIAB:ACCR INT PAY	0.1	0.1	0.1	0.1	0.0	0.1	0.1	0.1	0.1	0.1	0.1	0.1
OTH LIAB:DEFER'D I/E-OBS	0.0	0.0	0.0	0.0	0.0	0.0	0.0	0.0	0.0	0.0	0.0	0.0
OTH LIAB:ALL OTHER	1.9	1.9	1.9	1.9	1.9	1.9	1.9	1.9	1.9	1.9	1.9	1.9
OTHER LIABILITIES	2.7	2.7	2.7	2.7	2.7	2.7	2.7	2.7	2.7	2.7	2.6	2.6
COMMON STOCK & SURPLUS	1.5	1.5	1.5	1.5	1.5	1.5	1.5	1.4	1.4	1.4	1.4	1.4
RETAINED EARNINGS	4.6	4.6	4.6	4.6	4.6	4.6	4.6	4.6	4.6	4.6	4.6	4.6
TOTAL EQUITY	6.1	6.1	6.1	6.1	6.1	6.1	6.1	6.1	6.0	6.0	6.0	6.0
TOTAL LIAB & EQUITY	100.0	100.0	100.0	100.0	100.0	100.0	100.0	100.0	100.0	100.0	100.0	100.0
TOTAL EARNING ASSETS	89.1	89.3	89.8	90.0	89.4	89.3	89.3	90.2	89.4	90.2	90.3	90.1
TOTAL INT-BEAR LIAB	80.1	80.2	80.0	80.2	80.3	80.3	80.3	80.4	80.5	80.6	80.6	80.7

AVERAGE STATEMENT OF CONDITION - DETAIL
PERCENTAGE COMPOSITION
2001 ACTUAL

	JAN	FEB	MAR	APR	MAY	JUN	JUL	AUG	SEP	OCT	NOV	DEC
LIABILITIES & CAPITAL:												
BUSINESS DEMAND	8.9	8.9	8.8	8.8	8.8	8.7	8.7	8.6	8.6	8.5	8.5	8.5
PUBLIC DEMAND	1.7	1.7	1.7	1.7	1.7	1.7	1.7	1.7	1.7	1.7	1.7	1.7
DEMAND DEPOSITS	10.7	10.6	10.6	10.5	10.5	10.4	10.4	10.4	10.3	10.3	10.2	10.2
INTEREST-BEAR CHECKING	14.8	14.9	14.9	14.9	14.9	14.9	15.0	15.0	15.0	15.0	15.0	15.1
REGULAR SAVINGS	8.3	8.3	8.3	8.3	8.3	8.3	8.4	8.4	8.4	8.4	8.4	8.4
IBC & SAVINGS	23.2	23.2	23.2	23.2	23.3	23.3	23.3	23.4	23.4	23.4	23.4	23.4
MMDAs	20.2	20.3	20.4	20.4	20.5	20.5	20.6	20.7	20.7	20.8	20.8	20.9
SMALL CDs	6.6	6.6	6.6	6.6	6.6	6.6	6.6	6.5	6.5	6.5	6.5	6.5
LARGE CDs	20.3	20.4	20.4	20.4	20.4	20.5	20.5	20.5	20.5	20.6	20.6	20.6
PUBLIC CDs	8.7	8.7	8.7	8.7	8.7	8.7	8.7	8.7	8.6	8.6	8.6	8.6
OTHER CDS	0.7	0.7	0.7	0.7	0.7	0.7	0.7	0.7	0.7	0.7	0.7	0.7
INT RTE CONTRCTS-SWAPS	0.0	0.0	0.0	0.0	0.0	0.0	0.0	0.0	0.0	0.0	0.0	0.0
OTHER CDs	0.7	0.7	0.7	0.7	0.7	0.7	0.7	0.7	0.7	0.7	0.7	0.7
TOTAL CERTIFICATES	36.4	36.4	36.5	36.4	36.4	36.4	36.4	36.4	36.4	36.4	36.4	36.4
TOTAL DEPOSITS	90.5	90.5	90.7	90.7	90.7	90.7	90.8	90.8	90.8	90.8	90.8	90.9
TREASURY, TAX & LOAN	0.5	0.5	0.5	0.5	0.5	0.5	0.5	0.5	0.5	0.5	0.5	0.5
REPOS	0.1	0.1	0.0	0.1	0.1	0.1	0.0	0.0	0.1	0.1	0.1	0.0
FED FUNDS PURCHASED	0.3	0.3	0.3	0.3	0.3	0.3	0.3	0.3	0.3	0.3	0.3	0.2
SHORT-TERM BOR FUNDS	0.9	0.9	0.8	0.8	0.8	0.8	0.7	0.7	0.8	0.8	0.8	0.7
LONG-TERM DEBT	0.0	0.0	0.0	0.0	0.0	0.0	0.0	0.0	0.0	0.0	0.0	0.0
FHLB ADVANCES	0.0	0.0	0.0	0.0	0.0	0.0	0.0	0.0	0.0	0.0	0.0	0.0
LONG-TERM DEBT	0.0	0.0	0.0	0.0	0.0	0.0	0.0	0.0	0.0	0.0	0.0	0.0
OTH LIAB:ACCR INC TAXES	0.7	0.7	0.7	0.7	0.7	0.7	0.6	0.6	0.6	0.6	0.6	0.6
OTH LIAB:ACCR DIVID PAY	0.0	0.0	0.0	0.0	0.0	0.0	0.0	0.0	0.0	0.0	0.0	0.0
OTH LIAB:ACCR INT PAY	0.1	0.1	0.1	0.1	0.1	0.1	0.1	0.1	0.1	0.1	0.1	0.1
OTH LIAB:DEFER'D I/E-OBS	0.0	0.0	0.0	0.0	0.0	0.0	0.0	0.0	0.0	0.0	0.0	0.0
OTH LIAB:ALL OTHER	1.9	1.9	1.9	1.9	1.9	1.9	1.9	1.9	1.9	1.9	1.9	1.9
OTHER LIABILITIES	2.7	2.6	2.6	2.6	2.6	2.6	2.6	2.6	2.6	2.6	2.5	2.6
COMMON STOCK & SURPLUS	1.4	1.4	1.4	1.3	1.3	1.3	1.3	1.3	1.3	1.3	1.3	1.2
RETAINED EARNINGS	4.6	4.6	4.6	4.5	4.6	4.5	4.5	4.6	4.6	4.6	4.6	4.6
TOTAL EQUITY	5.9	5.9	5.9	5.9	5.9	5.9	5.8	5.9	5.8	5.8	5.8	5.8
TOTAL LIAB & EQUITY	100.0	100.0	100.0	100.0	100.0	100.0	100.0	100.0	100.0	100.0	100.0	100.0
TOTAL EARNING ASSETS	90.0	90.5	90.4	90.5	90.6	90.4	90.6	90.7	90.6	90.7	90.8	90.7
TOTAL INT-BEAR LIAB	80.7	80.8	80.8	80.9	81.0	81.1	81.1	81.2	81.2	81.3	81.4	81.4

STATEMENT OF INCOME - DETAIL
2000 ACTUAL

	JAN	FEB	MAR	APR	MAY	JUN	JUL	AUG	SEP	OCT	NOV	DEC
INTEREST INCOME:												
SHORT-TERM TREASURIES	153	143	153	149	159	162	177	186	189	204	206	222
LONG-TERM TREASURIES	283	282	282	282	283	285	286	289	289	288	289	290
US AGENCY SECURITIES	40	42	42	41	41	40	40	39	41	43	42	42
CMO CLASS B	0	0	0	0	0	0	0	0	0	0	0	0
OUR SECURITIZED MTG LOANS	0	0	0	0	0	0	0	0	0	0	0	
ASSET BACKED SECURITIES	40	42	42	41	41	40	40	39	41	43	42	42
TAX EXEMPTS	75	73	71	71	70	69	68	67	66	64	62	60
OTHER SECURITIES	20	21	22	22	22	22	22	23	24	24	24	24
FHLB STOCK	0	0	0	0	0	0	0	0	0	0	0	0
INT RTE CONTRACTS-SWAPS	0	0	0	0	0	0	0	0	0	0	0	0
INT RTE CONTRACTS-OPTIONS	0	0	0	0	0	0	0	0	0	0	0	
ALL OTHER SECURITIES	94	94	94	93	92	91	91	90	91	88	86	84
TOTAL SECURITIES	571	562	570	565	575	578	593	604	610	623	622	638
TERM FED FUNDS SOLD	0	0	0	0	0	0	0	0	0	0	0	0
OVERNIGHT FED FUNDS SOLD	48	48	43	52	39	31	26	45	39	61	63	67
TRADING ACCOUNT	0	0	0	0	0	0	0	0	0	0	0	0
SHORT-TERM INVESTMENTS	48	48	43	52	39	31	26	45	39	61	63	67
COM'L PARTIC PURCH-FIXED	0	0	0	0	0	0	0	0	0	0	0	0
DIRECT COM'L LOANS-FIXED	257	246	267	263	276	273	288	295	294	312	310	327
PART PUR - REQ'D-FIXED	0	0	0	0	0	0	0	0	0	0	0	0
PART SOLD - REQ'D-FIXED	0	0	0	0	0	0	0	0	0	0	0	0
COMML LNS-FIXED OPTION	0	0	0	0	0	0	0	0	0	0	0	0
COMMERCIAL LOANS-FIXED	257	246	267	263	276	273	288	295	294	312	310	327
COM'L PARTIC PURCH-FLOAT	0	0	0	0	0	0	0	0	0	0	0	0
COMMERCIAL LOANS-FLOAT	320	300	319	312	332	334	358	378	383	403	396	424
COMMERCIAL LOANS-FLOAT	320	300	319	312	332	334	358	378	383	403	396	424
MORTGAGE LOANS-FIXED	202	204	205	206	208	209	211	212	213	215	216	218
MORTGAGE LOANS-ADJ	171	162	175	172	180	176	184	187	184	193	190	201
HOME EQUITY LOANS	76	72	78	77	80	79	83	84	83	87	86	90
CONSUMER LOANS	374	359	391	388	410	407	429	434	426	445	436	458
CREDIT CARD LOANS	329	317	337	332	344	338	350	353	348	360	355	367
AUTO LOANS	10	10	11	11	12	12	12	13	13	13	13	14
TOTAL LOANS	1740	1670	1784	1760	1842	1828	1914	1957	1943	2029	2003	2100
TOTAL INTEREST INCOME	2359	2280	2397	2378	2455	2438	2534	2606	2592	2713	2688	2805

STATEMENT OF INCOME - DETAIL
2001 ACTUAL

	JAN	FEB	MAR	APR	MAY	JUN	JUL	AUG	SEP	OCT	NOV	DEC
INTEREST INCOME:												
SHORT-TERM TREASURIES	235	220	251	252	262	245	244	246	238	241	233	248
LONG-TERM TREASURIES	252	254	254	253	252	254	256	257	258	257	257	259
US AGENCY SECURITIES	44	44	47	50	49	49	48	48	49	51	50	50
CMO CLASS B	0	0	0	0	0	0	0	0	0	0	0	0
OUR SECURITIZED MTG LOANS	0	0	0	0	0	0	0	0	0	0	0	0
ASSET BACKED SECURITIES	44	44	47	50	49	49	48	48	49	51	50	50
TAX EXEMPTS	54	52	50	48	46	45	44	43	42	41	39	37
OTHER SECURITIES	24	25	25	25	25	25	26	27	27	27	27	27
FHLB STOCK	22	0	0	21	87	97	38	0	19	69	43	0
INT RTE CONTRACTS-SWAPS	0	0	0	0	0	0	0	0	0	0	0	0
INT RTE CONTRACTS-OPTIONS	0	0	0	0	0	0	0	0	0	0	0	0
ALL OTHER SECURITIES	99	77	75	94	158	167	108	70	88	136	109	64
TOTAL SECURITIES	631	594	627	650	721	715	656	620	633	685	649	620
TERM FED FUNDS SOLD	0	0	0	0	0	0	0	0	0	0	0	0
OVERNIGHT FED FUNDS SOLD	45	89	90	77	89	92	94	109	88	94	98	107
TRADING ACCOUNT	0	0	0	0	0	0	0	0	0	0	0	0
SHORT-TERM INVESTMENTS	45	89	90	77	89	92	94	109	88	94	98	107
COM'L PARTIC PURCH-FIXED	0	0	0	0	0	0	0	0	0	0	0	0
DIRECT COM'L LOANS-FIXED	341	343	347	354	360	365	369	371	373	375	376	377
PART PUR - REQ'D-FIXED	0	0	0	0	0	0	0	0	0	0	0	0
PART SOLD - REQ'D-FIXED	0	0	0	0	0	0	0	0	0	0	0	0
COMML LNS-FIXED OPTION	0	0	0	0	0	0	0	0	0		0	0
COMMERCIAL LOANS-FIXED	341	343	347	354	360	365	369	371	373	375	376	377
COM'L PARTIC PURCH-FLOAT	0	0	0	0	0	0	0	0	0	0	0	0
COMMERCIAL LOANS-FLOAT	434	407	475	474	494	474	483	475	454	473	461	481
COMMERCIAL LOANS-FLOAT	434	407	475	474	494	474	483	475	454	473	461	481
MORTGAGE LOANS-FIXED	219	220	223	226	228	231	234	236	239	242	244	246
MORTGAGE LOANS-ADJ	205	210	215	221	226	231	235	238	242	245	247	250
HOME EQUITY LOANS	106	108	110	112	114	116	118	120	121	123	125	126
CONSUMER LOANS	491	506	522	537	553	567	581	594	606	619	631	643
CREDIT CARD LOANS	368	343	378	372	387	381	396	401	396	411	395	411
AUTO LOANS	16	16	17	17	17	17	18	18	18	18	19	19
TOTAL LOANS	2180	2154	2287	2313	2380	2384	2433	2453	2449	2505	2499	2553
TOTAL INTEREST INCOME	2856	2836	3005	3040	3190	3191	3183	3183	3170	3285	3245	3280

STATEMENT OF INCOME - DETAIL
2000 ACTUAL

	JAN	FEB	MAR	APR	MAY	JUN	JUL	AUG	SEP	OCT	NOV	DEC
INTEREST EXPENSE:												
INTEREST-BEAR CHECKING	201	190	205	201	210	205	214	216	212	221	216	226
REGULAR SAVINGS	125	118	128	125	130	127	133	134	131	137	133	139
IBC & SAVINGS	326	308	333	325	340	332	347	350	343	358	350	365
MMDAs	315	300	314	314	344	353	368	373	380	407	412	454
SMALL CDs	108	102	110	106	110	108	113	114	111	116	113	118
LARGE CDs	411	376	388	369	392	398	434	459	467	500	497	534
PUBLIC CDs	197	178	182	172	181	181	196	206	207	219	216	230
OTHER CDS	12	12	12	12	13	12	13	13	13	14	14	14
INT RTE CONTRACTS-SWAPS	0	0	0	0	0	0	0	0	0	0	0	0
OTHER CDs	12	12	12	12	13	12	13	13	13	14	14	14
TOTAL CERTIFICATES	728	668	692	660	696	700	756	792	798	848	839	897
TREASURY, TAX & LOAN	10	9	9	10	10	11	11	12	12	12	12	13
REPOS	11	8	0	8	9	6	0	0	13	14	10	11
FED FUNDS PURCHASED	6	6	6	6	6	6	7	7	7	7	7	8
SHORT-TERM BOR FUNDS	27	22	15	24	25	23	18	19	32	33	29	31
LONG-TERM DEBT	0	0	0	0	0	0	0	0	0	0	0	0
FHLB ADVANCES	0	0	0	0	0	0	0	0	0	0	0	0
LONG-TERM DEBT	0	0	0	0	0	0	0	0	0	0	0	0
TOTAL INTEREST EXPENSE	1396	1299	1354	1323	1405	1408	1489	1534	1553	1646	1631	1748
NET INTEREST INCOME	963	981	1043	1055	1050	1029	1045	1071	1039	1067	1058	1057
PROVISION FOR LOAN LOSS	114	123	109	118	120	121	118	115	115	115	117	115
NET INT INCOME AFTER PROV	849	858	934	937	930	908	927	957	924	952	941	942
SERVICE CHARGES	95	96	97	98	99	100	101	102	103	104	106	107
OTHER INCOME	117	115	139	127	132	141	114	135	136	169	133	171
GAIN(LOSS) ON SECURITIES	0	0	0	0	0	0	0	0	0	0	0	0
TOTAL NON-INTEREST INC	212	211	236	225	231	241	215	238	239	273	239	278
SALARIES & BENEFITS	406	412	415	421	429	436	442	444	455	456	460	465
OCCUPANCY, FURN & EQUIP	116	118	118	120	122	124	125	125	128	128	129	130
PROMOTION EXPENSE	43	43	43	43	43	43	43	43	43	43	43	43
FDIC INSURANCE EXPENSE	0	0	0	0	0	0	0	0	0	0	0	0
DATA PROCESSING EXPENSE	111	112	113	114	115	116	117	119	120	121	122	123
FINANCING & HEDGING EXP	0	0	0	0	0	0	0	0	0	0	0	0
OTHER OPERATING EXPENSE	104	115	138	139	137	133	140	135	140	141	141	136
TOTAL NON-INTEREST EXP	781	801	828	836	846	853	867	866	886	889	895	898
NET INCOME BEFORE TAXES	279	268	342	326	315	297	275	328	277	336	285	322
STATE TAXES	16	15	17	16	17	17	15	16	15	17	14	16
FEDERAL TAXES	76	72	86	81	84	83	77	83	73	87	77	84
INCOME TAXES	91	87	103	97	100	100	92	100	87	103	85	100
NET INCOME	188	181	239	228	215	197	183	229	190	233	200	222

STATEMENT OF INCOME - DETAIL
2001 ACTUAL

	JAN	FEB	MAR	APR	MAY	JUN	JUL	AUG	SEP	OCT	NOV	DEC
INTEREST EXPENSE:												
INTEREST-BEAR CHECKING	229	209	234	229	239	234	244	247	241	252	246	257
REGULAR SAVINGS	141	129	144	141	147	143	150	151	148	154	150	157
IBC & SAVINGS	370	338	378	369	385	377	393	398	389	406	397	414
MMDAs	458	421	490	486	495	469	475	470	454	463	451	474
SMALL CDs	129	123	144	147	159	160	170	174	173	183	180	188
LARGE CDs	561	525	603	607	644	623	628	610	580	599	582	599
PUBLIC CDs	241	225	258	258	274	264	266	257	244	251	243	250
OTHER CDS	16	15	18	18	19	19	19	18	18	18	17	18
INT RTE CONTRACTS-SWAPS	0	0	0	0	0	0	0	0	0	0	0	0
OTHER CDs	16	15	18	18	19	19	19	18	18	18	17	18
TOTAL CERTIFICATES	947	889	1023	1030	1097	1067	1082	1060	1015	1051	1022	1054
TREASURY, TAX & LOAN	14	13	15	15	15	14	14	14	14	14	13	13
REPOS	4	4	0	2	2	2	0	0	2	2	2	0
FED FUNDS PURCHASED	8	8	8	8	8	8	8	8	8	8	7	7
SHORT-TERM BOR FUNDS	25	24	23	25	26	24	22	22	23	23	22	20
LONG-TERM DEBT	0	0	0	0	0	0	0	0	0	0	0	0
FHLB ADVANCES	0	0	0	0	0	0	0	0	0	0	0	0
LONG-TERM DEBT	0	0	0	0	0	0	0	0	0	0	0	0
TOTAL INTEREST EXPENSE	1800	1672	1914	1911	2002	1937	1972	1949	1880	1943	1892	1963
NET INTEREST INCOME	1056	1164	1091	1129	1188	1254	1211	1234	1290	1341	1353	1317
PROVISION FOR LOAN LOSS	134	125	130	131	132	134	135	137	138	140	141	137
NET INT INCOME AFTER PROV	922	1039	962	998	1055	1120	1076	1097	1152	1202	1212	1181
SERVICE CHARGES	108	109	110	111	112	114	115	116	117	119	120	121
OTHER INCOME	123	134	125	145	116	126	107	135	138	113	102	128
GAIN(LOSS) ON SECURITIES	0	0	0	0	0	0	0	0	0	0	0	0
TOTAL NON-INTEREST INC	231	243	235	256	228	240	222	251	255	232	222	249
SALARIES & BENEFITS	447	446	454	464	470	475	480	482	493	499	505	509
OCCUPANCY, FURN & EQUIP	118	118	120	122	123	124	125	126	128	129	131	131
PROMOTION EXPENSE	48	48	48	48	48	48	48	48	48	48	48	48
FDIC INSURANCE EXPENSE	0	0	0	0	0	0	0	0	0	0	0	0
DATA PROCESSING EXPENSE	125	127	128	129	130	131	133	134	135	136	138	139
FINANCING & HEDGING EXP	0	0	0	0	0	0	0	0	0	0	0	0
OTHER OPERATING EXPENSE	140	141	142	139	144	145	146	147	118	149	150	119
TOTAL NON-INTEREST EXP	877	879	891	901	915	923	931	937	922	962	971	945
NET INCOME BEFORE TAXES	276	403	306	353	369	436	367	412	485	471	463	484
STATE TAXES	14	20	15	18	18	22	18	21	24	24	23	24
FEDERAL TAXES	71	113	82	98	104	126	104	118	143	138	136	144
INCOME TAXES	85	133	97	115	122	147	122	139	167	162	159	168
NET INCOME	191	270	209	238	247	289	245	273	318	309	304	316

KEY RATIO REPORT - SUMMARY
2000 ACTUAL

	JAN	FEB	MAR	APR	MAY	JUN	JUL	AUG	SEP	OCT	NOV	DEC
PERFORMANCE:												
RETURN ON EQUITY %	13.04	13.25	13.83	13.62	13.25	13.57	12.32	12.82	11.98	12.95	11.37	12.21
RETURN ON ASSETS %	0.80	0.81	0.85	0.83	0.81	0.82	0.75	0.78	0.72	0.77	0.68	0.73
EARNINGS PER SHARE(ANN$)	0.87	0.90	0.94	0.93	0.91	0.94	0.86	0.90	0.84	0.92	0.81	0.87
COMMON DIV PER SHARE ($)	0.00	0.00	0.10	0.00	0.00	0.10	0.00	0.00	0.10	0.00	0.00	0.10
BOOK VALUE PER SHR(EOP$)	6.73	6.80	6.78	6.86	6.93	6.91	6.98	7.06	7.03	7.11	7.17	7.15
EARNING/TOTAL ASSETS %	89.15	89.28	89.84	90.01	89.40	89.25	89.34	90.17	89.37	90.20	90.29	90.15
INT BEAR/TOTAL DEPOSITS%	87.64	87.75	87.72	87.77	87.82	87.86	87.91	87.95	87.99	88.04	88.08	88.12
INTEREST MARGIN & OVERHEAD:												
AVG NATIONAL PRIME RATE	8.75	8.51	8.50	8.50	8.84	9.00	9.29	9.84	10.00	10.00	10.05	10.50
YIELD ON EARNING ASSETS	9.88	9.63	9.83	9.72	9.90	9.88	10.07	10.17	10.17	10.32	10.26	10.48
COST OF FUNDS RATE	6.27	6.14	6.01	5.98	6.09	6.26	6.37	6.50	6.69	6.80	6.90	7.09
SPREAD	3.61	3.49	3.82	3.74	3.81	3.62	3.71	3.67	3.49	3.53	3.36	3.39
INT MARGIN ON E.A. %	4.25	4.12	4.48	4.39	4.43	4.25	4.35	4.37	4.15	4.25	4.10	4.13
NET OVERHEAD TO E.A. %	2.29	2.53	2.34	2.47	2.39	2.45	2.50	2.37	2.52	2.27	2.49	2.24
LOAN POSITION:												
LOANS/TOTAL DEPOSITS %	69.55	69.48	69.91	70.11	70.30	70.48	70.57	70.56	70.54	70.50	70.47	70.36
LOANS TO EARNING ASSETS	69.99	69.98	70.28	70.06	70.76	71.17	71.43	70.79	71.00	70.35	70.38	70.39
LOSS RESERVE/LOANS %	1.71	1.70	1.71	1.70	1.70	1.69	1.69	1.69	1.69	1.69	1.69	1.69
LOSS PROVISION/LOANS %	0.66	0.75	0.61	0.68	0.66	0.68	0.63	0.61	0.63	0.61	0.63	0.59
NET CHARGE-OFFS/LOANS %	0.45	0.48	0.45	0.47	0.45	0.47	0.46	0.46	0.47	0.46	0.47	0.46
NONPERFORMING/LNS(EOP) %	1.44	1.45	1.45	1.45	1.45	1.45	1.46	1.46	1.47	1.48	1.48	1.49
CAPITAL LEVERAGE:												
CORE (TIER 1) RATIO %	9.12	9.15	8.94	9.02	9.01	8.92	8.95	8.96	8.80	8.88	8.83	8.77
TOTAL CAPITAL RATIO %	10.37	10.41	10.20	10.28	10.26	10.18	10.21	10.22	10.05	10.13	10.09	10.03
ASSET LEVERAGE RATIO %	5.88	5.91	5.88	5.85	5.90	5.85	5.84	5.88	5.82	5.76	5.80	5.75
EQUITY TO ASSETS %	6.11	6.10	6.13	6.08	6.09	6.07	6.06	6.08	6.01	5.98	5.99	5.96
DIVIDEND PAYOUT RATIO %	0.00	0.00	123.68	0.00	0.00	127.69	0.00	0.00	142.17	0.00	0.00	132.76
LIQUIDITY:												
CASH/TOTAL DEPOSITS %	8.28	8.26	7.39	7.37	8.17	8.15	8.12	7.30	8.08	7.27	7.25	7.24
PURCHASED FUNDS/E.A. %	33.21	33.18	33.07	32.82	33.00	33.06	33.08	32.74	32.80	32.46	32.44	32.47
NET FED FUNDS/EQUITY %	-37.25	-38.09	-33.56	-39.90	-26.75	-19.30	-14.49	-27.19	-22.00	-37.07	-37.81	-37.94
PER EMPLOYEE:												
SALARIES & BENEFITS ($)	23946	25664	24112	25044	24319	25237	24526	24629	25621	24878	25729	24940
TOTAL ASSETS ($MILLIONS)	1.64	1.64	1.64	1.64	1.63	1.62	1.62	1.63	1.62	1.64	1.64	1.64

KEY RATIO REPORT - SUMMARY
2001 ACTUAL

	JAN	FEB	MAR	APR	MAY	JUN	JUL	AUG	SEP	OCT	NOV	DEC
PERFORMANCE:												
RETURN ON EQUITY %	10.45	16.19	11.26	13.19	13.11	15.75	12.87	14.17	16.98	15.86	15.88	15.88
RETURN ON ASSETS %	0.62	0.96	0.67	0.78	0.77	0.92	0.75	0.83	0.99	0.92	0.93	0.93
EARNINGS PER SHARE(ANN$)	0.75	1.18	0.82	0.96	0.97	1.17	0.96	1.07	1.29	1.21	1.23	1.24
COMMON DIV PER SHARE ($)	0.00	0.00	0.10	0.00	0.00	0.10	0.00	0.00	0.10	0.00	0.00	0.10
BOOK VALUE PER SHR(EOP$)	7.21	7.30	7.27	7.35	7.43	7.43	7.51	7.60	7.61	7.71	7.81	7.81
EARNING/TOTAL ASSETS %	89.95	90.52	90.38	90.50	90.60	90.45	90.56	90.70	90.58	90.69	90.80	90.67
INT BEAR/TOTAL DEPOSITS%	88.19	88.25	88.32	88.37	88.43	88.48	88.53	88.58	88.63	88.69	88.74	88.79
INTEREST MARGIN & OVERHEAD:												
AVG NATIONAL PRIME RATE	10.50	10.93	11.50	11.50	11.50	11.07	10.98	10.50	10.50	10.50	10.50	10.50
YIELD ON EARNING ASSETS	10.59	10.76	10.88	11.01	11.27	11.33	11.06	10.93	10.92	11.05	10.94	10.83
COST OF FUNDS RATE	7.23	7.36	7.55	7.70	7.73	7.65	7.47	7.31	7.20	7.13	7.10	7.06
SPREAD	3.36	3.40	3.33	3.31	3.55	3.69	3.59	3.63	3.72	3.92	3.84	3.77
INT MARGIN ON E.A. %	4.10	4.18	4.13	4.13	4.36	4.48	4.37	4.39	4.46	4.66	4.57	4.49
NET OVERHEAD TO E.A. %	2.32	2.53	2.30	2.33	2.36	2.42	2.40	2.29	2.30	2.40	2.53	2.24
LOAN POSITION:												
LOANS/TOTAL DEPOSITS %	70.18	70.14	70.18	70.24	70.30	70.36	70.46	70.52	70.58	70.65	70.71	70.72
LOANS TO EARNING ASSETS	70.61	70.15	70.40	70.36	70.37	70.55	70.64	70.62	70.73	70.72	70.72	70.87
LOSS RESERVE/LOANS %	1.69	1.69	1.69	1.69	1.69	1.69	1.69	1.69	1.69	1.69	1.69	1.69
LOSS PROVISION/LOANS %	0.68	0.70	0.65	0.67	0.65	0.67	0.65	0.65	0.67	0.65	0.67	0.62
NET CHARGE-OFFS/LOANS %	0.44	0.48	0.44	0.45	0.44	0.45	0.44	0.44	0.45	0.44	0.45	0.44
NONPERFORMING/LNS(EOP) %	1.46	1.46	1.45	1.45	1.44	1.44	1.44	1.44	1.43	1.43	1.43	1.43
CAPITAL LEVERAGE:												
CORE (TIER 1) RATIO %	8.81	8.82	8.69	8.74	8.73	8.61	8.66	8.68	8.58	8.65	8.67	8.59
TOTAL CAPITAL RATIO %	10.07	10.08	9.95	10.00	9.98	9.87	9.92	9.94	9.84	9.90	9.92	9.85
ASSET LEVERAGE RATIO %	5.72	5.77	5.72	5.68	5.72	5.69	5.65	5.70	5.67	5.64	5.69	5.67
EQUITY TO ASSETS %	5.93	5.94	5.92	5.88	5.89	5.86	5.85	5.86	5.84	5.82	5.85	5.83
DIVIDEND PAYOUT RATIO %	0.00	0.00	145.90	0.00	0.00	105.65	0.00	0.00	95.78	0.00	0.00	96.47
LIQUIDITY:												
CASH/TOTAL DEPOSITS %	7.54	7.04	7.02	7.00	6.99	6.97	6.96	6.94	6.92	6.90	6.89	6.87
PURCHASED FUNDS/E.A. %	32.63	32.43	32.53	32.48	32.45	32.50	32.50	32.46	32.48	32.44	32.41	32.49
NET FED FUNDS/EQUITY %	-22.68	-47.72	-45.81	-38.06	-44.47	-47.69	-50.02	-59.94	-46.72	-51.42	-54.53	-60.49
PER EMPLOYEE:												
SALARIES & BENEFITS ($)	25027	27851	25337	26396	25726	26664	25882	25934	26906	26194	27148	26324
TOTAL ASSETS ($MILLIONS)	1.73	1.75	1.75	1.74	1.75	1.75	1.76	1.77	1.75	1.76	1.76	1.77

KEY RATIO REPORT - DETAIL
2000 ACTUAL

	JAN	FEB	MAR	APR	MAY	JUN	JUL	AUG	SEP	OCT	NOV	DEC
ASSET QUALITY:												
MOST BAL LOAN MIX (AVG)	10.16	10.34	10.30	10.38	10.45	10.52	10.60	10.70	10.80	10.90	11.01	11.03
RES/NON PERFORM (EOP)	1.20	1.20	1.19	1.19	1.19	1.18	1.18	1.17	1.17	1.16	1.16	1.15
NET CH-OFFS/LOANS(AVG)	0.45	0.48	0.45	0.47	0.45	0.47	0.46	0.46	0.47	0.46	0.47	0.46
INV MKT TO BOOK (EOP)	121.88	113.10	114.57	112.49	117.69	108.63	113.81	106.65	116.83	112.90	117.22	111.71
LIQUIDITY (AVG):												
LOANS/DEPOSITS (EOP)	69.62	69.79	70.00	70.19	70.37	70.56	70.55	70.54	70.50	70.47	70.44	70.25
S-T INVEST TO ASSETS	11.86	11.95	11.75	12.11	11.34	10.93	10.69	11.49	11.13	12.05	12.15	12.16
PURCHASED FUNDS/E.A.	33.21	33.18	33.07	32.82	33.00	33.06	33.08	32.74	32.80	32.46	32.44	32.47
NET BOR FUNDS/ASSETS	-1.14	-1.32	-1.53	-1.46	-0.67	-0.36	-0.36	-1.14	-0.24	-1.14	-1.34	-1.34
TOTAL LOANS/AVAIL DEP	88.01	87.77	87.27	87.38	88.38	88.47	88.44	87.42	88.13	87.11	86.94	86.72
CAPITAL ADEQUACY:												
EQUITY/ASSETS (EOP)	6.05	6.08	6.06	6.03	6.04	5.99	6.04	6.05	5.90	5.92	5.94	5.87
MARKET CAPITALIZATION	35760	35100	37650	38010	38160	38160	37440	38340	36540	38220	36570	37110
RISK BASED CAPITAL (EOP)	10.37	10.41	10.20	10.28	10.26	10.18	10.21	10.22	10.05	10.13	10.09	10.03
PE RATIO (EOP)	8.43	13.29	12.56	10.03	10.41	11.13	11.22	13.74	11.74	11.91	12.11	14.26
PROFITABILITY / EARNINGS (AVG):												
EARNINGS PER SHARE(ANN)	0.87	0.88	0.90	0.90	0.90	0.91	0.90	0.90	0.89	0.90	0.89	0.89
RETURN ON EQUITY	13.04	13.25	13.83	13.62	13.25	13.57	12.32	12.82	11.98	12.95	11.37	12.21
RETURN ON ASSETS	0.80	0.81	0.85	0.83	0.81	0.82	0.75	0.78	0.72	0.77	0.68	0.73
INT MARGIN ON E.A.	4.25	4.12	4.48	4.39	4.43	4.25	4.35	4.37	4.15	4.25	4.10	4.13
NET OVERHEAD TO E.A.	2.29	2.53	2.34	2.47	2.39	2.45	2.50	2.37	2.52	2.27	2.49	2.24
YIELD ON EARNING ASSETS	9.88	9.63	9.83	9.72	9.90	9.88	10.07	10.17	10.17	10.32	10.26	10.48
NET INCOME	221.66	434.65	673.16	901.49	1133.64	1364.67	1582.13	1810.83	2018.33	2250.88	2450.47	2672.68
GROWTH (%):												
TOTAL LOANS (YTD AVG)	13.45	13.96	14.21	14.37	14.48	14.54	14.56	14.54	14.48	14.40	14.30	14.18
TOTAL DEPOSITS(YTD AVG)	11.71	12.07	11.98	11.94	11.91	11.87	11.84	11.81	11.77	11.74	11.70	11.67
TOTAL EQUITY (YTD AVG)	-8.96	-1.92	1.04	2.54	3.52	4.17	4.67	5.05	5.33	5.57	5.75	5.90
BAL GROWTH (YTD AVG)	0.00	0.00	0.00	0.00	0.00	0.00	0.00	0.00	0.00	0.00	0.00	0.00
COMP GROWTH (YTD AVG)	0.00	0.00	0.00	0.00	0.00	0.00	0.00	0.00	0.00	0.00	0.00	0.00
TOTAL ASSETS ($EOP)	333582	335564	335452	341129	344151	346185	346956	350107	357223	360113	362291	365702
MEMO ITEMS:												
MKT VALUE OF INVST($MIL)	97	91	93	92	97	91	96	91	100	97	102	98
OUTSTANDING SHARES(000)	3000	3000	3000	3000	3000	3000	3000	3000	3000	3000	3000	3000
SAL & BENEFITS/EMP($)	23946	25664	24112	25044	24319	25237	24526	24629	25621	24878	25729	24940
ASSETS (AVG)/EMP($ MIL)	1.64	1.64	1.64	1.64	1.63	1.62	1.62	1.63	1.62	1.64	1.64	1.64
STOCK PRICE ($EOP)	11.92	11.70	12.55	12.67	12.72	12.72	12.48	12.78	12.18	12.74	12.19	12.37
BK VALUE PER SHARE (($EOP)	6.73	6.80	6.78	6.86	6.93	6.91	6.98	7.06	7.03	7.11	7.17	7.15

KEY RATIO REPORT - DETAIL
2001 ACTUAL

	JAN	FEB	MAR	APR	MAY	JUN	JUL	AUG	SEP	OCT	NOV	DEC
ASSET QUALITY:												
MOST BAL LOAN MIX (AVG)	10.95	10.79	10.61	10.46	10.32	10.18	10.03	9.89	9.74	9.60	9.46	9.38
RES/NON PERFORM (EOP)	1.18	1.18	1.19	1.19	1.19	1.19	1.20	1.20	1.20	1.20	1.20	1.21
NET CH-OFFS/LOANS(AVG)	0.44	0.48	0.44	0.45	0.44	0.45	0.44	0.44	0.45	0.44	0.45	0.44
INV MKT TO BOOK (EOP)	94.08	99.34	98.99	93.87	94.10	94.72	95.25	100.45	94.98	95.14	95.34	100.69
LIQUIDITY (AVG):												
LOANS/DEPOSITS (EOP)	70.15	70.16	70.23	70.29	70.35	70.41	70.48	70.54	70.60	70.66	70.72	70.68
S-T INVEST TO ASSETS	12.00	12.72	12.50	12.74	13.01	12.91	12.89	13.02	12.96	13.11	13.33	13.29
PURCHASED FUNDS/E.A.	32.63	32.43	32.53	32.48	32.45	32.50	32.50	32.46	32.48	32.44	32.41	32.49
NET BOR FUNDS/ASSETS	-0.70	-2.20	-2.21	-1.68	-2.06	-2.24	-2.44	-3.03	-2.18	-2.45	-2.65	-3.06
TOTAL LOANS/AVAIL DEP	86.79	86.18	86.19	86.22	86.25	86.26	86.37	86.40	86.43	86.46	86.48	86.48
CAPITAL ADEQUACY:												
EQUITY/ASSETS (EOP)	5.90	5.92	5.85	5.86	5.87	5.80	5.82	5.84	5.78	5.80	5.82	5.78
MARKET CAPITALIZATION	18960	37890	33900	27690	29040	32400	32310	40410	35580	36810	38160	45360
RISK BASED CAPITAL (EOP)	10.07	10.08	9.95	10.00	9.98	9.87	9.92	9.94	9.84	9.90	9.92	9.85
PE RATIO (EOP)	13.81	13.85	13.47	12.92	13.08	12.50	11.94	11.93	11.08	10.80	10.84	10.83
PROFITABILITY / EARNINGS (AVG):												
EARNINGS PER SHARE(ANN)	0.75	0.95	0.90	0.92	0.93	0.97	0.96	0.98	1.01	1.03	1.05	1.06
RETURN ON EQUITY	10.45	16.19	11.26	13.19	13.11	15.75	12.87	14.17	16.98	15.86	15.88	15.88
RETURN ON ASSETS	0.62	0.96	0.67	0.78	0.77	0.92	0.75	0.83	0.99	0.92	0.93	0.93
INT MARGIN ON E.A.	4.10	4.18	4.13	4.13	4.36	4.48	4.37	4.39	4.46	4.66	4.57	4.49
NET OVERHEAD TO E.A.	2.32	2.53	2.30	2.33	2.36	2.42	2.40	2.29	2.30	2.40	2.53	2.24
YIELD ON EARNING ASSETS	10.59	10.76	10.88	11.01	11.27	11.33	11.06	10.93	10.92	11.05	10.94	10.83
NET INCOME	191.19	461.61	670.66	908.40	1155.33	1444.01	1688.90	1961.70	2280.14	2589.48	2893.27	3209.41
GROWTH (%):												
TOTAL LOANS (YTD AVG)	12.50	12.21	12.16	12.10	12.05	11.99	11.96	11.96	11.98	12.02	12.08	12.15
TOTAL DEPOSITS(YTD AVG)	11.47	11.18	11.33	11.43	11.51	11.58	11.63	11.68	11.73	11.77	11.82	11.86
TOTAL EQUITY (YTD AVG)	7.36	7.35	7.36	7.33	7.32	7.33	7.36	7.39	7.45	7.54	7.65	7.77
BAL GROWTH (YTD AVG)	0.00	0.00	0.00	0.00	0.00	0.00	0.00	0.00	0.00	0.00	0.00	4.40
COMP GROWTH (YTD AVG)	0.00	0.00	0.00	0.00	0.00	0.00	0.00	0.00	0.00	0.00	0.00	31.90
TOTAL ASSETS ($EOP)	366817	370298	372824	376597	380232	383919	386804	390548	394867	398428	402309	405796
MEMO ITEMS:												
MKT VALUE OF INVST($MIL)	87	87	87	87	87	87	88	90	90	90	90	93
OUTSTANDING SHARES(000)	3000	3000	3000	3000	3000	3000	3000	3000	3000	3000	3000	3000
SAL & BENEFITS/EMP($)	25027	27851	25337	26396	25726	26664	25882	25934	26906	26194	27148	26324
ASSETS (AVG)/EMP($ MIL)	1.73	1.76	1.75	1.74	1.75	1.75	1.76	1.77	1.75	1.76	1.76	1.77
STOCK PRICE ($EOP)	6.32	12.63	11.30	9.23	9.68	10.80	10.77	13.47	11.86	12.27	12.72	15.12
BK VALUE PER SHARE (($EOP)	7.21	7.30	7.27	7.35	7.43	7.43	7.51	7.60	7.61	7.71	7.81	7.81

MONTHLY INTEREST RATE REPORT - DETAIL
2000 ACTUAL

	JAN	FEB	MAR	APR	MAY	JUN	JUL	AUG	SEP	OCT	NOV	DEC
EARNING ASSET YIELDS:												
SHORT-TERM TREASURIES	5.92	5.82	5.78	5.76	5.87	6.10	6.37	6.63	6.87	7.10	7.31	7.56
LONG-TERM TREASURIES	10.39	10.28	10.15	10.03	9.95	9.88	9.80	9.73	9.66	9.59	9.52	9.44
US AGENCY SECURITIES	12.78	12.55	12.54	12.52	12.51	12.49	12.47	12.46	12.33	12.21	12.19	12.18
CMO CLASS B	0.00	0.00	0.00	0.00	0.00	0.00	0.00	0.00	0.00	0.00	0.00	0.00
OUR SECURITIZED MTG LOANS	0.00	0.00	0.00	0.00	0.00	0.00	0.00	0.00	0.00	0.00	0.00	0.00
ASSET BACKED SECURITIES	12.78	12.55	12.54	12.52	12.51	12.49	12.47	12.46	12.33	12.21	12.19	12.18
TAX EXEMPTS	16.29	16.20	16.14	16.10	16.01	15.92	15.82	15.74	15.68	15.54	15.38	15.23
OTHER SECURITIES	11.16	11.09	11.07	11.07	11.07	11.07	11.07	11.08	11.09	11.09	11.09	11.09
FHLB STOCK	0.00	0.00	0.00	0.00	0.00	0.00	0.00	0.00	0.00	0.00	0.00	0.00
INT RTE CONTRACTS-SWAPS	0.00	0.00	0.00	0.00	0.00	0.00	0.00	0.00	0.00	0.00	0.00	0.00
INT RTE CONTRACTS-OPTIONS	0.00	0.00	0.00	0.00	0.00	0.00	0.00	0.00	0.00	0.00	0.00	0.00
ALL OTHER SECURITIES	15.42	15.27	15.15	15.12	15.04	14.96	14.88	14.77	14.69	14.57	14.42	14.29
TOTAL SECURITIES	9.58	9.44	9.34	9.27	9.24	9.28	9.32	9.36	9.41	9.43	9.43	9.46
TERM FED FUNDS SOLD	0.00	0.00	0.00	0.00	0.00	0.00	0.00	0.00	0.00	0.00	0.00	0.00
OVERNIGHT FED FUNDS SOLD	6.72	6.92	6.47	6.98	6.98	7.64	7.63	7.88	8.33	8.17	8.49	8.62
TRADING ACCOUNT	0.00	0.00	0.00	0.00	0.00	0.00	0.00	0.00	0.00	0.00	0.00	0.00
SHORT-TERM INVESTMENTS	6.72	6.92	6.47	6.98	6.98	7.64	7.63	7.88	8.33	8.17	8.49	8.62
COM'L PARTIC PURCH-FIXED	0.00	0.00	0.00	0.00	0.00	0.00	0.00	0.00	0.00	0.00	0.00	0.00
DIRECT COM'L LOANS-FIXED	8.76	8.26	8.88	8.63	8.97	8.75	9.12	9.24	9.08	9.53	9.34	9.79
PART PUR - REQ'D-FIXED	0.00	0.00	0.00	0.00	0.00	0.00	0.00	0.00	0.00	0.00	0.00	0.00
PART SOLD - REQ'D-FIXED	0.00	0.00	0.00	0.00	0.00	0.00	0.00	0.00	0.00	0.00	0.00	0.00
COM'L LOANS-OPTION CONTRACT	0.00	0.00	0.00	0.00	0.00	0.00	0.00	0.00	0.00	0.00	0.00	0.00
COMMERCIAL LOANS-FIXED	8.76	8.26	8.88	8.63	8.97	8.75	9.12	9.24	9.08	9.53	9.34	9.79
COM'L PARTIC PURCH-FLOAT	0.00	0.00	0.00	0.00	0.00	0.00	0.00	0.00	0.00	0.00	0.00	0.00
DIRECT COM'L LOANS-FLOAT	9.14	9.02	8.91	8.90	9.07	9.32	9.54	9.95	10.31	10.38	10.40	10.66
COMMERCIAL LOANS-FLOAT	9.14	9.02	8.91	8.90	9.07	9.32	9.54	9.95	10.31	10.38	10.40	10.66
MORTGAGE LOANS-FIXED	10.71	10.69	10.68	10.67	10.65	10.64	10.63	10.61	10.60	10.59	10.58	10.57
MORTGAGE LOANS-ADJ	8.97	8.41	8.99	8.70	8.98	8.68	8.99	9.02	8.77	9.09	8.85	9.24
HOME EQUITY LOANS	9.06	8.53	9.16	8.92	9.27	9.04	9.42	9.50	9.28	9.68	9.46	9.89
CONSUMER LOANS	8.91	8.42	9.08	8.87	9.25	9.06	9.46	9.56	9.35	9.77	9.56	10.01
CREDIT CARD LOANS	18.34	18.59	18.40	18.55	18.41	18.55	18.40	18.39	18.52	18.38	18.53	18.39
AUTO LOANS	9.17	8.72	9.46	9.29	9.75	9.59	10.07	10.24	10.07	10.58	10.41	10.96
TOTAL LOANS	10.12	9.82	10.14	10.01	10.23	10.16	10.41	10.54	10.51	10.75	10.65	10.94
TOTAL EARNING ASSETS	9.88	9.63	9.83	9.72	9.90	9.88	10.07	10.17	10.17	10.32	10.26	10.48

MONTHLY INTEREST RATE REPORT - DETAIL
2001 ACTUAL

	JAN	FEB	MAR	APR	MAY	JUN	JUL	AUG	SEP	OCT	NOV	DEC
EARNING ASSET YIELDS:												
SHORT-TERM TREASURIES	7.87	8.15	8.41	8.61	8.67	8.55	8.31	8.09	7.93	7.80	7.69	7.64
LONG-TERM TREASURIES	8.13	8.12	8.10	8.08	8.05	8.04	8.03	8.01	7.99	7.96	7.94	7.92
US AGENCY SECURITIES	13.05	13.04	12.92	12.81	12.80	12.79	12.77	12.76	12.62	12.49	12.48	12.47
CMO CLASS B	0.00	0.00	0.00	0.00	0.00	0.00	0.00	0.00	0.00	0.00	0.00	0.00
OUR SECURITIZED MTG LOANS	0.00	0.00	0.00	0.00	0.00	0.00	0.00	0.00	0.00	0.00	0.00	0.00
ASSET BACKED SECURITIES	13.05	13.04	12.92	12.81	12.80	12.79	12.77	12.76	12.62	12.49	12.48	12.47
TAX EXEMPTS	14.08	14.15	14.22	14.26	14.25	14.23	14.20	14.19	14.16	14.11	14.07	14.02
OTHER SECURITIES	11.09	11.08	11.08	11.08	11.08	11.08	11.04	11.01	11.01	11.01	11.01	11.01
FHLB STOCK	10.18	0.00	0.00	10.41	40.67	46.30	17.54	0.00	9.27	32.30	20.71	0.00
INT RTE CONTRACTS-SWAPS	0.00	0.00	0.00	0.00	0.00	0.00	0.00	0.00	0.00	0.00	0.00	0.00
INT RTE CONTRACTS-OPTIONS	0.00	0.00	0.00	0.00	0.00	0.00	0.00	0.00	0.00	0.00	0.00	0.00
ALL OTHER SECURITIES	12.80	13.40	13.42	12.83	18.91	20.17	14.17	13.24	12.38	17.20	14.74	13.03
TOTAL SECURITIES	8.96	9.02	9.11	9.20	10.04	10.15	9.22	8.85	8.78	9.33	8.94	8.54
TERM FED FUNDS SOLD	0.00	0.00	0.00	0.00	0.00	0.00	0.00	0.00	0.00	0.00	0.00	0.00
OVERNIGHT FED FUNDS SOLD	8.95	10.17	9.66	9.98	9.63	9.66	9.07	8.82	9.15	8.67	8.67	8.29
TRADING ACCOUNT	0.00	0.00	0.00	0.00	0.00	0.00	0.00	0.00	0.00	0.00	0.00	0.00
SHORT-TERM INVESTMENTS	8.95	10.17	9.66	9.98	9.63	9.66	9.07	8.82	9.15	8.67	8.67	8.29
COM'L PARTIC PURCH-FIXED	0.00	0.00	0.00	0.00	0.00	0.00	0.00	0.00	0.00	0.00	0.00	0.00
DIRECT COM'L LOANS-FIXED	10.19	10.22	10.30	10.40	10.49	10.56	10.58	10.58	10.54	10.50	10.45	10.40
PART PUR - REQ'D-FIXED	0.00	0.00	0.00	0.00	0.00	0.00	0.00	0.00	0.00	0.00	0.00	0.00
PART SOLD - REQ'D-FIXED	0.00	0.00	0.00	0.00	0.00	0.00	0.00	0.00	0.00	0.00	0.00	0.00
COM'L LOANS-OPTION CONTRACT	0.00	0.00	0.00	0.00	0.00	0.00	0.00	0.00	0.00	0.00	0.00	0.00
COMMERCIAL LOANS-FIXED	10.19	10.22	10.30	10.40	10.49	10.56	10.58	10.58	10.54	10.50	10.45	10.40
COM'L PARTIC PURCH-FLOAT	0.00	0.00	0.00	0.00	0.00	0.00	0.00	0.00	0.00	0.00	0.00	0.00
DIRECT COM'L LOANS-FLOAT	10.77	11.09	11.59	11.86	11.86	11.66	11.39	11.11	10.88	10.88	10.88	10.88
COMMERCIAL LOANS-FLOAT	10.77	11.09	11.59	11.86	11.86	11.66	11.39	11.11	10.88	10.88	10.88	10.88
MORTGAGE LOANS-FIXED	10.57	10.57	10.56	10.56	10.55	10.54	10.53	10.52	10.51	10.50	10.49	10.48
MORTGAGE LOANS-ADJ	9.30	9.42	9.55	9.68	9.80	9.89	9.94	9.95	9.97	9.98	9.97	9.95
HOME EQUITY LOANS	11.50	11.53	11.57	11.62	11.65	11.67	11.68	11.66	11.65	11.64	11.62	11.60
CONSUMER LOANS	10.67	10.87	11.06	11.26	11.44	11.60	11.74	11.85	11.96	12.06	12.15	12.23
CREDIT CARD LOANS	18.21	18.59	18.33	18.48	18.41	18.57	18.48	18.52	18.72	18.61	18.32	18.27
AUTO LOANS	12.12	12.20	12.29	12.37	12.45	12.51	12.55	12.56	12.58	12.59	12.59	12.58
TOTAL LOANS	11.27	11.44	11.59	11.75	11.81	11.85	11.83	11.80	11.80	11.80	11.78	11.78
TOTAL EARNING ASSETS	10.59	10.76	10.88	11.01	11.27	11.33	11.06	10.93	10.92	11.05	10.94	10.83

MONTHLY INTEREST RATE REPORT - DETAIL
2000 ACTUAL

	JAN	FEB	MAR	APR	MAY	JUN	JUL	AUG	SEP	OCT	NOV	DEC
COST OF FUNDS RATES:												
INTEREST-BEAR CHECKING	5.00	5.00	5.00	5.00	5.00	5.00	5.00	5.00	5.00	5.00	5.00	5.00
REGULAR SAVINGS	5.50	5.50	5.50	5.50	5.50	5.50	5.50	5.50	5.50	5.50	5.50	5.50
IBC & SAVINGS	5.18	5.18	5.18	5.18	5.18	5.18	5.18	5.18	5.18	5.18	5.18	5.18
MMDAs	5.85	5.79	5.69	5.81	6.10	6.39	6.36	6.37	6.62	6.79	7.01	7.39
SMALL CDs	5.81	5.82	5.80	5.77	5.74	5.76	5.79	5.79	5.80	5.81	5.82	5.83
LARGE CDs	7.46	7.17	6.89	6.71	6.82	7.08	7.40	7.74	8.06	8.25	8.38	8.64
PUBLIC CDs	7.45	7.14	6.88	6.72	6.83	7.07	7.39	7.76	8.06	8.24	8.39	8.62
OTHER CDS	6.64	6.64	6.58	6.52	6.52	6.58	6.60	6.65	6.77	6.87	6.97	7.12
INT RTE CONTRACTS-SWAPS	0.00	0.00	0.00	0.00	0.00	0.00	0.00	0.00	0.00	0.00	0.00	0.00
OTHER CDs	6.64	6.64	6.58	6.52	6.52	6.58	6.60	6.65	6.77	6.87	6.97	7.12
TOTAL CERTIFICATES	7.14	6.91	6.68	6.54	6.62	6.83	7.09	7.37	7.62	7.78	7.89	8.09
TREASURY, TAX & LOAN	6.58	6.33	6.33	6.62	6.84	7.26	7.50	7.76	7.94	8.05	8.10	8.51
REPOS	6.58	6.33	0.00	6.62	6.84	7.26	0.00	0.00	7.94	8.05	8.10	8.51
FED FUNDS PURCHASED	6.97	7.18	6.72	7.24	7.22	7.89	7.87	8.13	8.58	8.41	8.74	8.86
SHORT-TERM BOR FUNDS	6.66	6.53	6.47	6.77	6.93	7.43	7.63	7.89	8.07	8.13	8.25	8.59
LONG-TERM DEBT	0.00	0.00	0.00	0.00	0.00	0.00	0.00	0.00	0.00	0.00	0.00	0.00
FHLB ADVANCES	0.00	0.00	0.00	0.00	0.00	0.00	0.00	0.00	0.00	0.00	0.00	0.00
LONG-TERM DEBT	0.00	0.00	0.00	0.00	0.00	0.00	0.00	0.00	0.00	0.00	0.00	0.00
TOTAL INT-BEAR LIAB	6.27	6.14	6.01	5.98	6.09	6.26	6.37	6.50	6.69	6.80	6.90	7.09
NET INTEREST SPREAD	3.61	3.49	3.82	3.74	3.81	3.62	3.71	3.67	3.49	3.53	3.36	3.39
NET INTEREST INCOME	4.25	4.12	4.48	4.39	4.43	4.25	4.35	4.37	4.15	4.25	4.10	4.13
MARKET RATES:												
PRIME RATE (LG BKS)	8.75	8.51	8.50	8.50	8.84	9.00	9.29	9.84	10.00	10.00	10.05	10.50
FED FUNDS RATE(NATIONAL)	6.83	6.58	6.58	6.87	7.09	7.51	7.75	8.01	8.19	8.30	8.35	8.76
TREASURY BILL RATE 3 MO	5.90	5.69	5.69	5.92	6.27	6.50	6.73	7.02	7.23	7.34	7.68	8.09
TREASURY BILL RATE 6 MO	6.31	5.96	5.91	6.21	6.53	6.76	6.97	7.36	7.43	7.50	7.76	8.24
US GOVT YIELD (3YRS)	7.87	7.38	7.50	7.83	8.24	8.22	8.44	8.77	8.57	8.43	8.72	9.11
MUNICIPAL BOND YIELD	7.69	7.49	7.74	7.81	7.91	7.78	7.76	7.79	7.66	7.47	7.46	7.61
CONV MTG RATE (NEW)	9.10	9.12	9.15	9.13	8.95	9.26	9.17	9.06	9.26	9.10	9.43	9.39
90-DAY CD RATE(NATIONAL)	6.92	6.60	6.63	6.92	7.24	7.51	7.94	8.35	8.23	8.36	8.78	9.25
LONDON INTERBANK RATE	7.19	6.73	6.73	6.98	7.31	7.59	7.99	8.38	8.29	8.50	8.66	9.26

MONTHLY INTEREST RATE REPORT - DETAIL
2001 ACTUAL

	JAN	FEB	MAR	APR	MAY	JUN	JUL	AUG	SEP	OCT	NOV	DEC
COST OF FUNDS RATES:												
INTEREST-BEAR CHECKING	5.00	5.00	5.00	5.00	5.00	5.00	5.00	5.00	5.00	5.00	5.00	5.00
REGULAR SAVINGS	5.50	5.50	5.50	5.50	5.50	5.50	5.50	5.50	5.50	5.50	5.50	5.50
IBC & SAVINGS	5.18	5.18	5.18	5.18	5.18	5.18	5.18	5.18	5.18	5.18	5.18	5.18
MMDAs	7.34	7.39	7.66	7.76	7.55	7.31	7.07	6.91	6.81	6.65	6.62	6.64
SMALL CDs	6.31	6.62	6.96	7.30	7.58	7.80	7.97	8.12	8.25	8.38	8.47	8.52
LARGE CDs	8.95	9.18	9.43	9.69	9.85	9.75	9.40	9.04	8.80	8.70	8.63	8.51
PUBLIC CDs	8.93	9.18	9.41	9.67	9.85	9.76	9.41	9.03	8.79	8.70	8.63	8.51
OTHER CDS	7.31	7.61	7.88	8.10	8.32	8.44	8.43	8.25	8.07	7.89	7.67	7.47
INT RTE CONTRACTS-SWAPS	0.00	0.00	0.00	0.00	0.00	0.00	0.00	0.00	0.00	0.00	0.00	0.00
OTHER CDs	7.31	7.61	7.88	8.10	8.32	8.44	8.43	8.25	8.07	7.89	7.67	7.47
TOTAL CERTIFICATES	8.43	8.68	8.95	9.22	9.41	9.37	9.13	8.86	8.69	8.63	8.58	8.49
TREASURY, TAX & LOAN	8.87	9.11	9.60	9.59	9.56	9.28	8.99	8.74	8.77	8.59	8.30	8.20
REPOS	9.12	9.36	0.00	9.84	9.81	9.53	0.00	0.00	9.02	8.84	8.55	0.00
FED FUNDS PURCHASED	9.19	10.44	9.91	10.23	9.87	9.92	9.31	9.07	9.40	8.92	8.92	8.54
SHORT-TERM BOR FUNDS	9.00	9.55	9.71	9.82	9.68	9.50	9.10	8.85	8.99	8.72	8.52	8.32
LONG-TERM DEBT	0.00	0.00	0.00	0.00	0.00	0.00	0.00	0.00	0.00	0.00	0.00	0.00
FHLB ADVANCES	0.00	0.00	0.00	0.00	0.00	0.00	0.00	0.00	0.00	0.00	0.00	0.00
LONG-TERM DEBT	0.00	0.00	0.00	0.00	0.00	0.00	0.00	0.00	0.00	0.00	0.00	0.00
TOTAL INT-BEAR LIAB	7.23	7.36	7.55	7.70	7.73	7.65	7.47	7.31	7.20	7.13	7.10	7.06
NET INTEREST SPREAD	3.36	3.40	3.33	3.31	3.55	3.69	3.59	3.63	3.72	3.92	3.84	3.77
NET INTEREST INCOME	4.10	4.18	4.13	4.13	4.36	4.48	4.37	4.39	4.46	4.66	4.57	4.49
MARKET RATES:												
PRIME RATE (LG BKS)	10.50	10.93	11.50	11.50	11.50	11.07	10.98	10.50	10.50	10.50	10.50	10.50
FED FUNDS RATE(NATIONAL)	9.12	9.36	9.85	9.84	9.81	9.53	9.24	8.99	9.02	8.84	8.55	8.45
TREASURY BILL RATE 3 MO	8.29	8.48	8.83	8.70	8.40	8.22	7.92	7.91	7.72	7.59	7.65	7.64
TREASURY BILL RATE 6 MO	8.38	8.54	8.87	8.73	8.41	8.00	7.63	7.72	7.74	7.63	7.46	7.45
US GOVT YIELD (3YRS)	9.20	9.27	9.61	9.40	9.05	8.37	7.83	8.13	8.26	8.02	7.80	7.77
MUNICIPAL BOND YIELD	7.35	7.44	7.59	7.49	7.25	7.02	6.96	7.06	7.26	7.22	7.14	6.98
CONV MTG RATE (NEW)	10.53	10.77	9.99	10.17	10.18	10.09	10.06	9.83	9.87	9.77	9.78	9.70
90-DAY CD RATE(NATIONAL)	9.20	9.38	10.09	9.94	9.68	9.20	8.76	8.64	8.78	8.60	8.39	8.32
LONDON INTERBANK RATE	9.27	9.39	10.12	10.14	9.77	9.33	8.96	8.59	8.82	8.78	8.42	8.39

RISK-BASED CAPITAL REPORT - DETAIL
2000 ACTUAL

	JAN	FEB	MAR	APR	MAY	JUN	JUL	AUG	SEP	OCT	NOV	DEC
RISK-ADJUSTED ASSETS:												
CATEGORY I, 0%:												
CASH, RESERVES & DUE FROM	11977	18056	6944	13096	12053	18208	12136	13319	12278	13434	7395	13557
SHORT-TERM TREASURIES	30673	31037	31406	31779	32157	32539	32926	33317	33712	34112	34517	34927
LONG-TERM TREASURIES	32800	33100	33550	33800	34325	34775	35325	35850	35950	36075	36700	37050
US AGENCY SECURITIES	4063	4020	3977	3933	3889	3845	3800	3755	4210	4164	4117	4070
INT RTE CONTRACTS-OPTIONS	0	0	0	0	0	0	0	0	0	0	0	0
TRADING ACCOUNT	0	0	0	0	0	0	0	0	0	0	0	0
TOTAL - CATEGORY I	79514	86213	75877	82608	82424	89367	84187	86241	86151	87785	82729	89604
WTD TOTAL- CATEGORY I	0	0	0	0	0	0	0	0	0	0	0	0
CATEGORY II, 20%:												
ITEMS IN PROCESS	12477	11784	12652	11951	12834	12135	13019	12325	13211	12518	13407	12714
CMO CLASS B	0	0	0	0	0	0	0	0	0	0	0	0
OUR SECURITIZED MTG LOANS	0	0	0	0	0	0	0	0	0	0	0	0
FHLB STOCK	0	0	0	0	0	0	0	0	0	0	0	0
TERM FED FUNDS SOLD	0	0	0	0	0	0	0	0	0	0	0	0
OVERNIGHT FED FUNDS SOLD	12460	5475	11837	10223	9599	2193	6636	5656	9471	11098	14965	10220
CREDIT EQUIVALENT AMOUNTS:												
OFF-BALANCE SHEET ITEMS	5325	5470	5615	5760	5905	6050	6195	6340	6485	6630	6775	6920
TOTAL - CATEGORY II	30262	22729	30104	27934	28338	20378	25850	24321	29167	30246	35147	29855
WTD TOTAL- CATEGORY II	6052	4546	6021	5587	5668	4076	5170	4864	5833	6049	7029	5971
CATEGORY III, 50%:												
TAX EXEMPTS	10300	9950	9900	9900	9750	9800	9600	9550	9500	9100	8950	8650
MORTGAGE LOANS-FIXED	22716	22897	23080	23264	23449	23636	23825	24015	24206	24399	24594	24790
MORTGAGE LOANS-ADJ	22990	23271	23554	23841	24132	24426	24723	25024	25329	25638	25950	26266
CREDIT EQUIVALENT AMOUNTS:												
OFF-BALANCE SHEET ITEMS	2820	2892	2964	3036	3108	3180	3252	3324	3396	3468	3540	3612
TOTAL - CATEGORY III	58826	59010	59498	60041	60439	61042	61400	61913	62431	62605	63033	63317
WTD TOTAL-CATEGORY III	29413	29505	29749	30020	30220	30521	30700	30957	31216	31302	31517	31659
CATEGORY IV, 100%:												
OTHER SECURITIES	2108	2408	2408	2408	2408	2408	2408	2608	2608	2608	2608	2608
INT RTE CONTRACTS-SWAPS	0	0	0	0	0	0	0	0	0	0	0	0
COM'L PARTIC PURCH-FIXED	0	0	0	0	0	0	0	0	0	0	0	0
DIRECT COM'L LOANS-FIXED	35414	35854	36299	36749	37205	37666	38133	38605	39082	39565	40054	40153
PART PUR - REQ'D-FIXED	0	0	0	0	0	0	0	0	0	0	0	0
PART SOLD - REQ'D-FIXED	0	0	0	0	0	0	0	0	0	0	0	0
COM'L LOANS-OPTION CONTRACT	0	0	0	0	0	0	0	0	0	0	0	0
COM'L PARTIC PURCH-FLOAT	0	0	0	0	0	0	0	0	0	0	0	0
DIRECT COM'L LOANS-FLOAT	41506	41999	42497	43000	43509	44024	44545	45072	45604	46143	46688	47239
HOME EQUITY LOANS	10142	10218	10295	10372	10450	10529	10608	10688	10768	10849	10930	11013
CONSUMER LOANS	50709	51410	52119	52836	53562	54297	54441	54594	54656	54728	54809	54899
CREDIT CARD LOANS	21302	21509	21719	21930	22144	22360	22578	22798	23020	23244	23471	23700
AUTO LOANS	1361	1378	1396	1413	1431	1449	1468	1486	1505	1524	1544	1563
PROPERTY & EQUIPMENT	8247	8279	8311	8344	8377	8409	8442	8475	8509	8542	8575	8609
OREO & FORECLOSED ASSETS	496	507	518	530	541	553	565	577	589	601	614	619
OTHER ASSETS	5416	6031	6638	5441	6055	6689	5569	6213	6862	5648	6311	6989
TOTAL - CATEGORY IV	176700	179593	182200	183025	185683	188385	188757	191116	193204	193453	195603	197391
WTD TOTAL- CATEGORY IV	176700	179593	182200	183025	185683	188385	188757	191116	193204	193453	195603	197391
WTD NONCONFORMING ACCT	0	0	0	0	0	0	0	0	0	0	0	0
REDUCTION TO RISK ASSETS	0	0	0	0	0	0	0	0	0	0	0	0
GROSS RISK-WTD ASSETS	212166	213644	217969	218632	221570	222982	224627	226936	230253	230805	234149	235021

RISK-BASED CAPITAL REPORT - DETAIL
2001 ACTUAL

	JAN	FEB	MAR	APR	MAY	JUN	JUL	AUG	SEP	OCT	NOV	DEC
RISK-ADJUSTED ASSETS:												
CATEGORY I, 0%:												
CASH, RESERVES & DUE FROM	10079	10152	10223	10293	10365	10437	10510	10583	10658	10733	10810	10884
SHORT-TERM TREASURIES	35456	34943	35408	35917	35248	34572	34707	36810	36186	36638	37076	39373
LONG-TERM TREASURIES	37350	37600	37700	37550	37550	38150	38350	38750	38800	38700	38900	39400
US AGENCY SECURITIES	4030	3989	4649	4606	4563	4520	4477	4433	4889	4843	4796	4750
INT RTE CONTRACTS-OPTIONS	0	0	0	0	0	0	0	0	0	0	0	0
TRADING ACCOUNT	0	0	0	0	0	0	0	0	0	0	0	0
TOTAL - CATEGORY I	86915	86684	87980	88367	87726	87679	88043	90576	90533	90914	91582	94407
WTD TOTAL- CATEGORY I	0	0	0	0	0	0	0	0	0	0	0	0
CATEGORY II, 20%:												
ITEMS IN PROCESS	13199	13286	13379	13477	13576	13676	13777	13879	13982	14086	14191	14303
CMO CLASS B	0	0	0	0	0	0	0	0	0	0	0	0
OUR SECURITIZED MTG LOANS	0	0	0	0	0	0	0	0	0	0	0	0
FHLB STOCK	5000	0	0	5000	5044	5098	5093	0	5000	5031	5035	0
TERM FED FUNDS SOLD	0	0	0	0	0	0	0	0	0	0	0	0
OVERNIGHT FED FUNDS SOLD	8156	14207	12461	9868	10969	11297	12535	15574	11779	13397	13522	16363
CREDIT EQUIVALENT AMOUNTS:												
OFF-BALANCE SHEET ITEMS	7065	7210	7355	7500	7645	7790	7935	8080	8225	8370	8515	8660
TOTAL - CATEGORY II	33419	34702	33195	35844	37234	37862	39341	37533	38986	40884	41263	39326
WTD TOTAL- CATEGORY II	6684	6940	6639	7169	7447	7572	7868	7507	7797	8177	8253	7865
CATEGORY III, 50%:												
TAX EXEMPTS	8450	8050	7800	7350	7100	7050	6850	6750	6500	6450	6050	5750
MORTGAGE LOANS-FIXED	24798	25107	25419	25736	26056	26380	26708	27041	27377	27718	28063	28072
MORTGAGE LOANS-ADJ	26582	26902	27225	27553	27884	28220	28560	28903	29251	29603	29959	30320
CREDIT EQUIVALENT AMOUNTS:												
OFF-BALANCE SHEET ITEMS	3684	3756	3828	3900	3972	4044	4116	4188	4260	4332	4404	4476
TOTAL - CATEGORY III	63514	63814	64272	64538	65012	65694	66234	66882	67388	68103	68476	68618
WTD TOTAL-CATEGORY III	31757	31907	32136	32269	32506	32847	33117	33441	33694	34052	34238	34309
CATEGORY IV, 100%:												
OTHER SECURITIES	2608	2708	2708	2708	2708	2708	2908	2908	2908	2908	2908	2908
INT RTE CONTRACTS-SWAPS	0	0	0	0	0	0	0	0	0	0	0	0
COM'L PARTIC PURCH-FIXED	0	0	0	0	0	0	0	0	0	0	0	0
DIRECT COM'L LOANS-FIXED	40217	40339	40662	40989	41317	41649	41982	42318	42657	42998	43342	43688
PART PUR - REQ'D-FIXED	0	0	0	0	0	0	0	0	0	0	0	0
PART SOLD - REQ'D-FIXED	0	0	0	0	0	0	0	0	0	0	0	0
COM'L LNS-OPTION CONTRACT	0	0	0	0	0	0	0	0	0	0	0	0
COM'L PARTIC PURCH-FLOAT	0	0	0	0	0	0	0	0	0	0	0	0
DIRECT COM'L LOANS-FLOAT	47640	48044	48452	48863	49278	49696	50117	50542	50970	51402	51837	52276
HOME EQUITY LOANS	11178	11345	11515	11688	11863	12041	12221	12404	12590	12779	12970	13165
CONSUMER LOANS	55565	56239	56922	57613	58312	59020	59736	60461	61195	61937	62689	63450
CREDIT CARD LOANS	23931	24164	24399	24637	24877	25120	25365	25612	25861	26113	26368	26625
AUTO LOANS	1583	1603	1624	1644	1665	1686	1708	1729	1751	1774	1796	1819
PROPERTY & EQUIPMENT	8654	8700	8746	8792	8839	8885	8932	8979	9027	9074	9122	9170
OREO & FORECLOSED ASSETS	623	628	636	645	653	662	671	680	688	697	706	715
OTHER ASSETS	5701	6313	6958	5774	6513	7246	5836	6474	7126	5920	6588	7226
TOTAL - CATEGORY IV	197700	200083	202623	203353	206026	208712	209475	212108	214773	215603	218327	221043
WTD TOTAL- CATEGORY IV	197700	200083	202623	203353	206026	208712	209475	212108	214773	215603	218327	221043
WTD NONCONFORMING ACCT	0	0	0	0	0	0	0	0	0	0	0	0
REDUCTION TO RISK ASSETS	0	0	0	0	0	0	0	0	0	0	0	0
GROSS RISK-WTD ASSETS	236140	238931	241399	242791	245979	249132	250460	253055	256265	257832	260818	263217

RISK-BASED CAPITAL REPORT - DETAIL
2000 ACTUAL

	JAN	FEB	MAR	APR	MAY	JUN	JUL	AUG	SEP	OCT	NOV	DEC
CAPITAL:												
TIER 1, CORE CAPITAL:												
COMMON STOCK & SURPLUS	5000	5000	5000	5000	5000	5000	5000	5000	5000	5000	5000	5000
RETAINED EARNINGS	15181	15394	15337	15565	15798	15734	15951	16180	16092	16325	16524	16452
INCREASE: TIER 1 CAPITAL	0	0	00	0	0	0	0	0	0	0	0	
DECREASE: TIER 1 CAPITAL	-925	-925	-925	-925	-925	-925	-92	5-925	-925	-925	-925	-925
TOTAL TIER 1 CORE CAP	19256	19469	19412	19640	19873	19809	20026	20255	20167	20400	20599	20527
TIER 2, SUPPLEMENTARY CAPITAL:												
TIER 2 SUBJECT TO LIMITS	0	0	0	0	0	0	0	0	0	0	0	0
ADJUST TO % TIER 1 LIMIT	0	0	0	0	0	0	0	0	0	0	0	0
RESERVE FOR LOAN LOSSES	3575	3618	3647	3683	3720	3758	3791	3820	3849	3878	3907	3933
ALLOWANCE EXCESS	-923	-948	-922	-951	-951	-970	-983	-984	-971	-993	-980	-995
INCREASE: TIER 2 CAPITAL	0	0	0	0	0	0	0	0	0	0	0	0
SUBTOTAL	2652	2671	2725	2733	2770	2787	2808	2837	2878	2885	2927	2938
AMOUNT EXCEEDING TIER 1	0	0	0	0	0	0	0	0	0	0	0	0
TOTAL TIER 2 SUPP CAP	2652	2671	2725	2733	2770	2787	2808	2837	2878	2885	2927	2938
TIER 1 PLUS TIER 2	21908	22139	22137	22373	22642	22596	22834	23091	23045	23285	23526	23464
DECREASE: TOTAL CAPITAL	0	0	0	0	0	0	0	0	0	0	0	0
QUALIFYING TOTAL CAPITAL	21908	22139	22137	22373	22642	22596	22834	23091	23045	23285	23526	23464
GROSS RISK-WTD ASSETS	212166	213644	217969	218632	221570	222982	224627	226936	230253	230805	234149	235021
LESS: ALLOWANCE EXCESS	923	948	922	951	951	970	983	984	971	993	980	995
ADJUSTED RISK-WTD ASSETS	211243	212696	217047	217682	220619	222011	223644	225953	229282	229812	233169	234026
RISK-ADJUSTED CAPITAL RATIOS:												
CORE (TIER 1) RATIO	9.12	9.15	8.94	9.02	9.01	8.92	8.95	8.96	8.80	8.88	8.83	8.77
TOTAL CAPITAL RATIO	10.37	10.41	10.20	10.28	10.26	10.18	10.21	10.22	10.05	10.13	10.09	10.03
RISK-WTD TO TOTAL ASSETS	63.33	63.38	64.70	63.81	64.11	64.13	64.46	64.54	64.18	63.82	64.36	63.99

RISK-BASED CAPITAL REPORT - DETAIL
2001 ACTUAL

	JAN	FEB	MAR	APR	MAY	JUN	JUL	AUG	SEP	OCT	NOV	DEC
CAPITAL:												
TIER 1, CORE CAPITAL:												
COMMON STOCK & SURPLUS	5000	5000	5000	5000	5000	5000	5000	5000	5000	5000	5000	5000
RETAINED EARNINGS	16643	16913	16817	17055	17302	17286	17531	17803	17817	18126	18430	18441
INCREASE: TIER 1 CAPITAL	0	0	0	0	0	0	0	0	0	0	0	0
DECREASE: TIER 1 CAPITAL	-925	-925	-925	-925	-925	-925	-925	-925	-925	-925	-925	-925
TOTAL TIER 1 CORE CAP	20718	20988	20892	21130	21377	21361	21606	21878	21892	22201	22505	22516
TIER 2, SUPPLEMENTARY CAPITAL:												
TIER 2 SUBJECT TO LIMITS	0	0	0	0	0	0	0	0	0	0	0	0
ADJUST TO % TIER 1 LIMIT	0	0	0	0	0	0	0	0	0	0	0	0
RESERVE FOR LOAN LOSSES	3982	4020	4063	4106	4150	4194	4238	4283	4328	4374	4421	4462
ALLOWANCE EXCESS	-1030	-1034	-1045	-1071	-1075	-1079	-1107	-1120	-1125	-1151	-1161	-1172
INCREASE: TIER 2 CAPITAL	0	0	0	0	0	0	0	0	0	0	0	0
SUBTOTAL	2952	2987	3017	3035	3075	3114	3131	3163	3203	3223	3260	3290
AMOUNT EXCEEDING TIER 1	0	0	0	0	0	0	0	0	0	0	0	0
TOTAL TIER 2 SUPP CAP	2952	2987	3017	3035	3075	3114	3131	3163	3203	3223	3260	3290
TIER 1 PLUS TIER 2	23670	23975	23910	24165	24452	24475	24736	25042	25095	25424	25765	25806
DECREASE: TOTAL CAPITAL	0	0	0	0	0	0	0	0	0	0	0	0
QUALIFYING TOTAL CAPITAL	23670	23975	23910	24165	24452	24475	24736	25042	25095	25424	25765	25806
GROSS RISK-WTD ASSETS	236140	238931	241399	242791	245979	249132	250460	253055	256265	257832	260818	263217
LESS: ALLOWANCE EXCESS	1030	1034	1045	1071	1075	1079	1107	1120	1125	1151	1161	1172
ADJUSTED RISK-WTD ASSETS	235111	237897	240353	241720	244904	248052	249353	51936	255140	256680	259657	262045
RISK-ADJUSTED CAPITAL RATIOS:												
CORE (TIER 1) RATIO	8.81	8.82	8.69	8.74	8.73	8.61	8.66	8.68	8.58	8.65	8.67	8.59
TOTAL CAPITAL RATIO	10.07	10.08	9.95	10.00	9.98	9.87	9.92	9.94	9.84	9.90	9.92	9.85
RISK-WTD TO TOTAL ASSETS	64.09	64.24	64.47	64.19	64.41	64.61	64.46	64.51	64.61	64.42	64.54	64.58

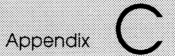
Monthly Financial Reports
for Years
2002 and 2003

Page

ENDING STATEMENT OF CONDITION - DETAIL

2002 ACTUAL

	JAN	FEB	MAR	APR	MAY	JUN	JUL	AUG	SEP	OCT	NOV	DEC
ASSETS:												
CASH, RESERVES & DUE FROM	10465	10543	10623	10704	10785	10868	10951	11035	11120	11207	11291	11388
ITEMS IN PROCESS	14403	14511	14620	14730	14841	14953	15066	15180	15296	15412	15522	15633
CASH, FLOAT & RESERVES	24868	25055	25243	25434	25626	25821	26017	26216	26416	26619	26813	27021
SHORT-TERM TREASURIES	39600	39073	39620	38974	39230	39392	40757	41997	42366	42735	44221	44290
LONG-TERM TREASURIES	40150	40600	41200	41750	41900	42250	42450	42400	42500	42400	42400	42200
US AGENCY SECURITIES	4703	4656	5008	4959	4909	4859	4809	5358	5305	5251	5198	5143
CMO CLASS B	0	0	0	0	0	0	0	0	0	0	0	0
OUR SECURITIZED MTG LOANS	0	0	0	0	0	0	0	0	0	0	0	0
ASSET BACKED SECURITIES	4703	4656	5008	4959	4909	4859	4809	5358	5305	5251	5198	5143
TAX EXEMPTS	5500	5250	5100	5000	4800	4550	4150	3850	3750	3550	3400	3200
OTHER SECURITIES	2908	2908	3024	3024	3024	3024	3024	3024	3124	3124	3124	3124
FHLB STOCK	0	0	0	0	0	0	0	0	0	0	0	0
INT RTE CONTRACTS-SWAPS	0	0	0	0	0	0	0	0	0	0	0	0
INT RTE CONTRACTS-OPTIONS	0	0	0	0	0	0	0	0	0	0	0	0
ALL OTHER SECURITIES	8408	8158	8124	8024	7824	7574	7174	6874	6874	6674	6542	6324
TOTAL SECURITIES	92861	92487	93952	93707	93863	94075	95190	96629	97045	97060	98343	97957
TERM FED FUNDS SOLD	0	0	0	0	0	0	0	0	0	0	0	0
OVERNIGHT FED FUNDS SOLD	17792	19044	17929	20043	20218	20364	20682	19589	20035	22041	21731	23529
TRADING ACCOUNT	0	0	0	0	0	0	0	0	0	0	0	0
SHORT-TERM INVESTMENTS	17792	19044	17929	20043	20218	20364	20682	19589	20035	22041	21731	23529
COM'L PARTIC PURCH-FIXED	0	0	0	0	0	0	0	0	0	0	0	0
DIRECT COM'L LOANS-FIXED	44037	44389	44743	45100	45459	45821	46186	46553	46924	47297	47673	48051
PART PUR - REQ'D-FIXED	0	0	0	0	0	0	0	0	0	0	0	0
PART SOLD - REQ'D-FIXED	0	0	0	0	0	0	0	0	0	0	0	0
COM'L LOANS-OPTION CONTRCT	0	0	0	0	0	0	0	0	0	0	0	0
COMMERCIAL LOANS-FIXED	44037	44389	44743	45100	45459	45821	46186	46553	46924	47297	47673	48051
COM'L PARTIC PURCH-FLOAT	0	0	0	0	0	0	0	0	0	0	0	0
DIRECT COM'L LOANS-FLOAT	52718	53164	53613	54067	54524	54984	55449	55917	56389	56865	57344	57828
COMMERCIAL LOANS-FLOAT	52718	53164	53613	54067	54524	54984	55449	55917	56389	56865	57344	57828
MORTGAGE LOANS-FIXED	28766	29124	29486	29853	30225	30601	30982	31367	31758	32153	32553	32958
MORTGAGE LOANS-ADJ	30685	31054	31428	31806	32189	32576	32968	33365	33766	34172	34584	34600
HOME EQUITY LOANS	13362	13562	13766	13972	14181	14394	14610	14828	15051	15276	15305	15338
CONSUMER LOANS	64220	64999	65788	66587	67395	68213	69041	69879	70727	71585	71835	71984
CREDIT CARD LOANS	26884	27146	27411	27678	27948	28220	28495	28773	29053	29336	29622	29911
AUTO LOANS	1842	1865	1889	1913	1937	1962	1987	2012	2038	2063	2090	2116
TOTAL LOANS	262514	265304	268124	270975	273857	276771	279716	282694	285705	288748	291006	292786
RESERVE FOR LOAN LOSSES	-4515	-4563	-4612	-4661	-4710	-4760	-4811	-4862	-4914	-4966	-5005	-5036
NET LOANS	257999	260741	263512	266314	269147	272010	274905	277832	280791	283782	286001	287750
PROPERTY & EQUIPMENT	9219	9268	9316	9366	9415	9465	9515	9565	9616	9666	9717	9769
OREO & FORECLOSED ASSETS	725	734	743	752	762	771	781	791	801	810	820	830
OTHER ASSETS	5921	6546	7203	5985	6651	7310	6057	6735	7408	6124	6795	7472
TOTAL OTHER ASSETS	15864	16548	17262	16103	16828	17546	16353	17091	17824	16601	17333	18071
TOTAL ASSETS	409384	413874	417899	421601	425682	429816	433148	437356	442111	446102	450220	454329

ENDING STATEMENT OF CONDITION - DETAIL
2003 FORECAST

	JAN	FEB	MAR	APR	MAY	JUN	JUL	AUG	SEP	OCT	NOV	DEC
ASSETS:												
CASH, RESERVES & DUE FROM	8434	8542	8655	8724	8794	8863	8934	9001	9066	9132	9200	9266
ITEMS IN PROCESS	7885	7956	8033	8070	8106	8143	8180	8215	8248	8281	8315	8349
CASH, FLOAT & RESERVES	16319	16498	16688	16794	16900	17006	17114	17216	17314	17413	17515	17615
SHORT-TERM TREASURIES	57231	53155	52555	52614	53666	53333	59362	59641	58542	57561	58237	58009
LONG-TERM TREASURIES	42400	42550	42950	43050	43200	43400	43400	43400	43300	43600	43800	44050
US AGENCY SECURITIES	5735	6330	6619	6705	6889	7171	7251	7579	7660	8040	8372	8501
CMO CLASS B	7750	7153	7153	7153	6628	6628	6628	6628	6628	6628	6628	6628
OUR SECURITIZED MTG LOANS	0	0	0	0	0	0	0	0	0	0	0	0
ASSET BACKED SECURITIES	13485	13484	13773	13859	13517	13798	13879	14207	14288	14668	14999	15129
TAX EXEMPTS	3100	3150	3000	3000	2850	2800	2650	2600	2550	2450	2450	2400
OTHER SECURITIES	3124	3574	3574	3574	3574	3574	4174	4174	4174	4174	4074	4074
FHLB STOCK	0	0	0	0	0	0	0	0	0	0	0	0
INT RTE CONTRACTS-SWAPS	0	0	0	0	0	0	0	0	0	0	0	0
INT RTE CONTRACTS-OPTIONS	0	0	0	0	0	0	0	0	0	0	0	0
ALL OTHER SECURITIES	6224	6724	6574	6574	6424	6374	6824	6774	6724	6624	6524	6474
TOTAL SECURITIES	119340	115913	115852	116097	116807	116905	123465	124022	122854	122453	123560	123662
TERM FED FUNDS SOLD	0	0	0	0	0	0	0	0	0	0	0	0
OVERNIGHT FED FUNDS SOLD	11283	17494	20339	19926	19380	21642	15111	17054	22129	25052	24871	25911
TRADING ACCOUNT	5000	5000	5000	5000	5000	5000	5000	5000	5000	5000	5000	5000
SHORT-TERM INVESTMENTS	16283	22494	25339	24926	24380	26642	20111	22054	27129	30052	29871	30911
COM'L PARTIC PURCH-FIXED	0	0	0	0	0	0	0	0	0	0	0	0
DIRECT COM'L LOANS-FIXED	48279	48520	48759	49228	49644	50110	50527	50698	50837	50949	51138	51299
PART PUR - REQ'D-FIXED	0	0	0	0	0	0	0	0	0	0	0	0
PART SOLD - REQ'D-FIXED	0	0	0	0	0	0	0	0	0	0	0	0
COM'L LOANS-OPTION CONTRACT	0	0	0	0	0	0	0	0	0	0	0	0
COMMERCIAL LOANS-FIXED	48279	48520	48759	49228	49644	50110	50527	50698	50837	50949	51138	51299
COM'L PARTIC PURCH-FLOAT	0	0	0	0	0	0	0	0	0	0	0	0
DIRECT COM'L LOANS-FLOAT	58138	58512	58800	59000	59300	59700	60100	60400	60700	61100	61500	61800
COMMERCIAL LOANS-FLOAT	58138	58512	58800	59000	59300	59700	60100	60400	60700	61100	61500	61800
MORTGAGE LOANS-FIXED	32427	31933	31408	30873	30338	29794	29259	28725	28227	27737	27272	26815
MORTGAGE LOANS-ADJ	35165	35746	36309	36864	37415	37959	38504	39045	39602	40160	40728	41297
HOME EQUITY LOANS	15389	15444	15501	15560	15622	15685	15751	15819	15890	15963	16039	16118
CONSUMER LOANS	72151	72324	72502	72739	73038	73398	73866	74439	75014	75440	75770	75956
CREDIT CARD LOANS	28841	30816	32372	33503	34206	34473	34299	33678	32605	31074	31472	31874
AUTO LOANS	2245	2370	2493	2614	2730	2844	2958	3070	3183	3295	3406	3515
TOTAL LOANS	292635	295665	298144	300382	302292	303963	305264	305876	306059	305719	307324	308674
RESERVE FOR LOAN LOSSES	-4918	-4801	-4852	-4899	-4938	-4974	-5002	-5019	-5026	-5020	-5030	-5055
NET LOANS	287717	290864	293292	295483	297354	298989	300263	300857	301034	300699	302294	303619
PROPERTY & EQUIPMENT	9796	9823	9851	9878	9906	9933	9961	9989	10017	10045	10073	10101
OREO & FORECLOSED ASSETS	940	1044	1150	1266	1376	1486	1605	1715	1826	1945	2057	2170
OTHER ASSETS	6286	7066	7870	6364	7171	7971	6462	7315	8153	6541	7375	8224
TOTAL OTHER ASSETS	17022	17933	18871	17508	18452	19391	18028	19019	19996	18530	19505	20494
TOTAL ASSETS	456681	463701	470043	470808	473894	478934	478981	483168	488327	489147	492746	496301

ENDING STATEMENT OF CONDITION - DETAIL
2002 ACTUAL

	JAN	FEB	MAR	APR	MAY	JUN	JUL	AUG	SEP	OCT	NOV	DEC
LIABILITIES & CAPITAL:												
BUSINESS DEMAND	34272	34431	34591	34752	34915	35079	35244	35410	35578	35747	35918	36090
PUBLIC DEMAND	6977	7029	7082	7136	7189	7244	7298	7353	7409	7465	7481	7501
DEMAND DEPOSITS	41249	41460	41673	41888	42104	42323	42542	42764	42987	43212	43399	43591
INTEREST-BEAR CHECKING	61537	62193	62855	63525	64202	64887	65578	66277	66983	67697	68419	69148
REGULAR SAVINGS	34106	34440	34778	35120	35464	35812	36164	36519	36877	37239	37604	37973
IBC & SAVINGS	95642	96633	97634	98645	99667	100699	101742	102796	103860	104936	106023	107122
MMDAs	85502	86543	87597	88664	89743	90836	91942	93061	94194	95341	96502	97677
SMALL CDs	26348	26543	26739	26936	27135	27335	27537	27741	27945	28152	28360	28969
LARGE CDs	84136	85022	85918	86823	87738	88662	89596	90540	91493	92457	93431	94416
PUBLIC CDs	34883	35146	35411	35678	35947	36219	36492	36767	37044	37324	37406	37506
OTHER CDS	2817	2851	2886	2921	2957	2993	3029	3066	3103	3141	3179	3217
INT RTE CONTRACTS-SWAPS	0	0	0	0	0	0	0	0	0	0	0	0
OTHER CDs	2817	2851	2886	2921	2957	2993	3029	3066	3103	3141	3179	3217
TOTAL CERTIFICATES	148184	149563	150954	152359	153777	155208	156654	158113	159586	161073	162376	164108
TOTAL DEPOSITS	370577	374199	377858	381555	385291	389066	392880	396734	400628	404563	408300	412497
TREASURY, TAX & LOAN	3793	3804	3815	3826	3836	3847	3858	3869	3880	3891	3902	3913
REPOS	0	500	500	500	500	500	0	0	500	500	500	0
FED FUNDS PURCHASED	1000	1000	1000	1000	1000	1000	1000	1000	1000	1000	1000	1000
SHORT-TERM BOR FUNDS	4793	5304	5315	5326	5336	5347	4858	4869	5380	5391	5402	4913
LONG-TERM DEBT	0	0	0	0	0	0	0	0	0	0	0	0
FHLB ADVANCES	0	0	0	0	0	0	0	0	0	0	0	0
LONG-TERM DEBT	0	0	0	0	0	0	0	0	0	0	0	0
OTH LIAB:ACCR INC TAXES	2481	2481	2481	2481	2481	2481	2481	2481	2481	2481	2481	2481
OTH LIAB:ACCR DIVID PAY	0	0	325	0	0	325	0	0	325	0	0	325
OTH LIAB:ACCR INT PAY	262	236	263	257	270	264	273	272	263	274	267	277
OTH LIAB:DEFER'D I/E-OBS	0	0	0	0	0	0	0	0	0	0	0	0
OTH LIAB:ALL OTHER	7559	7631	7703	7775	7847	7919	7992	8064	8137	8209	8282	8355
OTHER LIABILITIES	10302	10348	10771	10513	10598	10989	10745	10817	11206	10964	11030	11438
COMMON STOCK & SURPLUS	5000	5000	5000	5000	5000	5000	5000	5000	5000	5000	5000	5000
RETAINED EARNINGS	18712	19023	18955	19207	19457	19414	19664	19936	19897	20184	20487	20481
TOTAL EQUITY	23712	24023	23955	24207	24457	24414	24664	24936	24897	25184	25487	25481
TOTAL LIAB & EQUITY	409384	413874	417899	421601	425682	429816	433148	437356	442111	446102	450220	454329
TOTAL EARNING ASSETS	373167	376835	380005	384724	387938	391209	395588	398912	402785	407849	411080	414272
TOTAL INT-BEAR LIAB	334122	338043	341499	344993	348523	352090	355196	358839	363021	366742	370303	373819

ENDING STATEMENT OF CONDITION - DETAIL
2003 FORECAST

	JAN	FEB	MAR	APR	MAY	JUN	JUL	AUG	SEP	OCT	NOV	DEC
LIABILITIES & CAPITAL:												
BUSINESS DEMAND	36413	36505	36595	36679	36774	36888	37012	37111	37187	37269	37364	37452
PUBLIC DEMAND	7860	8233	8665	8697	8717	8717	8717	8717	8717	8717	8717	8717
DEMAND DEPOSITS	44273	44738	45260	45376	45490	45604	45728	45828	45903	45986	46081	46168
INTEREST-BEAR CHECKING	69148	69648	70148	70648	71148	71648	72148	72648	73148	73648	74148	74648
REGULAR SAVINGS	38022	38074	38128	38184	38242	38303	38367	38433	38501	38572	38645	38721
IBC & SAVINGS	107170	107722	108276	108832	109390	109951	110515	111081	111649	112220	112793	113369
MMDAs	98350	99000	99650	100300	100950	101600	102250	102900	103550	104200	104850	105500
SMALL CDs	29387	29905	30523	31140	31858	32576	33543	34495	35432	36369	37292	38214
LARGE CDs	94912	95310	95812	96317	96925	97435	97947	98462	98980	99501	100025	100551
PUBLIC CDs	39301	41163	43326	43483	43583	43583	43583	43583	43583	43583	43583	43583
OTHER CDS	3119	3136	3141	3181	3208	3351	3374	3397	3420	3444	3467	3491
INT RTE CONTRACTS-SWAPS	0	0	0	0	0	0	0	0	0	0	0	0
OTHER CDs	3119	3136	3141	3181	3208	3351	3374	3397	3420	3444	3467	3491
TOTAL CERTIFICATES	166719	169515	172801	174121	175574	176945	178447	179937	181416	182897	184366	185838
TOTAL DEPOSITS	416513	420974	425987	428629	431405	434101	436940	439746	442518	445303	448091	450876
TREASURY, TAX & LOAN	3934	3954	3975	3996	4017	4038	4059	4081	4102	4124	4145	4167
REPOS	0	1000	1000	1000	0	1000	0	0	1000	1000	500	0
FED FUNDS PURCHASED	1000	1000	1000	1000	1000	1000	1000	1000	1000	1000	1000	1000
SHORT-TERM BOR FUNDS	4934	5954	5975	5996	5017	6038	5059	5081	6102	6124	5645	5167
LONG-TERM DEBT	0	0	0	0	0	0	0	0	0	0	0	0
FHLB ADVANCES	0	0	0	0	0	0	0	0	0	0	0	0
LONG-TERM DEBT	0	0	0	0	0	0	0	0	0	0	0	0
OTH LIAB:ACCR INC TAXES	204	456	605	166	310	468	150	310	473	119	246	352
OTH LIAB:ACCR DIVID PAY	0	0	330	0	0	330	0	0	330	0	0	330
OTH LIAB:ACCR INT PAY	762	1520	2304	775	1561	2340	809	1640	2456	822	1634	2461
OTH LIAB:DEFER'D I/E-OBS	0	0	0	0	0	0	0	0	0	0	0	0
OTH LIAB:ALL OTHER	8384	8421	8458	8494	8531	8568	8605	8642	8679	8717	8754	8792
OTHER LIABILITIES	9351	10398	11696	9436	10401	11705	9564	10592	11938	9658	10635	11934
COMMON STOCK & SURPLUS	5000	5000	5000	5000	5000	5000	5000	5000	5000	5000	5000	5000
RETAINED EARNINGS	20883	21375	21385	21747	22071	22090	22417	22750	22769	23063	23375	23324
TOTAL EQUITY	25883	26375	26385	26747	27071	27090	27417	27750	27769	28063	28375	28324
TOTAL LIAB & EQUITY	456681	463701	470043	470808	473894	478934	478981	483168	488327	489147	492746	496301
TOTAL EARNING ASSETS	428258	434072	439335	441404	443480	447511	448840	451952	456043	458224	460756	463247
TOTAL INT-BEAR LIAB	377173	382191	386702	389249	390932	394535	396271	398999	402717	405440	407655	409874

228

AVERAGE STATEMENT OF CONDITION - DETAIL
PERCENTAGE COMPOSITION
2002 ACTUAL

	JAN	FEB	MAR	APR	MAY	JUN	JUL	AUG	SEP	OCT	NOV	DEC
ASSETS:												
CASH, RESERVES & DUE FROM	2.6	2.6	2.6	2.6	2.5	2.5	2.5	2.5	2.5	2.5	2.5	2.5
ITEMS IN PROCESS	3.5	3.5	3.5	3.5	3.5	3.5	3.5	3.5	3.5	3.5	3.5	3.5
CASH, FLOAT & RESERVES	6.2	6.1	6.1	6.1	6.1	6.0	6.0	6.0	6.0	6.0	6.0	6.0
SHORT-TERM TREASURIES	9.7	9.6	9.5	9.4	9.3	9.2	9.3	9.5	9.6	9.6	9.7	9.8
LONG-TERM TREASURIES	9.8	9.9	9.9	9.9	9.9	9.9	9.9	9.8	9.7	9.6	9.5	9.4
US AGENCY SECURITIES	1.2	1.1	1.2	1.2	1.2	1.2	1.1	1.2	1.2	1.2	1.2	1.2
CMO CLASS B	0.0	0.0	0.0	0.0	0.0	0.0	0.0	0.0	0.0	0.0	0.0	0.0
OUR SECURITIZED MTG LOANS	0.0	0.0	0.0	0.0	0.0	0.0	0.0	0.0	0.0	0.0	0.0	0.0
ASSET BACKED SECURITIES	1.2	1.1	1.2	1.2	1.2	1.2	1.1	1.2	1.2	1.2	1.2	1.2
TAX EXEMPTS	1.4	1.3	1.3	1.2	1.2	1.1	1.0	0.9	0.9	0.8	0.8	0.7
OTHER SECURITIES	0.7	0.7	0.7	0.7	0.7	0.7	0.7	0.7	0.7	0.7	0.7	0.7
FHLB STOCK	0.0	0.0	0.0	0.0	0.0	0.0	0.0	0.0	0.0	0.0	0.0	0.0
INT RTE CONTRACTS-SWAPS	0.0	0.0	0.0	0.0	0.0	0.0	0.0	0.0	0.0	0.0	0.0	0.0
INT RTE CONTRACTS-OPTIONS	0.0	0.0	0.0	0.0	0.0	0.0	0.0	0.0	0.0	0.0	0.0	0.0
ALL OTHER SECURITIES	2.1	2.0	2.0	1.9	1.9	1.8	1.7	1.6	1.6	1.5	1.5	1.4
TOTAL SECURITIES	22.8	22.6	22.5	22.5	22.3	22.1	22.0	22.1	22.1	22.0	21.9	21.8
TERM FED FUNDS SOLD	0.0	0.0	0.0	0.0	0.0	0.0	0.0	0.0	0.0	0.0	0.0	0.0
OVERNIGHT FED FUNDS SOLD	3.7	4.0	3.9	4.0	4.2	4.2	4.2	4.2	4.0	4.2	4.4	4.5
TRADING ACCOUNT	0.0	0.0	0.0	0.0	0.0	0.0	0.0	0.0	0.0	0.0	0.0	0.0
SHORT-TERM INVESTMENTS	3.7	4.0	3.9	4.0	4.2	4.2	4.2	4.2	4.0	4.2	4.4	4.5
COM'L PARTIC PURCH-FIXED	0.0	0.0	0.0	0.0	0.0	0.0	0.0	0.0	0.0	0.0	0.0	0.0
DIRECT COM'L LOANS-FIXED	10.8	10.8	10.8	10.8	10.7	10.7	10.7	10.7	10.7	10.7	10.6	10.6
PART PUR - REQ'D-FIXED	0.0	0.0	0.0	0.0	0.0	0.0	0.0	0.0	0.0	0.0	0.0	0.0
PART SOLD - REQ'D-FIXED	0.0	0.0	0.0	0.0	0.0	0.0	0.0	0.0	0.0	0.0	0.0	0.0
COM'L LOANS-OPTION CONTRACT	0.0	0.0	0.0	0.0	0.0	0.0	0.0	0.0	0.0	0.0	0.0	0.0
COMMERCIAL LOANS-FIXED	10.8	10.8	10.8	10.8	10.7	10.7	10.7	10.7	10.7	10.7	10.6	10.6
COM'L PARTIC PURCH-FLOAT	0.0	0.0	0.0	0.0	0.0	0.0	0.0	0.0	0.0	0.0	0.0	0.0
DIRECT COM'L LOANS-FLOAT	12.9	12.9	12.9	12.9	12.9	12.9	12.9	12.9	12.8	12.8	12.8	12.8
COMMERCIAL LOANS-FLOAT	12.9	12.9	12.9	12.9	12.9	12.9	12.9	12.9	12.8	12.8	12.8	12.8
MORTGAGE LOANS-FIXED	7.0	7.1	7.1	7.1	7.1	7.2	7.2	7.2	7.2	7.2	7.3	7.3
MORTGAGE LOANS-ADJ	7.5	7.5	7.6	7.6	7.6	7.6	7.6	7.7	7.7	7.7	7.7	7.7
HOME EQUITY LOANS	3.3	3.3	3.3	3.3	3.3	3.4	3.4	3.4	3.4	3.4	3.4	3.4
CONSUMER LOANS	15.7	15.8	15.8	15.8	15.9	15.9	16.0	16.0	16.1	16.1	16.1	16.0
CREDIT CARD LOANS	6.6	6.6	6.6	6.6	6.6	6.6	6.6	6.6	6.6	6.6	6.6	6.6
AUTO LOANS	0.5	0.5	0.5	0.5	0.5	0.5	0.5	0.5	0.5	0.5	0.5	0.5
TOTAL LOANS	64.3	64.4	64.5	64.6	64.6	64.7	64.8	64.9	64.9	65.0	65.0	64.9
RESERVE FOR LOAN LOSSES	-1.1	-1.1	-1.1	-1.1	-1.1	-1.1	-1.1	-1.1	-1.1	-1.1	-1.1	-1.1
NET LOANS	63.3	63.3	63.4	63.5	63.6	63.6	63.7	63.8	63.8	63.9	63.9	63.8
PROPERTY & EQUIPMENT	2.3	2.3	2.2	2.2	2.2	2.2	2.2	2.2	2.2	2.2	2.2	2.2
OREO & FORECLOSED ASSETS	0.2	0.2	0.2	0.2	0.2	0.2	0.2	0.2	0.2	0.2	0.2	0.2
OTHER ASSETS	1.6	1.5	1.7	1.6	1.5	1.6	1.6	1.5	1.6	1.5	1.4	1.6
TOTAL OTHER ASSETS	4.1	4.0	4.1	4.0	3.9	4.0	3.9	3.9	4.0	3.9	3.8	3.9
TOTAL ASSETS	100.0	100.0	100.0	100.0	100.0	100.0	100.0	100.0	100.0	100.0	100.0	100.0

AVERAGE STATEMENT OF CONDITION - DETAIL
PERCENTAGE COMPOSITION
2003 FORECAST

	JAN	FEB	MAR	APR	MAY	JUN	JUL	AUG	SEP	OCT	NOV	DEC
ASSETS:												
CASH, RESERVES & DUE FROM	2.2	1.8	1.8	1.9	1.9	1.9	1.9	1.9	1.9	1.9	1.9	1.9
ITEMS IN PROCESS	2.6	1.7	1.7	1.7	1.7	1.7	1.7	1.7	1.7	1.7	1.7	1.7
CASH, FLOAT & RESERVES	4.7	3.6	3.5	3.6	3.6	3.6	3.6	3.6	3.6	3.6	3.6	3.6
SHORT-TERM TREASURIES	11.1	12.0	11.3	11.2	11.3	11.3	11.8	12.4	12.2	11.9	11.8	11.8
LONG-TERM TREASURIES	9.3	9.2	9.1	9.2	9.2	9.1	9.1	9.0	9.0	8.9	8.9	8.9
US AGENCY SECURITIES	1.2	1.3	1.4	1.4	1.5	1.5	1.5	1.6	1.6	1.6	1.7	1.7
CMO CLASS B	1.7	1.5	1.5	1.5	1.4	1.4	1.4	1.4	1.4	1.4	1.4	1.3
OUR SECURITIZED MTG LOANS	0.0	0.0	0.0	0.0	0.0	0.0	0.0	0.0	0.0	0.0	0.0	0.0
ASSET BACKED SECURITIES	2.9	2.9	2.9	3.0	2.9	2.9	2.9	2.9	3.0	3.0	3.0	3.1
TAX EXEMPTS	0.7	0.7	0.7	0.6	0.6	0.6	0.6	0.5	0.5	0.5	0.5	0.5
OTHER SECURITIES	0.7	0.7	0.8	0.8	0.8	0.8	0.8	0.9	0.9	0.9	0.8	0.8
FHLB STOCK	0.0	0.0	0.0	0.0	0.0	0.0	0.0	0.0	0.0	0.0	0.0	0.0
INT RTE CONTRACTS-SWAPS	0.0	0.0	0.0	0.0	0.0	0.0	0.0	0.0	0.0	0.0	0.0	0.0
INT RTE CONTRACTS-OPTIONS	0.0	0.0	0.0	0.0	0.0	0.0	0.0	0.0	0.0	0.0	0.0	0.0
ALL OTHER SECURITIES	1.4	1.4	1.4	1.4	1.4	1.3	1.4	1.4	1.4	1.4	1.3	1.3
TOTAL SECURITIES	24.6	25.4	24.8	24.7	24.7	24.6	25.2	25.8	25.5	25.2	25.1	25.1
TERM FED FUNDS SOLD	0.0	0.0	0.0	0.0	0.0	0.0	0.0	0.0	0.0	0.0	0.0	0.0
OVERNIGHT FED FUNDS SOLD	2.8	3.5	4.4	4.0	3.9	4.0	3.5	3.1	3.7	4.5	4.8	4.8
TRADING ACCOUNT	1.1	1.1	1.1	1.1	1.1	1.1	1.0	1.0	1.0	1.0	1.0	1.0
SHORT-TERM INVESTMENTS	3.9	4.6	5.4	5.1	5.0	5.1	4.6	4.1	4.8	5.6	5.8	5.9
COM'L PARTIC PURCH-FIXED	0.0	0.0	0.0	0.0	0.0	0.0	0.0	0.0	0.0	0.0	0.0	0.0
DIRECT COM'L LOANS-FIXED	10.5	10.5	10.4	10.4	10.5	10.5	10.5	10.6	10.5	10.4	10.4	10.4
PART PUR - REQ'D-FIXED	0.0	0.0	0.0	0.0	0.0	0.0	0.0	0.0	0.0	0.0	0.0	0.0
PART SOLD - REQ'D-FIXED	0.0	0.0	0.0	0.0	0.0	0.0	0.0	0.0	0.0	0.0	0.0	0.0
COM'L LOANS-OPTION CONTRACT	0.0	0.0	0.0	0.0	0.0	0.0	0.0	0.0	0.0	0.0	0.0	0.0
COMMERCIAL LOANS-FIXED	10.5	10.5	10.4	10.4	10.5	10.5	10.5	10.6	10.5	10.4	10.4	10.4
COM'L PARTIC PURCH-FLOAT	0.0	0.0	0.0	0.0	0.0	0.0	0.0	0.0	0.0	0.0	0.0	0.0
DIRECT COM'L LOANS-FLOAT	12.7	12.6	12.5	12.6	12.6	12.5	12.5	12.6	12.5	12.5	12.5	12.5
COMMERCIAL LOANS-FLOAT	12.7	12.6	12.5	12.6	12.6	12.5	12.5	12.6	12.5	12.5	12.5	12.5
MORTGAGE LOANS-FIXED	7.1	7.0	6.8	6.6	6.5	6.3	6.2	6.0	5.9	5.7	5.6	5.5
MORTGAGE LOANS-ADJ	7.6	7.7	7.7	7.8	7.9	7.9	8.0	8.1	8.1	8.2	8.3	8.3
HOME EQUITY LOANS	3.4	3.3	3.3	3.3	3.3	3.3	3.3	3.3	3.3	3.3	3.3	3.3
CONSUMER LOANS	15.7	15.6	15.4	15.5	15.5	15.4	15.4	15.4	15.4	15.4	15.4	15.4
CREDIT CARD LOANS	6.4	6.5	6.7	7.0	7.2	7.2	7.2	7.1	6.8	6.5	6.4	6.4
AUTO LOANS	0.5	0.5	0.5	0.5	0.6	0.6	0.6	0.6	0.6	0.7	0.7	0.7
TOTAL LOANS	64.0	63.7	63.4	63.8	64.0	63.8	63.8	63.7	63.2	62.7	62.6	62.4
RESERVE FOR LOAN LOSSES	-1.1	-1.1	-1.0	-1.0	-1.0	-1.0	-1.0	-1.0	-1.0	-1.0	-1.0	-1.0
NET LOANS	62.9	62.6	62.4	62.8	62.9	62.8	62.7	62.7	62.1	61.7	61.6	61.4
PROPERTY & EQUIPMENT	2.1	2.1	2.1	2.1	2.1	2.1	2.1	2.1	2.1	2.1	2.1	2.0
OREO & FORECLOSED ASSETS	0.2	0.2	0.2	0.3	0.3	0.3	0.3	0.3	0.4	0.4	0.4	0.4
OTHER ASSETS	1.5	1.4	1.6	1.5	1.4	1.6	1.5	1.4	1.6	1.5	1.4	1.6
TOTAL OTHER ASSETS	3.8	3.8	3.9	3.9	3.8	4.0	3.9	3.9	4.0	4.0	3.9	4.1
TOTAL ASSETS	100.0	100.0	100.0	100.0	100.0	100.0	100.0	100.0	100.0	100.0	100.0	100.0

AVERAGE STATEMENT OF CONDITION - DETAIL
PERCENTAGE COMPOSITION
2002 ACTUAL

	JAN	FEB	MAR	APR	MAY	JUN	JUL	AUG	SEP	OCT	NOV	DEC
LIABILITIES & CAPITAL:												
BUSINESS DEMAND	8.4	8.4	8.3	8.3	8.3	8.2	8.2	8.2	8.1	8.1	8.0	8.0
PUBLIC DEMAND	1.7	1.7	1.7	1.7	1.7	1.7	1.7	1.7	1.7	1.7	1.7	1.7
DEMAND DEPOSITS	10.1	10.1	10.0	10.0	10.0	9.9	9.9	9.8	9.8	9.8	9.7	9.7
INTEREST-BEAR CHECKING	15.1	15.1	15.1	15.1	15.2	15.2	15.2	15.2	15.2	15.2	15.3	15.3
REGULAR SAVINGS	8.4	8.4	8.4	8.4	8.4	8.4	8.4	8.4	8.4	8.4	8.4	8.4
IBC & SAVINGS	23.5	23.5	23.5	23.5	23.5	23.5	23.6	23.6	23.6	23.6	23.7	23.7
MMDAs	20.9	21.0	21.0	21.1	21.2	21.2	21.3	21.3	21.4	21.4	21.5	21.6
SMALL CDs	6.5	6.5	6.4	6.4	6.4	6.4	6.4	6.4	6.4	6.3	6.3	6.4
LARGE CDs	20.6	20.6	20.7	20.7	20.7	20.7	20.8	20.8	20.8	20.8	20.8	20.9
PUBLIC CDs	8.6	8.5	8.5	8.5	8.5	8.5	8.5	8.5	8.4	8.4	8.4	8.3
OTHER CDS	0.7	0.7	0.7	0.7	0.7	0.7	0.7	0.7	0.7	0.7	0.7	0.7
INT RTE CONTRACTS-SWAPS	0.0	0.0	0.0	0.0	0.0	0.0	0.0	0.0	0.0	0.0	0.0	0.0
OTHER CDs	0.7	0.7	0.7	0.7	0.7	0.7	0.7	0.7	0.7	0.7	0.7	0.7
TOTAL CERTIFICATES	36.4	36.3	36.3	36.3	36.3	36.3	36.3	36.3	36.3	36.3	36.3	36.3
TOTAL DEPOSITS	90.9	90.9	90.9	90.9	91.0	91.0	91.1	91.1	91.1	91.1	91.1	91.2
TREASURY, TAX & LOAN	0.5	0.5	0.5	0.5	0.5	0.5	0.4	0.4	0.4	0.4	0.4	0.4
REPOS	0.0	0.1	0.1	0.1	0.1	0.1	0.0	0.0	0.1	0.1	0.1	0.0
FED FUNDS PURCHASED	0.2	0.2	0.2	0.2	0.2	0.2	0.2	0.2	0.2	0.2	0.2	0.2
SHORT-TERM BOR FUNDS	0.7	0.8	0.8	0.8	0.8	0.7	0.7	0.7	0.7	0.7	0.7	0.7
LONG-TERM DEBT	0.0	0.0	0.0	0.0	0.0	0.0	0.0	0.0	0.0	0.0	0.0	0.0
FHLB ADVANCES	0.0	0.0	0.0	0.0	0.0	0.0	0.0	0.0	0.0	0.0	0.0	0.0
LONG-TERM DEBT	0.0	0.0	0.0	0.0	0.0	0.0	0.0	0.0	0.0	0.0	0.0	0.0
OTH LIAB:ACCR INC TAXES	0.6	0.6	0.6	0.6	0.6	0.6	0.6	0.6	0.6	0.6	0.6	0.6
OTH LIAB:ACCR DIVID PAY	0.0	0.0	0.0	0.0	0.0	0.0	0.0	0.0	0.0	0.0	0.0	0.0
OTH LIAB:ACCR INT PAY	0.1	0.1	0.1	0.1	0.1	0.1	0.1	0.1	0.1	0.1	0.1	0.1
OTH LIAB:DEFER'D I/E-OBS	0.0	0.0	0.0	0.0	0.0	0.0	0.0	0.0	0.0	0.0	0.0	0.0
OTH LIAB:ALL OTHER	1.9	1.9	1.9	1.9	1.9	1.9	1.9	1.9	1.9	1.8	1.8	1.8
OTHER LIABILITIES	2.6	2.5	2.6	2.5	2.5	2.5	2.5	2.5	2.5	2.5	2.5	2.5
COMMON STOCK & SURPLUS	1.2	1.2	1.2	1.2	1.2	1.2	1.2	1.2	1.1	1.1	1.1	1.1
RETAINED EARNINGS	4.6	4.6	4.6	4.6	4.6	4.6	4.6	4.6	4.5	4.5	4.6	4.6
TOTAL EQUITY	5.8	5.8	5.8	5.8	5.8	5.7	5.7	5.7	5.7	5.7	5.7	5.7
TOTAL LIAB & EQUITY	100.0	100.0	100.0	100.0	100.0	100.0	100.0	100.0	100.0	100.0	100.0	100.0
TOTAL EARNING ASSETS	90.9	91.0	90.9	91.0	91.1	91.0	91.1	91.2	91.1	91.2	91.3	91.2
TOTAL INT-BEAR LIAB	81.5	81.6	81.6	81.7	81.8	81.8	81.9	81.9	82.0	82.1	82.1	82.2

AVERAGE STATEMENT OF CONDITION - DETAIL
PERCENTAGE COMPOSITION
2003 FORECAST

	JAN	FEB	MAR	APR	MAY	JUN	JUL	AUG	SEP	OCT	NOV	DEC
LIABILITIES & CAPITAL:												
BUSINESS DEMAND	8.4	8.3	8.2	7.9	7.8	7.8	7.8	7.8	7.7	7.7	7.7	7.6
PUBLIC DEMAND	1.9	2.0	2.0	1.9	1.8	1.8	1.8	1.8	1.8	1.8	1.8	1.8
DEMAND DEPOSITS	10.3	10.3	10.3	9.7	9.7	9.6	9.6	9.6	9.5	9.5	9.5	9.4
INTEREST-BEAR CHECKING	15.1	15.0	14.9	15.0	15.1	15.0	15.1	15.1	15.1	15.1	15.1	15.1
REGULAR SAVINGS	8.4	8.3	8.2	8.2	8.2	8.1	8.1	8.1	8.0	8.0	8.0	7.9
IBC & SAVINGS	23.5	23.3	23.1	23.2	23.2	23.2	23.2	23.2	23.1	23.0	23.1	23.0
MMDAs	21.4	21.4	21.2	21.3	21.4	21.3	21.3	21.4	21.3	21.3	21.4	21.3
SMALL CDs	6.4	6.4	6.5	6.6	6.7	6.8	6.9	7.1	7.2	7.4	7.5	7.7
LARGE CDs	20.7	20.6	20.4	20.5	20.5	20.5	20.5	20.5	20.4	20.4	20.4	20.3
PUBLIC CDs	8.4	8.7	9.0	9.3	9.2	9.2	9.1	9.1	9.0	8.9	8.9	8.8
OTHER CDS	0.7	0.7	0.7	0.7	0.7	0.7	0.7	0.7	0.7	0.7	0.7	0.7
INT RTE CONTRACTS-SWAPS	0.0	0.0	0.0	0.0	0.0	0.0	0.0	0.0	0.0	0.0	0.0	0.0
OTHER CDs	0.7	0.7	0.7	0.7	0.7	0.7	0.7	0.7	0.7	0.7	0.7	0.7
TOTAL CERTIFICATES	36.2	36.4	36.5	37.0	37.1	37.1	37.2	37.4	37.3	37.4	37.5	37.5
TOTAL DEPOSITS	91.5	91.4	91.2	91.2	91.4	91.2	91.3	91.5	91.2	91.2	91.4	91.3
TREASURY, TAX & LOAN	0.4	0.4	0.4	0.4	0.4	0.4	0.4	0.4	0.4	0.4	0.4	0.4
REPOS	0.0	0.1	0.2	0.2	0.1	0.1	0.1	0.0	0.1	0.2	0.2	0.1
FED FUNDS PURCHASED	0.2	0.2	0.2	0.2	0.2	0.2	0.2	0.2	0.2	0.2	0.2	0.2
SHORT-TERM BOR FUNDS	0.6	0.8	0.9	0.9	0.7	0.7	0.7	0.6	0.7	0.8	0.8	0.7
LONG-TERM DEBT	0.0	0.0	0.0	0.0	0.0	0.0	0.0	0.0	0.0	0.0	0.0	0.0
FHLB ADVANCES	0.0	0.0	0.0	0.0	0.0	0.0	0.0	0.0	0.0	0.0	0.0	0.0
LONG-TERM DEBT	0.0	0.0	0.0	0.0	0.0	0.0	0.0	0.0	0.0	0.0	0.0	0.0
OTH LIAB:ACCR INC TAXES	0.3	0.1	0.1	0.1	0.1	0.1	0.1	0.0	0.1	0.1	0.0	0.1
OTH LIAB:ACCR DIVID PAY	0.0	0.0	0.0	0.0	0.0	0.0	0.0	0.0	0.0	0.0	0.0	0.0
OTH LIAB:ACCR INT PAY	0.1	0.2	0.4	0.3	0.2	0.4	0.3	0.3	0.4	0.3	0.3	0.4
OTH LIAB:DEFER'D I/E-OBS	0.0	0.0	0.0	0.0	0.0	0.0	0.0	0.0	0.0	0.0	0.0	0.0
OTH LIAB:ALL OTHER	1.8	1.8	1.8	1.8	1.8	1.8	1.8	1.8	1.8	1.8	1.8	1.8
OTHER LIABILITIES	2.3	2.1	2.4	2.3	2.1	2.3	2.2	2.1	2.3	2.2	2.1	2.3
COMMON STOCK & SURPLUS	1.1	1.1	1.1	1.1	1.1	1.1	1.0	1.0	1.0	1.0	1.0	1.0
RETAINED EARNINGS	4.5	4.6	4.6	4.6	4.7	4.6	4.7	4.7	4.7	4.7	4.7	4.7
TOTAL EQUITY	5.6	5.7	5.6	5.7	5.7	5.7	5.7	5.8	5.7	5.7	5.8	5.8
TOTAL LIAB & EQUITY	100.0	100.0	100.0	100.0	100.0	100.0	100.0	100.0	100.0	100.0	100.0	100.0
TOTAL EARNING ASSETS	92.5	93.7	93.5	93.6	93.6	93.5	93.5	93.6	93.4	93.5	93.6	93.4
TOTAL INT-BEAR LIAB	81.8	81.9	81.7	82.4	82.5	82.3	82.5	82.6	82.4	82.6	82.7	82.6

STATEMENT OF INCOME - DETAIL
2002 ACTUAL

	JAN	FEB	MAR	APR	MAY	JUN	JUL	AUG	SEP	OCT	NOV	DEC
INTEREST INCOME:												
SHORT-TERM TREASURIES	256	231	258	251	259	252	264	269	262	268	260	268
LONG-TERM TREASURIES	263	267	271	276	279	282	284	286	288	289	290	290
US AGENCY SECURITIES	49	49	50	51	50	50	49	51	53	52	52	51
CMO CLASS B	0	0	0	0	0	0	0	0	0	0	0	0
OUR SECURITIZED MTG LOANS	0	0	0	0	0	0	0	0	0	0	0	0
ASSET BACKED SECURITIES	49	49	50	51	50	50	49	51	53	52	52	51
TAX EXEMPTS	35	33	32	31	30	29	27	25	24	23	22	21
OTHER SECURITIES	27	27	27	28	28	28	28	28	28	29	29	29
FHLB STOCK	0	0	0	0	0	0	0	0	0	0	0	0
INT RTE CONTRACTS-SWAPS	0	0	0	0	0	0	0	0	0	0	0	0
INT RTE CONTRACTS-OPTIONS	0	0	0	0	0	0	0	0	0	0	0	0
ALL OTHER SECURITIES	62	60	59	59	58	57	55	52	52	51	50	49
TOTAL SECURITIES	629	606	638	637	647	640	651	659	654	660	651	658
TERM FED FUNDS SOLD	0	0	0	0	0	0	0	0	0	0	0	0
OVERNIGHT FED FUNDS SOLD	103	112	112	115	121	124	124	122	121	126	127	124
TRADING ACCOUNT	0	0	0	0	0	0	0	0	0	0	0	0
SHORT-TERM INVESTMENTS	103	112	112	115	121	124	124	122	121	126	127	124
COM'L PARTIC PURCH-FIXED	0	0	0	0	0	0	0	0	0	0	0	0
DIRECT COM'L LOANS-FIXED	378	377	377	376	376	377	377	378	379	380	382	384
PART PUR - REQ'D-FIXED	0	0	0	0	0	0	0	0	0	0	0	0
PART SOLD - REQ'D-FIXED	0	0	0	0	0	0	0	0	0	0	0	0
COMML LOANS-FIXED OPTION	0	0	0	0	0	0	0	0	0	0	0	0
COMMERCIAL LOANS-FIXED	378	377	377	376	376	377	377	378	379	380	382	384
COM'L PARTIC PURCH-FLOAT	0	0	0	0	0	0	0	0	0	0	0	0
COMMERCIAL LOANS-FLOAT	476	424	471	459	479	467	487	491	479	499	487	508
COMMERCIAL LOANS-FLOAT	476	424	471	459	479	467	487	491	479	499	487	508
MORTGAGE LOANS-FIXED	248	253	256	259	262	265	268	271	274	278	281	284
MORTGAGE LOANS-ADJ	251	252	253	254	255	257	260	263	265	268	270	271
HOME EQUITY LOANS	128	130	132	134	136	138	140	142	144	146	147	147
CONSUMER LOANS	655	667	680	693	707	721	733	746	758	769	777	780
CREDIT CARD LOANS	416	390	426	420	435	428	443	447	440	455	449	465
AUTO LOANS	19	19	20	20	20	21	21	21	21	22	22	22
TOTAL LOANS	2572	2511	2613	2614	2670	2674	2729	2759	2762	2817	2814	2860
TOTAL INTEREST INCOME	3305	3230	3362	3366	3438	3437	3504	3540	3537	3604	3593	3641

STATEMENT OF INCOME - DETAIL
2003 FORECAST

	JAN	FEB	MAR	APR	MAY	JUN	JUL	AUG	SEP	OCT	NOV	DEC
INTEREST INCOME:												
SHORT-TERM TREASURIES	302	295	314	304	317	309	336	355	341	346	334	347
LONG-TERM TREASURIES	292	293	296	298	298	299	300	300	299	299	300	301
US AGENCY SECURITIES	61	65	68	69	69	70	71	72	73	74	76	77
CMO CLASS B	59	54	54	54	50	50	50	50	50	50	50	50
OUR SECURITIZED MTG LOANS	0	0	0	0	0	0	0	0	0	0	0	0
ASSET BACKED SECURITIES	120	119	122	123	119	120	121	122	123	124	126	127
TAX EXEMPTS	20	20	20	19	19	18	17	17	16	16	15	15
OTHER SECURITIES	28	30	32	32	32	32	35	38	38	38	37	37
FHLB STOCK	0	0	0	0	0	0	0	0	0	0	0	0
INT RTE CONTRACTS-SWAPS	0	0	0	0	0	0	0	0	0	0	0	0
INT RTE CONTRACTS-OPTIONS	0	0	0	0	0	0	0	0	0	0	0	0
ALL OTHER SECURITIES	48	50	52	51	51	50	52	54	54	53	52	52
TOTAL SECURITIES	762	758	783	775	785	779	809	831	816	822	812	826
TERM FED FUNDS SOLD	0	0	0	0	0	0	0	0	0	0	0	0
OVERNIGHT FED FUNDS SOLD	78	99	124	114	113	116	103	89	110	135	143	146
TRADING ACCOUNT	34	34	34	34	34	34	34	34	34	34	34	34
SHORT-TERM INVESTMENTS	112	133	158	148	147	150	137	123	144	169	177	180
COM'L PARTIC PURCH-FIXED	0	0	0	0	0	0	0	0	0	0	0	0
DIRECT COM'L LOANS-FIXED	403	405	406	409	412	416	419	422	423	424	425	427
PART PUR - REQ'D-FIXED	0	0	0	0	0	0	0	0	0	0	0	0
PART SOLD - REQ'D-FIXED	0	0	0	0	0	0	0	0	0	0	0	0
COMML LOANS-FIXED OPTION	0	0	0	0	0	0	0	0	0	0	0	0
COMMERCIAL LOANS-FIXED	403	405	406	409	412	416	419	422	423	424	425	427
COM'L PARTIC PURCH-FLOAT	0	0	0	0	0	0	0	0	0	0	0	0
COMMERCIAL LOANS-FLOAT	494	442	493	479	497	484	503	506	492	511	498	518
COMMERCIAL LOANS-FLOAT	494	442	493	479	497	484	503	506	492	511	498	518
MORTGAGE LOANS-FIXED	283	278	274	270	265	260	256	251	246	242	238	234
MORTGAGE LOANS-ADJ	271	271	271	272	272	272	273	273	274	274	275	276
HOME EQUITY LOANS	147	147	147	147	148	148	148	148	149	149	150	150
CONSUMER LOANS	780	779	779	779	779	780	781	784	787	789	791	790
CREDIT CARD LOANS	457	450	518	524	554	546	563	557	530	525	503	524
AUTO LOANS	23	24	25	26	27	28	29	30	31	32	33	34
TOTAL LOANS	2857	2797	2914	2905	2953	2934	2972	2971	2933	2948	2913	2953
TOTAL INTEREST INCOME	3731	3688	3855	3829	3885	3863	3918	3925	3893	3939	3902	3959

STATEMENT OF INCOME - DETAIL
2002 ACTUAL

	JAN	FEB	MAR	APR	MAY	JUN	JUL	AUG	SEP	OCT	NOV	DEC
INTEREST EXPENSE:												
INTEREST-BEAR CHECKING	260	237	266	260	271	265	277	280	274	286	280	292
REGULAR SAVINGS	159	145	162	158	165	161	168	170	166	173	169	177
IBC & SAVINGS	418	382	427	418	436	426	445	450	440	459	449	469
MMDAs	516	508	578	567	589	576	598	593	570	586	562	572
SMALL CDs	189	170	188	181	188	182	190	191	186	193	188	196
LARGE CDs	594	536	598	588	619	605	627	625	604	628	614	639
PUBLIC CDs	247	222	247	242	254	248	256	254	245	254	247	255
OTHER CDS	17	16	18	18	19	19	20	20	19	20	19	19
INT RTE CONTRACTS-SWAPS	0	0	0	0	0	0	0	0	0	0	0	0
OTHER CDs	17	16	18	18	19	19	20	20	19	20	19	19
TOTAL CERTIFICATES	1048	944	1051	1029	1079	1054	1092	1089	1054	1095	1068	1109
TREASURY, TAX & LOAN	13	12	13	13	13	13	13	13	13	13	12	12
REPOS	0	2	2	2	2	2	0	0	2	2	2	0
FED FUNDS PURCHASED	7	7	7	7	7	7	7	7	7	7	7	6
SHORT-TERM BOR FUNDS	20	20	22	21	22	22	20	20	21	22	20	18
LONG-TERM DEBT	0	0	0	0	0	0	0	0	0	0	0	0
FHLB ADVANCES	0	0	0	0	0	0	0	0	0	0	0	0
LONG-TERM DEBT	0	0	0	0	0	0	0	0	0	0	0	0
TOTAL INTEREST EXPENSE	2002	1854	2078	2035	2126	2078	2154	2152	2085	2162	2100	2168
NET INTEREST INCOME	1303	1376	1285	1331	1311	1359	1350	1388	1451	1442	1493	1473
PROVISION FOR LOAN LOSS	152	148	149	151	153	154	156	158	159	161	149	141
NET INT INCOME AFTER PROV	1151	1228	1135	1180	1159	1205	1194	1230	1292	1281	1345·	1332
SERVICE CHARGES	122	124	125	126	128	129	130	132	133	135	136	138
OTHER INCOME	133	132	131	107	133	142	123	131	120	134	117	134
GAIN(LOSS) ON SECURITIES	0	0	0	0	0	0	0	0	0	0	0	0
TOTAL NON-INTEREST INC	255	256	256	233	261	271	253	263	253	269	253	272
SALARIES & BENEFITS	507	514	524	529	535	544	552	566	579	589	595	601
OCCUPANCY, FURN & EQUIP	136	138	140	141	142	144	146	149	152	154	155	156
PROMOTION EXPENSE	53	53	53	53	53	53	53	53	53	53	53	53
FDIC INSURANCE EXPENSE	0	0	0	0	0	0	0	0	0	0	0	0
DATA PROCESSING EXPENSE	141	143	144	145	147	148	149	151	152	154	155	157
FINANCING & HEDGING EXP	0	0	0	0	0	0	0	0	0	0	0	0
OTHER OPERATING EXPENSE	156	157	138	160	161	152	163	155	165	155	168	140
TOTAL NON-INTEREST EXP	993	1005	999	1028	1038	1042	1064	1073	1102	1104	1127	1107
NET INCOME BEFORE TAXES	413	479	392	385	382	435	384	420	444	446	471	497
STATE TAXES	21	24	20	19	19	22	19	21	22	22	24	25
FEDERAL TAXES	121	143	116	114	113	131	115	127	135	136	145	153
INCOME TAXES	142	167	135	133	132	152	134	148	157	158	168	178
NET INCOME	271	312	257	252	250	282	250	272	286	287	303	319

STATEMENT OF INCOME - DETAIL
2003 FORECAST

	JAN	FEB	MAR	APR	MAY	JUN	JUL	AUG	SEP	OCT	NOV	DEC
INTEREST EXPENSE:												
INTEREST-BEAR CHECKING	294	266	297	289	301	293	305	307	300	312	304	316
REGULAR SAVINGS	179	162	180	174	180	175	181	181	175	182	176	182
IBC & SAVINGS	473	428	476	463	481	468	486	488	475	493	480	498
MMDAs	606	532	593	577	600	585	608	612	596	620	604	628
SMALL CDs	199	181	202	197	207	203	213	218	216	228	225	238
LARGE CDs	637	573	635	617	642	625	649	652	635	659	641	666
PUBLIC CDs	264	250	293	293	304	294	304	304	294	304	294	304
OTHER CDS	19	18	20	19	20	20	21	22	21	22	21	22
INT RTE CONTRACTS-SWAPS	0	0	0	0	0	0	0	0	0	0	0	0
OTHER CDs	19	18	20	19	20	20	21	22	21	22	21	22
TOTAL CERTIFICATES	1119	1022	1149	1128	1173	1142	1188	1196	1166	1213	1182	1230
TREASURY, TAX & LOAN	11	10	11	11	12	11	12	12	11	12	12	12
REPOS	0	3	6	6	3	3	3	0	3	6	4	1
FED FUNDS PURCHASED	6	6	6	6	6	6	6	6	6	6	6	6
SHORT-TERM BOR FUNDS	18	19	24	23	21	20	21	18	21	24	22	20
LONG-TERM DEBT	0	0	0	0	0	0	0	0	0	0	0	0
FHLB ADVANCES	0	0	0	0	0	0	0	0	0	0	0	0
LONG-TERM DEBT	0	0	0	0	0	0	0	0	0	0	0	0
TOTAL INTEREST EXPENSE	2216	2001	2242	2191	2275	2215	2303	2315	2258	2350	2288	2376
NET INTEREST INCOME	1516	1688	1613	1637	1610	1648	1615	1610	1635	1588	1615	1583
PROVISION FOR LOAN LOSS	0	1	171	168	163	159	152	142	131	119	134	150
NET INT INCOME AFTER PROV	1516	1687	1442	1469	1448	1488	1463	1468	1504	1470	1481	1434
SERVICE CHARGES	138	139	140	141	142	143	144	145	146	147	148	149
OTHER INCOME	143	133	146	156	132	145	132	150	139	115	129	139
GAIN(LOSS) ON SECURITIES	0	0	0	0	0	0	0	0	0	0	0	0
TOTAL NON-INTEREST INC	281	272	286	297	274	288	276	295	286	262	277	288
SALARIES & BENEFITS	605	612	622	627	637	645	653	661	669	675	683	692
OCCUPANCY, FURN & EQUIP	148	150	152	154	156	158	160	162	164	165	167	169
PROMOTION EXPENSE	52	52	52	52	52	52	52	52	52	52	52	52
FDIC INSURANCE EXPENSE	66	67	68	68	69	70	70	71	72	73	73	74
DATA PROCESSING EXPENSE	153	154	155	156	157	158	159	160	161	162	163	164
FINANCING & HEDGING EXP	0	0	0	0	0	0	0	0	0	0	0	0
OTHER OPERATING EXPENSE	140	150	147	140	144	146	131	134	123	143	130	134
TOTAL NON-INTEREST EXP	1166	1186	1197	1198	1216	1230	1227	1241	1241	1271	1269	1286
NET INCOME BEFORE TAXES	631	773	532	568	506	547	512	522	549	461	489	436
STATE TAXES	32	39	27	28	25	27	26	26	27	23	24	22
FEDERAL TAXES	197	243	165	177	157	171	160	163	172	143	153	136
INCOME TAXES	229	282	192	205	182	198	185	189	199	166	177	158
NET INCOME	402	491	340	362	323	349	327	333	349	294	312	279

KEY RATIO REPORT - SUMMARY
2002 ACTUAL

	JAN	FEB	MAR	APR	MAY	JUN	JUL	AUG	SEP	OCT	NOV	DEC
PERFORMANCE:												
RETURN ON EQUITY %	13.52	17.02	12.61	12.74	12.09	14.06	11.99	12.90	13.97	13.50	14.55	14.72
RETURN ON ASSETS %	0.79	0.99	0.73	0.73	0.70	0.81	0.69	0.74	0.80	0.76	0.83	0.83
EARNINGS PER SHARE(ANN$)	1.06	1.35	1.01	1.02	0.98	1.15	0.98	1.07	1.16	1.13	1.23	1.25
COMMON DIV PER SHARE ($)	0.00	0.00	0.11	0.00	0.00	0.11	0.00	0.00	0.11	0.00	0.00	0.11
BOOK VALUE PER SHR(EOP$)	7.90	8.01	7.99	8.07	8.15	8.14	8.22	8.31	8.30	8.39	8.50	8.49
EARNING/TOTAL ASSETS %	90.86	91.04	90.93	91.03	91.13	91.01	91.11	91.21	91.10	91.20	91.31	91.19
INT BEAR/TOTAL DEPOSITS%	88.84	88.89	88.95	89.00	89.05	89.10	89.15	89.20	89.25	89.29	89.34	89.40
INTEREST MARGIN & OVERHEAD:												
AVG NATIONAL PRIME RATE	10.11	10.00	10.00	10.00	10.00	10.00	10.00	10.00	10.00	10.00	10.00	10.00
YIELD ON EARNING ASSETS	10.78	10.81	10.74	10.77	10.75	10.78	10.75	10.74	10.76	10.71	10.70	10.62
COST OF FUNDS RATE	7.13	7.23	7.25	7.26	7.27	7.26	7.22	7.14	7.07	7.02	6.97	6.90
SPREAD %	3.65	3.57	3.49	3.51	3.48	3.52	3.53	3.60	3.69	3.70	3.72	3.72
INT MARGIN ON E.A. %	4.39	4.33	4.24	4.25	4.23	4.26	4.26	4.33	4.40	4.40	4.42	4.40
NET OVERHEAD TO E.A. %	2.35	2.65	2.32	2.55	2.37	2.43	2.43	2.41	2.59	2.43	2.62	2.39
LOAN POSITION:												
LOANS/TOTAL DEPOSITS %	70.78	70.89	70.95	71.00	71.06	71.12	71.18	71.24	71.30	71.36	71.34	71.14
LOANS TO EARNING ASSETS	70.82	70.76	70.91	70.92	70.94	71.10	71.15	71.16	71.27	71.28	71.20	71.14
LOSS PROVISION/LOANS %	0.69	0.73	0.66	0.68	0.66	0.68	0.66	0.66	0.68	0.66	0.62	0.57
NET CHARGE-OFFS/LOANS %	0.45	0.49	0.45	0.46	0.45	0.46	0.45	0.45	0.46	0.45	0.46	0.45
LOSS RESERVE/LOANS %	1.69	1.69	1.69	1.69	1.69	1.69	1.69	1.69	1.69	1.69	1.69	1.70
NONPERFORMING/LNS(EOP) %	1.42	1.42	1.42	1.41	1.41	1.41	1.40	1.40	1.40	1.40	1.40	1.40
CAPITAL LEVERAGE:												
TIER 1 RISK BASED CAP %	8.65	8.65	8.53	8.57	8.56	8.44	8.49	8.50	8.38	8.43	8.46	8.38
TOTAL RISK BASED CAP %	9.90	9.91	9.79	9.82	9.81	9.70	9.75	9.76	9.64	9.68	9.71	9.64
ASSET LEVERAGE %	5.63	5.68	5.63	5.59	5.62	5.58	5.54	5.58	5.54	5.50	5.54	5.52
EQUITY TO ASSETS %	5.81	5.83	5.80	5.77	5.77	5.74	5.72	5.72	5.69	5.67	5.68	5.66
DIVIDEND PAYOUT %	0.00	0.00	126.53	0.00	0.00	115.10	0.00	0.00	113.56	0.00	0.00	102.04
LIQUIDITY:												
CASH/TOTAL DEPOSITS %	6.79	6.70	6.69	6.67	6.66	6.64	6.63	6.61	6.60	6.59	6.57	6.56
PURCHASED FUNDS/E.A. %	32.43	32.33	32.36	32.33	32.31	32.35	32.34	32.31	32.32	32.29	32.25	32.26
NET FED FUNDS/EQUITY %	-59.52	-64.40	-63.29	-65.09	-69.10	-69.44	-70.07	-68.75	-67.11	-70.65	-73.18	-75.66
PER EMPLOYEE:												
SALARIES & BENEFITS ($)	26731	29805	27141	28111	27299	28439	27680	28062	29361	28671	29726	28832
TOTAL ASSETS ($MILLIONS)	1.82	1.82	1.82	1.82	1.83	1.83	1.83	1.83	1.82	1.83	1.83	1.83

KEY RATIO REPORT - SUMMARY
2003 FORECAST

	JAN	FEB	MAR	APR	MAY	JUN	JUL	AUG	SEP	OCT	NOV	DEC
PERFORMANCE:												
RETURN ON EQUITY %	18.45	24.51	15.19	16.60	14.15	15.68	14.14	14.20	15.32	12.40	13.44	11.57
RETURN ON ASSETS %	1.04	1.39	0.86	0.94	0.81	0.89	0.81	0.82	0.88	0.71	0.78	0.67
EARNINGS PER SHARE(ANN$)	1.58	2.14	1.34	1.47	1.27	1.42	1.28	1.31	1.42	1.15	1.26	1.09
COMMON DIV PER SHARE ($)	0.00	0.00	0.11	0.00	0.00	0.11	0.00	0.00	0.11	0.00	0.00	0.11
BOOK VALUE PER SHR(EOP$)	8.63	8.79	8.79	8.92	9.02	9.03	9.14	9.25	9.26	9.35	9.46	9.44
EARNING/TOTAL ASSETS %	92.51	93.71	93.54	93.57	93.63	93.47	93.54	93.59	93.43	93.50	93.56	93.39
INT BEAR/TOTAL DEPOSITS%	88.69	88.72	88.74	89.36	89.40	89.44	89.48	89.52	89.56	89.61	89.66	89.70
INTEREST MARGIN & OVERHEAD:												
AVG NATIONAL PRIME RATE	10.00	10.00	10.00	10.00	10.00	10.00	10.00	10.00	10.00	10.00	10.00	10.00
YIELD ON EARNING ASSETS	10.56	10.59	10.53	10.57	10.54	10.54	10.49	10.46	10.42	10.33	10.31	10.28
COST OF FUNDS RATE	6.98	6.90	6.90	6.90	6.90	6.89	6.89	6.88	6.88	6.88	6.88	6.87
SPREAD %	3.59	3.69	3.64	3.67	3.65	3.65	3.60	3.57	3.54	3.46	3.44	3.40
INT MARGIN ON E.A. %	4.40	4.56	4.51	4.49	4.47	4.47	4.42	4.38	4.35	4.26	4.24	4.20
NET OVERHEAD TO E.A. %	2.45	2.79	2.44	2.50	2.51	2.59	2.50	2.48	2.58	2.60	2.64	2.54
LOAN POSITION:												
LOANS/TOTAL DEPOSITS %	69.95	69.64	69.51	69.92	69.95	69.93	69.82	69.59	69.25	68.79	68.51	68.41
LOANS TO EARNING ASSETS	69.16	67.96	67.74	68.17	68.31	68.25	68.17	68.04	67.60	67.11	66.91	66.86
LOSS PROVISION/LOANS %	0.00	0.00	0.68	0.68	0.64	0.64	0.59	0.55	0.52	0.46	0.53	0.57
NET CHARGE-OFFS/LOANS %	0.47	0.52	0.48	0.49	0.48	0.50	0.48	0.48	0.50	0.48	0.49	0.48
LOSS RESERVE/LOANS %	1.70	1.65	1.60	1.60	1.61	1.61	1.61	1.62	1.62	1.62	1.62	1.61
NONPERFORMING/LNS(EOP) %	1.39	1.39	1.38	1.38	1.38	1.38	1.39	1.39	1.40	1.41	1.41	1.41
CAPITAL LEVERAGE:												
TIER 1 RISK BASED CAP %	8.62	8.62	8.51	8.61	8.64	8.56	8.69	8.75	8.69	8.82	8.85	8.77
TOTAL RISK BASED CAP %	9.88	9.88	9.77	9.87	9.90	9.82	9.95	10.00	9.95	10.08	10.11	10.02
ASSET LEVERAGE %	5.47	5.55	5.52	5.52	5.57	5.56	5.56	5.62	5.60	5.58	5.63	5.60
EQUITY TO ASSETS %	5.62	5.66	5.63	5.66	5.71	5.70	5.71	5.75	5.73	5.73	5.77	5.75
DIVIDEND PAYOUT %	0.00	0.00	96.98	0.00	0.00	94.55	0.00	0.00	94.42	0.00	0.00	118.43
LIQUIDITY:												
CASH/TOTAL DEPOSITS %	5.18	3.89	3.89	3.91	3.91	3.91	3.91	3.91	3.91	3.91	3.90	3.90
PURCHASED FUNDS/E.A. %	31.69	31.51	31.69	32.01	32.01	31.93	31.85	31.81	31.67	31.57	31.52	31.46
NET FED FUNDS/EQUITY %	-46.25	-58.33	-73.51	-66.58	-65.07	-66.64	-58.53	-49.49	-61.64	-75.75	-79.58	-80.81
PER EMPLOYEE:												
SALARIES & BENEFITS ($)	28858	32157	29233	30403	29657	30845	30044	30238	31449	30632	31857	31030
TOTAL ASSETS ($MILLIONS)	1.85	1.86	1.87	1.87	1.86	1.87	1.86	1.86	1.87	1.88	1.88	1.88

KEY RATIO REPORT - DETAIL
2002 ACTUAL

	JAN	FEB	MAR	APR	MAY	JUN	JUL	AUG	SEP	OCT	NOV	DEC
ASSET QUALITY:												
MOST BAL LOAN MIX (AVG)	9.24	9.02	8.88	8.73	8.59	8.44	8.30	8.15	8.01	7.86	7.76	7.78
RES/NON PERFORM (EOP)	1.21	1.21	1.21	1.22	1.22	1.22	1.22	1.23	1.23	1.23	1.23	1.23
NET CH-OFFS/LOANS(AVG)	0.45	0.49	0.45	0.46	0.45	0.46	0.45	0.45	0.46	0.45	0.46	0.45
INV MKT TO BOOK (EOP)	100.44	100.14	99.91	99.74	99.85	100.17	100.31	100.37	100.29	100.54	100.93	101.25
LIQUIDITY (AVG):												
LOANS/DEPOSITS (EOP)	70.84	70.90	70.96	71.02	71.08	71.14	71.20	71.26	71.31	71.37	71.27	70.98
S-T INVEST TO ASSETS	13.44	13.60	13.42	13.40	13.50	13.46	13.57	13.71	13.68	13.86	14.13	14.34
PURCHASED FUNDS/E.A.	32.43	32.33	32.36	32.33	32.31	32.35	32.34	32.31	32.32	32.29	32.25	32.26
NET BOR FUNDS/ASSETS	-2.99	-3.23	-3.15	-3.24	-3.47	-3.48	-3.56	-3.49	-3.32	-3.51	-3.66	-3.85
TOTAL LNS/AVAIL DEP	86.44	86.43	86.46	86.49	86.52	86.55	86.58	86.61	86.64	86.67	86.58	86.24
CAPITAL ADEQUACY:												
EQUITY/ASSETS (EOP)	5.79	5.80	5.73	5.74	5.75	5.68	5.69	5.70	5.63	5.65	5.66	5.61
MARKET CAPITALIZATION	43920	49860	45660	42630	42390	40890	38340	38310	35910	34980	35760	36060
RISK BASED CAPITAL (EOP)	9.90	9.91	9.79	9.82	9.81	9.70	9.75	9.76	9.64	9.68	9.71	9.64
PE RATIO (EOP)	12.01	12.84	12.51	12.71	13.00	12.93	13.07	13.56	13.65	13.79	14.26	14.11
PROFITABILITY / EARNINGS (AVG):												
EARNINGS PER SHARE(ANN)	1.06	1.20	1.13	1.10	1.08	1.09	1.07	1.07	1.08	1.08	1.10	1.11
RETURN ON EQUITY	13.52	17.02	12.61	12.74	12.09	14.06	11.99	12.90	13.97	13.50	14.55	14.72
RETURN ON ASSETS	0.79	0.99	0.73	0.73	0.70	0.81	0.69	0.74	0.80	0.76	0.83	0.83
INT MARGIN ON E.A.	4.39	4.33	4.24	4.25	4.23	4.26	4.26	4.33	4.40	4.40	4.42	4.40
NET OVERHEAD TO E.A.	2.35	2.65	2.32	2.55	2.37	2.43	2.43	2.41	2.59	2.43	2.62	2.39
YIELD ON EARNING ASSETS	10.78	10.81	10.74	10.77	10.75	10.78	10.75	10.74	10.76	10.71	10.70	10.62
NET INCOME	270.64	582.29	839.14	1091.21	1341.10	1623.47	1873.32	2145.12	2431.31	2718.42	3021.32	3339.83
GROWTH (%):												
TOTAL LOANS (YTD AVG)	13.18	13.31	13.38	13.41	13.43	13.44	13.45	13.46	13.47	13.48	13.47	13.43
TOTAL DEPOSITS(YTD AVG)	12.24	12.24	12.25	12.26	12.27	12.27	12.28	12.30	12.31	12.32	12.32	12.33
TOTAL EQUITY (YTD AVG)	9.42	9.50	9.58	9.63	9.64	9.64	9.62	9.59	9.55	9.49	9.43	9.37
BAL GROWTH (YTD AVG)	0.00	0.00	0.00	0.00	0.00	0.00	0.00	0.00	0.00	0.00	0.00	4.20
COMP GROWTH (YTD AVG)	0.00	0.00	0.00	0.00	0.00	0.00	0.00	0.00	0.00	0.00	0.00	34.00
TOTAL ASSETS ($EOP)	409384	413874	417899	421601	425682	429816	433148	437356	442111	446102	450220	454329
MEMO ITEMS:												
MKT VALUE OF INVST($MIL)	93	93	94	93	94	94	95	97	97	98	99	99
OUTSTANDING SHARES(000)	3000	3000	3000	3000	3000	3000	3000	3000	3000	3000	3000	3000
SAL & BENEFITS/EMP($)	26731	29805	27141	28111	27299	28439	27680	28062	29361	28671	29726	28832
ASSETS (AVG)/EMP($ MIL)	1.82	1.82	1.82	1.82	1.82	1.83	1.83	1.83	1.82	1.83	1.83	1.83
STOCK PRICE ($EOP)	14.64	16.62	15.22	14.21	14.13	13.63	12.78	12.77	11.97	11.66	11.92	12.02
BK VALUE PER SHARE ($EOP)	7.90	8.01	7.99	8.07	8.15	8.14	8.22	8.31	8.30	8.39	8.50	8.49

KEY RATIO REPORT - DETAIL
2003 FORECAST

	JAN	FEB	MAR	APR	MAY	JUN	JUL	AUG	SEP	OCT	NOV	DEC
ASSET QUALITY:												
MOST BAL LOAN MIX (AVG)	7.94	8.06	8.14	8.28	8.62	8.87	8.98	9.00	9.05	9.17	9.27	9.34
RES/NON PERFORM (EOP)	1.21	1.17	1.18	1.18	1.18	1.18	1.18	1.18	1.17	1.17	1.16	1.16
NET CH-OFFS/LOANS(AVG)	0.47	0.52	0.48	0.49	0.48	0.50	0.48	0.48	0.50	0.48	0.49	0.48
INV MKT TO BOOK (EOP)	101.30	101.34	101.33	101.31	101.29	101.28	101.19	101.17	101.14	101.12	101.08	101.06
LIQUIDITY (AVG):												
LOANS/DEPOSITS (EOP)	70.26	70.23	69.99	70.08	70.07	70.02	69.86	69.56	69.16	68.65	68.59	68.46
S-T INVEST TO ASSETS	13.92	15.47	15.64	15.20	15.21	15.27	15.35	15.46	15.94	16.46	16.62	16.64
PURCHASED FUNDS/E.A.	31.69	31.51	31.69	32.01	32.01	31.93	31.85	31.81	31.67	31.57	31.52	31.46
NET BOR FUNDS/ASSETS	-2.17	-2.76	-3.50	-3.13	-3.19	-3.27	-2.81	-2.42	-3.01	-3.71	-4.01	-4.17
TOTAL LNS/AVAIL DEP	83.77	82.51	82.77	83.32	83.32	83.23	83.02	82.67	82.19	81.57	81.17	80.98
CAPITAL ADEQUACY:												
EQUITY/ASSETS (EOP)	5.67	5.69	5.61	5.68	5.71	5.66	5.72	5.74	5.69	5.74	5.76	5.71
MARKET CAPITALIZATION	56580	70830	62310	61350	60000	58950	58020	59400	59790	58740	60330	58410
RISK BASED CAPITAL (EOP)	9.88	9.88	9.77	9.87	9.90	9.82	9.95	10.00	9.95	10.08	10.11	10.02
PE RATIO (EOP)	12.01	12.83	12.51	12.70	12.99	12.93	13.07	13.56	13.65	13.79	14.26	14.11
PROFITABILITY / EARNINGS (AVG):												
EARNINGS PER SHARE(ANN)	1.57	1.84	1.66	1.61	1.54	1.52	1.48	1.46	1.46	1.42	1.41	1.38
RETURN ON EQUITY	18.45	24.51	15.19	16.60	14.15	15.68	14.14	14.20	15.32	12.40	13.44	11.57
RETURN ON ASSETS	1.04	1.39	0.86	0.94	0.81	0.89	0.81	0.82	0.88	0.71	0.78	0.67
INT MARGIN ON E.A.	4.40	4.56	4.51	4.49	4.47	4.47	4.42	4.38	4.35	4.26	4.24	4.20
NET OVERHEAD TO E.A.	2.45	2.79	2.44	2.50	2.51	2.59	2.50	2.48	2.58	2.60	2.64	2.54
YIELD ON EARNING ASSETS	10.56	10.59	10.53	10.57	10.54	10.54	10.49	10.46	10.42	10.33	10.31	10.28
NET INCOME	402.43	893.78	1234.07	1596.51	1919.97	2269.01	2596.20	2928.97	3278.47	3572.58	3884.42	4163.07
GROWTH (%):												
TOTAL LOANS (YTD AVG)	12.08	11.75	11.57	11.42	11.23	11.03	10.78	10.49	10.16	9.76	9.38	9.03
TOTAL DEPOSITS(YTD AVG)	13.39	13.39	13.44	13.25	13.05	12.86	12.66	12.46	12.27	12.07	11.88	11.68
TOTAL EQUITY (YTD AVG)	8.93	9.19	9.46	9.68	9.87	10.03	10.18	10.32	10.44	10.55	10.63	10.68
BAL GROWTH (YTD AVG)	4.46	4.20	3.98	3.57	3.18	2.83	2.48	2.15	2.11	2.31	2.50	2.66
COMP GROWTH (YTD AVG)	34.40	34.33	34.47	34.34	34.15	33.91	33.62	33.27	32.88	32.39	31.89	31.39
TOTAL ASSETS ($EOP)	456681	463701	470043	470808	473894	478934	478981	483168	488327	489147	492746	496301
MEMO ITEMS:												
MKT VALUE OF INVST($MIL)	121	117	117	118	118	118	125	125	124	124	125	125
OUTSTANDING SHARES(000)	3000	3000	3000	3000	3000	3000	3000	3000	3000	3000	3000	3000
SAL & BENEFITS/EMP($)	28858	32157	29233	30403	29657	30845	30044	30238	31449	30632	31857	31030
ASSETS (AVG)/EMP($ MIL)	1.85	1.86	1.87	1.87	1.86	1.87	1.86	1.87	1.87	1.87	1.88	1.88
STOCK PRICE ($EOP)	18.86	23.61	20.77	20.45	20.00	19.65	19.34	19.80	19.93	19.58	20.11	19.47
BK VALUE PER SHARE ($EOP)	8.63	8.79	8.79	8.92	9.02	9.03	9.14	9.25	9.26	9.35	9.46	9.44

MONTHLY INTEREST RATE REPORT - DETAIL
2002 ACTUAL

	JAN	FEB	MAR	APR	MAY	JUN	JUL	AUG	SEP	OCT	NOV	DEC
EARNING ASSET YIELDS:												
SHORT-TERM TREASURIES	7.63	7.66	7.72	7.78	7.81	7.79	7.75	7.67	7.55	7.41	7.27	7.12
LONG-TERM TREASURIES	7.92	7.92	7.94	7.98	8.01	8.03	8.05	8.09	8.13	8.17	8.20	8.23
US AGENCY SECURITIES	12.45	12.44	12.32	12.20	12.19	12.18	12.17	11.98	11.82	11.81	11.80	11.78
CMO CLASS B	0.00	0.00	0.00	0.00	0.00	0.00	0.00	0.00	0.00	0.00	0.00	0.00
OUR SECURITIZED MTG LOANS	0.00	0.00	0.00	0.00	0.00	0.00	0.00	0.00	0.00	0.00	0.00	0.00
ASSET BACKED SECURITIES	12.45	12.44	12.32	12.20	12.19	12.18	12.17	11.98	11.82	11.81	11.80	11.78
TAX EXEMPTS	13.97	13.93	13.94	13.97	13.97	13.94	13.91	13.92	13.94	13.97	14.03	14.10
OTHER SECURITIES	11.01	11.01	10.98	10.95	10.95	10.95	10.95	10.95	10.95	10.95	10.95	10.95
FHLB STOCK	0.00	0.00	0.00	0.00	0.00	0.00	0.00	0.00	0.00	0.00	0.00	0.00
INT RTE CONTRACTS-SWAPS	0.00	0.00	0.00	0.00	0.00	0.00	0.00	0.00	0.00	0.00	0.00	0.00
INT RTE CONTRACTS-OPTIONS	0.00	0.00	0.00	0.00	0.00	0.00	0.00	0.00	0.00	0.00	0.00	0.00
ALL OTHER SECURITIES	12.96	12.91	12.86	12.84	12.82	12.77	12.69	12.64	12.60	12.58	12.57	12.57
TOTAL SECURITIES	8.50	8.49	8.50	8.54	8.55	8.53	8.49	8.45	8.40	8.35	8.28	8.20
TERM FED FUNDS SOLD	0.00	0.00	0.00	0.00	0.00	0.00	0.00	0.00	0.00	0.00	0.00	0.00
OVERNIGHT FED FUNDS SOLD	8.08	8.95	8.12	8.37	8.03	8.41	8.00	7.98	8.31	7.96	7.92	7.17
TRADING ACCOUNT	0.00	0.00	0.00	0.00	0.00	0.00	0.00	0.00	0.00	0.00	0.00	0.00
SHORT-TERM INVESTMENTS	8.08	8.95	8.12	8.37	8.03	8.41	8.00	7.98	8.31	7.96	7.92	7.17
COM'L PARTIC PURCH-FIXED	0.00	0.00	0.00	0.00	0.00	0.00	0.00	0.00	0.00	0.00	0.00	0.00
DIRECT COM'L LOANS-FIXED	10.33	10.24	10.14	10.05	9.97	9.90	9.84	9.78	9.73	9.69	9.65	9.62
PART PUR - REQ'D-FIXED	0.00	0.00	0.00	0.00	0.00	0.00	0.00	0.00	0.00	0.00	0.00	0.00
PART SOLD - REQ'D-FIXED	0.00	0.00	0.00	0.00	0.00	0.00	0.00	0.00	0.00	0.00	0.00	0.00
COM'L LNS-OPTION CONTRACT	0.00	0.00	0.00	0.00	0.00	0.00	0.00	0.00	0.00	0.00	0.00	0.00
COMMERCIAL LOANS-FIXED	10.33	10.24	10.14	10.05	9.97	9.90	9.84	9.78	9.73	9.69	9.65	9.62
COM'L PARTIC PURCH-FLOAT	0.00	0.00	0.00	0.00	0.00	0.00	0.00	0.00	0.00	0.00	0.00	0.00
DIRECT COM'L LOANS-FLOAT	10.68	10.43	10.39	10.38	10.38	10.39	10.38	10.38	10.39	10.38	10.38	10.39
COMMERCIAL LOANS-FLOAT	10.68	10.43	10.39	10.38	10.38	10.39	10.38	10.38	10.39	10.38	10.38	10.39
MORTGAGE LOANS-FIXED	10.47	10.45	10.45	10.44	10.44	10.43	10.43	10.42	10.41	10.40	10.40	10.39
MORTGAGE LOANS-ADJ	9.89	9.79	9.70	9.62	9.57	9.54	9.52	9.51	9.49	9.46	9.43	9.39
HOME EQUITY LOANS	11.58	11.57	11.57	11.57	11.59	11.60	11.60	11.59	11.58	11.56	11.54	11.52
CONSUMER LOANS	12.31	12.39	12.48	12.57	12.66	12.75	12.83	12.89	12.94	12.98	13.00	13.02
CREDIT CARD LOANS	18.33	18.81	18.38	18.53	18.40	18.54	18.39	18.38	18.51	18.37	18.51	18.37
AUTO LOANS	12.57	12.57	12.59	12.61	12.63	12.66	12.66	12.66	12.66	12.64	12.61	12.57
TOTAL LOANS	11.75	11.74	11.68	11.69	11.68	11.70	11.69	11.70	11.71	11.69	11.70	11.68
TOTAL EARNING ASSETS	10.78	10.81	10.74	10.77	10.75	10.78	10.75	10.74	10.76	10.71	10.70	10.62

MONTHLY INTEREST RATE REPORT - DETAIL
2003 FORECAST

	JAN	FEB	MAR	APR	MAY	JUN	JUL	AUG	SEP	OCT	NOV	DEC
EARNING ASSET YIELDS:												
SHORT-TERM TREASURIES	7.00	6.98	7.00	7.03	7.03	7.03	7.03	7.03	7.03	7.03	7.03	7.03
LONG-TERM TREASURIES	8.28	8.29	8.30	8.30	8.30	8.29	8.29	8.28	8.27	8.25	8.24	8.23
US AGENCY SECURITIES	13.44	12.81	12.46	12.27	12.10	11.90	11.72	11.54	11.35	11.19	10.99	10.85
CMO CLASS B	9.08	9.08	9.08	9.08	9.08	9.08	9.08	9.08	9.08	9.08	9.08	9.08
OUR SECURITIZED MTG LOANS	0.00	0.00	0.00	0.00	0.00	0.00	0.00	0.00	0.00	0.00	0.00	0.00
ASSET BACKED SECURITIES	10.89	10.79	10.69	10.62	10.61	10.54	10.46	10.38	10.30	10.23	10.14	10.07
TAX EXEMPTS	14.17	14.21	14.25	14.29	14.26	14.23	14.21	14.17	14.11	14.03	13.96	13.94
OTHER SECURITIES	10.93	10.89	10.86	10.86	10.86	10.86	10.83	10.79	10.79	10.79	10.79	10.79
FHLB STOCK	0.00	0.00	0.00	0.00	0.00	0.00	0.00	0.00	0.00	0.00	0.00	0.00
INT RTE CONTRACTS-SWAPS	0.00	0.00	0.00	0.00	0.00	0.00	0.00	0.00	0.00	0.00	0.00	0.00
INT RTE CONTRACTS-OPTIONS	0.00	0.00	0.00	0.00	0.00	0.00	0.00	0.00	0.00	0.00	0.00	0.00
ALL OTHER SECURITIES	12.56	12.49	12.43	12.43	12.39	12.35	12.22	12.10	12.06	12.00	11.97	11.96
TOTAL SECURITIES	8.25	8.19	8.22	8.23	8.21	8.20	8.16	8.13	8.12	8.11	8.10	8.08
TERM FED FUNDS SOLD	0.00	0.00	0.00	0.00	0.00	0.00	0.00	0.00	0.00	0.00	0.00	0.00
OVERNIGHT FED FUNDS SOLD	7.17	7.94	7.17	7.41	7.17	7.41	7.17	7.17	7.41	7.17	7.41	7.17
TRADING ACCOUNT	8.16	8.16	8.16	8.16	8.16	8.16	8.16	8.16	8.16	8.16	8.16	8.16
SHORT-TERM INVESTMENTS	7.45	7.99	7.37	7.57	7.38	7.57	7.40	7.42	7.57	7.35	7.54	7.34
COM'L PARTIC PURCH-FIXED	0.00	0.00	0.00	0.00	0.00	0.00	0.00	0.00	0.00	0.00	0.00	0.00
DIRECT COM'L LOANS-FIXED	10.05	10.04	10.03	10.02	10.01	10.00	10.00	10.00	10.00	10.00	10.00	10.00
PART PUR - REQ'D-FIXED	0.00	0.00	0.00	0.00	0.00	0.00	0.00	0.00	0.00	0.00	0.00	0.00
PART SOLD - REQ'D-FIXED	0.00	0.00	0.00	0.00	0.00	0.00	0.00	0.00	0.00	0.00	0.00	0.00
COM'L LNS-OPTION CONTRACT	0.00	0.00	0.00	0.00	0.00	0.00	0.00	0.00	0.00	0.00	0.00	0.00
COMMERCIAL LOANS-FIXED	10.05	10.04	10.03	10.02	10.01	10.00	10.00	10.00	10.00	10.00	10.00	10.00
COM'L PARTIC PURCH-FLOAT	0.00	0.00	0.00	0.00	0.00	0.00	0.00	0.00	0.00	0.00	0.00	0.00
DIRECT COM'L LOANS-FLOAT	10.03	9.89	9.89	9.89	9.89	9.89	9.89	9.89	9.89	9.89	9.89	9.89
COMMERCIAL LOANS-FLOAT	10.03	9.89	9.89	9.89	9.89	9.89	9.89	9.89	9.89	9.89	9.89	9.89
MORTGAGE LOANS-FIXED	10.39	10.39	10.39	10.39	10.39	10.39	10.39	10.39	10.39	10.39	10.39	10.39
MORTGAGE LOANS-ADJ	9.32	9.17	9.04	8.91	8.79	8.67	8.56	8.45	8.35	8.25	8.16	8.07
HOME EQUITY LOANS	11.49	11.46	11.43	11.40	11.38	11.35	11.32	11.30	11.27	11.25	11.22	11.20
CONSUMER LOANS	13.00	12.97	12.93	12.89	12.84	12.80	12.75	12.71	12.66	12.61	12.57	12.52
CREDIT CARD LOANS	18.31	19.68	19.31	19.36	19.25	19.34	19.26	19.30	19.44	19.42	19.57	19.46
AUTO LOANS	12.50	12.42	12.34	12.27	12.21	12.15	12.10	12.06	12.01	11.98	11.94	11.90
TOTAL LOANS	11.65	11.73	11.71	11.71	11.69	11.68	11.63	11.60	11.56	11.49	11.46	11.43
TOTAL EARNING ASSETS	10.56	10.59	10.53	10.57	10.54	10.54	10.49	10.46	10.42	10.33	10.31	10.28

MONTHLY INTEREST RATE REPORT - DETAIL
2002 ACTUAL

	JAN	FEB	MAR	APR	MAY	JUN	JUL	AUG	SEP	OCT	NOV	DEC
COST OF FUNDS RATES:												
INTEREST-BEAR CHECKING	5.00	5.00	5.00	5.00	5.00	5.00	5.00	5.00	5.00	5.00	5.00	5.00
REGULAR SAVINGS	5.50	5.50	5.50	5.50	5.50	5.50	5.50	5.50	5.50	5.50	5.50	5.50
IBC & SAVINGS	5.18	5.18	5.18	5.18	5.18	5.18	5.18	5.18	5.18	5.18	5.18	5.18
MMDAs	7.14	7.70	7.82	7.82	7.78	7.76	7.70	7.55	7.41	7.28	7.13	6.94
SMALL CDs	8.48	8.39	8.30	8.22	8.17	8.14	8.14	8.14	8.13	8.11	8.09	8.05
LARGE CDs	8.36	8.26	8.24	8.29	8.35	8.35	8.28	8.16	8.07	8.04	8.04	8.01
PUBLIC CDs	8.36	8.26	8.24	8.29	8.35	8.36	8.28	8.16	8.07	8.04	8.04	8.01
OTHER CDS	7.34	7.31	7.32	7.36	7.47	7.59	7.66	7.68	7.63	7.54	7.38	7.17
INT RTE CONTRACTS-SWAPS	0.00	0.00	0.00	0.00	0.00	0.00	0.00	0.00	0.00	0.00	0.00	0.00
OTHER CDs	7.34	7.31	7.32	7.36	7.47	7.59	7.66	7.68	7.63	7.54	7.38	7.17
TOTAL CERTIFICATES	8.36	8.27	8.23	8.26	8.30	8.30	8.24	8.15	8.07	8.04	8.04	8.00
TREASURY, TAX & LOAN	7.98	7.99	8.03	8.01	7.93	8.04	7.90	7.88	7.95	7.86	7.56	7.06
REPOS	0.00	8.24	8.28	8.26	8.18	8.29	0.00	0.00	8.20	8.11	7.81	0.00
FED FUNDS PURCHASED	8.32	9.22	8.37	8.63	8.27	8.66	8.24	8.22	8.57	8.20	8.17	7.42
SHORT-TERM BOR FUNDS	8.10	8.40	8.16	8.23	8.06	8.25	8.02	8.00	8.16	7.99	7.77	7.18
LONG-TERM DEBT	0.00	0.00	0.00	0.00	0.00	0.00	0.00	0.00	0.00	0.00	0.00	0.00
FHLB ADVANCES	0.00	0.00	0.00	0.00	0.00	0.00	0.00	0.00	0.00	0.00	0.00	0.00
LONG-TERM DEBT	0.00	0.00	0.00	0.00	0.00	0.00	0.00	0.00	0.00	0.00	0.00	0.00
TOTAL INT-BEAR LIAB	7.13	7.23	7.25	7.26	7.27	7.26	7.22	7.14	7.07	7.02	6.97	6.90
NET INTEREST SPREAD	3.65	3.57	3.49	3.51	3.48	3.52	3.53	3.60	3.69	3.70	3.72	3.72
NET INTEREST INCOME	4.39	4.33	4.24	4.25	4.23	4.26	4.26	4.33	4.40	4.40	4.42	4.40
MARKET RATES												
PRIME RATE (LG BKS)	10.11	10.00	10.00	10.00	10.00	10.00	10.00	10.00	10.00	10.00	10.00	10.00
FED FUNDS RATE(NATIONAL)	8.23	8.24	8.28	8.26	8.18	8.29	8.15	8.13	8.20	8.11	7.81	7.31
TREASURY BILL RATE 3 MO	7.64	7.76	7.87	7.78	7.78	7.74	7.66	7.44	7.38	7.19	7.07	6.81
TREASURY BILL RATE 6 MO	7.52	7.72	7.83	7.82	7.82	7.64	7.57	7.36	7.33	7.20	7.04	6.76
US GOVT YIELD (3YRS)	8.13	8.39	8.63	8.78	8.69	8.40	8.26	8.22	8.27	8.07	7.74	7.47
MUNICIPAL BOND YIELD	7.10	7.22	7.29	7.39	7.35	7.24	7.19	7.32	7.43	7.49	7.18	7.09
CONV MTG RATE (NEW)	9.91	9.88	10.03	10.17	10.28	10.13	10.08	10.11	9.90	9.98	9.90	9.76
90-DAY CD RATE(NATIONAL)	8.16	8.22	8.35	8.42	8.35	8.23	8.10	7.97	8.06	8.06	8.03	7.82
LONDON INTERBANK RATE	8.22	8.24	8.37	8.44	8.35	8.23	8.09	7.99	8.07	8.06	8.04	7.87

MONTHLY INTEREST RATE REPORT - DETAIL
2003 FORECAST

	JAN	FEB	MAR	APR	MAY	JUN	JUL	AUG	SEP	OCT	NOV	DEC
COST OF FUNDS RATES:												
INTEREST-BEAR CHECKING	5.00	5.00	5.00	5.00	5.00	5.00	5.00	5.00	5.00	5.00	5.00	5.00
REGULAR SAVINGS	5.50	5.50	5.50	5.50	5.50	5.50	5.50	5.50	5.50	5.50	5.50	5.50
IBC & SAVINGS	5.18	5.18	5.18	5.18	5.18	5.18	5.17	5.17	5.17	5.17	5.17	5.17
MMDAs	7.28	7.03	7.03	7.03	7.03	7.03	7.03	7.03	7.03	7.03	7.03	7.03
SMALL CDs	8.01	7.94	7.86	7.79	7.72	7.65	7.60	7.56	7.52	7.48	7.44	7.41
LARGE CDs	7.93	7.86	7.82	7.82	7.82	7.82	7.82	7.82	7.82	7.82	7.82	7.82
PUBLIC CDs	8.10	8.11	8.16	8.22	8.22	8.22	8.22	8.22	8.22	8.22	8.22	8.22
OTHER CDS	7.16	7.32	7.42	7.48	7.51	7.52	7.52	7.52	7.52	7.52	7.52	7.52
INT RTE CONTRACTS-SWAPS	0.00	0.00	0.00	0.00	0.00	0.00	0.00	0.00	0.00	0.00	0.00	0.00
OTHER CDs	7.16	7.32	7.42	7.48	7.51	7.52	7.52	7.52	7.52	7.52	7.52	7.52
TOTAL CERTIFICATES	7.97	7.92	7.91	7.91	7.90	7.88	7.87	7.86	7.85	7.84	7.83	7.82
TREASURY, TAX & LOAN	6.81	6.81	6.81	6.81	6.81	6.81	6.81	6.81	6.81	6.81	6.81	6.81
REPOS	0.00	6.81	6.81	6.81	6.81	6.81	6.81	0.00	6.81	6.81	6.81	6.81
FED FUNDS PURCHASED	7.42	8.21	7.42	7.66	7.42	7.66	7.42	7.42	7.66	7.42	7.66	7.42
SHORT-TERM BOR FUNDS	7.01	7.21	6.96	7.02	6.98	7.05	6.98	7.01	7.05	6.96	7.03	6.99
LONG-TERM DEBT	0.00	0.00	0.00	0.00	0.00	0.00	0.00	0.00	0.00	0.00	0.00	0.00
FHLB ADVANCES	0.00	0.00	0.00	0.00	0.00	0.00	0.00	0.00	0.00	0.00	0.00	0.00
LONG-TERM DEBT	0.00	0.00	0.00	0.00	0.00	0.00	0.00	0.00	0.00	0.00	0.00	0.00
TOTAL INT-BEAR LIAB	6.98	6.90	6.90	6.90	6.90	6.89	6.89	6.88	6.88	6.88	6.88	6.87
NET INTEREST SPREAD	3.59	3.69	3.64	3.67	3.65	3.65	3.60	3.57	3.54	3.46	3.44	3.40
NET INTEREST INCOME	4.40	4.56	4.51	4.49	4.47	4.47	4.42	4.38	4.35	4.26	4.24	4.20
MARKET RATES												
PRIME RATE (LG BKS)	10.00	10.00	10.00	10.00	10.00	10.00	10.00	10.00	10.00	10.00	10.00	10.00
FED FUNDS RATE(NATIONAL)	7.31	7.31	7.31	7.31	7.31	7.31	7.31	7.31	7.31	7.31	7.31	7.31
TREASURY BILL RATE 3 MO	6.81	6.81	6.81	6.81	6.81	6.81	6.81	6.81	6.81	6.81	6.81	6.81
TREASURY BILL RATE 6 MO	6.76	6.76	6.76	6.76	6.76	6.76	6.76	6.76	6.76	6.76	6.76	6.76
US GOVT YIELD (3YRS)	7.47	7.47	7.47	7.47	7.47	7.47	7.47	7.47	7.47	7.47	7.47	7.47
MUNICIPAL BOND YIELD	7.09	7.09	7.09	7.09	7.09	7.09	7.09	7.09	7.09	7.09	7.09	7.09
CONV MTG RATE (NEW)	9.76	9.76	9.76	9.76	9.76	9.76	9.76	9.76	9.76	9.76	9.76	9.76
90-DAY CD RATE(NATIONAL)	7.82	7.82	7.82	7.82	7.82	7.82	7.82	7.82	7.82	7.82	7.82	7.82
LONDON INTERBANK RATE	7.87	7.87	7.87	7.87	7.87	7.87	7.87	7.87	7.87	7.87	7.87	7.87

RISK-BASED CAPITAL REPORT - DETAIL
2002 ACTUAL

	JAN	FEB	MAR	APR	MAY	JUN	JUL	AUG	SEP	OCT	NOV	DEC
RISK-ADJUSTED ASSETS:												
CATEGORY I, 0%:												
CASH, RESERVES & DUE FROM	10465	10543	10623	10704	10785	10868	10951	11035	11120	11207	11291	11388
SHORT-TERM TREASURIES	39600	39073	39620	38974	39230	39392	40757	41997	42366	42735	44221	44290
LONG-TERM TREASURIES	40150	40600	41200	41750	41900	42250	42450	42400	42500	42400	42400	42200
US AGENCY SECURITIES	4703	4656	5008	4959	4909	4859	4809	5358	5305	5251	5198	5143
INT RTE CONTRACTS-OPTIONS	0	0	0	0	0	0	0	0	0	0	0	0
TRADING ACCOUNT	0	0	0	0	0	0	0	0	0	0	0	0
TOTAL - CATEGORY I	94917	94872	96451	96386	96824	97369	98967	100790	101291	101593	103109	103022
WTD TOTAL- CATEGORY I	0	0	0	0	0	0	0	0	0	0	0	0
CATEGORY II, 20%:												
ITEMS IN PROCESS	14403	14511	14620	14730	14841	14953	15066	15180	15296	15412	15522	15633
CMO CLASS B	0	0	0	0	0	0	0	0	0	0	0	0
OUR SECURITIZED MTG LOANS	0	0	0	0	0	0	0	0	0	0	0	0
FHLB STOCK	0	0	0	0	0	0	0	0	0	0	0	0
TERM FED FUNDS SOLD	0	0	0	0	0	0	0	0	0	0	0	0
OVERNIGHT FED FUNDS SOLD	17792	19044	17929	20043	20218	20364	20682	19589	20035	22041	21731	23529
CREDIT EQUIVALENT AMOUNTS:												
OFF-BALANCE SHEET ITEMS	8805	8950	9095	9240	9385	9530	9675	9820	9965	10110	10255	10400
TOTAL - CATEGORY II	41001	42506	41644	44013	44444	44847	45424	44589	45296	47563	47508	49562
WTD TOTAL- CATEGORY II	8200	8501	8329	8803	8889	8969	9085	8918	9059	9513	9502	9912
CATEGORY III, 50%:												
TAX EXEMPTS	5500	5250	5100	5000	4800	4550	4150	3850	3750	3550	3400	3200
MORTGAGE LOANS-FIXED	28766	29124	29486	29853	30225	30601	30982	31367	31758	32153	32553	32958
MORTGAGE LOANS-ADJ	30685	31054	31428	31806	32189	32576	32968	33365	33766	34172	34584	34600
CREDIT EQUIVALENT AMOUNTS:												
OFF-BALANCE SHEET ITEMS	4548	4620	4692	4764	4836	4908	4980	5052	5124	5196	5268	5340
TOTAL - CATEGORY III	69499	70048	70706	71423	72049	72635	73080	73634	74398	75071	75805	76098
WTD TOTAL-CATEGORY III	34749	35024	35353	35712	36025	36317	36540	36817	37199	37536	37902	38049
CATEGORY IV, 100%:												
OTHER SECURITIES	2908	2908	3024	3024	3024	3024	3024	3024	3124	3124	3124	3124
INT RTE CONTRACTS-SWAPS	0	0	0	0	0	0	0	0	0	0	0	0
COM'L PARTIC PURCH-FIXED	0	0	0	0	0	0	0	0	0	0	0	0
DIRECT COM'L LOANS-FIXED	44037	44389	44743	45100	45459	45821	46186	46553	46924	47297	47673	48051
PART PUR - REQ'D-FIXED	0	0	0	0	0	0	0	0	0	0	0	0
PART SOLD - REQ'D-FIXED	0	0	0	0	0	0	0	0	0	0	0	0
COM'L LNS-OPTION CONTRACT	0	0	0	0	0	0	0	0	0	0	0	0
COM'L PARTIC PURCH-FLOAT	0	0	0	0	0	0	0	0	0	0	0	0
DIRECT COM'L LOANS-FLOAT	52718	53164	53613	54067	54524	54984	55449	55917	56389	56865	57344	57828
HOME EQUITY LOANS	13362	13562	13766	13972	14181	14394	14610	14828	15051	15276	15305	15338
CONSUMER LOANS	64220	64999	65788	66587	67395	68213	69041	69879	70727	71585	71835	71984
CREDIT CARD LOANS	26884	27146	27411	27678	27948	28220	28495	28773	29053	29336	29622	29911
AUTO LOANS	1842	1865	1889	1913	1937	1962	1987	2012	2038	2063	2090	2116
PROPERTY & EQUIPMENT	9219	9268	9316	9366	9415	9465	9515	9565	9616	9666	9717	9769
OREO & FORECLOSED ASSETS	725	734	743	752	762	771	781	791	801	810	820	830
OTHER ASSETS	5921	6546	7203	5985	6651	7310	6057	6735	7408	6124	6795	7472
TOTAL - CATEGORY IV	221836	224582	227496	228443	231296	234164	235144	238077	241129	242147	244326	246423
WTD TOTAL- CATEGORY IV	221836	224582	227496	228443	231296	234164	235144	238077	241129	242147	244326	246423
WTD NONCONFORMING ACCT	0	0	0	0	0	0	0	0	0	0	0	0
REDUCTION TO RISK ASSETS	0	0	0	0	0	0	0	0	0	0	0	0
GROSS RISK-WTD ASSETS	264785	268107	271178	272957	276209	279451	280768	283812	287387	289196	291730	294385

RISK-BASED CAPITAL REPORT - DETAIL
2003 FORECAST

	JAN	FEB	MAR	APR	MAY	JUN	JUL	AUG	SEP	OCT	NOV	DEC
RISK-ADJUSTED ASSETS:												
CATEGORY I, 0%:												
CASH, RESERVES & DUE FROM	8434	8542	8655	8724	8794	8863	8934	9001	9066	9132	9200	9266
SHORT-TERM TREASURIES	57231	53155	52555	52614	53666	53333	59362	59641	58542	57561	58237	58009
LONG-TERM TREASURIES	42400	42550	42950	43050	43200	43400	43400	43400	43300	43600	43800	44050
US AGENCY SECURITIES	5735	6330	6619	6705	6889	7171	7251	7579	7660	8040	8372	8501
TRADING ACCOUNT	5000	5000	5000	5000	5000	5000	5000	5000	5000	5000	5000	5000
TOTAL - CATEGORY I	118801	115577	115779	116094	117549	117767	123947	124622	123569	123334	124608	124826
WTD TOTAL- CATEGORY I	0	0	0	0	0	0	0	0	0	0	0	0
CATEGORY II, 20%:												
ITEMS IN PROCESS	7885	7956	8033	8070	8106	8143	8180	8215	8248	8281	8315	8349
CMO CLASS B	7750	7153	7153	7153	6628	6628	6628	6628	6628	6628	6628	6628
OUR SECURITIZED MTG LOANS	0	0	0	0	0	0	0	0	0	0	0	0
FHLB STOCK	0	0	0	0	0	0	0	0	0	0	0	0
TERM FED FUNDS SOLD	0	0	0	0	0	0	0	0	0	0	0	0
OVERNIGHT FED FUNDS SOLD	11283	17494	20339	19926	19380	21642	15111	17054	22129	25052	24871	25911
CREDIT EQUIVALENT AMOUNTS:												
OFF-BALANCE SHEET ITEMS	10642	10703	10756	10823	10894	10981	11063	11110	11154	11205	11264	11310
TOTAL - CATEGORY II	37559	43307	46282	45972	45009	47394	40982	43006	48159	51165	51078	52198
WTD TOTAL- CATEGORY II	7512	8661	9256	9194	9002	9479	8196	8601	9632	10233	10216	10440
CATEGORY III, 50%:												
TAX EXEMPTS	3100	3150	3000	3000	2850	2800	2650	2600	2550	2450	2450	2400
MORTGAGE LOANS-FIXED	32427	31933	31408	30873	30338	29794	29259	28725	28227	27737	27272	26815
MORTGAGE LOANS-ADJ	35165	35746	36309	36864	37415	37959	38504	39045	39602	40160	40728	41297
CREDIT EQUIVALENT AMOUNTS:												
OFF-BALANCE SHEET ITEMS	5321	5352	5378	5411	5447	5491	5531	5555	5577	5602	5632	5655
TOTAL - CATEGORY III	76013	76180	76095	76149	76051	76043	75944	75926	75956	75950	76082	76167
WTD TOTAL-CATEGORY III	38007	38090	38048	38074	38025	38022	37972	37963	37978	37975	38041	38083
CATEGORY IV, 100%:												
OTHER SECURITIES	3124	3574	3574	3574	3574	3574	4174	4174	4174	4174	4074	4074
INT RTE CONTRACTS-SWAPS	0	0	0	0	0	0	0	0	0	0	0	0
INT RTE CONTRACTS-OPTIONS	0	0	0	0	0	0	0	0	0	0	0	0
COM'L PARTIC PURCH-FIXED	0	0	0	0	0	0	0	0	0	0	0	0
DIRECT COM'L LNS-FIXED	48279	48520	48759	49228	49644	50110	50527	50698	50837	50949	51138	51299
PART PUR - REQ'D-FIXED	0	0	0	0	0	0	0	0	0	0	0	0
PART SOLD - REQ'D-FIXED	0	0	0	0	0	0	0	0	0	0	0	0
COM'L LNS-OPTION CONTRACT	0	0	0	0	0	0	0	0	0	0	0	0
COM'L PARTIC PURCH-FLOAT	0	0	0	0	0	0	0	0	0	0	0	0
DIRECT COM'L LNS-FLOAT	58138	58512	58800	59000	59300	59700	60100	60400	60700	61100	61500	61800
HOME EQUITY LOANS	15389	15444	15501	15560	15622	15685	15751	15819	15890	15963	16039	16118
CONSUMER LOANS	72151	72324	72502	72739	73038	73398	73866	74439	75014	75440	75770	75956
CREDIT CARD LOANS	28841	30816	32372	33503	34206	34473	34299	33678	32605	31074	31472	31874
AUTO LOANS	2245	2370	2493	2614	2730	2844	2958	3070	3183	3295	3406	3515
PROPERTY & EQUIPMENT	9796	9823	9851	9878	9906	9933	9961	9989	10017	10045	10073	10101
OREO & FORECLOSED ASSETS	940	1044	1150	1266	1376	1486	1605	1715	1826	1945	2057	2170
OTHER ASSETS	6286	7066	7870	6364	7171	7971	6462	7315	8153	6541	7375	8224
TOTAL - CATEGORY IV	245189	249493	252872	253726	256565	259175	259704	261298	262400	260526	262903	265130
WTD TOTAL- CATEGORY IV	245189	249493	252872	253726	256565	259175	259704	261298	262400	260526	262903	265130
WTD NONCONFORMING ACCT	0	0	0	0	0	0	0	0	0	0	0	0
REDUCTION TO RISK ASSETS	0	0	0	0	0	0	0	0	0	0	0	0
GROSS RISK-WTD ASSETS	290707	296244	300176	300995	303592	306676	305872	307863	310010	308734	311160	313653

RISK-BASED CAPITAL REPORT - DETAIL
2002 ACTUAL

	JAN	FEB	MAR	APR	MAY	JUN	JUL	AUG	SEP	OCT	NOV	DEC
CAPITAL:												
TIER 1, CORE CAPITAL:												
COMMON STOCK & SURPLUS	5000	5000	5000	5000	5000	5000	5000	5000	5000	5000	5000	5000
RETAINED EARNINGS	18712	19023	18955	19207	19457	19414	19664	19936	19897	20184	20487	20481
INCREASE: TIER 1 CAPITAL	0	0	0	0	0	0	0	0	0	0	0	0
DECREASE: TIER 1 CAPITAL	-925	-925	-925	-925	-925	-925	-925	-925	-925	-925	-925	-925
TOTAL TIER 1 CORE CAP	22787	23098	23030	23282	23532	23489	23739	24011	23972	24259	24562	24556
TIER 2, SUPPLEMENTARY CAPITAL:												
TIER 2 SUBJECT TO LIMITS	0	0	0	0	0	0	0	0	0	0	0	0
ADJUST TO % TIER 1 LIMIT	0	0	0	0	0	0	0	0	0	0	0	0
RESERVE FOR LOAN LOSSES	4515	4563	4612	4661	4710	4760	4811	4862	4914	4966	5005	5036
ALLOWANCE EXCESS	-1205	-1212	-1222	-1249	-1258	-1267	-1302	-1315	-1322	-1352	-1359	-1356
INCREASE: TIER 2 CAPITAL	0	0	0	0	0	0	0	0	0	0	0	0
SUBTOTAL	3310	3351	3390	3412	3453	3493	3510	3548	3592	3615	3647	3680
AMOUNT EXCEEDING TIER 1	0	0	0	0	0	0	0	0	0	0	0	0
TOTAL TIER 2 SUPP CAP	3310	3351	3390	3412	3453	3493	3510	3548	3592	3615	3647	3680
TIER 1 PLUS TIER 2	26096	26450	26420	26694	26985	26983	27249	27559	27565	27874	28209	28236
DECREASE: TOTAL CAPITAL	0	0	0	0	0	0	0	0	0	0	0	0
QUALIFYING TOTAL CAPITAL	26096	26450	26420	26694	26985	26983	27249	27559	27565	27874	28209	28236
GROSS RISK-WTD ASSETS	264785	268107	271178	272957	276209	279451	280768	283812	287387	289196	291730	294385
LESS: ALLOWANCE EXCESS	1205	1212	1222	1249	1258	1267	1302	1315	1322	1352	1359	1356
ADJUSTED RISK-WTD ASSETS	263580	266895	269956	271709	274952	278184	279467	282497	286066	287844	290371	293029
RISK-ADJUSTED CAPITAL RATIOS:												
CORE (TIER 1) RATIO	8.65	8.65	8.53	8.57	8.56	8.44	8.49	8.50	8.38	8.43	8.46	8.38
TOTAL CAPITAL RATIO	9.90	9.91	9.79	9.82	9.81	9.70	9.75	9.76	9.64	9.68	9.71	9.64
RISK-WTD TO TOTAL ASSETS	64.38	64.49	64.60	64.45	64.59	64.72	64.52	64.59	64.70	64.52	64.50	64.50

RISK-BASED CAPITAL REPORT - DETAIL
2003 FORECAST

	JAN	FEB	MAR	APR	MAY	JUN	JUL	AUG	SEP	OCT	NOV	DEC
CAPITAL:												
TIER 1, CORE CAPITAL:												
COMMON STOCK & SURPLUS	5000	5000	5000	5000	5000	5000	5000	5000	5000	5000	5000	5000
RETAINED EARNINGS	20883	21375	21385	21747	22071	22090	22417	22750	22769	23063	23375	23324
INCREASE: TIER 1 CAPITAL	0	0	0	0	0	0	0	0	0	0	0	0
DECREASE: TIER 1 CAPITAL	-925	-925	-925	-925	-925	-925	-925	-925	-925	-925	-925	-925
TOTAL TIER 1 CORE CAP	24958	25450	25460	25822	26146	26165	26492	26825	26844	27138	27450	27399
TIER 2, SUPPLEMENTARY CAPITAL:												
TIER 2 SUBJECT TO LIMITS	0	0	0	0	0	0	0	0	0	0	0	0
ADJUST TO % TIER 1 LIMIT	0	0	0	0	0	0	0	0	0	0	0	0
RESERVE FOR LOAN LOSSES	4918	4801	4852	4899	4938	4974	5002	5019	5026	5020	5030	5055
ALLOWANCE EXCESS	-1285	-1098	-1100	-1136	-1144	-1141	-1178	-1171	-1150	-1161	-1141	-1134
INCREASE: TIER 2 CAPITAL	0	0	0	0	0	0	0	0	0	0	0	0
SUBTOTAL	3634	3703	3752	3762	3795	3833	3823	3848	3875	3859	3889	3921
AMOUNT EXCEEDING TIER 1	0	0	0	0	0	0	0	0	0	0	0	0
TOTAL TIER 2 SUPP CAP	3634	3703	3752	3762	3795	3833	3823	3848	3875	3859	3889	3921
TIER 1 PLUS TIER 2	28592	29153	29212	29585	29941	29998	30315	30673	30719	30998	31340	31320
DECREASE: TOTAL CAPITAL	0	0	0	0	0	0	0	0	0	0	0	0
QUALIFYING TOTAL CAPITAL	28592	29153	29212	29585	29941	29998	30315	30673	30719	30998	31340	31320
GROSS RISK-WTD ASSETS	290707	296244	300176	300995	303592	306676	305872	307863	310010	308734	311160	313653
LESS: ALLOWANCE EXCESS	1285	1098	1100	1136	1144	1141	1178	1171	1150	1161	1141	1134
ADJUSTED RISK-WTD ASSETS	289422	295146	299076	299859	302448	305535	304694	306692	308859	307573	310019	312519
RISK-ADJUSTED CAPITAL RATIOS:												
CORE (TIER 1) RATIO	8.62	8.62	8.51	8.61	8.64	8.56	8.69	8.75	8.69	8.82	8.85	8.77
TOTAL CAPITAL RATIO	9.88	9.88	9.77	9.87	9.90	9.82	9.95	10.00	9.95	10.08	10.11	10.02
RISK-WTD TO TOTAL ASSETS	63.38	63.65	63.63	63.69	63.82	63.79	63.61	63.48	63.25	62.88	62.92	62.97

GRAPHIC
ANALYSIS

Return on Equity

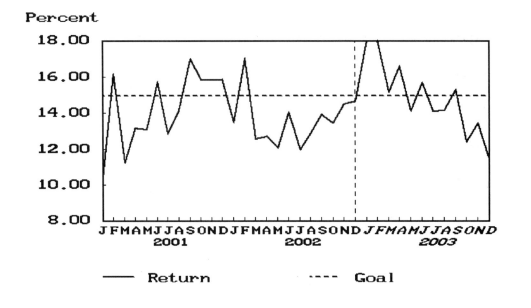

Return on Assets

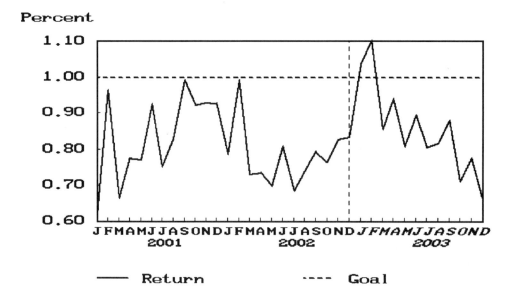

Price/Earnings Ratio

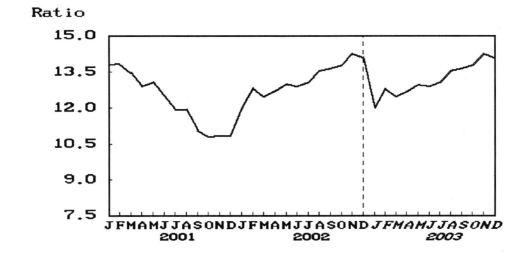

Total Risk-Based Capital %

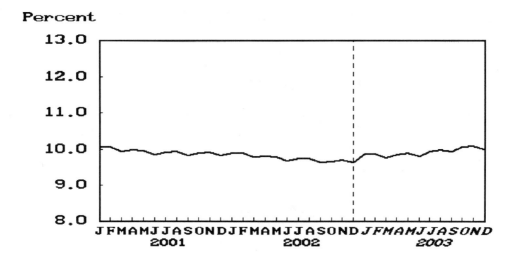

Loans to Available Deposits

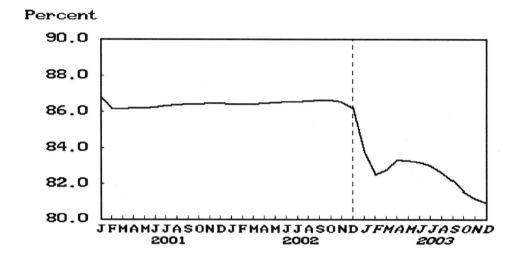

Loan Mix - 2003

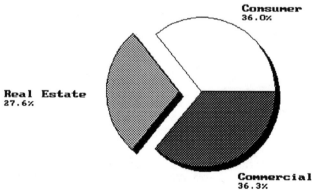

Interest Spread

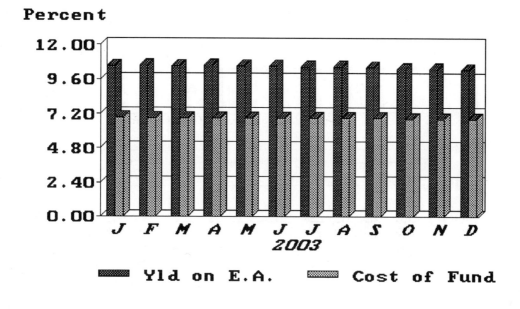

Percent

Yld on E.A.   Cost of Fund

Interest Margin and Net Overhead to Earning Assets

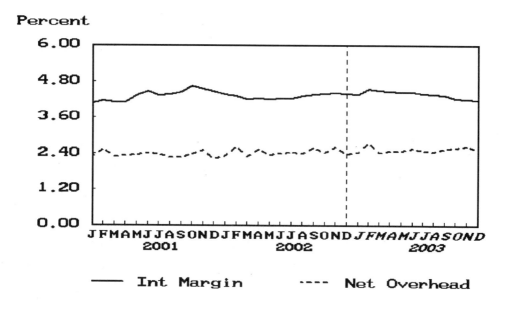

Percent

Int Margin   ---- Net Overhead

Loan Quality Characteristics

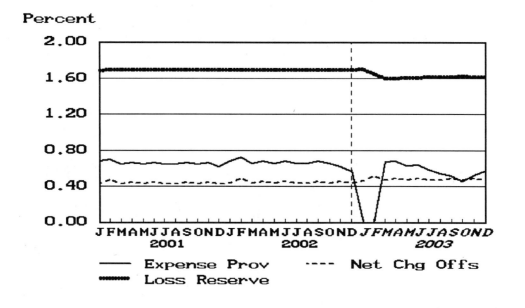

Loans and Deposits to Equity

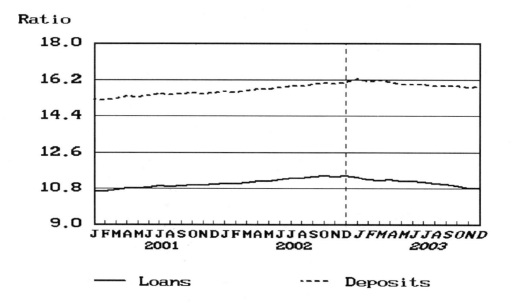

DETAIL
KEY RATIOS
REPORT DEFINITIONS

ASSET QUALITY:

Most Bal Loan Mix (AVG).

The difference between the highest and the lowest mix of commercial, consumer, and real estate loans to total loans. Balance growth does not measure the amount of growth but merely the spread between the greatest and the least. It shows the ability of management to diversify (instead of concentrate) in all industries.

Reserves/Non-Performing (EOP).

Reserve for loan losses divided by non-performing loans. This ratio indicates the extent to which principal losses from non-performing loans are covered by the loan loss reserves. The higher the ratio, the greater the strength of the reserve.

Net Charge-Offs/Loans (AVG).

Actual net charge-offs for the time period divided by average gross total loans. Actual charge-offs can be calculated by subtracting the increase in the ending reserve for loan losses balance from the loan loss provision. For periodic reports, the net charge-offs are annualized on a daily basis. Gives a direct indication of actual loan losses as a percentage of average gross loans.

Invest Market to Book (EOP).

Ratio of market value, calculated above, to the book value of the securities. All securities are assumed to be purchased at par value. Indicates the amount of interest rate risk that exists in securities portfolios.

LIQUIDITY (AVG %):

Loans/Deposits (EOP).

Gross total loans divided by total deposits. Indicates the extent to which deposit dollars have been committed to loans.

S-T Investments to Assets.

Short-term treasuries plus overnight federal funds sold are divided by average total assets. Reflects the amount of assets that are invested in short maturity and low risk assets.

Purchased Funds/E.A.

Purchased funds includes large CDs, public CDs, and short-term borrowings divided by total earning assets. Indicates the bank's dependence upon funds obtained in competitive money markets as a method of financing earning assets.

Net Short Bor Funds/Total Assets.

Net borrowed funds includes short-term borrowed funds less overnight federal funds sold. Indicates the extent of exposure the bank has assumed by financing assets from the short-term market.

Total Loans/Available Deposits.

Total loans divided by total deposits less cash float, reserves and public deposits. Indicates the extent (if any) to which sources other than collected deposits net of reserve are being used to fund loans.

CAPITAL ADEQUACY:

Equity to Assets (EOP)

Total equity divided by total assets.

Market Capitalization.

Number of shares outstanding times stock price.

Risk-Based Capital (EOP).

Total qualifying (core and supplemental) capital divided by risk-weighted assets and off-balance sheet items. This ratio was developed by regulators to determine capital adequacy based on the credit risk inherent in the bank's assets. Effective December 31, 1992, a minimum of 8% total risk-based capital was required. The guidelines also require a core (or Tier 1) capital ratio of 4%, computed as risk-weighted assets and off-balance sheet items divided by core capital.

P/E Ratio (EOP).

Market price per share divided by earnings per share (EPS), expressed as a multiple. Shares of common stock which are highly regarded by investors generally sell at a higher P/E ratio, or multiple, than less highly regarded common stock.

EARNINGS/PROFITABILITY:

Earnings Per Share ($).

Annualized net income divided by average number of shares of stock outstanding.

Return on Equity.

Annualized net income divided by the average total equity capital. Reflects the bank's ability to generate a return on the shareholders' book equity.

Return on Assets.

Annualized net income divided by the average total assets. Reflects the bank's ability to generate a return on the total resources available to management.

Interest Margin on E.A.

Annualized taxable-equivalent interest income less interest expense divided by average gross earning assets. Reflects the yield on earning assets adjusted for the cost of the interest-bearing instruments.

Net Overhead to E.A.

Annualized non-interest expense, excluding loan loss provision, less non-interest income divided by average gross earning assets. The ratio shows the yield that must be earned on earning assets just to cover the net operating expenses of the bank.

Yield on Earning Assets.

Annualized taxable-equivalent interest income divided by average gross earning assets.

Net Income.

Year-to-date net income.

GROWTH (YTD AVG %):

Total Loans.

For annual growth rates, the change in average total loans from the prior year is divided by the prior year's average total loans. For periodic growth rates, a year-to-date average change in total loans is divided by a year-to-date average of total loans for the prior year.

Total Deposits.

For annual growth rates, the change in average total deposits from the prior year is divided by the prior year's average total deposits. For periodic growth rates, a year-to-date average change in total deposits is divided by a year-to-date average of total deposits for the prior year.

Total Equity.

For annual growth rates, the change in average total equity from the prior year is divided by the prior year's average total equity. For periodic growth rates, a year-to-date average change in total equity is divided by a year-to-date average of total equity for the prior year.

Balanced Growth.

The difference between the highest and the lowest growth rates of total loans, total deposits, and total equity. Balanced growth does not measure the amount of growth, but merely the spread between greatest and least. Shows the ability of management to control and to balance the growth rates of three key elements.

Composite Growth.

The sum of the growth rates of total loans, total deposits, and total equity. Shows the ability of management to generate aggregate growth in the three areas of loans, deposits, and equity.

Total Assets ($EOP).

The dollar amount of total assets as of a point in time.

MEMO ITEMS:

Market Value of Invst ($ Mil).

Represents the average market value of U.S. Treasuries (short- and long-term) and tax-exempt securities. Market value is calculated using standard present value computations, the market rate of interest for each type of security, and the time to maturity.

Outstanding Shares (000).

Average number of shares of common stock outstanding.

Salaries & Benefits/Emp($).

Actual total salaries and benefits expense divided by number of employees.

Assets/Emp ($ Mil).

Average total assets divided by the number of employees.

Stock Price (EOP).

The earnings per share times the price/earnings ratio. In actuality, this reflects the price which a buyer and a seller can agree upon as fair. In the simulation, it is the hypothetical price derived from earnings per share and a calculated price/earnings ratio.

Book Value per Share (EOP).

The dollar value of equity as reported on the historical balance sheet (as opposed to market value) divided by the number of outstanding shares of stock.

SUMMARY
KEY RATIOS
REPORT DEFINITIONS

PERFORMANCE:

Return on Equity.

Annualized net income divided by the average total equity capital. Reflects the bank's ability to generate a return on the shareholders' book equity.

Return on Assets.

Annualized net income divided by the average total assets. Reflects the bank's ability to generate a return on the total resources available to management.

Earnings Per Share ($).

Annualized net income divided by average number of shares of stock outstanding.

Common Div Per Share ($).

Dividend per share of common stock.

Book Value per Share (EOP).

The dollar value of equity as reported on the historical balance sheet (as opposed to market value) divided by the number of outstanding shares of stock.

Earning/Total Assets.

Average gross earning assets divided by average total assets. Indicates the percentage of total assets that are employed directly in generating revenue.

Interest Bearing/Total Deposits.

Total interest bearing checking, savings and time deposits divided by total deposits. Indicates the percentage of deposits supplied through instruments with explicit interest costs attached.

INTEREST MARGIN AND OVERHEAD:

Average National Prime Rate.	Average prime rate of several large New York banks.
Yield on Earning Assets.	Annualized taxable-equivalent interest income divided by average gross earning assets.
Cost of Funds Rate.	Annualized interest expense divided by average interest-bearing deposits.
Spread.	The arithmetic difference between the yield in earning assets and the cost of funds rate.
Interest Margin on E.A.	Annualized taxable-equivalent interest income less interest expense divided by average gross earning assets. Reflects the yield on earning assets adjusted for the cost of the interest-bearing instruments.
Net Overhead to E.A.	Annualized non-interest expense, excluding loan loss provision, less non-interest income divided by average gross earning assets. The ratio shows the yield that must be earned on earning assets just to cover the net operating expenses of the bank.

LOAN POSITION:

Loans/Total Deposits.	Gross total loans divided by the total deposits. Indicates the extent to which deposit dollars have been committed to loans.
Loans/Earning Assets.	Gross total loans divided by total earning assets.
Loss Reserve/Loans (%).	Average reserve for loan losses divided by average gross total loans. Reflects the bank's policy of maintaining a minimum reserve for loan losses. Adjustments needed to keep the percentage at the minimum reserve (for loan loss write-offs and for loan balance growth) will generate a debit to the loan loss provision (expense).
Loss Provision/Loans (%).	The expense account, loan loss provision, is divided by average gross total loans. For periodic reports, the loan loss provision is annualized on a daily basis. The expense is the sum of net charge-offs and the adjustment to the reserve for loan losses due to growth in loan balances. Gives the relationship between the loan loss expense and the average gross loans.

| Net Charge-Offs/Loans (AVG). | Actual net charge-offs for the time period divided by average gross total loans. Actual charge-offs can be calculated by subtracting the increase in the ending reserve for loan losses balance from the loan loss provision. For periodic reports, the net charge-offs are annualized on a daily basis. Gives a direct indication of actual loan losses as a percentage of average gross loans. |
| NonPerforming/Loans (EOP). | Non-accrual loans, other real estate owned, and renegotiated loans divided by the sum of gross loans and other real estate owned. |

CAPITAL LEVERAGE:

Core (Tier 1) Ratio.	Risk-weighted assets and off-balance sheet items divided by total qualifying core capital.
Total Capital Ratio.	Total capital divided by total risk-weighted assets.
Asset Leverage Ratio.	Core capital divided by average quarterly assets less any intangibles.
Equity to Assets.	Total equity divided by total assets.
Dividend Payout Ratio.	Dividends paid divided by net income.

LIQUIDITY:

Cash/Total Deposits (%).	Total cash divided by total deposits. For this and all other liquidity ratios, annual ratios use twelve month averages; and periodic ratios use the specific month's average account balance. Indicates amount of cash available to cover possible deposit withdrawals.
Purchased Funds/E.A..	Purchased funds includes large CDs, public CDs, and short-term borrowings divided by total earning assets. Indicates the bank's dependence upon funds obtained in competitive money markets as a method of financing earning assets.
Net Fed Funds/Equity (%).	Net federal funds (purchased less sold) divided by total equity. Indicates the extent of exposure the bank has assumed by financing assets from the federal funds market.

PER EMPLOYEE:

| Salaries & Benefits/Emp($). | Actual total salaries and benefits expense divided by number of employees. |
| Total Assets ($ Mil). | Average total assets divided by number of employees. |

Interest Variance Analysis

The interest variance computations needed to generate the interest variance analysis reports illustrated in Chapter Two are explained here. The reports present a comparison of two sets of assets, yields and mixes or of liabilities, cost of funds rates and mixes. The comparison identifies the reasons the two sets of figures differ — the variances.

The basic variances identified are rate, size, and mix. Generally, the comparisons are of actual to plan, "what-if" to base, year to year, or month to month.

The analysis focused on interest margin, which is interest income minus interest expense. The computations calculate separate sets of variances for interest income and interest expense. For reporting purposes, however, the variances are usually shown together.

Basic Formulas

Designations of the variance components are given below.

R — *Rate*. Annual (or annualized) interest rates are used.

S — *Size*. The total amount of average earning assets is used for both interest income and interest expense computations.

M — *Mix*. The mix of the total amount of earning assets is composed of interest-earning assets and interest-paying liabilities, each expressed as a percentage of total earning assets.

In the illustration below, the subscripts indicate time periods; and the symbol Δ (delta) is used to indicate change from one time period to another.

The computations for interest income for period 2 can be expressed as

(1) R_2 X S_2 X M_2 = Interest Income$_2$ (II$_2$)

and for period 1 as

(2) R_1 X S_1 X M_1 = Interest Income$_1$ (II$_1$)

Thus, Interest Income$_2$ minus Interest Income$_1$ equals the change in interest income and is expressed as

$$II_2 - II_1 = \Delta II_{2,1}$$

The symbol R_2 represents the set of annual interest rate yields for all interest-bearing assets (i) for period 2. S_2 is the total average earning assets for period 2. And M_2 is the set of percentages of total average earning assets that each asset represents.

If this bank had ten different earning-asset accounts, the expression, above for period 2, would appear as follows:

Asset	Rates		Size		Mix		Interest Income
1	$R_{2,1}$	X	S_2	X	$M_{2,1}$	=	$II_{2,1}$
2	$R_{2,2}$	X	S_2	X	$M_{2,2}$	=	$II_{2,2}$
.	.		.		.		.
.	.		.		.		.
.	.		.		.		.
10	$R_{2,10}$	X	S_2	X	$M_{2,10}$	=	$II_{2,10}$
Total	R_2	X	S_2	X	100%	=	II_2

Variances The basic variance analysis has three components, one related to each component of interest income. To explain the change in interest income using the three components, a systematic and logical sequence is used.

Rate Variance To evaluate the impact of interest rate changes alone, the size and mix components are held constant while rates are changed. Formulas (3) and (4) illustrate the calculation of interest incomes that lead to the rate variance:

(3) R_2 X S_2 X M_2 = (II$_2$) = Interest Income for Period 2

minus

(4) R_1 X S_2 X M_2 = Interest Income (asks "what-if" interest rates in Period 1 continued unchanged into Period 2)

equals the *Rate Variance.*

Notice that the only difference between formulas 3 and 4 is the subscript for rate.

Size Variance
By continuing the above analysis, the impact of more or fewer earning assets can be measured as the size component as follows:

(4) R_1 X S_2 X M_2 = Interest Income (asks "what-if" interest rates in Period 1 continued unchanged into Period 2)

minus

(5) R_1 X S_1 X M_2 = Interest Income (asks "what-if" interest rates and earning assets in Period 1 continued unchanged into Period 2)

equals the *Size Variance*.

Notice that the only difference between formulas 4 and 5 is the subscript for size. The size variance, then, is the change in size of total earning assets with interest rates and the asset mix held constant. The same formulas also work for interest expense on the liability side.

Mix Variance
The formulas will appear as follows:

(5) R_1 X S_1 X M_2 = Interest Income (asks "what-if" interest rates and earning assets in Period 1 continued unchanged into Period 2)

minus

(6) R_1 X S_1 X M_1 = (II_1) = Interest Income for Period 1

equals the *Mix Variance*.

Notice that by formula 6 the transition from Period 2 to Period 1 is complete. The mix variance results from changes in specific percentages that each loan and investment account represents of earning assets. The total mix variance can be broken down into variances for individual investment and loan accounts. The same formulas and analysis can be done for interest-paying liabilities.

Thus, the total change in interest income (Interest Income$_{2,1}$) between Period 2 and Period 1 is explained by the three components which can be added —— Rate Variance $_{2,1}$ + Size Variance $_{2,1}$ + Mix Variance $_{2,1}$.

The same calculation sequence is used for interest-paying liabilities. While interest-paying liabilities do not equal earning assets, the earning assets total is used. Funding of the difference between earning assets and interest-paying liabilities comes from interest-free funds.

The computations above assume that the numbers of days or months for the two time periods being compared are the same. For example, December and January are compared, or two 365-day years are compared.

Other Computational Issues

Interest margin variance analysis is an analytical tool identifying direction and magnitude of variances. Different computational options can yield different variance numbers, but rarely will the direction or relative size of variances change. Accuracy is less critical than cause and effect. Also, simplification at the expense of purity generally creates more powerful and usable analyses.

The foregoing computations contain four unstated assumptions that should be highlighted:

- the three variances are calculated in sequence;
- joint variances among the three variances are ignored and combined into one of the three;
- a specific order of calculation is used — rate, size, and then mix;
- the analysis moves from "actual" to "plan," "this year" to "last year," and "what-if" to "base" periods (e.g., Period 2 to Period 1 in the above illustration).

Explaining the Entire Variance

The first assumption means that 100% of the difference between Periods 2 and Period 1 is explained. As the subscripts change from Period 2 (for all factors in formula 3) to Period 1 (for all factors in formula 6) sequentially, the total change in interest income is explained. Thus,

$$\text{Interest Income}_2 - \text{Interest Income}_1 =$$
$$\text{Rate Variance} + \text{Size Variance} + \text{Mix Variance}.$$

If all three variances had been calculated from the same base (either Period 1 or Period 2), the sum of the three variances would only rarely equal the interest income change. If for example, the following calculations are made:

$$(R_2 \times S_1 \times M_1) - (R_1 \times S_1 \times M_1) = \text{Rate Variance}$$
$$(R_1 \times S_2 \times M_1) - (R_1 \times S_1 \times M_1) = \text{Size Variance}$$
$$(R_1 \times S_1 \times M_2) - (R_1 \times S_1 \times M_1) = \text{Mix Variance}$$

The sum of the rate, size, and mix variances will not equal Period 2 interest income minus Period 1 interest income.

Joint Variance

The second assumption is related to linking the primary and secondary, or joint, variances. Different variance dollar amounts can be generated simply by varying the calculation sequence. The differences are generally minor and result from combining the joint variances (e.g., the interaction of interest rate and mix changes, called a rate/mix variance) with the primary variance, either the rate, size, or mix variance. The first primary variance calculated always absorbs three of the four secondary variances. Figure F-1 illustrates the joint variances and how they are combined when a rate, size, and mix sequence is used.

Calculation Order

The calculation order rarely matters. Custom in cost accounting and other variance analysis work separates the price-related variances (the rate variance here) first. Also, in traditional financial institution variance analysis, size and mix variances are at times combined into a volume variance. The sequence suggested here — rate, size, and mix — is commonly used but is not the only one seen in practice.

Joint Variances Identification

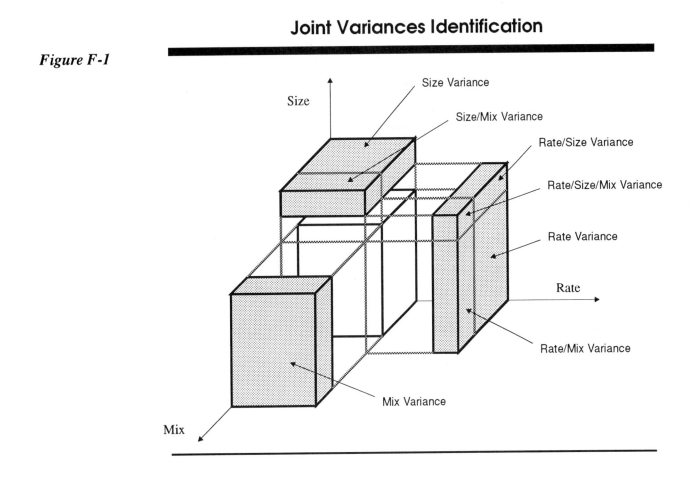

Base Period   The fourth assumption establishes the base period. The finishing point (Period 1) is the base period with the starting point (Period 2) being the new interest income level. The same philosophy is used to calculate growth rates. Generally, the older time period, the plan, or the original forecast is considered to be the base period, Period 1. The more recent time period, actual results, or "what-if" alternative is the Period 2 figure. A consistent rule is helpful to understand the comparisons, but is not essential nor unbreakable.

Annualized Interest   The computations use annualized yields and rates, whether the comparisons are for months, quarters, years, or any time period. Some assets earn interest on a daily basis and others on a monthly basis. To find annual yields for daily earning assets, a 365-day year is used (except for leap years) and the specific number of days in each month is used. For level payment assets, interest is earned by the month and is annualized using 12 months.

Accrual Days Variance   Another complicating issue arises when monthly comparisons are made and the months being compared have a different number of accrual days. For example, an analysis that compares February to January would be distorted by the fact that one month has 28 or 29 days and the other has 31 days. This is solved by separating out the 3 (or 2) days difference in earning power via an accrual days variance. By inserting the accrual days variable between the rate and the size variables, the formulas would then appear as follows:

(7) R_1 X A_2 X S_2 X M_2 = Interest Income (assumes interest rates in Period 1 continued unchanged into Period 2)

minus

(8) R_1 X A_1 X S_2 X M_2 = Interest Income (assumes interest rates and accrual days in Period 1 continued unchanged into Period 2)

equals the *Accrual Days Variance*.

Interest Margin Variance Analysis
February Forecast versus January Forecast — 2003

Figure F-2

INTEREST INCOME CHANGE DUE TO:	MIX	SIZE	ACCRUAL DAYS	RATE	TOTAL CHANGE
SHORT-TERM TREASURIES	19	7	-32	-1	-6
LONG-TERM TREASURIES	-5	7	0	0	2
ASSET BACKED SECURITIES	-3	3	0	-1	-1
ALL OTHER SECURITIES	1	2	0	0	2
TOTAL SECURITIES	15	18	-32	-6	-4
SHORT-TERM INVESTMENTS	18	3	-10	9	20
COMMERCIAL LOANS-FIXED	-7	9	0	0	2
COMMERCIAL LOANS-FLOAT	-8	11	-48	-6	-52
MORTGAGE LOANS-FIXED	-11	6	0	0	-4
MORTGAGE LOANS-ADJ	-2	6	0	-4	0
HOME EQUITY LOANS	-3	3	0	0	0
CONSUMER LOANS	-15	17	0	-2	0
CREDIT CARD LOANS	-3	10	-45	31	-7
AUTO LOANS	1	1	0	0	1
TOTAL LOANS	-49	64	-95	21	-59
TOTAL EARNING ASSETS	0	86	-137	8	-43

INTEREST EXPENSE CHANGE DUE TO:	MIX	SIZE	ACCRUAL DAYS	RATE	TOTAL CHANGE
IBC & SAVINGS	-9	11	-46	0	-45
MMDAs	-10	14	-59	-19	-74
SMALL CDs	-1	4	-20	-2	-18
LARGE CDs	-11	14	-62	-5	-64
PUBLIC CDs	6	6	-27	1	-14
OTHER CDs	-1	0	-2	0	-2
TOTAL CERTIFICATES	-7	25	-110	-6	-98
SHORT-TERM BOR FNDS	3	0	-2	1	2
LONG-TERM DEBT	0	0	0	0	0
TOTAL INT-BEAR LIAB	-25	50	-217	-23	-215
NET INTEREST MARGIN	129	38	87	-82	172

Figure F-2 presents a comparative analysis of February 2003 and January 2003. The impact of a three day difference is a February savings of $87,000. More liabilities than assets pay daily interest. Leap year versus non-leap year analysis would also have an accrual days variance, but it would probably be immaterial. In variance analysis where the accrual days are equal, the accrual days variance will be zero.

Taxable Equivalent

Income from any tax-exempt securities account is shown on the statement of income as the actual dollars earned on the investment. Yields on any tax-exempt securities are listed on the interest rate reports as the taxable-equivalent basis, meaning that the rate of return is adjusted to make it appear equivalent to a taxable security.

In interest variance analysis reports, the interest income from any tax-exempt securities is also shown on a taxable-equivalent basis. This is to allow the interest margin analysis to be independent of the tax status of specific accounts.

Sum of Variances versus Variance of Sum

On the interest variance reports, the variances reported at subtotal levels of data detail (e.g., total securities, total loans, total earning aessets) reflect the application of the variance formulas to the totals. As such, the sum of the variances reported at the detail account level will not foot to the variance reported at the aggregate level. Although the sum of the variances will generally approximate the variance of the sum, the potential for significant disparity does exist. Such instances typically indicate data anomalies at the detail level.

SEC Method for Calculating Interest Variance

The 1975 issued Guide 61, *Guides for the Preparation and Filing of Registration Statements Under the Securities Act of 1933 - Statistical Disclosures by Bank Holding Companies*. The relevant instructions for interest variance analysis are the following:

VII. Interest Rates and Interest Differential

B. For the latest two fiscal years and any interim period reported on, present (1) the dollar amount of change in interest income and (2) the dollar amount of change in interest expense. The changes should be segregated for each major category of interest-earning asset and interest-bearing liability into amounts attributable to (a) changes in volume (change in volume times old rate), (b) changes in rates (change in rate times old volume, and (c) changes in rate/volume (change in rate times the change in volume). The rate/volume variances should be allocated on a consistent basis between rate and volume variances and the basis of allocation disclosed in a note to the table.

The SEC approach differs from the earlier three and four variance methods. Only two variances are requested — rate and volume variance. The two variances are first computed from the base period and the residual joint variance is then allocated. The computations are shown below.

The interest income $(R_1 \times V_1) = $ Interest Income$_1$ (II_1),
for Period 1
and for period 2 $(R_2 \times V_2) = $ Interest Income$_2$ (II_2),
is calculated as follows:

R is the annualized interest rate, and
V is the average earning asset balance for the period.

The interest income variance is:

$(R_2 \times V_2) - (R_1 \times V_1) = \Delta II_{2,1}$.

To calculate the volume variance, the first step is to use $(V_2 \times R_1)$,
and to subtract $- (V_1 \times R_1)$,
which gives the *main* portion of the *volume variance* = a_m.
This is item (a) in the SEC guide quoted above.

To calculate the rate variance, the first step is to use $(R_2 \times V_1)$
and to subtract $- (R_1 \times V_1)$
which gives the *main* portion of the *rate variance* $= b_m$.
This is item (b) in the SEC guide quoted above.

These two main portions are not equal to the change in interest income from period 1 to period 2 ($\Delta II_{2,1}$). The remainder is item (c) in the SEC guide. Thus, $(a_m) + (b_m) + (c) = II_{2,1}$.

Item (c) is then allocated to the volume and rate variances on a proportional basis. The volume variance portion of item (c) is the absolute value of (a_m) divided by the sum of the absolute values of (a_m) and (b_m). The computations follow.

$$\frac{|a_m|}{|a_m| + |b_m|} \times c = a_c$$

The rate variance portion of item (c) is:

$$\frac{|b_m|}{|a_m| + |b_m|} \times c = b_c$$

The total volume and rate variances can now be shown as:

$a_m + a_c = $ *SEC Volume Variance*

$b_m + b_c = $ *SEC Rate Variance*

Present Value/ Duration Analysis

Duration analysis is used in asset/liability management to identify the repricing timing of assets and liabilities. A mismatch between the duration of assets and liabilities means that a change in reinvestment rates will have different effects on the present values of assets and liabilities. A comparison between the duration of the assets and liabilities indicates the direction in which long-term book income will change in relationship to changes in the future level of interest rates.

Under an active management team, if the general level of rates is expected to increase, the balance sheet should be managed so that the duration of the future liabilities will exceed the duration of future assets thus causing future book income to increase. If the direction of change in interest rates is unknown, the balance sheet should be managed so that the duration of the assets equals the duration of the liabilities so future book income will be immune to changes in futures rates.

Calculations The present value of a single cash flow is computed by dividing the cash flow by a discount factor which represents the amount by which $1 will grow at a specified interest rate from the present to the time of the cash flow. The discount factor is the quantity one plus the reinvestment rate multiplied by itself for the number of years until the flow occurs (i.e., for cash flows in Figure G-1, $(1 + .10) = 1.10$, $\$100 / 1.10 = \$90.91$ and $(1 + .10) \times (1 + .10) = 1.211$, $\$200 / 1.211 = \$165.29$). The multiplicative series of the one plus the reinvestment rate factor is more easily represented and computed by raising the factor to the power of the number of years to the flow:

$$(1 + .10) \times (1 + .10) = (1 + .10)^2$$

Present Value The present value of a series of cash flows is computed by summing the present value of each individual flow in the series. The sum represents today's worth of the future cash flows in terms of the assumed future reinvestment rates.

By investing the present value at the reinvestment rate and letting the interest compound until the time of the last cash flow, the compounded amount will equal the sum of the cash flows plus interest earned on the cash flows. This compounded amount is called the *future value* of the series. The difference between the future value and the sum of the cash flows is the amount of interest earned on the cash flows. It is this interest which is at risk when the reinvestment rate changes.

Present Value Analysis

Figure G-1

Year	Cash Flow	Reinvest Rate	Beginning Present Value	Compound Interest	End of Period Future Value
1	$100.00	10.00%	$ 90.91	$ 46.41	$1,171.78
2	200.00	10.00	165.29	66.20	1,288.96
3	300.00	10.00	225.39	63.00	1,417.86
4	400.00	10.00	273.21	40.00	1,559.65
5	500.00	10.00	310.46	0.00	1,715.61
	$1,500.00	10.00%	$1,065.26	$ 215.61	

Compound Interest Cash Flows	$ 215.61
Principal Cash Flows	1,500.00
Total Receipts	$1,715.61

Figure G-1 shows a series of cash flows which have the present value of $1,065.26 and will grow to $1,715.61 in five years when invested at 10.0%. The future value of $1,715.61 is the sum of the original cash flows, $1,500, and the amount of interest earned on the reinvested cash flows. The "Present Value" column is computed by dividing the "Cash Flow" column by one plus the "Reinvest Rate" column raised to the power in the "Year" column ($273.21 = 400 / (1.10)^4$). The "Compound Interest" column is the total interest earned in the future by the associated cash flow (for the cash flow of $300.00, $63.00 interest will be earned in years 4 and 5; i.e., $63.00 = 300 \times (1.10) \times (1.10) - \$300$). The "Future Value" column is computed by multiplying the total present value of $1,065.26 by one plus the average reinvestment rate raised to the power of the number of years outstanding ($1,715.61 = $1,065.26 x (1.10)^5).

The compound interest of $215.61 earned by reinvesting the flows in Figure G-1 will change if the reinvestment rates change. If a lower reinvestment rate is used the present value will be higher and the amount of compound interest earned will be lower.

The analysis of the entire balance sheet depicts the book value of equity. The present value of equity is the difference between assets and liabilities. This difference is called the market value of equity, or sometimes the market value of portfolio equity (i.e. the net worth of the firm). To compute this net value, however, present values must be established for the non-rate-related accounts such as cash, fixed assets, other assets, and other liabilities. Some of these accounts can be handled easier than others. For example, the fixed assets may contain the corporation's office building. An appraisal can be obtained to provide a value for it. However, in general these accounts do not often have any meaningful cash flows associated with them. The present values of these accounts are customarily set equal to the book values (with some exceptions if desired, as stated above), thus implying that they have a duration of zero. But since these accounts do not mature, they could also have a duration of a very long time period and accompanying present values of zero. In either event, the present value of these accounts is not meaningful because it is not based on the discounting of future cash flows. Since the present value of equity must include the present values of these non-rate-related accounts, its interpretation can be questionable.

Duration Duration was defined by Frederick Macaulay in 1938 as the weighted average term to maturity of a bonds cash flows.[1] Duration is computed by weighting the discounted cash flows by the time to receipt and dividing the weighted sum by the present value. Mathematically, duration is computed as:

$$\text{Duration} = \frac{\sum_{i=1}^{n} \left(\text{Time} \times \frac{\text{Cash Flow}_i}{(1 + \text{Rate})^{time}} \right)}{\sum_{i=1}^{n} \frac{\text{Cash Flow}_i}{(1 + \text{Rate})^{time}}}$$

Expressed in words, duration is the sum of time multiplied by the present value of each cash flow in period i divided by the sum of the present value of all cash flows, where:

cash flow$_i$ = the cash flow occurring in period i,
time = length of time in years until the cash flow in period i occurs,
rate = the annual reinvestment interest rate, and
n = the number of items in the cash flow series for the asset or liability.

[1] Fabozzi, Frank J., *Fixed Income Mathematics*, Probus Publishing Company, Illinois, 1988, p. 170.

Duration Calculation (from Figure G-1)

Figure G-2

Year	Present Value	Year x PV
1	$ 90.91	$ 90.91
2	165.29	330.58
3	225.39	676.17
4	273.21	1,092.84
5	310.46	1,552.30
	$1,065.26	$3,742.80

Duration in years = $3,742.80/$1,065.26 = 3.52

Figure G-2 completes the duration equation. $90.91 x 1 = $90.91, $165.29 x 2 = $330.58 ... $310.46 x 5 = $1,552.30. The cash flows are time weighted and summed. Then the sum of the time weighted cash flows are divided by the sum of the present values. $3,742.80 / $1,065.26 = 3.52 years. The duration value is in terms of the instrument's cash flow periods. It can be adjusted to an annual number by dividing the duration value by the number of cash flows per year (in this case it is already an annual number).

The duration number for total assets is obtained by weighting each individual instrument/portfolios duration by the present value of total assets. The duration number for liabilities is obtained in the same fashion except for weighting them by the present value of total liabilities. If the numbers are equal to each other then the balance sheet is said to be matched. If this is the case then the future value of the assets and liabilities will change in tandem with changes in interest rates.

If the duration of assets does not match the duration of liabilities, then management has the choice of taking steps to shorten maturities on one side of the balance sheet or lengthen them on the other. It could be that management wants to create an asset-sensitive or liability-sensitive institution. The proper adjustment of the balance sheet as evaluated through duration could achieve this.

The duration of equity as shown in Figure G-3 is:

$$\text{Duration }_{Equity} = \frac{(\text{Present Value }_{Assets} \text{ X Duration }_{Assets} - \text{Present Value }_{Liabilities} \text{ X Duration }_{Liabilities})}{\text{Present Value }_{Equity}}$$

PRESENT VALUE AND DURATION REPORT
Community Regional National Bank
December 31, 2003   Dollars in Thousands

Figure G-3

	BOOK VALUE	PRESENT VALUE	DURATION (MONTHS)	INT. RATE ELASTICITY	DISC. CASH FLOW YIELD
ASSETS:					
CASH	17615	17615	0.0	0.00	0.00
SHORT-TERM TREASURIES	58009	57967	1.1	-0.09	7.94
LONG-TERM TREASURIES	44050	43808	21.1	-1.66	8.58
US AGENCY SECURITIES	8501	8545	42.4	-3.39	9.54
CMO CLASS B	6628	6318	78.6	-6.22	9.80
TAX EXEMPTS	2400	2374	16.2	-1.28	8.19
OTHER SECURITIES	4074	4066	54.4	-4.13	11.19
TOTAL SECURITIES	123662	123078	17.1	-1.35	9.28
SHORT-TERM INVESTMENTS	30911	30653	17.1	-1.31	8.86
DIRECT COM'L LOANS-FIXED	51299	51327	6.0	-0.49	9.91
DIRECT COM'L LOANS-FLOAT	61800	61838	0.5	-0.04	8.67
MORTGAGE LOANS-FIXED	26815	25941	46.8	-3.73	11.23
MORTGAGE LOANS-ADJ	41297	40892	5.0	-0.41	10.44
HOME EQUITY LOANS	16118	16235	18.3	-1.49	10.58
CONSUMER LOANS	75956	76289	12.7	-1.04	11.99
CREDIT CARD LOANS	31874	32070	3.2	-0.26	15.38
AUTO LOANS	3515	3461	16.1	-1.31	12.91
TOTAL LOANS	308674	308053	10.3	-0.83	11.36
RESERVE FOR LOAN LOSSES	-5055	0	0.0	0.00	0.00
NET LOANS	303619	308053	10.3	-0.83	11.36
OTHER ASSETS	20494	19569	0.0	0.00	0.00
TOTAL ASSETS	496301	498969	11.7	-0.93	10.37
LIABILITIES:					
BUSINESS DEMAND	37452	36387	4.9	-0.41	6.93
PUBLIC DEMAND	8717	8648	1.5	-0.12	6.53
INTEREST-BEAR CHECKING	74648	74596	5.4	-0.45	5.14
REGULAR SAVINGS	38721	38370	14.2	-1.17	6.24
MMDAs	105500	106352	5.4	-0.44	5.19
SMALL CDs	38214	38482	15.3	-1.26	6.80
LARGE CDs	100551	100648	1.5	-0.13	7.09
PUBLIC CDs	43583	43654	1.5	-0.12	6.91
OTHER CDS	3491	3505	3.0	-0.25	5.94
TOTAL CERTIFICATES	185838	186289	4.4	-0.36	6.85
TOTAL DEPOSITS	450876	450642	5.6	-0.46	6.08
SHORT-TERM BORROWINGS	5167	5167	0.0	0.00	0.00
OTHER LIABILITIES	11934	11934	0.0	0.00	0.00
TOTAL LIABILITIES	467977	467744	5.4	-0.45	6.08
TOTAL EQUITY	28324	31225	105.8	-8.17	

276

Modified
Duration

Once the duration numbers have been obtained the next step would be to calculate how the present values will change given changes in the interest rates, Figure G-4 Price/Yield Equation. Modified duration is a term used to measure the present value sensitivity to changes in rate (It is also the first derivative of the price/yield equation). This predicts the movement of the price (present value) per 100 basis point rise in rates. The sign will be negative because the present/market value decreases when rates increase. Modified duration gives a good approximation of the change in price for small changes in rates. Modified duration gives the tangent line to the price/yield relationship at the current price and yield. The differential equation for modified duration, in the most useful form is:

$$\frac{\text{Change in Present Value}}{\text{Present Value}} \times 100 = \frac{\text{Macaulay's Duration}}{1 + \text{Reinvestment Rate}}$$

Modified duration has limitations. It assumes that the yield curve is flat and that changes to rates are the same for all maturities. This is known as parallel shifts to the yield curve. There are several other more complex forms of the modified duration equation to take into account these limitations, but this form works just about as well as any of them for practical purposes.

Price/Yield Equation

Figure G-4

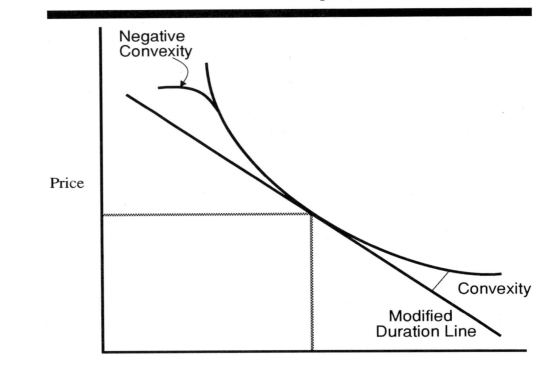

Interest-Rate Elasticity

Sometimes modified duration and interest-rate elasticity are considered to be the same thing. However a more detailed analysis of the price/yield relationship considers convexity (the second derivative of the price/yield equation). The accuracy of modified duration as an approximation of the price change will depend directly on a convexity. The more convex the instrument, the less accurate modified duration will be as a predictor of price change given a change in rates. Convexity is the speed with which the tangent line to the price/yield equation moves away from the equation itself. Convexity can have a positive or negative value. On bonds with no options it will be positive, on callable bonds it can be negative. Interest-rate elasticity is the sum of modified duration and convexity and thus is a more accurate measure of price change given a change in interest rates.

Discount Rate

After estimates of cash flows have been made (probability, amount and timing) a discount rate must be obtained. The easiest way to obtain a discount rate is to use the marginal rate for similar instruments. For a loan, this would be the rate at which new loans of similar type are being made. This marginal (or incremental rate) must be adjusted for current credit quality if it is an existing loan that is being discounted. If an incremental rate is not readily available a rate may be built-up. Starting from the Treasury yield curve a risk-free rate whose maturity is equal to the term of the cash flow is selected. Then this rate is adjusted upward for current credit quality considerations; other adjustments are made to cover the servicing costs of carrying the loan and to cover any prepayment options on the loan. This built-up rate should approximate the incremental rate (if available) as the incremental rate needs to cover these costs implicitly. Any differences should be accounted for by a difference in the credit quality or prepayments.

As mentioned earlier if a market price is available it should be used. However in order to calculate the above discussed numbers (duration, modified duration and interest-rate elasticity), cash flows and a discount rate are needed. These can be obtained by estimating the cash flows and their timing, then backing into a discount rate that sets the present value of the estimated cash flows equal to the market price. This is an internal rate of return concept. With this discount rate, estimates of duration, modified duration and interest-rate elasticity may now be made.

Time Horizon   The methodology can be employed for a past, present or future balance sheet. Duration analysis when applied to a past or present balance sheet is called "static duration" and when applied to a future balance sheet is called "forward duration". A duration analysis of a forecast as compared to a duration analysis of history shows the effect of planned new business on the timing of the asset and liability cash flows. If the forecast asset and liability durations imply too great a level of interest-rate risk, presumably the cash flow timings of the planned business may be changed. The analysis can also be made over a series of dates to show the direction of change. The data requirements for computing duration depend on whether the analysis horizon is to be static or a future point in time.

Static Duration   Static duration requires, at the minimum, the historical end-of-period balances, future maturity and repricing flows of the historical balances, and the cash flows associated with the contracted interest received or paid until the accounts mature or reprice, for all market-rate sensitive asset and liability accounts. If the analysis is to include all rate-related accounts, then the above data must be included for the additional accounts. An analysis which includes the non-rate-related asset and liability accounts must include the data for these accounts.

Forward Duration   To calculate forward duration, additional data must exist that identifies the maturity/repricing flows associated with the end-of-period balances contained in the forecast balance sheet. In addition to the scheduled transactions, there must also be data for new transactions which specify the incremental funds added between the present time and the forecast date. The amounts of the new transactions must cross-foot to the end-of-period balances held in the forecast after accounting for the amounts of the maturing transactions. Also, the subsequent maturity/repricing of the new funds must be specified along with the new transactions so the future cash flows can be associated with the correct forecasted end-of-period balances.

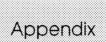

TECHNICAL
OPERATING
INSTRUCTIONS

Start-Up

Prior to entering team decisions, the following should appear on the screen:

```
11/05/92                    COMMERCIAL BANK                       MONTHLY
Enhanced
                        INTEGRATED PLANNING MODEL
   1 UPDATE HISTORY                  6 Batch Operation
   2 DEVELOP FORECASTS               7 MODEL ADMINISTRATION
   3 FINANCIAL REPORTING             8 GAME ADMINISTRATION
   4 Presentation Graphics           9 EXIT MODEL
   5 Data Inquiry

                        Enter Selection  1 █

                        Press Esc to EXIT MODEL


      Press ↑, ↓, →, or ← to select item or enter number and press ↵.
```

The top line of this screen shows today's date, the entity's name and the Model Type (Monthly, Quarterly, etc). The body of the screen lists the selections available to the operator.

The operator can use the cursor arrows to move among the selections or type the number of the correct selection. When the operator makes a selection, and moves from the main menu to a submenu, the names of the previous menus remain on the screen. This creates a map which enables the operator to retrace the different steps.

The operator should select "Batch Operations" from the Integrated Planning Menu. The following pages discuss the options available to the user in "Batch Operations".

When the students have finished a decision they should print their decisions and goals. Then they should run the Batch File "BCKUPDEC" after inserting the Backup Diskette into the Backup Drive.

Batch Operation

The following screen is representative of Batch Operation.

```
Batch Operation                                    CRNB (QUARTERLY)



                        1 = Execute a Batch file
                        2 = Create a Batch file




Press Esc to exit selection
_____

Option   1
```

Always select "Execute a Batch File".

The following is a flow chart for Batch Operation.

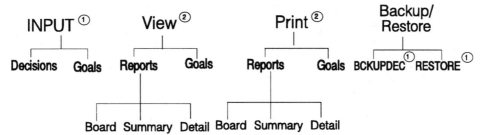

Batch Operation

① Actual Batch File Name

② To view or print any reports (or graph any goals), see the following pages for actual batch file name.

Select or type in the Batch File name and press "Enter" key twice.

Report Batch Files

REPORT NAME	VIEW ①	PRINT ①
Summary/ Comparative ②		
Statement of Condition - EOP	VCOMEOP	PCOMEOP
Statement of Condition - AVG	VCOMBSAD	PCOMBSAD
Statement of Condition - % Comp	VCOMBSAP	PCOMBSAP
Risk-Based Capital	VCOMRBC	PCOMRBC
Income Statement	VCOMIEA	PCOMIEA
Rate Report	VCOMRTE	PCOMRTE
Key Ratios	VCOMKEY	PCOMKEY
Interest Variance	VCOMINVR	PCOMINVR
All reports above		PCOMALL ③
Detail/ Periodic w/Total		
Statement of Condition - EOP	VDETEOP	PDETEOP
Statement of Condition - AVG	VDETBSAD	PDETBSAD
Statement of Condition - % Comp	VDETBSAP	PDETBSAP
Risk-Based Capital	VDETRBC	PDETRBC
Income Statement	VDETIEA	PDETIEA
Sources/Uses of Funds	VDETCASH	PDETCASH
Key Ratios	VDETKEY	PDETKEY
Rate Report	VDETRTE	PDETRTE
New Yields and Rates	VDETNEWR	PDETNEWR
P/E Ratio	VDETPE	PDETPE
All reports above		PDETALL ③
Other		
Gap		PGAP ③
Duration		PDUR ③
Fair Market Value		PFMV ③
SFAS107 - 1Year	VSFAS1YR	PSFAS1YR ③
SFAS107 - 2Year	VSFAS2YR	PSFAS2YR ③
Line of Business - Summary	VLOBS	PLOBS
Line of Business - Detail	VLOBD	PLOBD

REPORT NAME	VIEW ④	PRINT ④
Board Level Statements ②		
Income Statement	VSUMIEA	PSUMIEA
Key Ratios	VSUMKEY	PSUMKEY
Statement of Condition - % Comp	VSUMBSA	PSUMBSA
Statement of Condition - EOP	VSUMEOP	PSUMEOP
Rate Report	VSUMRTE	PSUMRTE

① The screen will freeze at the *Financial Reporting* menu. If printing, a beep will let you know the report is completed; you will come back to *Batch Operation*. If viewing, press *Alt X* to return to *Batch Operation*.

② These reports compare your team's forecast (what-if) vs the original forecast for 2003 for your choice of time period (3, 6, 9, or 12 months).

③ These reports take several minutes longer in running than the rest of the reports.

④ The screen will freeze at the *Presentation Graphics* menu. A beep will let you know the report is completed. If printing, this will return you to *Batch Operation*.

Graph Batch Files

GOALS		VIEW ①	PRINT ①
Asset Quality	Balanced Loan Mix	VGOAL1A	PGOAL1A
	Res/Non-Performing	VGOAL1B	PGOAL1B
	Lowest Net Loan Charge-offs	VGOAL1C	PGOAL1C
	Highest Market/Book-Inv	VGOAL1D	PGOAL1D
Liquidity	Highest S-T Fds/Assets	VGOAL2A	PGOAL2A
	Lowest Purch Fds/E.A.	VGOAL2B	PGOAL2B
	Lowest Net Short Borr Fds/Assets	VGOAL2C	PGOAL2C
	Lowest Gross Loans/Net Avail Dep	VGOAL2D	PGOAL2D
Capital Adequacy	Highest Equity/Assets	VGOAL4A	PGOAL4A
	Highest Market Capitalization	VGOAL4B	PGOAL4B
	Highest RBC	VGOAL4C	PGOAL4C
	Highest PE Ratio	VGOAL4D	PGOAL4D
Earnings	Highest Net Int Margin/E.A.	VGOAL5A	PGOAL5A
	Lowest Net Overhead/E.A.	VGOAL5B	PGOAL5B
	Highest Yield on E.A.	VGOAL5C	PGOAL5C
	Highest Total of Net Income	VGOAL5D	PGOAL5D
Growth	Most Balanced Growth	VGOAL6A	PGOAL6A
	Highest Composite Growth	VGOAL6B	PGOAL6B
	Highest Total Assets 12/31/03	VGOAL6C	PGOAL6C
	Highest Growth in Total Deposits	VGOAL6D	PGOAL6D

① The screen will freeze at the *Presentation Graphics* menu. A beep will let you know the graph is completed. If printing, this will return you to *Batch Operation*. If viewing, press *Enter* to return to *Batch Operation*.

Adjustable-Rate Mortgages — Interest rate on the mortgage is subject to change. In the simulation case, the rate adjusts on the loan's anniversary date to the 1-year Treasury Bill BEY plus 100 basis points. (See also, *Real Estate (ARM)*).

ALCO (*Asset/Liability Management Committee*) — The small group of the bank's board of directors and managers whose responsibility includes setting goals for earnings, liquidity, capital, asset quality, interest sensitivity, and growth.

Allowance - Loss on Loans — See Loan Loss Reserve.

Asset Quality Risk — The possibility that principal value paid out in the past will not be repaid in the future, or that investable funds will not generate adequate yields.

Average Daily Balance — Used to determine individual balances for use in calculating many ratios and in generating an average balance statement of condition. Actual days and balances are used to calculate monthly and annual average balances.

Average Maturity — Weighted average of a portfolio of any group of statement of condition accounts. Weighting uses months to maturity and the dollar amounts. Weighting can be done for each account, groups of accounts, or for the entire balance sheet.

Basis Point — A term used to measure interest rate levels and differentials — one hundredth of one percent — 0.01 percent.

Book Value — The original cost of an asset, plus or minus any premium, discount, or amortization adjustments.

Borrowed Funds —— Includes funds acquired from lenders in the form of debt, either short or long term, at money market interest rates.

Break-Even Yield —— The yield on a bank's earning assets necessary to cover its total interest and non-interest expense, net of non-interest income.

CAMEL —— An acronym for Capital, Asset Quality, Management, Earnings, and Liquidity. The term is used to refer to the Federal regulatory agencies' composite rating system for financial institutions. Each of the five categories is rated and then a summary overall rating is derived. A rating of "1" is the highest rating, and a "5" is the lowest.

Capital Adequacy —— The level of capital funds required to support the institutional structure and to provide protection against unanticipated and excessive losses.

Capital Multiplier —— The relationship of a bank's total assets to capital, expressed as a multiple of assets to capital.

Certificates of Deposit (CDs) —— A time deposit certificate issued by a bank in recognition of an interest-earning time deposit.

Chart of Accounts —— Listing of asset, liability, equity, revenue, and expense accounts used in the bank's general ledger system.

Clearings —— The interbank presentation of checks, offsetting of counter claims, and settlement of resulting balances.

Compensating Balances —— The amount of funds a borrower must leave on deposit with a bank as a result of a loan contract.

Core Capital —— Refer to Appendices B and C.

Core Deposits —— Deposits (including demand deposits, savings deposits, and small denomination time deposits) acquired from the bank's natural market area and, typically, implying customer allegiance. In the simulation case, defined as IBC, Regular Savings, and MMDA; in the real world, sometimes defined more broadly.

Cost of Funds Rate —— Interest expense divided by total interest-bearing deposits.

Credit Risk —— The possibility that the funds paid or committed to borrowers will not be repaid as agreed upon at the time the contract was made.

Delinquent Loans —— Loans with repayment over two months past due.

Duration —— Process of measuring the present values of future cash flows for all statement of condition accounts.

Earning Assets —— Bank funds which have been loaned or invested at a rate of interest.

Eurocurrency —— U.S. currency that is deposited in foreign banks or in foreign branches of domestic banks.

Federal Funds —— Bank deposits at a Federal Reserve Bank in excess of Federal Reserve System requirements, which may be sold by one bank to another on a very short-term basis at an agreed upon rate of interest.

Federal Funds Purchased —— Very short-term borrowing used to provide liquidity. The liability could be in the form of a repurchase agreement, other bank borrowings, or other short maturity borrowings.

Federal Funds Sold —— Very short-term investments used to generate earnings on idle funds. The asset could be in the form of reverse repurchase agreements, Treasury bills, deposits in banks, and other highly liquid investments.

Fixed-Rate Mortgages —— The interest rate committed at origination date and is held constant through the final mortgage payment.

Float —— The dollar amount of deposits which are in the process of collection from the banks upon which they were drawn.

Floating Rate —— An interest rate, in an asset or liability contract, that will move up or down when a defined external market rate changes.

Incremental Rate —— Interest rate at which new earning assets or interest-paying liabilities are acquired.

Interest Margin (dollars) —— The dollar differential between gross interest revenues and gross interest expense dollars (sometimes referred to as Net Interest Income).

Interest Margin (percent) —— The interest margin dollars divided by total earning assets.

Interest Margin (Taxable Equivalent) —— Some loans and investments made by banks result in interest income which is exempt from income taxes. Investments in municipal bonds are in this category. The taxable equivalent interest margin is the amount that would have been necessary for a bank to earn on a fully taxable basis in order to equal a given tax-exempt margin.

Interest-Rate Risk —— The possibility that interest rates will change unexpectedly in the future and thereby create a loss of net interest income; also net asset value; or both.

Interest-Rate Swap —— An agreement between two parties to exchange interest payments related to a specific type and amount of principal on their respective balance sheets.

Interest Sensitivity —— The relationship of changes in interest income and interest expense to fluctuations in interest rates over a defined time horizon.

Interest Spread —— The difference between a bank's earning assets yield and cost of funds rate.

Large CD's —— $100,000 or more certificates of deposit attractively priced relative to the money market rates to draw funds into the bank.

Level Payment Loan —— A loan agreement that provides for a fixed sum to be paid periodically during the term of the loan. Part of the fixed payment is credited to interest, and the balance is used to reduce the principal of the loan.

Liquid Assets —— Two definitions: First, as defined by regulators, is cash and most investments with a maturity of one year or less. Second, as defined for liquidity planning, those assets which are scheduled to mature, run-off, or be sold within a specific liquidity time period.

Liquidity —— The ability of a bank to meet the credit needs of the market place and the depositors' demand for cash.

Liquidity Ratio —— In the simulation case, the ratio of liquid assets to volatile funds.

Liquidity Risk —— Is the possibility that the bank will not have adequate cash funds to meet the bank's needs.

Loan Commitment —— A promise to lend a specified amount of money at a specified time.

Loan Loss Provision —— The expense item on a bank's income statement that reflects both current and anticipated loan loss experience (sometimes referred to as Provision for Loan Loss).

Loan Loss Reserve —— A valuation reserve set up to provide for possible losses on a bank's loans. The reserve is classified as a contra-asset on a bank's statement of condition, not as an equity account (sometimes referred to as Allowance-Loss on Loans or Reserve for Loan Loss).

Loan Participations —— The participation of a non-originating bank in a loan, through the purchase of all or part of the loan from the originating bank.

Long-Term Debt —— Funds with initial maturity longer than one year. Notes, mortgages, and other instruments could require periodic or "balloon" repayments and interest payments.

Maturing Rates —— Interest income rate or interest expense rate on funds maturing or "running-off" in a given time period.

Money Market Accounts Deposits (MMDA) —— Deposits that can be withdrawn on demand with transaction limits and that pay an interest rate that moves with and is equal to some function of a money market rate.

Municipal Bonds —— Bonds sold by political subdivisions such as states, cities, and counties. The interest paid on these bonds to the holder is exempt from federal income tax.

Mutual Funds —— Investment acquired by placing funds on deposit with a mutual fund manager. Generally, this account's yield will increase or decrease as interest rates move up and down respectively. Funds are readily accessible.

Notional Value —— The benchmark or reference value of a trade, where no principal is actually expected to change; used in interest rate swaps, caps, floors, etc.

Pledging Requirements —— The regulatory requirement, in many jurisdictions, that public deposits have specified types of securities pledged as collateral for those deposits.

Price/Earnings Ratio (P/E) —— The relationship of the market price of a share of common stock to the earnings per share of the stock, expressed as multiple. Shares of common stock which are highly regarded by investors generally sell at a higher price/earnings ratio, or multiple, than less highly regarded common stock.

Primary Capital —— Total equity capital plus reserves for loan losses. Usually expressed as a percentage of gross total assets (total assets with the reduction of the reserve for loan losses added back in).

Prime Rate —— The interest rate charged on large loans by banks to their best-known and most creditworthy customers.

Provision for Loan Loss —— See Loan Loss Provision.

Purchased Funds —— Includes all borrowed funds and any deposits that are large and highly sensitive to money market interest rate changes.

Real Estate (ARM) —— Adjustable-rate real estate mortgages. In the simulation case, rate adjustments to the current new mortgage rate occur on the annual anniversary of the loan.

Real Estate (FRM) —— Fixed-rate to maturity real estate mortgages.

Reserve for Loan Loss —— See Loan Loss Reserve.

Reliable Funds —— Borrowings and deposits that will not mature nor likely be withdrawn within a specific liquidity timeframe.

Repurchase Agreement —— A contract between a buyer and a seller of securities, wherein the seller agrees to buy back the securities at an agreed price after a stated period of time.

Risk Assets —— Those bank assets which are subject to diminution in value due to risks (such as credit risk, interest rate risk, or liquidity risk).

Rollover —— The process of selling new securities to pay off those maturing, extending the maturity on an existing loan, or replacing a maturing CD with another CD.

Runoff —— The maturation of loans, investments, or liabilities which results in a reduction in these accounts on a bank's statement of condition.

Simulation —— The technique of utilizing representative operating data to produce conditions that are likely to occur in actual performance.

Taxable-Equivalent Yield —— The taxable-equivalent yield is the pre-tax yield that would have been necessary on a security, had the income been taxable, to equate it with the actual tax-exempt yield earned by the recipient.

Tax-Exempt Securities —— State and municipal bonds which are exempt from federal income taxation.

Tier 1 Capital —— Refer to Appendices B and C.

Treasury Bills —— Debt instruments of the U.S. Government issued for specific periods.

Volatile Funds —— Borrowings and deposits scheduled to mature, "runoff", or likely be withdrawn within a specific liquidity timeframe.

Yield on Earning Assets —— Gross interest income on all earning assets (gross loans and investments) divided by earning assets.

BIBLIOGRAPHY

Adams, John P. Bank Investments. Third ed. Washington, D.C.: American Bankers Association, 1986.

Arthur Andersen & Co., Accounting for Securitization Transactions by Sellers/Issuers., 1989.

Bailey, John M., and Charlene G. Valenza. "Regulating Capital Adequacy." Bank Management, February 1990, pp. 30-33.

Baughn, William H., Thomas I. Storrs, and Charles E. Walker, eds. The Bankers' Handbook. Third ed. Homewood, IL: Dow Jones-Irwin, 1988.

Bartlett, William W. Mortgage-Backed Securities: Products, Analysis, Trading. Englewood Cliffs, NJ: Prentice Hall, 1989.

Bierwag, Gerald O. Duration Analysis: Managing Interest Rate Risk. Cambridge, MA: Ballinger Publishing Company, 1987.

Carl, Bernard J., and Andrew E Furer. "Mortgage Securities Take on New Shapes in REMICs." Savings Institutions, January 1987.

Comptroller of the Currency, Administrator of National Banks, under the general guidance of Thomas M. Fitzgerald, District Administrator. Risk Management, 1992 - 1993.

Comptroller's Handbook for National Bank Examiners. Washington, D.C.: Office of the Comptroller of the Currency, March 1990.

Cook, Timothy Q., and Timothy D. Rowe, eds. Instruments of the Money Market. Sixth ed. Richmond, VA: Federal Reserve Bank of Richmond, 1986.

Dean, Julie F. "Trading Versus Investing: A New "Hot Button" with Regulators." The Journal of Bank Accounting and Auditing, Summer 1989, pp. 15-17.

Douglas, Livingston G., C.F.A. Bond Risk Analysis. New York: NYIF Corp., 1990

"Government-Sponsored Enterprises Created by Congress." The Washington Post, 15 Oct. 1989, p. H-4.

Ernst & Young, Financial Services Industries Practice. Financial Instruments: Ernst & Young's Letter on Capital Markets Developments. New York, Vol. 3, No. 1., July 1990.

Ernst & Young. 1993 SEC Guidelines, Rules, and Regulations. USA: Warren, Gorham, Lamont, 1992.

Fabozzi, Frank J. Fixed Income Mathematics. Chicago: Probus Publishing Company, 1988.

Fabozzi, Frank J., ed. The Handbook of Mortgage-Backed Securities. Chicago: Probus Publishing Company, 1988.

Farin, Thomas A. Interest Rate Risk Measurement and TB-13. Chicago: Financial Managers Society, June 1989.

Federal Deposit Insurance Corporation. FDIC News Release: FDIC Approves Policy Statement on Risk-Based Capital. Washington, D.C.: PR-53-89 (March 14, 1989), 202-898-6996.

Federal Financial Institutions Examination Council. Uniform Bank Performance Report Peer Group Data as of 12/31/89. Washington, D.C.: FDIC Public Disclosure Group, 1990.

Gardner, Mona J. and Mills, Dixie L. Managing Financial Institutions: An Asset/Liability Approach. Third ed. USA: The Dryden Press, 1991.

"Glossary of Selected Financial Instruments." Journal of Accountancy, November 1979, pp. 59-60.

Gooch, William K. and Sally A. Brown. Mortgage-Backed Derivative Products. Chicago: Financial Managers Society, May 1989.

Goy, Zwen A., ed. Handbook of Securities of the United States Government and Federal Agencies and Related Money Market Instruments. 33rd ed. New York: The First Boston Corporation, 1988.

Griffin, Kubik, Stephens, & Thompson, Inc. "CMO Yield/Maturity Relationships." Profitable Banker. Bank Administration Institute, August 1989, Vol. 1, No. 8, p.6.

Heagey, Thomas C. "Hedging on the Rise. "Bank Administration, October 1989, pp. 24, 26, 28.

Houle, David A. "CMOs: Restructuring Square Cash Flows to Fit Round Portfolio Holes." Bank Accounting & Finance, Fall 1989, pp. 19-23.

Hull, John. Options, Futures, and Other Derivative Securities. Englewood Cliffs, NJ: Prentice Hall, Inc., 1989.

Johnson, Hazel J. The Bank Valuation Handbook. Chicago: Bankers Publishing Company, 1993.

Katz, Jane W. Secondary Mortgage Market. Chicago: Financial Managers Society, 1990.

Kellison, Stephen G. The Theory of Interest, Second Edition. Richard D. Irwin, Inc., 1991

Multinational Banking Department. An Overview of Interest Rate Risk: An OCC Staff Paper. Washington, D.C.: Office of the Comptroller of the Currency, December 1989.

Onak, Michael, E. "Swaps Alternatives." Bank Administration, November 1989, pp. 38-44.

Olson, Ronald L., Harold M. Sollenberger, and William E. O'Connell, Jr. Advanced Financial Planning for Commercial Banks. Greenbelt, MD: Ivy Press Inc., 1984.

Phares, Kurt. "Market-to-Market Trading." Financial Manager's Statement, July/August 1990, pp. 34-35.

Spang, William, and Maryn Fisher. "Agencies Issue Risk-Based Capital Rules." The Journal of Bank Accounting & Auditing, Summer 1989, pp. 36-44.

Stigum, Marcia, and Frank J. Fabozzi. The Dow Jones-Irwin Guide to Bond and Money Market Investments. Homewood, IL: Dow Jones-Irwin, 1987.

Tate, Christine A. Asset Securitization and the Banking Industry. Chicago: Financial Managers Society, 1992.

INDEX

Q, R

S, T

U, V, W, X, Y, Z,

ABOUT OLSON RESEARCH ASSOCIATES, INC.

In 1970, Olson Research Associates, Inc. was one of the first to offer computerized financial planning models to commercial banks. Today, twenty-three years later, Olson Research, recognized as the industry leader in innovative modeling for asset/liability management, has expanded to serve commercial banks, thrifts, and credit unions throughout the United States and Canada.

The Financial Planning Model of 1970 has been succeeded by seven generations of financial models. The most recent of these generations has produced the Asset/Liability Management Model, Budgeting & Management Reporting Model, Strategic Planning Model and the ability to combine all three of the above models into a fully integrated system.

An addition to the Financial Planning Model is the Regulatory Analysis Model (RAM), introduced in 1992. The RAM is designed to help banks comply with the requirements of FASB's SFAF #107 and FDICIA's Section 121 and 305.

In addition to offering models, Olson Research also develops and delivers educational, consulting and financial performance evaluation services to the financial services industry. The simulation case and all of the reports in this text utilize a financial simulation model built by Olson Research.